3/06

THE GEOLOGICAL EVOLUTION OF AUSTRALIA AND NEW ZEALAND

THE
GEOLOGICAL EVOLUTION
OF
AUSTRALIA & NEW ZEALAND

by

D. A. BROWN
K. S. W. CAMPBELL
K. A. W. CROOK

All of Department of Geology, Australian National University, Canberra

1966

THE QUEEN'S AWARD
TO INDUSTRY 1966

PERGAMON PRESS
OXFORD · LONDON · EDINBURGH · NEW YORK
TORONTO · SYDNEY · PARIS · BRAUNSCHWEIG

Pergamon Press Ltd., Headington Hill Hall, Oxford
4 & 5 Fitzroy Square, London W.1
Pergamon Press (Scotland) Ltd., 2 & 3 Teviot Place, Edinburgh 1
Pergamon Press Inc., Maxwell House, Fairview Park, Elmsford,
New York 10523
Pergamon of Canada Ltd., 207 Queen's Quay West, Toronto 1
Pergamon Press (Aust.) Pty. Ltd., 19a Boundary Street,
Rushcutters Bay, Sydney, N.S.W. 2011, Australia
Pergamon Press S.A.R.L., 24 rue des Écoles, Paris 5^e
Vieweg & Sohn GmbH, Burgplatz 1, Braunschweig

Printed in Great Britain by A. Wheaton & Co., Exeter

08 012277 9 (flexicover)
08 012278 7 (hard cover)

Contents

Preface

KNOWLEDGE of the geology of the Australasian region has expanded apace since the end of World War II as a result of two main factors—the extensive programme of reconnaissance mapping being carried out by the Commonwealth Bureau of Mineral Resources and the various State Geological Surveys, and the 1:250,000 mapping project of the New Zealand Geological Survey, on the one hand, and the increased activity of oil and mining companies, particularly in geophysical and drilling work, on the other. All phases of this work are still proceeding and no doubt will continue, perhaps at an increasing rate. Consequently in a book of this kind, all that can be offered is a single (and somewhat arbitrary) cross-section of a continuously and rapidly developing spectrum of ideas. Many of the data that have been collected are not yet available in published form, being either in oil company files or awaiting publication by governmental agencies, so that some of the opinions expressed here will have to be modified almost before the book is published. Under such circumstances, publication at the present time needs some justification.

This work is not intended to be a detailed compendium of the stratigraphy of Australia and New Zealand, though it is hoped that it may in some measure meet the need for an up-to-date teaching aid in this field. It may, in particular, be used to assist students to obtain a knowledge of the stratigraphy of their own country, so as to supplement and illustrate the courses on stratigraphic principles that have formed an increasing part of formal teaching in stratigraphy in recent years. For Australia, it cannot, of course, replace David and Browne's *Geology of the Commonwealth of Australia* as a source of information. This excellent work, however, was issued in 1950 (and is now out of print), too early to incorporate the major post-war advances in knowledge. Moreover, the State geology volumes being issued by the Geological Society of Australia are in the nature of reference works rather than textbooks, and to date there are none available for New South Wales, Victoria, or the Northern Territory. Other works, such as *The Geology of Australian Ore Deposits* and *The Economic Geology of New Zealand*, published by the Australasian Institute of Mining and Metallurgy for the Eighth Commonwealth Mining and Metallurgical Conference, are concerned with special aspects of Australasian geology.

vii

In so far as New Zealand is concerned, there is no modern text available of a kind suitable for teaching the regional stratigraphy to undergraduate students, though reference may be made to the valuable summaries accompanying the series of 1 : 250,000 geological maps now in process of publication. Presumably teachers and students in overseas universities also have a need for a textbook such as this at the undergraduate level, though it is hoped that the method of presentation will make the subject matter intelligible to the interested layman also. For the reason, too, that we expect the book to be consulted by non-Australasians, we have used the metric system of measurement throughout.

The task of compilation and interpretation of available data for the Australian sections has been very laborious owing to the vast size of, and vigorous activity in, the fields of geological investigation in the Commonwealth. The almost daily changes in the geological picture, as new data come from the host of exploratory ventures in the search for petroleum alone, made the task especially difficult. We should like to pay a special tribute here to all those officers of the Bureau of Mineral Resources who gave much of their time in helpful advice and constructive criticism of our work as it developed.

For New Zealand, the task was markedly more simple. The relatively small country and the good coverage of geological mapping with a wealth of well-founded interpretation and palaeogeographical reconstruction very greatly reduced the labour involved. Again, we make our acknowledgement of the great assistance rendered by the officers of the New Zealand Geological Survey.

So far as is possible, we have tried to integrate the geological events in both countries, drawing attention to the similarities and contrasts between them. Indeed, some critics may find it difficult to justify such a treatment when, on practically every count except geographical juxtaposition (if one may use this term to describe the present separation of some 2000 km), there is such a difference between these two lands. On the one hand, there is a relatively stable coign of continental proportions, in a sense geologically senile and sclerotic, and on the other, there is a small, seismically active chain of mountains, recently emergent from the Pacific Ocean, geosynclinal in nature for most of its decipherable history, a veritable Peter Pan of the geological world. It is, however, this geosynclinal character that links eastern Australia with New Zealand, separated as they now are by a broad seaway, the bottom of which is apparently composed of oceanic crust. For in Palaeozoic times, when the similarities in depositional events and faunas between these two areas were most apparent, both were the sites of geosynclinal troughs. Since then, however, the links have largely been severed as the Tasman Orthogeosyncline of eastern Australia passed through orogenic phases and became stabilized.

It will be seen that in general we have concentrated on the interpretation, rather than on presentation, of the raw data. This is a consequence of our belief that Geology is ultimately a history of the Earth, and as such should be presented as a continuously unfolding narrative. In doing this we have been acutely conscious of the inadequacy of the data on which many of our interpretations have been based. But we believe that uninterpreted data are of little value and that the method used imparts something of the excitement and intellectual stimulus which is Geology.

It will be obvious that the emphasis of the book is on the stratigraphical, sedimentological, and palaeontological aspects of our subject, this bias reflecting our own research interests. We have not, however, ignored the petrological or structural aspects, and wherever possible we have consulted with our colleagues on these matters.

In an attempt to cover the ground as completely as possible we have not only made use of published sources, but have also consulted (a) the Record series of the Bureau of Mineral Resources which is on limited distribution, and (b) the well completion reports of various oil companies in Australia drilling with the aid of government subsidy. Certain unpublished theses, which are acknowledged in the text, have also been consulted. We are indebted to the authors of these for permission to quote their works.

To acknowledge the individual help of our colleagues in the geological fraternity of both Australia and New Zealand, would occupy a great deal of space. We must therefore, apologize for acknowledging this invaluable aid in a collective fashion. In addition to the staffs of the Bureau of Mineral Resources and the New Zealand Geological Survey, we also extend our grateful appreciation and thanks to our colleagues in the Departments of Geology of various Commonwealth and Dominion universities, in the State Geological Surveys, and in the C.S.I.R.O. Divisions of Land Research and Soils. At the same time, we accept full responsibility for all statements and interpretations made in this book.

In the Australian sections of the book, one author (K. S. W. C.) was responsible for the chapters on the Palaeozoic Systems and the marine portion of the Tertiary System. Another (K. A. W. C.) wrote the Precambrian, Mesozoic and Quaternary chapters and the account of the non-marine Tertiary. The New Zealand sections were compiled by the third author (D. A. B.).

In a book of this nature not every statement of fact or interpretation can be documented. In general we have quoted only the latest general work that deals with a particular sequence. Furthermore the principal references to each sequence or basin are generally quoted early in the discussion, and are not again referred to. Data not available by January 1965 have not been included in the text figures, though data available up to January 1966 may be referred to in the text.

The recommendations of the *Australian Code of Stratigraphic Nomenclature* (4th edition, 1964) and the practice of the New Zealand Geological Survey have been followed in matters of stratigraphic nomenclature in this book. The terminology of terrigenous sandy sediments used is a simplified form of that published by Crook (1960).

MAPS

We have not included geological maps of Australia and New Zealand in this volume, both for reasons of economy and because their inclusion would duplicate unnecessarily the excellent publications of governmental authorities which are readily available.

For Australia the most recent maps are the *Tectonic Map of Australia* (1960) (scale 1:2,534,400), with explanatory notes, available from the Director, Bureau of Mineral Resources, P.O. Box 378, Canberra City, A.C.T. (price $A3.00), and the map *Geology* (2nd edition, 1966) in the *Atlas of Australian Resources*, 2nd series (scale 1:6,000,000) available from booksellers, or the Department of National Development, P.O. Box 850, Canberra City, A.C.T. (price $A0.50).

For New Zealand, the New Zealand Geological Survey, P.O. Box 30368, Lower Hutt, has produced the *Geological Map of New Zealand* (1958) on a scale of 1:2,000,000 (price $NZ 0·50).

CHAPTER 1

The Precambrian Systems

ROCKS of Precambrian age outcrop over large areas of Australia, principally in Western Australia, South Australia, and the Northern Territory, and are known from all States except Victoria. A wide variety of lithologies is represented, including essentially unmetamorphosed sandstones, shales, and dolomites, acid to basic volcanics and intrusives, and highly deformed schists and gneisses of sedimentary and igneous derivation. Probably the most striking feature of the Australian Precambrian is the widespread occurrence of thick sequences of sedimentary and volcanic rocks, up to about 2300 m.y. old, in a state of preservation comparable to that typical of Phanerozoic shelf sequences.

Although attempts have been made in the past to systematize our knowledge of the Australian Precambrian, these have largely failed to stand the test of time. Only now, principally as the result of a concerted effort of regional mapping and radiometric dating conducted by the Commonwealth Bureau of Mineral Resources, the State Geological Surveys of South Australia and of Western Australia, and the Department of Geophysics and Geochemistry, Australian National University, is a coherent, comprehensive, and soundly based stratigraphic scheme emerging.

This scheme (Dunn *et al.*, 1966), in summary, recognizes that a fourfold time-stratigraphic subdivision of the Australian Precambrian is feasible. It is based on a combination of radiometric dates on selected sediments, volcanics, and some granites and metamorphics, lithological correlation using characteristic successions of lithologies, and geotectonic evolution as marked by certain widely occurring "tectono-magmatic events", involving the initiation or renewal of deposition over large areas and widespread volcanism and intrusive activity.

The nomenclature of these time-rock units is still in a state of flux. Dunn *et al.* (1966) use the term Archaean, and divide the Proterozoic into three units, the senses of which differ from both overseas and earlier Australian usages. A local nomenclature has therefore been proposed for the Proterozoic systems in Australia and will be used herein. Rocks known to be older than Proterozoic will be termed Archaean.

The Archaean in Australia has not yet been subdivided into time-rock units. Of the Proterozoic systems the two youngest have been named and defined, but there has been no formal definition or local name published for the oldest. Only the youngest system has been formally subdivided into series. The nomenclatural styles used in this chapter reflect these variations in nomenclature and definition.

The oldest subdivision of the Precambrian, the Archaean, is best represented in Western Australia, and comprises most, but not all, of the Precambrian high-grade metamorphic terrains. Some low-grade metamorphic rocks occur; essentially unmetamorphosed strata are unknown.

The oldest of the Proterozoic systems, here termed the "Nullaginian System", is best developed in the Pilbara region of Western Australia and the Katherine–Darwin region of the Northern Territory, where thick successions of sedimentary and volcanic rocks occur. Metamorphosed equivalents occur elsewhere in the Northern Territory and in Queensland. Present estimates of the age limits of this system are: top, *c.* 1800 m.y., base, *c.* 2300 m.y. (Dunn *et al.*, 1966).

The next youngest, the Carpentarian System, is probably the most widely distributed of the Proterozoic systems. Thick unmetamorphosed sequences occur throughout much of the northern half of the continent, and metamorphic complexes of similar age are well developed in South Australia and western New South Wales. The base of the system is defined, and the top is taken as the base of the Adelaidean System. The presently accepted age limits for this system are top, *c.* 1400 m.y., base, *c.* 1800 m.y. (Dunn *et al.*, 1966), although that for the top is subject to considerable uncertainty (Compston *et al.*, 1966).

The youngest of the Proterozoic systems, the Adelaidean System, which is well developed in South Australia and is represented in all States except Victoria, is widely known for the evidence of glaciation that it contains, and for the remarkable assemblage of fossils that has been described from its uppermost parts. This system, the base of which is defined, accumulated during the time interval between the end of the Carpentarian Period and the beginning of the Cambrian Period.

A considerable part of the Precambrian on the Australian mainland has been assigned to the Archaean or to one or other of the Proterozoic time-rock units by Dunn *et al.* (1966), who record the nature and sources of relevant radiometric data. Age attributions in this chapter and in the correlation chart (see Table 1.5) largely follow those of Dunn *et al.* (1966). The degree of certainty with which a particular rock unit can be assigned to a particular system varies, principally with the amount and quality of the radiometric data available. Data collection is still in progress and Table 1.5 (p. 38) should not therefore be taken as final. It is nevertheless much more accurate than earlier correlation charts of the Australian Precambrian.

For most of the metamorphic and plutonic complexes on the mainland, some uncertainty exists as to whether the age of their oldest parts can be regarded as established, and in some cases their ages can only be guessed at.

Almost all of the mapped sedimentary sequences in the Australian Precambrian, which are treated herein at the level of groups, have been mapped at formation or even member level.

New Zealand has no undoubted Precambrian rocks, but certain weakly metamorphosed sediments and some gneisses in Westland and south Nelson are probably of this age.

STRATIGRAPHY

Archaean

Structurally complex plutonic and high-grade metamorphic rocks occupy much of the southwestern part of the Australian continent (Prider, 1965), where they are known as the Yilgarn and Pilbara Systems. Many radiometric dates on these rocks exceed 2500 m.y. (Wilson *et al.*, 1960). Similar rocks also appear from beneath Proterozoic strata at several points in the Northern Territory and in the north of Western Australia (Fig. 1.1.)

The **Yilgarn "System"** is widespread in the southwestern part of Western Australia forming, with associated granites, a Precambrian Shield. The Yilgarn "System" is particularly well developed near Kalgoorlie (Sofoulis, 1963). It consists principally of granitic gneiss with large intrusive granite bodies (Prider, 1954), some of which may be younger than Archaean. Charnockitic granulites occur in many places (Wilson, 1958). Greenstones—metamorphosed basic igneous rocks and their derivatives—form several narrow north-trending belts, and broader areas, within the more acid rocks (Prider, 1961). In the Kalgoorlie district, and elsewhere, quartzites and high-grade pelitic schists are intercalated between greenstone units. The greenstones form the locus of the main gold-mineralization in Western Australia.

The **Pilbara "System"** is well developed in the Pilbara Goldfield district and adjacent areas in Western Australia (Noldart and Wyatt, 1962; Ryan, 1964). The lithologies characteristic of the Yilgarn "System" are repeated in the Pilbara "System". Three rock units have been recognized. The first, the "Granitic Complex", which is believed to contain the oldest rocks, comprises gneiss, migmatite, and granite, in part in the form of mantled gneiss domes. Granites of more than one age are present, for some intrude the other units of the Pilbara "System". All, however, are pre-"Nullaginian".

The second unit, comprising the greenstones and associated jaspilites of the Pilbara "System", is the Warrawoona "Series". This unit is believed to be separated from the third and youngest unit of the "system", the Mosquito Creek "Series", by a disconformity. Jaspilite, coarse conglomerate, and breccia are prominent in the Mosquito Creek "Series", together with some foliated argillite and sandstone. The overall metamorphic grade is lower than that of the Warrawoona "Series". "Nullaginian" strata unconformably overlie the Pilbara "System".

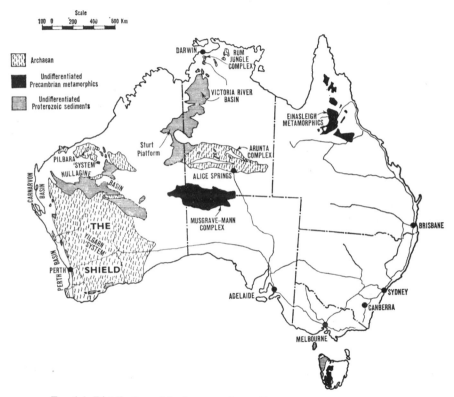

Fig. 1.1. Distribution of Archaean and undifferentiated Precambrian rocks.

Towards the coast, in the West Pilbara Goldfield, the Warrawoona and Mosquito Creek "Series" have not been recognized, equivalent strata being mapped as the Roebourne Group (Ryan, 1965). This comprises acid and basic volcanics, metamorphosed towards the base, overlain by jaspilite and shale, grading eastward into an entirely sedimentary sequence consisting largely of quartz-rich greywacke and shale, estimated to be 12,000 m thick. Further east, as the Pilbara Goldfield is approached, volcanics and chemical sediments reappear in the succession.

The "Nullaginian" Agicondi "Series" of the Pine Creek Geosyncline overlies a crystalline basement, which, in the vicinity of Rum Jungle, consists primarily of granite, gneiss, and migmatite, known as the **Rum Jungle Complex**. Exposures of this unit resemble mantled gneiss domes (Rhodes, 1965). Elsewhere the basement consists of schist, granulite, migmatite, and greenstone.

The **Arunta Complex,** which outcrops widely in the Macdonnell and Harts Ranges of Central Australia, forms the basement on which the Adelaidean strata of the Amadeus Basin rest. It also underlies the "?Nullaginian" Warramunga Group of the Warramunga Geosyncline. The Arunta Complex consists of high-grade metamorphics, gneiss, migmatite, granite, aplite, and pegmatite. The metamorphics include basic and calcareous granulites, calc-silicate rocks, amphibolites, and schists (Joklik, 1955). Low-grade retrogressive metamorphics occur in some areas. Radiometric dates from the Arunta Complex vary considerably (Wilson *et al.*, 1960), probably in part as a result of this late metamorphism.

"Nullaginian System"

In their *Geology of the Commonwealth of Australia*, David and Browne (1950) described their Nullagine Series—a unit not precisely defined—as probably coeval with the Precambrian strata of the Adelaide Geosyncline. This correlation, of long standing among Australian geologists, was not adopted for the Tectonic Map of Australia, Walpole (1962*a*) pointing out that the Nullagine "System", as he termed it, could be much older than the rocks of the Adelaide Geosyncline. This has subsequently been shown to be the case (Leggo *et al.*, 1965), and the greater part of the old Nullagine Series is now referred to the as yet unnamed time-rock unit, that is here termed the "Nullaginian System". Some parts of the old Nullagine Series are thought to be post-"Nullaginian" and will be described, using their recently proposed rock-unit names, elsewhere in this chapter.

The "Nullaginian System" in the **Nullagine Basin** (Fig. 1.2) comprises the Mount Bruce Super-Group, which contains the Fortescue, Hamersley, and Wyloo Groups (MacLeod *et al.*, 1963; Daniels, 1966). The super-group overlies the Archaean Pilbara "System" with strong angular unconformity.

The Fortescue Group reaches 4200 m in thickness in the Hamersley region, and consists predominantly of basic pillow lavas and pyroclastics, with some quartz sandstone and arkose at the base and shale and jaspilite towards the top. Further north, near Nullagine, the group is much thinner (360 m), and polymictic conglomerate and pisolitic limestone with *Collenia* are present (De la Hunty, 1963).

The Hamersley Group is predominantly of chemical origin and probably accumulated under very stable conditions. It comprises up to 2400 m of jaspilite, chert, dolomite, and shale, with dolerite and dacite near the top. There are three iron formations, predominantly of jaspilite, and these constitute a major reserve of iron ore (Campana *et al.*, 1964). Much of the sequence is banded, and seams of crocidolite occur in the iron formations and are mined in some localities (Finucane, 1964).

Fig. 1.2. Distribution of "Nullaginian" strata.

The Wyloo Group consists predominantly of quartz-rich terrigenous clastics, ranging in grainsize from shale to conglomerate. Jaspilite fragments in the conglomerates suggest derivation from outcrops of the Hamersley Group to the north. One basalt flow, and a dolomite with *Collenia* and *Newlandia,* occur within the unit. The total thickness of the Wyloo Group exceeds 3250 m. Deposition is believed to have taken place in a variety of environments during a period of tectonic instability (Daniels, 1966).

The **Pine Creek Geosyncline** of the Northern Territory (Fig. 1.2) contains a probably "Nullaginian" sequence, the Agicondi "Series", which is noted for its facies changes (Walpole, 1962*b*; Malone, 1962; Walpole and Crohn, 1965). It lies unconformably on the Rum Jungle Complex and coeval rocks. Granites intruding the Agicondi "Series" have been dated (Hurley *et al.*, 1961), but the dates obtained must be regarded as minimum ages. They suggest that the sediments are older than 1700 m.y.

The Agicondi "Series" comprises four major units. The oldest (Batchelor Group) is up to 1500 m thick and comprises alternations of clastic and dolomitic sediments. The clastics include muddy quartz sandstone and arkoses, siltstones, and conglomerates. Algal bioherms, dolutites, and dolomite breccias form the dolomitic component. Chert lenses occur within them. The unit was deposited in shallow water on the western margin of the geosyncline (see Fig. 1.3) and was derived from the northwest.

The Goodparla Group, about 3000 m thick, contains a uraninite ore body near Rum Jungle. The group conformably overlies the Batchelor Group where the latter is developed, and elsewhere rests directly on the Archaean basement. It was derived predominantly from the northeast and three facies have been recognized. The marginal facies, which is developed in the east, consists of ripple-marked and cross-stratified arkose, quartz-rich sandstone and siltstone, with conglomerate developed locally above basement highs. Lenses of silicified dolomite are intercalated. This facies apparently represents a shelf environment.

Basinwards (westwards) the marginal facies intertongues with a transitional facies, deposited in a slope environment. This transitional facies consists of muddy quartz arenites intertonguing with siltstones. These may be turbidites. Some silicified dolomite is present.

The trough facies of the Goodparla consists of interbedded chert, siltstone, and dolomite. Sedimentation units are thin and extensive.

Because of the facies relationships within the Goodparla there is some intertonguing of the trough facies of the Goodparla and the Finniss River Group.

The Finniss River Group, like the Goodparla, exhibits strong facies changes, but it is derived from the west (Fig. 1.3). Two facies which interfinger are recognized. The western or marginal facies, reaching 1500 m in thickness, contains quartz conglomerates, muddy quartz arenites, and siltstones. The arenites exhibit graded bedding, ripple marks, and load casts, and sedimentation units are thin and extensive; they may therefore be turbidites.

In the trough facies of the Finniss River Group, up to 2400 m thick, siltstones are prominent. However, the trough facies includes some extensive tongues of coarser sediment which extend basinwards from the marginal

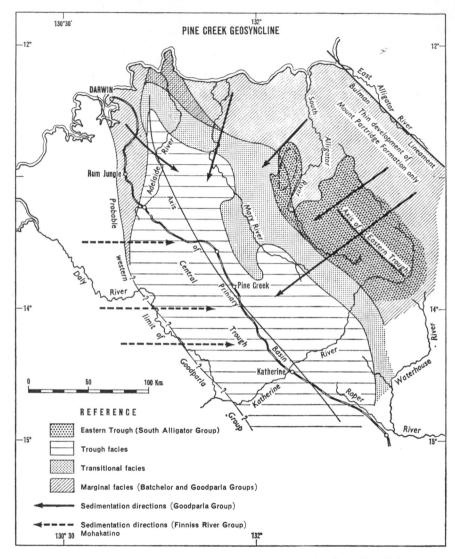

FIG. 1.3. Pine Creek Geosyncline: provenance and distribution of Batchelor, Goodparla, and Finniss River Groups. (After Walpole, 1962*b*.)

facies in the west. Locally the marginal and trough facies contain volcanic units near their tops. They comprise rhyolite and tuffs in the west and basic lavas and tuffs in the east.

The marginal facies of the group is overlain conformably by the Chilling Sandstone, a unit that extends west and southwest far beyond the limits of the Pine Creek Geosyncline. This comprises 450 m of cross-stratified and ripple-marked quartz-rich sandstone which accumulated in a shallow-water environment (Randal, 1962).

The Finniss River Group is absent from the eastern part of the geosyncline. There the Goodparla Group is overlain by the South Alligator Group. Locally the contact may be a disconformity or angular unconformity. The South Alligator Group, which is about 6000 m thick, is limited westwards by an Archaean basement ridge, along which is developed a discontinuous reef facies comprising algal dolomite bioherms with siltstones and chert lenses. Eastwards this gives way to chert, which may be altered dolomite. The major part of the group is developed farther east, and interfingers with the other facies. It consists of siltstone with rare arenite interbeds. The terrigenous sediments in the South Alligator Group were derived from the east.

Walpole (1962a) considers that after the deposition of the Batchelor and Goodparla Groups in the main trough of the geosyncline, there was uplift of the highlands to the west which provided material for the Finniss River Group. Faulting also occurred along an old basement high in the east to form the ridge on which the South Alligator reefs then developed, with the subsiding South Alligator Trough forming to the east of the ridge.

The whole Pine Creek Geosyncline sequence was folded after the deposition of the South Alligator Group and the Chilling Sandstone.

Probable "Nullaginian" strata (Halls Creek Group) outcrop southwest of the Pine Creek Geosyncline in Western Australia (Fig. 1.2), and are here regarded as having accumulated in a depression termed the **Halls Creek Trough.** The geometry of this feature, and its relations to the Pine Creek and Warramunga Geosynclines, remain to be elucidated.

The Halls Creek Group comprises basic volcanics, quartz-rich conglomerate and greywacke, shale, and some limestone and dolomite. Metamorphism is predominantly greenschist facies, but reaches granulite facies locally. The group is intruded by granites, gabbros, and ultrabasics of the Lamboo Complex (Gemuts, 1965).

To the southeast of the Halls Creek Trough, in **The Granites–Tanami Region,** Northern Territory, possible equivalents of the Halls Creek Group outcrop (Spence, 1964/102). These comprise shales, some hematitic, and greywackes locally metamorphosed and intruded by granite.

To the south of the Pine Creek Geosyncline, in the Tennant Creek district, the **Warramunga Geosyncline** (Fig. 1.2) contains a sequence of probable "Nullaginian" age, the Warramunga Group. This comprises more than 900 m of quartz-rich greywacke, shale, and siltstone that passes southeastwards into a quartz-rich sandstone sequence (Ivanac, 1954; Crohn and Oldershaw, 1964/79). The sequence is strongly deformed but weakly metamorphosed. For the most part the group is thought to have accumulated in moderately deep water, with the sandstone portion being a shallow-water shelf deposit. The group is overlain unconformably by Carpentarian strata.

In the northeast Northern Territory and western Queensland the **basement rocks of the McArthur Basin, South Nicholson Basin, and Mount Isa Geosyncline** are believed to be of "Nullaginian" age (Fig. 1.2). These, the Grindall, Murphy, and Yaringa Metamorphics respectively,

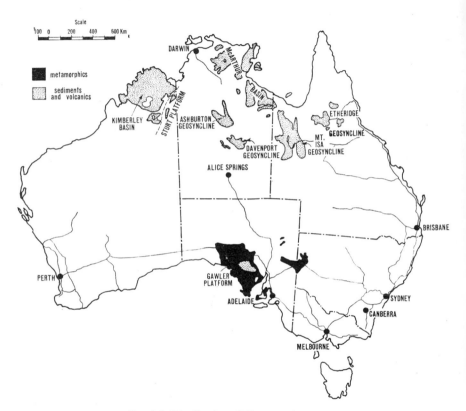

Fig. 1.4. Distribution of Carpentarian strata.

consist of schists and gneisses. The first two units are intruded by granites which have been dated (McDougall *et al.*, 1965).

The Grindall Metamorphics are overlain unconformably by a sedimentary sequence, the Ritarango Beds, comprising up to 3000 m of quartz-rich and lithic sandstone and conglomerate. This may be an equivalent of the South Alligator Group. Alternatively, it may be of early Carpentarian age.

Carpentarian System

This system was named by McDougall *et al.* (1965), part of the sequence in the McArthur Basin of the Northern Territory being taken as the type sequence. They recognized the base of the Cliffdale Volcanics as the base of the system, but did not define any top. A convenient top has, however, been provided by Thomson's (1966) definition of a base for the Adelaidean System, in rocks in the Adelaide Geosyncline that are known to be much younger than the Cliffdale Volcanics.

The **McArthur Basin** sequence extends from Arnhem Land to the Queensland border (Fig. 1.4) (Dunn *et al.*, in prep. and lies unconformably on "Nullaginian" basement rocks. The Carpentarian in the McArthur Basin comprises more than 8500 m of dominantly shallow-water sediments, with volcanics prominent towards the base (Fig. 1.5A, B). The sediments form the Tawallah Group and the overlying McArthur Group and their equivalents (Table 1.1).

In many places (Fig. 1.5A), acid to intermediate volcanics and pyroclastics with some feldspar-rich terrigenous sediments (Edith River, Cliffdale, Scrutton, Spencer Creek, and Fagan Volcanics) were the first rocks to be deposited in the McArthur Basin. Locally they reach 1200 m in thickness and are separated from overlying units by minor unconformities.

SYSTEM	McARTHUR BASIN					SOUTH NICHOLSON BASIN (& precursor)
	NORTH COAST	NORTH WEST	NORTH EAST	CENTRAL	SOUTH EAST	
ADELAIDEAN	WESSEL GROUP					
	MALAY ROAD GROUP	MAIWOK SUB-GROUP ROPER GROUP		MAIWOK SUB-GROUP ROPER GROUP		SOUTH NICHOLSON GROUP
CARPENTARIAN	WILBERFORCE BEDS	MOUNT RIGG GROUP	? ? HABGOOD GROUP ?	McARTHUR GROUP	? ?	BLUFF RANGE BEDS
	MOUNT BONNER SANDSTONE	KATHERINE RIVER GROUP	PARSONS RANGE GROUP	TAWALLAH GROUP	? ?	CARRARA RANGE FORMATION
	SPENCER CREEK VOLCANICS	EDITH RIVER VOLCANICS	FAGAN VOLCANICS RITARANGO BEDS	SCRUTTON VOLCANICS	CLIFFDALE VOLCANICS	
"NULLAGINIAN"	GRANITE AND METAMORPHIC BASEMENT					

TABLE 1.1. GENERALIZED STRATIGRAPHIC TABLE FOR THE McARTHUR AND SOUTH NICHOLSON BASINS. (Dunn, P. R. and Roberts, H. G., pers. comm.)

That part of the Katherine River Group above the Edith River Volcanics consists of up to 4500 m of arkosic and quartz sandstone and dolomite interbedded with intermediate and basic volcanics and pyroclastics. The sediments are ripple-marked and cross-stratified on a medium scale and represent shallow-water deposition on the western marginal platform of the McArthur Basin (Fig. 1.5A). Instability, caused by the continual volcanicity, produced local unconformities and slumping throughout the group.

To the east an important trough developed in which 6000 m of sediment (Parsons Range Group) accumulated. The lower portion is dominantly quartzose sandstone and subarkose. Siltstone and fine quartzose sandstone are more prominent in the upper part, and dolomite occurs towards the top. The topmost 150 m consists of cross-stratified and ripple-marked quartzose sandstone.

On Groote Eylandt to the east the equivalent sequence is much thinner (c. 600 m). Quartz-rich sandstones with medium-scale cross-stratification predominate, with local conglomerates containing volcanic pebbles. Similar sandstone (Mount Bonner) and younger banded siltstones and shales (basal Habgood Group) occur in the northeast coastal region of Arnhem Land.

In the southeastern part of the basin the equivalent Tawallah Group reaches 4200 m in maximum thickness. It is lithologically similar to the Katherine River Group, and accumulated on the southern part of the eastern marginal platform of the basin (Fig. 1.5A).

A local positive block, the "Murphy Tectonic Ridge" separated the group from its possible equivalent (Carrara Range Formation) to the south (Fig. 1.5A), where the sequence is thin because of breaks in deposition, only the upper, volcanic-rich part of the sequence, being present.

Following the deposition of the Tawallah Group and its equivalents, the margins of the McArthur Basin were uplifted and eroded. The succeeding McArthur Group was deposited unconformably on the Tawallah Group in the southeast, as was the Mount Rigg Group on the Katherine River Group in the northwest (Fig. 1.5B). Only in the axial part of the basin was deposition continuous. There the McArthur Group lies conformably on the Tawallah and Parsons Range Groups and in the northeast the Habgood Group spans this interval without any break.

Deposition of the McArthur Group and equivalents was marked by a regional decrease in terrigenous detritus that culminated in widespread deposition of carbonate mud (now dolomite) with scattered algal biostromes. Locally, basic volcanics were extruded.

The axial part of the basin, already trough-like in the north-central region (Fig. 1.5A) was then accentuated by rapid sinking between two north-trending hinge-lines to form the Batten Trough (Fig. 1.5B). A reef dolomite developed on the western hinge-line with back-reef carbonate mud, algal

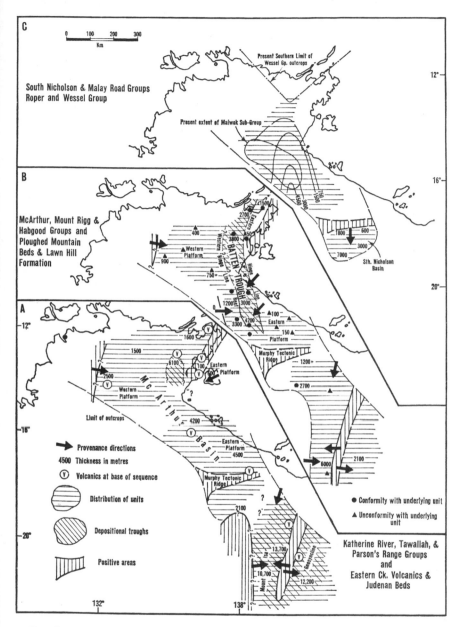

Fig. 1.5. Evolution of the McArthur and South Nicholson Basins and the Mount Isa Geosyncline. (Compiled using data contained in the explanatory notes to map sheets C53/14 to 16, D53/1 to 12 and 14 to 16, E53/2 to 4, 7 to 8 and 11 to 12 (1 : 250,000 geological series), and from Carter *et al.*, 1961.)

biostromes and quartz-rich silts, muds, and sands to the west. Locally, halite crystals were incorporated in the sediments. In the south the shoreline lay about 80 km west of the reef. East of the reef a thick succession of silt, carbonates, chert, sand, and chert breccia accumulated in which slump structures and graded bedding are common. Further east across the eastern hinge-line the water shallowed onto an extensive platform, where the section is much thinner. Breakdown of the reef then occurred, carbonate muds with biostromes being deposited in the southeast of the basin and quartz-rich sand, chert, and chert breccia with some algal and oolitic carbonates in the north and southwest. Basic volcanics accompanied these rocks in the northwest.

The McArthur Group is thickest (4200 m) in the southern part of the Batten Trough. It reaches 3300 m thick on the western platform in the south, but on the eastern platform it is less than 300 m thick, except in the north-coastal region (Fig. 1.5).

South of the Murphy Tectonic Ridge a sequence of carbonates and terrigenous clastics (Bluff Range Beds) possibly accumulated at the same time as the McArthur Group. The sequence lies conformably on volcanics of the Carrara Range Formation.

An orogeny at the end of the Carpentarian Period brought deposition of the McArthur Group and Bluff Range Beds to a close and modified the depositional framework for the succeeding units which are regarded as Adelaidean and which lie unconformably on the older units.

Southeast of the McArthur Basin, a thick Carpentarian succession, notable for the ore bodies it contains, accumulated in the **Mount Isa Geosyncline** (Fig. 1.5A, B). Carter *et al.* (1961) have recognized many units (Fig. 1.6) and described the evolution of this geosyncline in detail. The summary that follows is based on their work. Radiometric data (Richards *et al.*, 1963; Webb *et al.*, 1963) indicate that deposition in the Mount Isa Geosyncline was probably contemporaneous with part of that in the South Nicholson and McArthur Basins. The following correlation has been suggested (H. G. Roberts, pers. comm.); Tawallah Group = Leander Quartzite + Eastern Creek Volcanics + Judenan Beds; McArthur Group = Ploughed Mountain Beds + Lawn Hill Formation. The correlated units are lithologically similar.

The sequence in the Mount Isa Geosyncline lies unconformably on the "?Nullaginian" Yaringa Metamorphics. The oldest unit in the sequence, the Leichhardt Metamorphics, comprises amphibolite facies metamorphics. Originally these rocks were rhyolite and dacite, with intercalated terrigenous sediments, which marked a phase of acid volcanism.

The rhyolitic and dacitic volcanism continued, forming the Argylla Formation some 3000 m thick, the first unit for which a palaeogeography

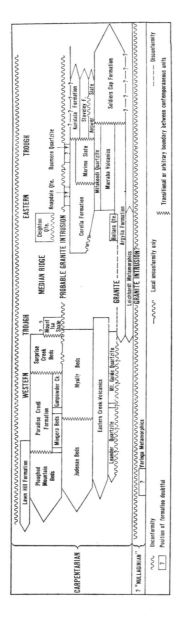

FIG. 1.6. Schematic representation of stratigraphic relationships in the Mount Isa Geosyncline. (After Carter *et al.*, 1961, modified.)

has been established (Fig. 1.7A). The lavas intertongue eastwards with a sandstone–shale sequence (Soldiers Cap Formation). The whole complex has subsequently been metamorphosed; the lavas have reached the greenschist facies whereas the sediments reach high in the amphibolite facies.

The Ewen Granite, which has been dated by Richards *et al.* (1963) as 1775 m.y., was intruded into the Argylla Formation before the onset of the next phase of volcanicity.

The area occupied by the acid volcanics was next covered by up to 2400 m of quartz-rich sands (Leander, Mount Guide, and Ballara Quartzites) which were initially derived from the west. In the eastern region of the geosyncline deposition of the Soldiers Cap Formation continued unbroken.

A fundamental modification to the geosyncline then took place, with the rise of a median meridional ridge (Fig. 1.7B). The eastern and western troughs of the geosyncline so formed persisted throughout the duration of the geosyncline, and have different sedimentary and tectonic histories. A change in the source of the quartz-rich sand in the western part of the geosyncline from west to east and northeast heralded the rise of this ridge.

The median ridge soon became the site of basic volcanicity, and both troughs of the geosyncline received a great thickness of interbedded basalt and sediment (Eastern Creek and Marraba Volcanics), some 3000 m in the eastern and 6000 m in the western trough (Fig. 1.7C). The basalts extended far across the eastern trough where they became intercalated with the sandstone–shale sequence of the Soldiers Cap Formation. The median ridge continued to rise during the period of volcanicity, and most of the volcanics were eroded from it.

As the volcanicity waned, some 1200 m of quartz-rich sands (Mitakoodi Quartzite), with occasional basalt intercalations, spread over the eastern trough and interfingered with the Soldiers Cap Formation. The close of the volcanicity is recorded in the overlying shale unit (now slate) which contains rare basalt flows in its basal portion.

After the deposition of the quartz-rich sands there was considerable movement in the eastern trough, with two subsidiary geanticlines rising within it. This movement brought to a close the deposition of the Soldiers Cap Formation. The western trough was little affected, only local unconformities on the western margin of the median ridge being produced.

After the movement, about 3000 m of thin-bedded dolomite with some shale and sandstone and dolomite breccia (Corella Formation) were deposited in the eastern trough (Fig. 1.7D). The unit now consists largely of calc–silicate rocks and schists. Lithologies change towards the south, where quartz-rich sand and mud (now quartzite, schist, and slate) accumulated with the dolomite.

The relation of the Corella Formation and its equivalents to the Soldiers Cap Formation and other older units varies from place to place. Conformity, disconformity, and angular unconformity all occur. This complexity is due to the variable deformation of the eastern trough, some parts having risen above sealevel whereas others apparently suffered only submarine erosion. The breccia in the base of the Corella Formation is probably a

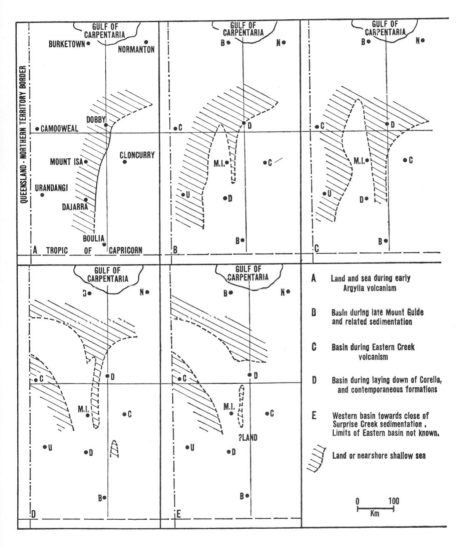

FIG. 1.7. Evolution of the Mount Isa Geosyncline. (After Carter *et al.*, 1961.)

record of this movement. The Corella Formation contains an important uraninite–allanite ore body at Mary Kathleen (Hughes and Munro, 1965).

Following the deposition of the Corella Formation and its equivalents a further sheet of quartz-rich sand (Roxmere and Knapdale Quartzites), reaching perhaps 1800 m in thickness, spread over the eastern trough. The strata are ripple-marked and cross-stratified, suggesting deposition in shallow water.

The equivalents in the western trough of the Corella Formation and its overlying quartzites are the Judenan and Myally Beds, which form a facies assemblage. The Myally Beds occur closest to the median ridge and are also well developed in the north of the trough. They consist of 6000 m of quartz-rich sandstone with minor siltstone and shale. Conglomerate and arkose occur near the base and rhyolite and basalt near the top. The Judenan is developed to the west and south of the Myally. It consists of 1800 m of muddy quartz-rich sandstone, siltstone, and shale, and is less well sorted than the Myally. Rhyolite and basalt occur in the upper part. The chief source for the Judenan and Myally Beds lay to the north of the trough (Fig. 1.5A).

Deposition of the Roxmere and Knapdale Quartzites in the eastern trough, and of the Judenan and Myally Beds in the western, was terminated by a major orogeny that deformed the whole of the eastern trough to a greater or lesser extent, and also affected the eastern margin of the western trough. Granite intrusions into the sediments of the eastern trough probably accompanied this deformation (Fig. 1.6).

With this deformation, sedimentation in the eastern trough diminished appreciably. After a period of erosion during which the land surface became strongly dissected, quartz-rich sands and gravels (Deighton Quartzite) again spread over the eastern trough from the west, to a thickness of 2100 m. No further sedimentation appears to have occurred prior to the orogeny that terminated the history of the geosyncline at the end of the Carpentarian Period.

In the western trough more than 6000 m of sediment accumulated in the interval between the two orogenies. Terrigenous detritus was contributed from the north and west, and from the median ridge to the east (Figs. 1.5B and 1.7E). The deepest water in the trough apparently lay to the south, close to the ridge. In this there accumulated a thin-bedded shale–dolomitic siltstone sequence (Mount Isa Shale), exhibiting small-scale cross-stratification, convolute bedding, and slump breccias (Bennett, 1965). Currents flowed from both east and west. The Mount Isa Shale, at Mount Isa, contains important galena–sphalerite–pyrite and chalcopyrite–pyrite ore bodies.

Elsewhere in the trough the Surprise Creek and Ploughed Mountain Beds and their equivalents accumulated. They consist of quartz-rich sandstone, often muddy, siltstone, shale, and dolomite. The multiplicity of sources produced marked facies changes, dolomite being best developed in the central and northern parts of the trough. Algal bioherms are extremely well developed in some places. The eastern parts of the trough received quartz-rich sand and gravel, particularly in the south. Towards the western margin siltstone and shale became prominent except in the southwest where conglomerate, arkose, and quartzites (Mingera Beds) were deposited. Ripple marks, medium-scale cross-stratification, and mudcracks suggest deposition in shallow water.

The interbedded dolomite–shale–sandstone sequence extends northwest-wards, towards the McArthur Basin (Fig. 1.5B). In this part of the trough the Ploughed Mountain Beds were followed conformably by a quartz-rich sandstone (Lawn Hill Formation) with rhyolite in its lower part and siltstone and shale towards its top.

A major orogeny terminated deposition of the Lawn Hill Formation, both the western and eastern troughs being deformed. Subsequent deposition was limited to local accumulation of quartz-rich sandstone and conglomerates of Adelaidean or possibly Cambrian age.

In northern Queensland some 9000 m of strata were deposited in the **Etheridge Geosyncline** (White, 1961, 1962). These are probably Carpentarian (Richards *et al.*, 1967), and lie unconformably on older Precambrian rocks.

Deposition in the Etheridge Geosyncline probably took place principally in deep water. The finer-grained parts of the Etheridge and Langdon River Formations—shale, chert, and calcareous quartz siltstone—are regarded as pelagic sediments. They accumulated in the western trough and the central part of the eastern trough of the geosyncline. Some shallower water deposition of quartz sandstone and siltstone took place close to basement outcrops and in the northeast of the geosyncline.

Later volcanicity gave rise to a thin sequence of acid lavas, the Croydon Volcanics. These may be roughly contemporaneous with the rhyolite in the Lawn Hill Formation of the Mount Isa Geosyncline.

The sequence was later folded and intruded by granite, and by ultrabasic rocks along its eastern margin.

Carpentarian deposition was also widespread in the northwest of Western Australia in the **Kimberley Basin** (Fig. 1.4) (Dow *et al.*, 1964/104; Roberts *et al.*, 1965/156; Gellatly *et al.*, 1965/210). This basin occupies the Kimberley Division of Western Australia, and is bounded on the southwest and southeast by a mobile belt which contains sequences comparable to those of the basin proper, but containing many unconformities. Some of these mobile belt sequences are notably thicker than their equivalents elsewhere, and appear to have accumulated in sub-basins peripheral to the main basin.

The lowest Carpentarian unit, the Whitewater Volcanics, comprises about 2000 m of acid volcanics and tuffs, and lies unconformably on the Halls Creek Group and Lamboo Complex. It is overlain unconformably by a conformable sequence of three groups, aggregating 5700 m in maximum thickness, all of which are shallow water deposits, some possibly being ter-restrial. This sequence is extensively intruded by sills of the ?Adelaidean Hart Dolerite. The oldest unit, the Speewah Group (maximum 2300 m) contains a threefold rhythm of quartz sandstone, subarkose or arkose, and olive to fawn siltstone and shale with minor acid volcanics. The overlying Kimberley Group (maximum 3300 m) is predominantly quartz sandstone, with basic

	KIMBERLEY BASIN		STURT PLATFORM
		LUBBOCK SUB-BASIN	
ADELAIDAN		LOUISA DOWNS GROUP	Albert Edward Group
	MOUNT HOUSE GROUP	KUNIANDI GROUP	Duerdin Group
		GLIDDEN GROUP	Helicopter Siltstone / Wade Ck. Sandstone
CARPENTARIAN		COLOMBO SANDSTONE	Bungle Bungle Dolomite / Mt. Parker Sandstone
	BASTION GROUP	CROWHURST GROUP	
	KIMBERLEY GROUP		Red Rock Beds
	SPEEWAH GROUP		
	WHITEWATER VOLCANICS		

TABLE 1.2. GENERALIZED STRATIGRAPHIC TABLE FOR KIMBERLEY BASIN AND STURT PLATFORM. (From Roberts *et al.*, 1965/156, modified)

volcanics towards the base and red and green shales and some stromatolitic dolomite towards the top. At Yampi Sound, in the southwest of the basin, these shales and the overlying sandstones pass into 600 m of hematitic quartz-ite and iron-formation (Harms, M.Sc. thesis, 1959) which are mined as iron ores (Reid, 1965).

The uppermost unit, the Bastion Group (maximum 1400 m), comprises purple and green shale and siltstone, quartz sandstone, and some dolomite. Equivalent and lithologically similar strata (Crowhurst Group, maximum about 150 m) occur in southern part of the mobile zone in what is here termed the **Lubbock Sub-Basin** (Table 1.2).

In the northeastern extremity of the mobile belt, strata equivalent to at least the Speewah Group, and possibly to the whole of the overlying sequence as well, accumulated in what may have been a separate sub-basin. These, the Carr Boyd Group, aggregate about 9000 m in thickness and consist primarily of alternations of quartz sandstone and red, green, or black siltstone and shale. There are several unconformities within the group, at the base of sandstone units.

The youngest Carpentarian unit in the Kimberley Basin, the Colombo Sandstone (maximum 90 m) occurs in the southern part of the basin and consists of poorly sorted quartz sandstone. It unconformably overlies the Crowhurst Group, and is unconformably overlain by the Adelaidean Louisa Downs Group.

To the east of the mobile zone on the eastern margin of the Kimberley basin, Carpentarian strata were deposited on an extensive north–south trending structure, here termed the **Sturt Platform.** The relationship of this feature to the Victoria River Basin to the north (Fig. 1.1) has yet to be determined.

The oldest strata, the Red Rock Beds (Dow *et al.*, 1964/104) may be equivalents of the Carr Boyd Group in the Kimberley Basin. They comprise 3300 m of shallow-water quartzite and red siltstone lying unconformably on the Halls Creek Group. Unconformably above this unit there occur some 300 m of cross-stratified quartz sandstone of shallow-water origin (Mount Parker Sandstone). This may be an equivalent of the Colombo Sandstone in the Kimberley Basin (Table 1.2). It is overlain conformably by about 1400 m of stromatolitic dolomite, and grey shale and quartz sandstone (Bungle Bungle Dolomite). The sequence is overlain unconformably by the Adelaidean Wade Creek Sandstone.

The sequence in the **Davenport Geosyncline**, known as the Hatches Creek Group (Smith *et al.*, 1961), lies unconformably on the Warramunga Group. It consists largely of quartz-rich sandstones which are argillaceous towards the base of the sequence, and some shale and siltstone. Porphyritic rhyolite, andesite, and basalt flows are present in the lower parts of the sequence. Small- to medium-scale cross-stratification and ripple-marks are abundant in the sandstones. The total thickness of the sequence exceeds 7500 m.

The group is unmetamorphosed except in the vicinity of shear zones and igneous intrusions. Gabbro and granophyre masses locally intrude the sequence (Ryan, 1961) and both quartz–porphyry and granite intrusions are recorded by Smith *et al.* (1961); almost all of these masses are restricted to axial culminations of folds. The granite is younger than the porphyry in at least one locality. Minimum ages have been determined by Hurley *et al.* (1961).

The **Ashburton Geosyncline**, which lies north of Tennant Creek, contains a sequence exceeding 3300 m in thickness, which is very similar to the Hatches Creek Group. It comprises quartz-rich sandstone and conglomerate with small- to medium-scale cross-stratification (Ivanac, 1954). Some basalt is interbedded with the sandstones, and quartz–porphyry intrusions are present. The nature of the contact between this sequence and the underlying Warramunga Group is somewhat obscure, but is probably unconformable. Both the Hatches Creek Group and the sequence in the Ashburton Geosyncline are overlain unconformably by Cambrian strata.

Metamorphic complexes of probable Carpentarian age occur in the south of South Australia and extend across the border into New South Wales (Fig. 1.4). All are overlain unconformably by Adelaidean strata. The **Willyama Complex** of the Broken Hill district, New South Wales, has been the subject of much study because of the large silver–lead–zinc ore bodies that it contains. The complex consists of high-grade metamorphic rocks among which schists, amphibolites, gneisses, and banded iron-formations are prominent (Binns, 1964). A detailed form-stratigraphy has been worked out for part of the complex, and a complicated structural picture has emerged (Gustafson *et al.*, 1950; Lewis *et al.*, 1965). The complex is polymetamorphic and yields a wide range of radiometric dates (Binns, 1963; Richards and Pidgeon, 1963).

The **Mount Painter Complex**, which lies about 250 km northwest of Broken Hill, is similar to the Willyama Complex and comprises quartzite, schists, gneisses, and potash granites. It is intruded by Lower Palaeozoic granodiorites (Compston *et al.*, 1966), and contains some uranium ore bodies.

On the western side of the Adelaide Geosyncline the **Gawler Platform** is composed of metamorphic rocks which are Carpentarian or older. Two units, apparently conformable and together aggregating a maximum of 10,000 m in thickness, have been recognized. The older, the Flinders Group, has a maximum thickness of 9000 m and consists dominantly of gneisses and migmatites with some quartzites, dolomites, and minor meta-igneous amphibolites.

The overlying Hutchison Group is up to 6000 m thick. In it mica schists are predominant, together with bedded amphibolite, hematite quartzite, and dolomite. The iron-ore deposits west of Whyalla occur in probable equivalents of this unit.

The oldest deposits on the Gawler Platform, which lie unconformably on the Flinders and Hutchison Groups and their equivalents (Thomson, 1966), are of late Carpentarian age. The oldest of these, the Corunna Conglomerate, consists of conglomerate, sandstone, red shale, and dolomite. It is cut by intrusive phases of the predominantly extrusive Gawler Range Volcanics, which consists of rhyolite and quartz-porphyry. Both of these units are geographically separated from Adelaidean strata by older rocks, and their age relationships to the Adelaidean have been determined by Compston *et al.* (1966) using radiometric methods.

Adelaidean System

The Adelaide (or Adelaidean*) System (or Series) is a unit of long standing among Australian geologists, having been introduced by David (1922) to describe the thick sequence of Precambrian sediments that conformably underlies the Cambrian in the Adelaide Geosyncline. The base of the System, in this, its type area, has been defined (Thomson, 1966) as the base of the Callanna Beds near Wooltana. Strata coeval with the type Adelaidean occur in many Australian sedimentary basins (Dunn *et al.*, 1966) (Fig. 1.8).

The radiometric age of the base of the Adelaidean System (and hence of the top of the Carpentarian System) is not firmly established. The strata in the type area for the base of the system, near Wooltana, are metamorphosed, and the Wooltana Volcanics give only a minimum age of 850 m.y. (Compston *et al.*, 1966). The basement in the nearby Mount Painter and Olary districts sets an upper limit of 1600 m.y.

Petrographically similar volcanics near Roopena 340 km southwest on Eyre Peninsula, have been dated at 1345 ± 30 m.y. (Compston *et al.*, 1966). They are geographically separated from the main Adelaide Geosyncline sequence by older rocks, but have been correlated with the Wooltana Volcanics (Thomson, 1966). The presently accepted age of *c.* 1400 m.y. for the base of the system rests on this correlation. Other possibilities are discussed by Compston *et al.* (1966).

The Precambrian part of the **Adelaide Geosyncline** sequence exceeds 15,000 m in maximum thickness. It is remarkable that, in spite of its great thickness, turbidites are absent from the sequence, and volcanics are limited in amount. In this geosyncline the Adelaidean System has been divided into four major time-rock units, known as the Willouran, Torrensian, Sturtian, and Marinoan Series (Glaessner and Parkin, eds., 1958). A rock-unit terminology (Table 1.3) has been proposed by Thomson *et al.* (1964) who have provided a valuable summary of the stratigraphy.

Sediments of Willouran age form the base of the sequence (Callanna Beds and equivalents) and lie unconformably on a crystalline basement. They comprise up to 3600 m of siltstone, slate, dolomite, and quartz sandstone. At

---

*There has been some unwillingness to use the adjectival form, as Howchin (1929) had applied the term *Adelaidean Stage* to a unit in the Tertiary. This later term, the homonymy of which Howchin was aware (Howchin, 1935), is clearly inadmissible under Article 12(ii) of the *Australian Code of Stratigraphic Nomenclature* (1964). Ludbrook (1963) has clarified the situation by introducing the term *Yatalan Stage* to describe the Tertiary unit.

Wooltana, west of Lake Frome, the Callanna Beds consist of some 600 m of metasomatized trachyte with some andesite and rhyolite (Wooltana Volcanics) and minor phyllite and marble overlying a basal quartzite (Crawford, 1963). Similar volcanics, believed to be of Willouran age, occur in the northwestern part of the geosyncline, in the east near Broken Hill, and on the western edge of the Stuart Shelf 45 km southwest of Port Augusta (Roopena Volcanics) (Thomson, 1966).

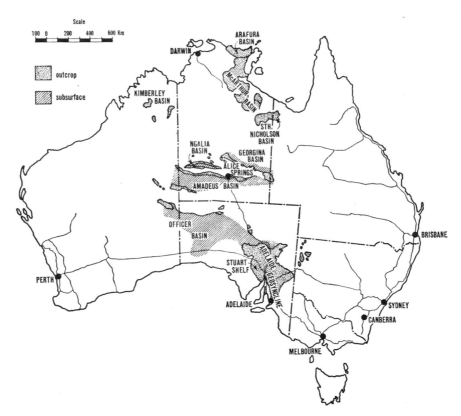

Fig. 1.8. Distribution of Adelaidean Strata.

Willouran strata are best developed in the northwestern and southern parts of the Adelaide Geosyncline (Fig. 1.9A). Sequences are thickest in the northwest. The Willouran is absent in the Everard Range near the South Australia–Northern Territory border, and is overlapped by the Sturtian strata on the flanks of the Mount Painter Complex.

	TIME – ROCK UNITS	ROCK UNITS		UNCONFORMITIES
CAMBRIAN SYSTEM — LOWER CAMBRIAN SERIES		PARACHILNA AND MOUNT TERRIBLE FORMATIONS (limestones with archaeocyathids) Shelf facies	KANMANTOO GROUP (greywackes) Trough facies	local
ADELAIDEAN SYSTEM — MARINOAN SERIES		POUND QUARTZITE / A B C RANGE QUARTZITE / upper glacial beds / interglacial beds	WILPENA GROUP	
STURTIAN SERIES		YUDNAMUTANA SUB-GROUP AND EQUIVALENTS = lower glacial beds	UMBERATANA GROUP AND EQUIVALENTS	local / local
TORRENSIAN SERIES		ALDGATE SANDSTONE, COPLEY QUARTZITE AND EQUIVALENTS	BURRA GROUP AND EQUIVALENTS	slight
WILLOURAN SERIES		WOOLTANA VOLCANICS	CALLANNA BEDS, RIVER WAKEFIELD GROUP, AND EQUIVALENTS	strong
CARPENTARIAN		Crystalline basement : Mount Painter Complex, Willyama Complex, etc.		

TABLE 1.3. SIMPLIFIED STRATIGRAPHIC SCHEME FOR THE ADELAIDE GEOSYNCLINE. (After Thomson *et al.*, 1964)

South and east of Adelaide the Willouran is represented by a sequence of some thousands of metres of phyllite, quartzite, and dolomite (River Wakefield Group), which occurs beneath the Burra Group near Riverton, 50 km north of Adelaide.

The Willouran Series is succeeded by the Torrensian Series. In some places Torrensian strata lie unconformably on the Willouran.

The Burra Group, the most widespead unit in the Torrensian Series, commences with a basal sandstone–conglomerate unit, usually quartz-rich, up to 1950 m thick. This is overlain by an argillite–carbonate succession in which dolomites, limestones, and magnesites occur. In the Burra region limestone predominates in the lower part of the succession (Dickinson, 1942). West of Copley, magnesites with interbedded quartzite or arkose beds occur scattered throughout the argillite sequence. These quartzites become prominent only in the Adelaide region where they form a massive unit in the middle of the sequence.

Forbes (1960, 1961) considered the magnesite, which is widespread, and best developed in the Copley area, to be possibly the result of reaction between alkaline water of continental origin and sea water in an area of paralic sedimentation. Palaeocurrent indicators suggest highlands to the north and west, with marine conditions prevailing in the southeast.

The Burra Group, like the Callanna Beds, is thicker in the western and northwestern regions of the geosyncline than elsewhere, the area of maximum accumulation extending from near Leigh Creek to within a few kilometres of Adelaide. In this region its thickness exceeds 3000 m with a maximum of more than 4200 m. To the northeast, east and south of this area, the Burra Group thins, and is overlapped by the Umberatana Group on the Mount Painter inlier, and in the Olary region. Westward the Burra Group thins rapidly onto the Stuart Shelf where it is apparently overlapped by Marinoan strata (Fig. 1.9B).

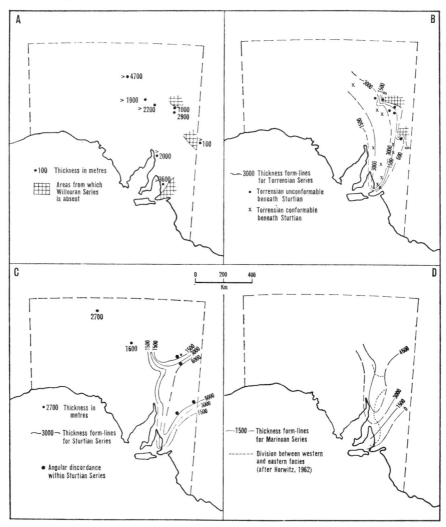

Fig. 1.9. Evolution of the Adelaide Geosyncline through Willouran, Torrensian, Sturtian, and Marinoan Epochs (A, B, C, D respectively). Isopachs constructed from thicknesses measured on maps of the 1 : 63,360 Geological Atlas of South Australia.

The thinning of the Burra Group to the east and northeast is partly the result of erosion prior to deposition of the Umberatana Group. In these regions (Fig. 1.9B), but not elsewhere, there is unconformity between the Burra Group and the overlying Umberatana Group, and the Burra Group remains either as a thin veneer over the basement, or as isolated pockets, which are the troughs of synclines.

The Umberatana Group approaches its thickest development in the areas where it lies unconformably on the Burra Group. Erosion of the Burra Group in the east presumably occurred therefore during the late Torrensian when the upper part of the thick Torrensian sequence to the west was still accumulating. At this time, then, the geosyncline was cannibalistic.

The lower part of the Umberatana Group (Table 1.3), which here forms the Sturtian Series, has long been regarded as a partly glacigenic sequence. It commonly commences with massive boulder bed which may locally be underlain by or be interbedded with quartzites. One glacial pavement has been recognized (Mirams, 1964). Tillites occur higher in the sequence and contain facetted and striated erratics of granite, gneiss, quartzite, limestone, slate, and rarely amphibolite. Laminated silty shale, locally varved, together with dolomite, sandstone, and conglomerate, may also be present. The dominantly glacigenic lower part of the sequence is known throughout much of the geosyncline as the Yudnamutana Sub-Group.

The overlying interglacial sequence consists chiefly of laminated blue–grey silty shale and minor arkose, in the lower part, with green siltstone, dolomite, and muddy sandstones above containing local developments of iron-formation. In the Adelaide region a limestone is developed at the top of the sequence.

The Sturtian thickens markedly north and northeast from Adelaide (Fig. 1.9c) reaching a maximum in excess of 6000 m. The thickness of tillite and tillitic sandstone within the sequence increases in a somewhat similar manner, reaching a maximum of 2100 m near Mount Fitton.

At several localities some angular discordance appears to exist within the Sturtian Series (Fig. 1.9c). In the Mount Painter district this falls within the Yudnamutana Sub-Group, whereas 30 km to the north, and perhaps also in the Olary district, the angular discordance appears at the top of the sub-group. These discordances are known only from the eastern and north-eastern regions of the geosyncline.

The Sturtian is the most widespread of the units in the Adelaide Geosyn-cline. Outliers have been mapped far to the northwest of the Flinders Ranges in the Everard Range. Here basalt flows occur with the tillites. The massive Anabama Granite intrudes Sturtian strata in the Olary region (Mirams, 1961), and is probably of Early Palaeozoic age (Compston *et al.*, 1966).

The Marinoan Series, which succeeds the Sturtian, has in the past been recognized as a post-glacial sequence (Glaessner and Parkin, eds., 1958, p. 13), with its basal unit characteristically a purple and green shale or slate. However, Webb and Horwitz (1959) have shown that the upper glacial sequence recognized in various parts of South Australia which had previously been regarded as of late Sturtian age, is of early Marinoan age.

It has recently been pointed out that the lower Marinoan is not everywhere characterized by red beds (Horwitz, 1962). These merely form a "western facies" of the unit, which is also characterized by stromatolitic limestones and a general absence of boulder tillite. On the opposite side of a transitional zone characterized by a poverty of coarse detritus, the "eastern facies" is developed (Fig. 1.9D). In this the rocks are usually grey, arenites are matrix-rich, boulder tillite is common, and the limestones lack stromatolites. These differences are considered to be related to differences of source, the western facies being derived from the Shield to the west and the eastern facies from an eastern source (Horwitz, 1962).

The remainder of the Marinoan (Wilpena Group) consists of purple and green shales and siltstones, quartzite, and limestones which are commonly dolomitic and contain stromatolites. Commonly there are two prominent quartzite units, the ABC Range Quartzite in the middle of the sequence, and the Pound Quartzite at the top which contains the medusoid-octocoral-annelid fauna described by Glaessner and Daily (1959). Limestones and dolomites are prominent between these two quartzites.

The Marinoan is thickest (more than 4500 m) in a north-trending zone coinciding with the Flinders Ranges. It thins southwards to zero against the older Precambrian inliers of the Adelaide Hills. To the west the Marinoan thins on to the Stuart Shelf, being 2700 m thick west of Lake Torrens (Fig. 1.9D).

The Marinoan, in general, passes conformably into the overlying Cambrian strata, but south and east of Adelaide there is some evidence of unconformity between the Marinoan and the Cambrian (Horwitz *et al.*, 1959; Thomson and Horwitz, 1961).

The Adelaidean strata of the **Officer Basin** are very poorly known. The area closest to the Stuart Shelf from which they have been recorded is near Maralinga, South Australia. There 300 m of chocolate and green shale of probable Marinoan age occur in the subsurface (Ludbrook, 1961*a*; Coats, 1965).

?Adelaidean strata (Townsend Range "Series") outcrop on the northern margin of the basin on both sides of the South Australia–Western Australia border (Johnson, 1963; Horwitz and Sofoulis, 1963). Quartzite with some shale and limestone, which is probably Marinoan, lies unconformably on a sequence of basic volcanics, conglomerate, quartzite, and limestone which may be of Willouran age. The ?Willouran lies with strong unconformity on the older Precambrian Musgrave–Mann Complex.

The **Amadeus Basin,** which extends across the southern part of the Northern Territory (Fig. 1.8), contains a sequence, with extensive Adelaidean sediments at the base, which has been the subject of much study (Prichard and Quinlan, 1962; Wells *et al.*, 1965*a, b, c, d*; Forman, 1965; Forman *et al.*, 1965; Ranford *et al.*, 1965). The basin is bounded on the north and south by areas of granite–gneiss and schist—the Arunta and Musgrave–Mann Complexes (Fig. 1.1). The margins of the basin are structurally complex, both the metamorphic basement and part of the sedimentary cover having been involved in recumbent folds.

SYSTEM	WEST		SOUTH	NORTH EAST
CAMBRIAN	///////		///////	PERTAOORRTA GROUP
			MT. CURRIE CONGL.	
ADELAIDEAN	MAURICE FORMATION		WINNALL BEDS	PERTATATAKA FORMATION
	SIR FREDERICK CONGLOMERATE	ELLIS SANDSTONE		
	CARNEGIE FORMATION	BOORD FORMATION	ININDIA BEDS	AREYONGA FORMATION
	Disconformity BITTER SPRINGS FORMATION		?PINYINNA BEDS	Disconformity BITTER SPRINGS FORMATION
	HEAVITREE QUARTZITE		DEAN QUARTZITE	HEAVITREE QUARTZITE

TABLE 1.4. STRATIGRAPHIC SCHEME—AMADEUS BASIN. (Wells *et al.*, 1965*a, c*; Forman, 1965)

The basement is commonly gneiss, granite, and schist with which the Adelaidean is generally unconformable. However, in the Petermann Ranges a metamorphic gradation occurs between the underlying gneisses and granites and the basal sedimentary unit (Dean Quartzite) which is regionally metamorphosed (Forman, 1965). Weakly to moderately metamorphosed acid and basic volcanics form the basement over wide areas in the west and southwest, and locally the sediments appear conformable with the volcanics.

The Adelaidean reaches more than 3600 m in maximum thickness towards the southern margin of the basin and 2000 m at the northern **margin.**

The sequence (Table 1.4), comprises marine quartzite and carbonates overlain by sandstone, siltstone, shale, limestone, dolomite, and boulder beds, of fluviatile, glacial, and marine origin. Shallow-water conditions appear to have been maintained throughout the history of the basin.

The lowest unit consists of a basal orthoquartzite (Heavitree and Dean Quartzites), up to 450 m thick, locally underlain by siltstones and conglomerates which are thought to represent valley fill. Medium-scale cross-stratification, ripple marks, and locally, mud-cracks, are common. These are succeeded conformably by a carbonate-dominated succession up to 750 m thick (Bitter Springs Formation, Pinyinna Beds) comprising bedded fetid dolomite and limestone, with stromatolitic dolomite and limestone, chert, shale, halite (subsurface), and gypsum in places. Basic volcanics occur locally in the eastern part of the basin. The Bitter Springs and Pinyinna Beds have behaved incompetently, giving rise to numerous diapiric structures and a disharmonic structural relationship between the strata below and above the unit.

The overlying parts of the sequence in places lie disconformably on the Bitter Springs Formation, but relationships appear to be conformable on the south side of the basin.

The Areyonga and Boord Formations and Inindia Beds, which reach 2100 m in thickness, succeed the carbonate unit. They are in part glacigenic, and should probably be correlated with the Sturtian glacials of the Adelaide Geosyncline and the tillites of the Duerdin Group. Tillites, tillitic sandstones, muddy sandstones, and conglomerates are widely but sporadically developed. Fine-grained material apparently consists mainly of rock flour. The erratic blocks reach more than 60 cm in diameter. Many blocks are striated and are associated in the siltstone with distorted lamination. The upper part of the Areyonga lacks tillitic rocks, being composed of poorly sorted, pebbly, cross-stratified, quartz-rich sandstone.

Interbedded, red–brown, cross-stratified sandstone and siltstone (Carnegie Formation) occupy an equivalent position in the sequence in the southwest of the trough and interfinger with the Boord Formation to the north. The Boord Formation and the Inindia Beds contain limestone, including calcilutites and oolitic and stromatolitic types, dolomite, oolitic chert, siltstone, and minor sandstone.

In the southern and western parts of the trough the Inindia Beds and their equivalents are overlain unconformably by the Winnall Beds and its equivalents (Table 1.4). To the northeast the Areyonga Formation is conformably overlain by the Pertatataka Formation, which is more or less an equivalent of the Winnall Beds. This changing relationship is believed to reflect tectonism affecting the southern and western parts of the basin, an event which may be further reflected in the presence in the west of the

Sir Frederick Conglomerate, a coarse equivalent of the lower part of the Winnall Beds.

There is an increase in maximum thicknesses from north to south and west. The Pertataka Formation reaches 1200 m, the Winnall Beds 2400 m, and the Sir Frederick Conglomerate–Ellis Sandstone–Maurice Formation section may be as thick as 3900 m. The increases in thicknesses are matched by a change from green, red, and red–brown sandstone, siltstone, and shale with some white quartz sandstone and limestone (Pertataka) to red–brown and white, partly feldspathic, quartz-rich sandstone and siltstone (Winnall, Ellis, Maurice) and quartzite cobble conglomerate (Sir Frederick). Some sandstones in the Winnall Beds are pebbly with abundant detrital chert.

The Pertataka Formation shows close similarities to the "eastern facies" of the Marinoan Series in the Adelaide Geosyncline, and Wells *et al.*, (1965/108) have recognized in it a boulder bed which they believe to be of glacial origin.

The Adelaidean strata are separated from overlying Cambrian strata by a major regional unconformity in the south, although they are generally conformable with the Cambrian in the north. The unconformity is considered by Forman (1965) to reflect a major orogeny that occurred in the late Adelaidean or Early Cambrian and was most pronounced along the southern margin of the basin.

The **Ngalia Basin** which lies within the Arunta Complex, and the **Georgina Basin** which is situated on its north side, contain Adelaidean sediments resting on a basement of granite and Archaean meta-sediments. The strata on the southern margin of the Georgina Basin are best known (Smith, 1960/73, 1964; Smith and Milligan, 1963/46; Smith and Vine, 1960/71).

The lowest unit, not everywhere present, is considered to be glacigenic. It consists of green siltstone with boulders up to 1 m in diameter, some of which are striated, with some quartz-rich sandstone, arkose, and dolomite. The unit thickens eastwards from 45 m near Huckitta to more than 540 m on the Queensland border.

A sequence of red and green shales, quartz-rich sandstones, arkose, siltstone, and stromatolitic dolomite (Mopunga Group) overlies the glacigenic unit, possibly disconformably. It contains Cambrian fossils near its top. This sequence exhibits ripple marks and medium-scale cross-stratification, and in part, at least, was derived from the Arunta Block to the south-west. Near Huckitta its thickness exceeds 1500 m, and it thins eastwards. Similar rocks extend northwest to Barrow Creek, but are little known. Tindale (1933) claims that the 420 m of strata in the Giles Range, still further west, are similar to those of the Mopunga Group.

In the Ngalia Basin P. J. Cook (pers. comm.) has recognized a sequence of 450 m of quartz sandstone, with ripple marks and medium-scale cross-stratification, which lies unconformably on the ?Archaean basement south of Yuendumu. This sequence is believed to be Adelaidean, and is overlain unconformably by Lower Cambrian strata.

The most complete Adelaidean sequence in the **Kimberley Basin** of Western Australia occurs in the Lubbock Sub-Basin which forms its southernmost part. The sequence (Roberts *et al.*, 1965/156) comprises three groups, the lowest of which, the Glidden Group (maximum 550 m) lies unconformably on the Carpentarian Kimberley Group. It is a shallow-water deposit, consisting principally of quartz sandstone and subarkose with some dark green to black shale and siltstone.

The next youngest unit, the Kuniandi Group, consists of up to 1200 m of purple, green and grey siltstone, muddy quartz-rich sandstone and subarkose, with a prominent tillite and some dolomite, siltstone, and sandstone forming the lowermost formation (Landrigan Tillite). The tillite comprises boulders, cobbles, and pebbles of a variety of rock types including quartzite, granite, and dolomite set in a red or green muddy sand matrix. Some of the larger phenoclasts are polished and striated.

The Kuniandi Group lies unconformably on the Kimberley Group and is overlain unconformably by the Upper Adelaidean Louisa Downs Group. The relationships between the Kuniandi and Glidden Groups shown in Table 1.2 are a matter of inference.

The uppermost unit in the sequence, the **Louisa Downs Group**, exceeds 4000 m in maximum thickness. Like the Kuniandi, it commences with a tillite-bearing unit, the Egan Formation. This can be broadly subdivided into a lower arkose–siltstone–sandy limestone sequence, a middle tillite consisting predominantly of quartzite phenoclasts, with some of dolomite and rarely of granite in a purple grey or green muddy sand matrix, and an upper dolomite sequence. The tillite locally rests on a polished and striated pavement. Higher formations in the group consist of quartz-rich arenites and purple, green, and grey siltstone and shale. The group is regarded largely as a marine deposit, formed in shallow water except for the upper parts which have many of the features of turbidites, and may be deeper water deposits. It is overlain unconformably by the Cambrian Antrim Plateau Volcanics.

Certain of the units of the Lubbock Sub-Basin sequence extend northwards into the southern part of the Kimberley Basin proper. However, over much of the main part of the basin Adelaidean strata are missing, probably due to erosion. Those that are preserved, the Mount House Group (maximum 750 m), are equivalents of the Kuniandi Group to the south, and like it lie unconformably on the Kimberley Group. The Walsh Tillite (Guppy *et al.*, 1958) at the base reaches 60 m in thickness and is generally similar to the Landrigan Tillite. It overlies a striated pavement in places, as for example at Police Creek (Harms, M.Sc. thesis, 1959). The upper parts of the group consist dominantly of red and green shale, although quartz sandstone and stromatolitic dolomite are locally prominent.

On the **Sturt Platform**, to the east of the Kimberley Basin a sequence similar to that in the Lubbock Sub-Basin was deposited (Table 1.2). The Wade Creek Sandstone, and the Helicopter Siltstone conformably overlying it, form the lowest units (Dow *et al.*, 1964/104). They comprise about 670 m of quartz sandstone and green and grey siltstone and shale of probable shallow-water origin. The unit lies unconformably on the Carpentarian Bungle Bungle Dolomite.

The Helicopter Siltstone is overlain unconformably by the Duerdin Group, a correlative of the Mount House Group. The basal units of the Duerdin Group comprise two tillites, each ranging from 0 to 150 m in thickness, and separated by a minor unconformity (Dow, 1965). Striated and smoothed pavements are known, and the ice moved from the northeast. The boulders include many lithologies characteristic of the Lamboo Complex. These tillites are believed to be equivalents of the Walsh and Landrigan Tillites in the Kimberley Basin. The upper tillite is followed by 600 m of siltstone and dolomitic sandstone.

This is succeeded unconformably by about 1500 m of sediments (Albert Edward Group), with quartz-rich sandstone prominent at the base and purple, green, and grey shales with some sandstone overlying. No tillite is known to occur in the group. The Cambrian Antrim Plateau Volcanics lie unconformably on this sequence.

The **McArthur and South Nicholson Basins** (Fig. 1.5c) in the northeastern Northern Territory were also the sites of Adelaidean sedimentation (Table 1.1) (Dunn *et al.*, in prep.) the sediments having been dated by McDougall *et al.* (1965).

In the South Nicholson Basin over 6000 m of muds, quartz-rich silts, and sands which are commonly glauconitic (South Nicholson Group) accumulated. This group thins markedly towards the old Murphy Tectonic Ridge which separates the South Nicholson and McArthur Basins.

In the McArthur Basin a somewhat similar sequence with local carbonates (Roper Group) was deposited. The locus of maximum sedimentation lies slightly west of that of earlier units (Fig. 1.5c). Ripple marks and medium-scale cross-stratification are common, suggesting shallow-water conditions. The sequence becomes more silty towards the north. In the west-central part of the basin additional strata of similar lithology (Maiwok Sub-Group) overlie the main part of the Roper Group.

In the north-coastal region of Arnhem Land there occur up to 1500 m of strata (Malay Road Group), coeval with and similar to the main part of the Roper Group.

Folding, following the deposition of the Roper, Malay Road, and South

Nicholson Groups, terminated sedimentation. Only in the north was there any subsequent Precambrian deposition. There, in the **Arafura Basin,** more than 1350 m of younger Adelaidean terrigenous stable shelf sediments (Wessel Group) which have been dated radiometrically (McDougall *et al.*, 1965), lie unconformably on older units (Table 1.1). They consist principally of ripple-marked quartz sandstone and grey–green and purple shale, with minor chert and chert breccia near the top of the sequence. The sequence was folded some time before the Cretaceous.

Undifferentiated Precambrian Rocks

METAMORPHIC COMPLEXES

Several metamorphic complexes, which are believed on stratigraphic grounds to be of Precambrian age, have not been dated radiometrically. These occur in South Australia, Queensland, Tasmania, and New Zealand.

In the northwest of South Australia, extending across the Northern Territory border, there is a large area of crystalline rocks known as the **Musgrave–Mann Complex.** This is in part pre-Adelaidean, but along its northern margin, rocks of the complex were involved with Adelaidean strata in an ep-Adelaidean diastrophic movement with accompanying granitization. Part of the complex in this region may therefore consist of transformed Adelaidean strata (Forman, 1965). The Musgrave–Mann Complex (Fig. 1.1) consists of gneisses, quartzites, and acid to basic granulites, some of which are charnockitic. These are extensively intruded by granites, and by basic and ultrabasic plutonics which form the Giles Complex. Some anorthosite masses also occur.

To the southeast the **Peake Metamorphics** consisting of migmatite, granite-gneiss, mica-schist, slate, quartzite, and basic metamorphics, appear beneath the Adelaidean Willouran Series in the Peake and Denison Ranges (Glaessner and Parkin, eds., 1958).

Similar rocks, forming the **Barossa and Houghton Complexes,** occur as inliers in the Adelaide Hills. These rocks lie unconformably beneath Adelaidean or Cambrian strata.

In Queensland the **Einasleigh Metamorphics**, which form the basement for the Carpentarian sequence in the Etheridge Geosyncline, consist of migmatites, banded granulites, amphibolites, gneisses, and mica-schists (White, 1961).

The highlands of **western Tasmania** contain large areas of strongly deformed meta-sediments and meta-volcanics (Fig. 1.1). Massive and schistose quartzites, garnet-, mica-, and albite-schists, phyllites, and amphibolites predominate, and the sequence probably exceeds 6000 m in thickness. These rocks are separated from the relatively unmetamorphosed younger

Precambrian strata of western Tasmania by a major unconformity (Spry and Banks, eds., 1962). The precise age of the metamorphics is unknown.

In the north Westland and south Nelson regions of **New Zealand**, well-banded granitic gneisses are grouped together under the name Constant Gneiss (Table 1.5). These gneisses appear to have fold directions unrelated to those of the ?Precambrian Greenland–Waiuta sedimentaries and are believed to be the possible source rocks of the latter. There is no direct evidence to show that all the isolated outcrops of these gneisses do, in fact, form a related group of formations or that they are of pre-Palaeozoic age. They include a very wide variety of ortho- and paragneisses, and so far no age determinations have been made either on them or on the alkaline and calc-alkaline granites (e.g. the Tuhua Granite) with which they are associated.

SEDIMENTARY SEQUENCES

Precambrian sediments that cannot yet be referred to a particular system are limited in their occurrence to the Northern Territory, Western Australia, Tasmania, and New Zealand.

The **Victoria River Basin** lies to the northeast of the Kimberley Basin (Fig. 1.1), and contains an incompletely known sequence (Traves, 1955; Randal, 1962) lying unconformably on "Nullaginian" and older units.

The basal unit (Victoria River Group) is widespread. It consists of up to 1350 m of quartz sandstone and siltstone, limestone, dolomite, and shale. The sandstone commonly carries asymmetrical ripple-marks, and some is cross-stratified. Desiccation cracks and intraformational shale-clast conglomerates have been observed. The dolomite contains algal bioherms.

The succession is somewhat complicated by facies changes, but in the north it begins with 300 m of sandstone, containing some limestones at the base. This unit is overlain by a similar thickness of chocolate and green siltstones and dolomite. The upper 750 m of the sequence consists of interbedded quartzose sandstone, subarkose, siltstone, and dolomite, with quartz–sandstone and dolomite predominant at the top.

The Victoria River Group is overlain unconformably by the Tolmer Group, up to 800 m thick. The basal 600 m, the Buldiva Sandstone, consists of quartzose sandstone with ripple-marks and cross-stratification. It was deposited in a shallow epeiric sea. This sandstone is followed by dolomite and silicified limestone which passes up into a sandstone–siltstone–carbonate unit in which impressions of halite crystals occur.

The Tolmer Group is overlain unconformably by the Cambrian Antrim Plateau Volcanics.

To the south of the Victoria River basin, on the **Sturt Platform**, the

Gardiner Formation outcrops (Smith, J. W., 1963/120). This is dominantly quartz-rich sandstone with some chocolate shale and dolomite. This unit, together with quartz-rich sandstones and conglomerates of the Kearney and Phillipson Beds, extends southwards towards the western end of the Amadeus Basin. All the units exhibit ripple marks and medium-scale cross-stratification. Their relationships to the Adelaidean and Carpentarian strata elsewhere on the Sturt Platform are not known.

The area in **central Western Australia** that lies between the Nullagine and Amadeus Basins has been only partly mapped, in a reconnaissance fashion (Wells, 1963/59). Much of the region contains outcrops of Mesozoic strata, with surficial Cainozoic deposits. Inliers of Precambrian sediments occur in both the east at Iragana Hills and west at Constance Headland, with small outcrops at a few places between, particularly in diapiric structures (Fig. 1.1).

The Precambrian at Iragana Hills exceeds 3600 m in thickness, and consists of red–brown kaolinitic sandstone with minor red–brown siltstone. It resembles the Adelaidean Carnegie Formation of the Amadeus Basin. The Precambrian at Constance Headland is also predominantly quartz sandstone with some oligomictic conglomerate. Stromatolitic dolomite, gypsum, and some sandstone and siltstone occur in the Woolnough Hills Diapir, and resembles the Adelaidean Bitter Springs Formation of the Amadeus Basin.

There can be little doubt that Precambrian strata extend in the subsurface throughout much of central Western Australia.

In the southern part of the **Nullagine Basin**, the "Nullaginian" Wyloo Group is overlain unconformably by younger Precambrian strata (Daniels, 1966) (Fig. 1.1). The lower unit, the Bresnahan Group is a sequence of quartz sandstone and arkose, with conglomerate at the base. It is incompletely known, may reach 12,000 m in thickness, and is believed to have accumulated rapidly in shallow water.

A younger unit, lying unconformably on the Bresnahan Group, consists of about 600 m of dolomite, shale, and quartzite (Bangemall Group). The presence in the group of *Collenia* establishes its age as Precambrian, and it may be late Adelaidean.

In the northeastern part of the basin the equivalent of the lower part of the Bangemall Group—or perhaps of part of the Bresnahan Group—is the Pinjian Chert Breccia (Noldart and Wyatt, 1962). This is a regolithic mantle that reaches 60 m in thickness as fillings of ancient valleys cut in the "Nullaginian". It is overlain disconformably by the Manganese Group, an equivalent of the Bangemall Group. This comprises some 550 m of chocolate, red, and green shales in which syngenetic braunite pellets and secondary manganese oxides are widespread. Sandstones within the group are quartz-rich and exhibit medium-scale cross-stratification. A basal conglomerate overlies the Pinjian Chert Breccia, or the "Nullaginian" where the breccia is absent.

The youngest of the Precambrian strata are 120 m of quartz-rich conglomerates and cross-stratified sandstones which lie unconformably on the Manganese Group.

Unfossiliferous sediments which are probably Precambrian (Moora and Yandanooka Groups, Billeranga Beds, Cardup Shale) occur sporadically on the **eastern margin of the Perth Basin** in Western Australia (Fig. 1.1) (McWhae *et al.*, 1958; Glover, 1960; Logan and Chase, 1961). They lie unconformably on a crystalline Archaean basement. The thickness of each is about 1000 m except for the Yandanooka Group which reaches 9000 m. Volcanic detritus is prominent in the Yandanooka and lower Moora Groups, forming conglomerate and lithic sandstones. Arkosic detritus appears only locally in the Yandanooka Group, but is more common elsewhere. Orthoquartzite, chert, shale, and stromatolitic dolomite occur in all units except the Yandanooka, and are accompanied by acid volcanics in the Billeranga Beds.

Ripple-marks, mud cracks, medium-scale cross-stratification, stromatolites, and rare oolites all suggest shallow-water conditions, but Glover (1960) considers that the dominantly siltstone portion (upper 7500 m) of the Yandanooka Group was deposited in somewhat deeper water than the other units.

Radiometric data (Compston and Pidgeon, 1962) suggest that the Cardup Shale is most probably Adelaidean in age.

On the **southeastern margin of the Carnarvon Basin** ?Precambrian sediments rest unconformably on a crystalline Precambrian basement (Perry and Dickins, 1960). The oldest sedimentary unit, the Nilling Beds, consists of an unknown thickness of quartz sandstone. This is overlain, also unconformably, by the Badgeradda Group, which comprises more than 3000 m of cross-stratified quartz sandstone and siltstone. This unit is probably a shallow-water deposit. Neither fossils nor other evidence for the age of the group have been found.

On the **southern margin of the Shield** more than 900 m of quartzite and phyllite with some mica schist (Stirling Range Beds) lies unconformably on the crystalline Precambrian basement. They are regarded as shallow-water deposits derived from the westsouthwest (Clarke *et al.*, 1954).

Thick sequences of unmetamorphosed Precambrian rocks overlie the older metamorphosed Precambrian in **western Tasmania** (Spry and Banks, eds., 1962). The older Precambrian apparently formed a north-trending geanticline (Fig. 1.1) and younger Precambrian quartzite, slate, and siltstone was deposited both to the west and east of it. Dolomite occurs at the top of most sequences, with chert and basic volcanics locally on the western side of the geanticline. The dolomite transgresses westwards onto the geanticline in the south. Away from the geanticline the succession exceeds 3000 m in thickness, reaching 3900 m in northwestern Tasmania (Rocky Cape Group) where a derivation of sediment from the south is suggested. These younger Precambrian strata are not in general conformable with the overlying Cambrian Dundas Group and occupy somewhat different depositional areas.

In **New Zealand** a Precambrian age has been assigned to certain unfossiliferous greywackes and argillites occurring in the Westland and south Nelson regions. These sedimentary rocks, which are remarkably uniform and similar lithologically, are provisionally divided into two groups on the basis of markedly contrasting regional strike, namely, (a) a western group (Greenland) striking northwest, and (b) an eastern group (Waiuta) striking north and northnortheast. Both groups occur to the west of the Alpine Fault, and the quartz veins that transect them have been a considerable source of gold. A sequence of hornfelses and schists in the South Westland region (Martins Bay Formation) is also included here.

The evidence so far adduced to support a Precambrian age for these rocks is by no means conclusive. It is based on the following observations: (a) although the argillite members of the Greenland and Waiuta Groups are fine-grained and apparently suitable for the preservation of fossils, none has so far been found in them; (b) both the Greenland and Waiuta rocks lack carbon, their shales being dominantly pale green in colour; (c) these rocks lack the complex distortions impressed on the Lower Palaeozoic rocks of northwest Nelson and were deposited in an environment quite different from that of the latter. From evidence in the Reefton area, a pre-Middle Devonian age must be assigned to the Waiuta argillites and greywackes because of the marked divergence in strike and considerably greater degree of alteration of these rocks as compared with the sediments of the Reefton Group (Middle Devonian) against which they abut in faulted contact.

Suggate (1957, p. 28), in his discussion of the age of these rocks, points out that the absence of quartz lodes from the younger Reefton Group implies their emplacement in pre-Devonian times in the Waiuta rocks.

SEDIMENTARY FACIES AND CLIMATE

At present comment and interpretation are feasible for only the most outstanding features of the Proterozoic systems. Probably the most striking feature of these systems is that, despite their wide extent and great thickness, greywackes form only a minor component of their make-up. Greywacke-suite sediments are best developed in the "Nullaginian", and occur in the Pine Creek and Warramunga Geosynclines. They have not been recorded in the Nullagine Basin. In the Carpentarian System, greywacke-suite sediments are very poorly represented. Some may occur in the Etheridge Geosyncline, but the evidence here is inconclusive. In the western trough of the Mount Isa Geosyncline the upper Carpentarian Mount Isa Shale may contain elements of this suite; and in the Batten Trough of the McArthur

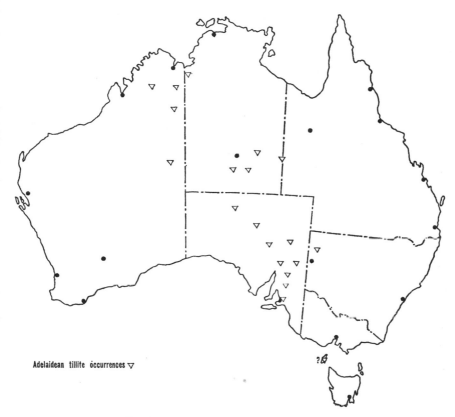

Adelaidean tillite occurrences ▽

Fig. 1.10. Distribution of Adelaidean tillites.

Basin approximately coeval deposits—part of the McArthur Group—are probably greywacke-suite carbonates. The Adelaidean is apparently entirely devoid of greywacke-suite sediments.

If the conventional interpretation of greywacke-suite sediments as deep-water turbidity current deposits is accepted, the implication of the poor development of this suite is that deep-water deposition was characteristic of the Proterozoic in Australia only in the Northern Territory during the

"Nullaginian" Period. In general, at other times and places, deposition took place under shallow marine or terrestrial conditions.

Although considerable thicknesses of these shallow-water deposits accumulated, the time spans for their accumulation were also considerable. Sedimentation rates were either very slow, or many hiatuses remain to be recognized within the sequences.

The tectonic significance of these observations has yet to be assessed.

The Carpentarian System is remarkable for the general similarity of its successions over a very large area, extending in an arc some 1200 km from western Queensland to the Kimberleys in Western Australia. The similarity arises both from the distribution of acid and basic lavas throughout the sequences, and from the tendency for quartz-rich terrigenous detritus to be abundant in the middle parts of the sequences, with dolomite predominant in the upper parts. These similarities may be of tectonic or climatic significance, or both. In particular, the widespread accumulation at this time of carbonates, including stromatolitic reefs, suggest, if uniformitarian principles can be applied to this distant time, that a tropical climate then prevailed over northern Australia.

Among the Adelaidean strata, the Sturtian and Marinoan tillites probably excite the greatest interest. The Adelaidean tillites are typical bouldery, matrix-rich diamictites, and outcrops occur at many points, possibly from King Island, Tasmania, and certainly from near Adelaide, South Australia, northwestwards to the Kimberley Basin in Western Australia (Dow, 1965) a maximum distance of some 2000 km (Fig. 1.10). There, and in South Australia, the tillites lie, in some places, on glacial pavements. The weight of evidence for a glacigenic origin for these rocks is now such that this Adelaidean glaciation must be regarded as established beyond doubt. The extent of the glacials, and their occurrence at more than one level in several successions, suggests that the Adelaidean glaciation was comparable with those of the Late Palaeozoic and Pleistocene in its magnitude.

PALAEOGEOGRAPHY

Palaeogeographic interpretations of the data now available are, of necessity, tentative. The new data have, however, enabled a considerable advance to be made from the maps produced by David and Browne (1950) and Noakes (1956). The new maps (Figs. 1.11—1.13) give some idea of the maximum extent of marine sedimentation during each period. However, they should strictly not be compared with similar maps for later periods, since the time span depicted on each is of the same order as the whole of the Phanerozoic Eon.

PALAEONTOLOGY

Stromatolites are the most common Precambrian fossils, and they appear to be of some value for correlation (Edgell, 1964a). Four floral assemblages have been recognized, the youngest of which, comprising *Conophyton inclinatum* and *Collenia frequens*, is Upper Adelaidean. Radiometric data conflict with Edgell's correlation chart at several points, and suggest that his *C. undosa*,

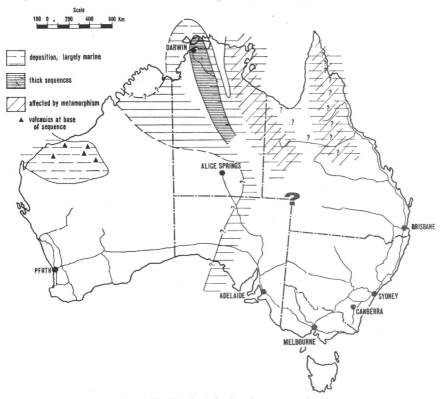

FIG. 1.11. "Nullaginian" palaeogeography.

C. australasica, Newlandia lamellosa assemblage is "Nullaginian", as are his older *Collenia* assemblages. This would accord with the overseas range of *C. undosa*, and *C. australasica* would then be a long-ranging form, rather than *C. undosa* as Edgell suggests.

Siliceous triact spicules have been described from the Carpentarian McArthur Group of the McArthur Basin (Dunn, 1964). Sandstones with abundant burrows (*Skolithos*) occur sporadically (e.g. in the Adelaidean Wessel Group) and problematical fossils are found occasionally (see e.g. Logan and Chase, 1961).

Specifically determinable metazoan organic remains appear only in the uppermost Adelaidean rocks. To date they are known from the Pound Quartzite in the Adelaide Geosyncline, from the Amadeus Basin and from the Kimberley Basin and its environs. The fauna includes medusoids, octocorals (*Rangea, Charnia*), annelids (*Spriggina, Dickinsonia*), and invertebrates

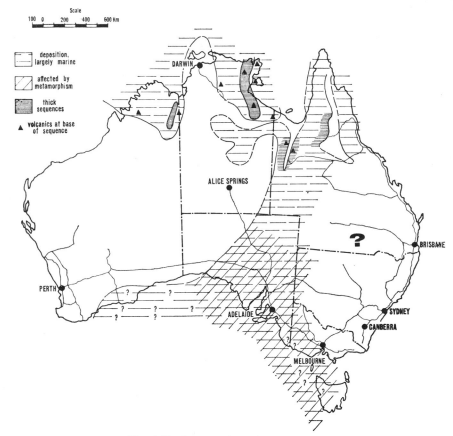

FIG. 1.12. Carpentarian palaeogeography.

of unknown affinities (*Parvancornia, Tribrachidium*). Some of these forms are known from late Precambrian strata in other continents (Glaessner, 1962).

TECTONISM AND IGNEOUS ACTIVITY

Igneous activity, both intrusive and extrusive, was a recurrent phenomenon from Archaean to Early Adelaidean times, as was tectonism (Fig. 1.14). Only the major igneous and tectonic events will be discussed here.

The units that have been recognized within the "Pilbara System" suggest that at least two separate phases of folding and granite intrusion affected these Archaean strata before their final deformation, metamorphism, and intrusion in the ep-Archaean orogeny. These Archaean events are known to span at least the period about 2300–3000 m.y. (see Leggo *et al.*, 1965), and some of them may be older still.

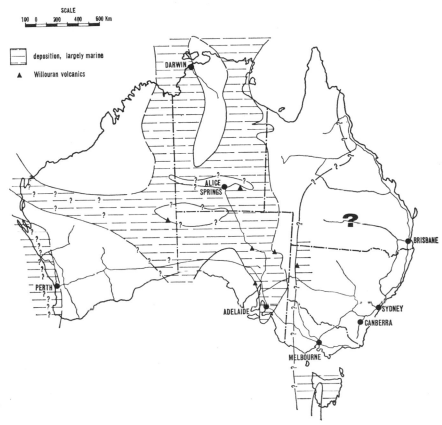

Fig. 1.13. Adelaidean palaeogeography.

It seems probable that, with careful field work and radiometric dating, much more of the Archaean history of the continent will be unravelled. It is quite possible that further time-rock units older than the "Nullaginian" will be established.

Following the ep-Archaean orogeny basic vulcanicity became general in the Nullagine Basin (Fortescue Group). Subsequently there was some acid volcanism in this basin and in the Pine Creek Geosyncline.

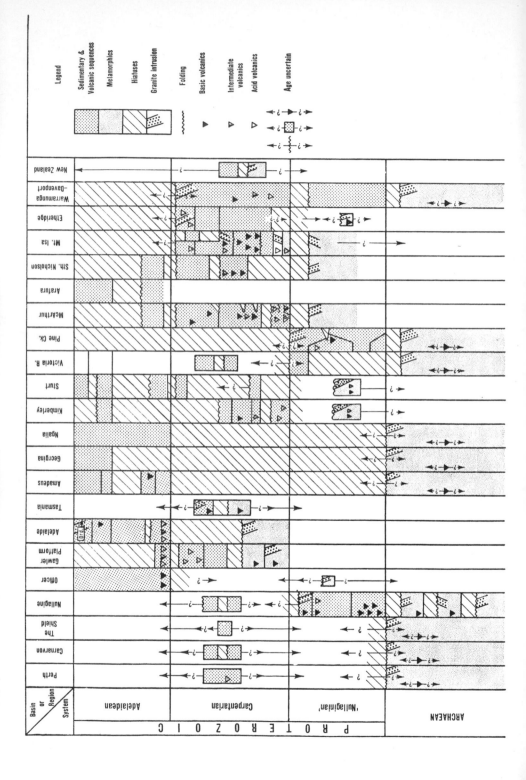

The epi-"Nullaginian" orogeny, about 1800 m.y. ago, was marked by metamorphism in the northeast of the Northern Territory, and in Queensland (Fig. 1.12). In these places, and in the Pine Creek Geosyncline, granite intrusion was widespread. Granite intrusion also occurred in the Nullagine Basin.

The succeeding volcanism, which extended from the Mount Isa Geosyncline to the Kimberley Basin, was acid in character. It gave way to basic volcanism in the east later in the Carpentarian but acid volcanism recurred towards the end of the period in this region. Numerous local unconformities are recorded from most Carpentarian sequences, particularly in the lower parts, suggesting a continuation of tectonic instability. Granite intrusion took place twice during the Carpentarian in the Mount Isa Geosyncline, but, with the exception of the metamorphosed areas in South Australia, other areas were not affected.

Regional metamorphism during the Carpentarian Period appears to have been restricted to the eastern half of the continent. The Leichhardt Metamorphics in the Mount Isa Geosyncline, and in South Australia the Willyama and Mount Painter Complexes, and the metamorphics of the Gawler Platform each result from a Carpentarian metamorphism.

A major orogeny deformed the Carpentarian sequences in northern Australia before Adelaidean strata were deposited. This, the epi-Carpentarian orogeny, was followed by granite intrusion in the Etheridge Geosyncline. It does not appear to have been an epoch in which regional metamorphism occurred. The Adelaidean Period commenced with limited acid to basic volcanism in the Adelaide Geosyncline, Stuart Shelf, and Officer and Amadeus Basins, but this soon ceased. Thereafter Australia appears to have been free from volcanism until the Cambrian, except for a minor Sturtian occurrence in the Adelaide Geosyncline.

The Adelaidean was a tectonically quiet period for the most part, with unconformities of restricted extent. However, the final deformation of the McArthur and South Nicholson Basins occurred during this period, prior to the deposition of the Wessell Group, and there was some folding in the Kimberley Basin and the Sturt Platform. Dolerite sills were emplaced in parts of northern Australia. Granite intrusion, dated at 750 m.y. (McDougall and Leggo, 1965), occurred on King Island, Tasmania.

The end of the Adelaidean went unmarked by tectonism or igneous activity except in the southwest Amadeus Basin, where a major orogeny mobilized the basement and granitized part of the Adelaidean sequence.

Most Adelaidean sequences were folded during the Palaeozoic, that in the Adelaide Geosyncline being involved in post-Middle Cambrian folding and granite emplacement (see Fig. 2.8).

CHAPTER 2

The Cambrian System

THE Early Cambrian depositional areas in Australia accord, in general, with those of the late Adelaidean. In the Adelaide Geosyncline, the central eastern part of the Amadeus Basin, and the southern part of the Georgina Basin, there is conformity at the base of the Cambrian. Elsewhere there was little or no Early Cambrian deposition. Over the northwestern quadrant of the continent, Lower Cambrian tholeiitic basalts were poured out, the thickest sections being in the Ord and Daly River Basins. Terrigenous and carbonate deposits accumulated in the Adelaide Geosyncline and Amadeus Basin, and volcanics, greywackes, and shales in the Tasman Orthogeosyncline. By Middle Cambrian times shallow-water sedimentation had extended over much of the Ord, Daly River, and Georgina Basins; in the Tasman Orthogeosyncline and the Amadeus Basin sedimentation continued as in the earlier parts of the period; but the Adelaide Geosyncline was deformed and sedimentation ceased. Upper Cambrian sediments covered much the same areas as those of the Middle Cambrian except in the Daly River Basin which became land.

Tectonically the period was one of quiet except in the Tasman Orthogeosyncline and the Adelaide Geosyncline. In Victoria and Tasmania there is a complex record of deformation and volcanism different from that known in any other part of the continent. The folding of the Adelaide Geosyncline produced only minor deformation in the west, but in the east there was strong overfolding and thrusting. These movements began in the Middle Cambrian but probably extended into the Ordovician. Elsewhere in Australia the only Cambrian movements were epeirogenic.

The Cambrian rocks of New Zealand are known only from the South Island. These comprise strongly deformed basic volcanics, terrigenous sediments, and fossiliferous limestones. The fossiliferous part of the sequence is Middle Cambrian, but representatives of both lower and upper series are probably present also.

STRATIGRAPHY

Australia

ORD AND DALY RIVER BASINS

The Early Cambrian saw sheets of tholeiitic basalt (the Antrim Plateau Basalts) extruded over wide areas in the Ord and Daly River Basins and their environs. The basalts reach a maximum thickness of about 1000 m, and rest unconformably on Proterozoic and Archaean strata.

Cambrian sediments of the **Ord Basin** are preserved in three main subsidiary basins, the **Argyle, Rosewood**, and **Hardman Basins**, which are fault-bounded. These are post-depositional basins, remnants of a sedimentary sheet which covered wide areas. Probably marine conditions were continuous across the Bonaparte, Ord, and Daly River Basins at times. The Negri Group, of Middle Cambrian age, rests with disconformity on the

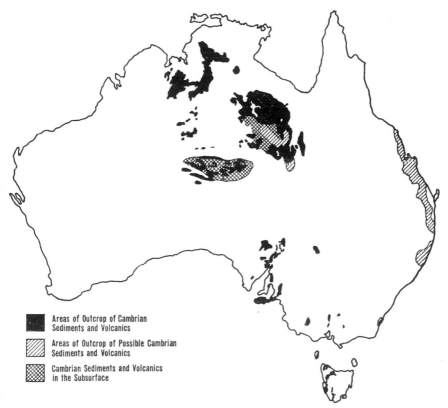

Areas of Outcrop of Cambrian
Sediments and Volcanics

Areas of Outcrop of Possible Cambrian
Sediments and Volcanics

Cambrian Sediments and Volcanics
in the Subsurface

FIG. 2.1. Distribution of Cambrian Strata.

underlying basalts. It consists of interbedded shales (some of them gypsiferous) and thin-bedded limestones, the maximum thickness being about 1000 m (Traves, 1956). *Girvanella* is common, and the trilobite *Redlichia forresti* is followed by *Xystridura* and the brachiopod *Billingsella*. The conformably overlying Elder Sandstone (450 m) is a fine- to medium-grained

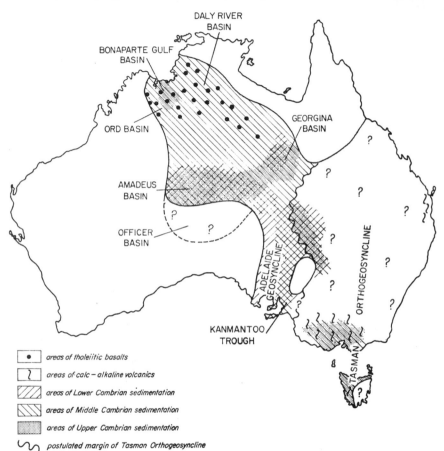

FIG. 2.2. Cambrian palaeogeography.

sandstone, in places shaly and containing mud pellets, and showing ample evidence of its shallow-water origin. It is unfossiliferous but its lower parts are considered to be late Middle Cambrian or Late Cambrian, and its upper parts Devonian (Veevers *et al.*, 1964c).

The Daly River Basin is not readily delineated because of Mesozoic cover. There is little doubt that there was continuity of sedimentation between this and the Barkly Tableland region of the Georgina Basin during at least some of the Middle Cambrian. The Daly River Group, which is correlated with the Negri Group, is disconformable on the Antrim Plateau Basalts in places, but elsewhere it overlaps them to rest directly on the Agicondi "Series". Only about 350 m of limestones, shales, and sandstones are present in the northwest of the basin, but it is probable that this increases considerably in the southeast. No rocks corresponding with the Elder Sandstone have been found. A very widespread sheet of limestone, the Montejinni Limestone, 25 m thick, occurs to the south of the main outcrop of the Daly River Group and is isolated from it by Mesozoic rocks. It lies on Antrim Plateau Basalts and is correlated with the lower Daly River and lower Negri Groups.

It is concluded that in both basins during the early Middle Cambrian the water was shallow, and at times the circulation was sufficiently restricted to permit evaporites to form. The sea gained access through both the Bonaparte Gulf and Georgina Basins. Later in the Middle Cambrian the Daly River Basin became land, and the arenaceous deposits of the Ord Basin were formed in a gulf opening into the Bonaparte Gulf Basin (Öpik, 1956c).

Bonaparte Gulf Basin

The Bonaparte Gulf Basin is a relatively small discordant structure, covering approximately 20,000 sq km of the present land surface. The stratigraphy indicates that a large segment of the original basin is beneath the sea to north and west of the present outcrop. The overall structure is simple, with the oldest rocks around the basin margin in the south and progressively younger rocks northwards; the eastern edge is faulted. The basin originated in the Cambrian, and had a long history extending into the Triassic (Traves, 1955, 1956; Öpik, 1956c; McWhae *et al.*, 1958). The oldest rocks are the Antrim Plateau Basalts which are much thinner and more restricted in outcrop than in the Ord Basin. Disconnected remnants of this formation lie on the Precambrian between the two basins.

Middle and Upper Cambrian sediments (the Carlton Group) form a sequence overlying the basalt without an apparent structural break. They are thickest (almost 1000 m) at the western end of the basin and thin towards the east where Upper Devonian rests on Antrim Plateau Basalts (Veevers *et al.*, 1964c). The bulk of this group consists of reddish quartzose sandstone, with an abundance of glauconitic sandstones towards the top, and inter-bedded dolomitic limestones at intervals throughout. Some of the limestones are oolitic, and many of the sandstones are cross-stratified. Five formations have been named in the group (the uppermost one being Ordovician), and the most recent work has indicated three unnamed formations at the base (Veevers *et al.*, 1964*c*). Fossils occur throughout the sequence, but they are in profusion in the limestones. The hyolithoid *Biconulites* in the lowest limestone indicates a correlation with part of the Negri Group. Towards the middle of the section the Skewthorpe Formation contains upper Middle Cambrian species of damesellid trilobites, and the higher parts have Upper Cambrian saukiid and kaolishaniid trilobites (Öpik, pers. comm.).

The Bonaparte Gulf Basin began to subside at approximately the same time as the nearby Ord and Daly River Basins, but its subsidence was more profound and longer lasting. A feature worthy of note is the higher sandstone–limestone ratio in the sediments of this basin compared with the neighbouring basins, presumably because of the presence of a source area where the Precambrian was not covered by Antrim Plateau Basalt. This was either the western part of the Kimberley Basin, or the area at present covered by the sea to the north of the Bonaparte Gulf Basin, or both.

GEORGINA BASIN

The Georgina Basin is a shallow stable structure, covering some 270,000 sq km. Cambrian sediments were deposited in most places on deformed and eroded Archaean to Carpentarian rocks, though there is apparent conformity on Adelaidean sediments at some localities in the southwest of the basin. As here used the term Georgina Basin embraces the Barkly Basin of the Northern Territory (Noakes and Traves, 1954), and the Oban and Undilla Basins (Öpik, 1956*a*) and Burke River Structural Belt (Öpik, 1961*b*) of Queensland. Its boundaries are easily defined by contact with Archaean to Carpentarian rocks, except in the northwest, where Mesozoic cover obscures a probable connexion with the Daly River Basin. It had a sedimentary history extending from the Adelaidean to the Devonian. Outcrops are isolated and generally poor, dips are low, and the thickness exposed at any locality small, making lithological mapping difficult. The interpretation of the Cambrian sequence has been particularly dependent on biostratigraphic studies, but as some of the units, especially the dolomites, contain few fossils, varying interpretations of some areas are currently held.

During the Cambrian, subsidence was in general slight, but it was by no means uniform. Certain regions, some of which have been given basin status (see above), subsided more rapidly than others. For example, near the southern end of the basin there are up to 1200 m of Middle and Upper Cambrian strata, and there are over 1000 m of upper Middle and Upper Cambrian in the Burke River Structural Belt, whereas elsewhere successions of 100–200 m are quite common. Major disconformities are to be found in almost every section (Öpik, 1956*a*; Hill and Denmead, eds., 1960).

Lower Cambrian sediments are not common. Some unfossiliferous dolomites referred to the Camooweal Dolomite, are known to underlie the Middle Cambrian in the Queensland section. In the southwest of the basin the archaeocyathid-bearing Mount Baldwin Formation, which overlies the Adelaidean Grant Bluff Formation with apparent conformity, is the earliest Cambrian formation (Smith, 1967/61). Basalts and agglomerates (e.g. the Helen Springs and Peaker Piker Volcanics) underlie the Middle Cambrian part of the Barkly Tableland (Noakes and Traves, 1954; Smith and Roberts, 1963). In the northern part of this tableland the thin Bukalara Sandstone is thought to be of the same age (Dunn, 1963).

Middle Cambrian sediments are far more widespread and are the basal Cambrian units over most of the basin. In general they are thicker than either the Lower or the Upper Cambrian. Limestones, dolomites, and siliceous siltstones and shales form the bulk of the sediments in the Queensland part of the basin, but rapid changes in facies and in thickness have necessitated a complex rock-unit nomenclature. Two of the best known sections are in the Undilla Basin, and between Camooweal and Urandangi east of the Northern Territory border, where the sequence is as shown in Fig. 2.3 (Öpik, 1956a; Noakes *et al.*, 1959; Hill and Denmead, eds., 1960; Randal and Brown, 1962/49). The Camooweal Dolomite is here considered to range in age from Early Cambrian to early Middle Cambrian. The limestones in this region are usually thin-bedded, grey to buff in colour, and sometimes cross-stratified or oolitic. Interbeds of marl and silicified siltstone occur. The dolomites also are thin-bedded, frequently with micro cross-stratification, in part friable and vuggy, and with frequent stringers and nodules of chert. The shaly units, e.g. the Inca Formation, are laminated and siliceous, and contain beds of spongolite. The typical faunal sequence is best known from the Undilla Basin. The Thorntonia Limestone is characterized by *Redlichia idonea* towards the base and *Xystridura* and *Pagetia* higher up. The Currant Bush Limestone fauna has not been described, but it is known to include the trilobites *Koptura*, *Anomocare*, and *Mapania* in the upper half, and *Doryagnostus* and *Ptychagnostus punctuosus* near the top. In the V-Creek Limestone *Papyriaspis*, *Goniagnostus nathorsti*, and *Lejopyge laevigata* are of major importance. The last agnostids also occur in the Mail Change and Split Rock formations where they are joined by *Crepicephalina*.

In the Northern Territory the Middle Cambrian is referred to the Marqua Beds (Casey and Tomlinson, 1956; Smith, 1963), or the Arthur Creek or Sandover Beds (Smith, 1964). Each of these units is 300–400 m thick, and probably contains several disconformities. They are composed of flaggy, blue to black limestones and silicified shales but, in addition, there are many quartzose calcareous sandstone units which are not present further east. Presumably this indicates a source area in the southwest of the basin, and a very flat stable area to the east and northeast from which almost no detritus was derived.

Further north in the Barkly Tableland there is a veneer of silicified shale, chert, fine-grained sandstones, and some limestone, generally less than 100 m thick but locally up to 400 m (Öpik, 1956*b*; Reynolds, 1963/159). This

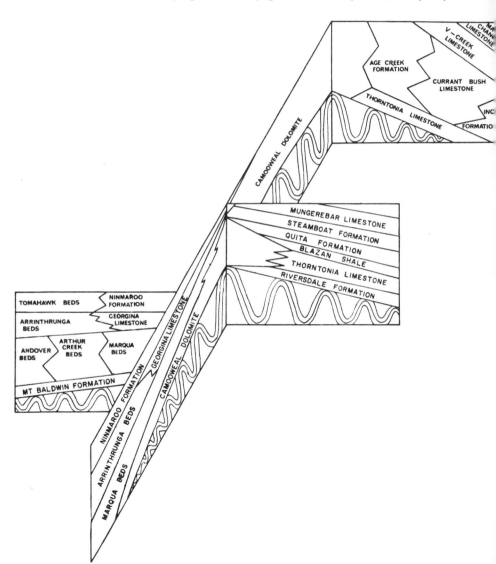

Fig. 2.3. Correlation diagram showing probable relationships between the various Cambrian and Ordovician lithological units in the Georgina Basin.

was deposited during the early Middle Cambrian in a very shallow transgression across a variety of Precambrian rocks.

There are abundant faunas, especially trilobites and brachiopods, in all these Middle Cambrian sequences, though the greatest profusion occurs in the limestones and shales in Queensland. The dolomites are almost barren of fossils, but the sandier units in the west contain a magnificently preserved fauna of both agnostids and polymerids on several horizons.

The Upper Cambrian is restricted to the southern and eastern parts of the basin, but even there it does not form a continuous sheet. The thickest and most continuous sections occur in the southwest overlying the Arthur Creek Beds, and in the Burke River Structural Belt in the extreme east. There is also an important, thin, sheet-like unit, the Georgina Limestone, over much of the southern part of the basin in the vicinity of the Queensland border. Two units are recognized in the southwest—the Arrinthrunga Formation and the Tomahawk Beds. The Arrinthrunga Formation is up to 900 m thick and is made up of thin-bedded, variously coloured limestones, and dolomites with some quartz sandstone, especially towards the top. There is ample evidence of its shallow-water origin—ripple marks, cross-stratification, mud cracks, and halite casts (Smith, 1967/61). Fossils are not common, but lower Upper Cambrian trilobites have been found near the base. Only the *lower* parts of the Tomahawk Beds are Cambrian. They are predominantly quartzose sandstone, often glauconitic, with interbeds of siltstone and dolomite. The fauna is abundant and indicates a very late Cambrian age.

In the Burke River Structural Belt, which is a meridionally oriented sunkland, a thick Upper Cambrian succession is preserved. About 1000 m of sediment are exposed, but this figure is probably increased in the south where the Cambrian is covered by the Ordovician, and the sunkland becomes a sedimentary trough. Five units span the entire Upper Cambrian, apparently without a break. They are the Pomegranate Limestone, O'Hara Shale, Chatsworth Limestone, Gola Beds, and the lower part of the Ninmaroo Formation. The Pomegranate and O'Hara are partly equivalent, as also are the Chatsworth Limestone and Gola Beds. Lithologically both the limestones and shales are closely similar to the Middle Cambrian in the Undilla area. Trilobites are abundant throughout. *Glyptagnostus, Pseudagnostus, Olenus*, and *Eugonocare* occur in both the O'Hara Shale and Pomegranate Limestone, and *Kolishania, Pagodia*, and *Pseudagnostus* in the Gola Beds.

AMADEUS AND NGALIA BASINS

The Amadeus Basin had a complex sedimentary history during the Cambrian Period as a result of varying rates of subsidence and differing tectonic responses in various sectors. The stratigraphic units do not thin out,

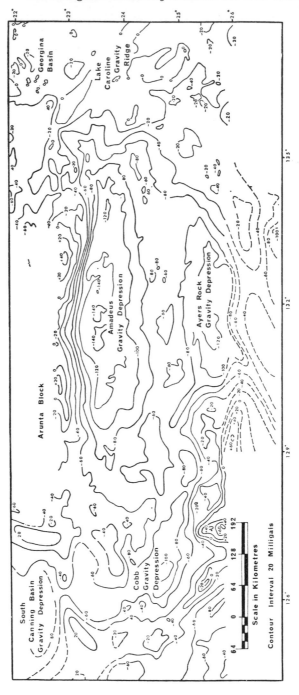

FIG. 2.4. Bouguer anomaly map of Amadeus Basin showing the relations with the Georgina and Canning Basins. Modified from B.M.R. Geophysical Maps. Published with permission.

nor do they show evidence of shoreline deposition along the present (faulted) northern boundary of the basin (Prichard and Quinlan, 1962). An open seaway must have occupied part of the site of the present Arunta Block, and there was probably continuity of sedimentation between the Amadeus, Georgina, and possibly the Ngalia Basins during at least part of the period. The entire Cambrian section is marine in the east of the basin, whereas in the west it is at least partly terrestrial. Access to the sea was therefore probably through the Georgina Basin, and during the Early and early Middle Cambrian through the Adelaide Geosyncline also. The sea is unlikely to have entered through the Canning Basin where, in any case, there is as yet no certain evidence of Cambrian sediments (Veevers and Wells, 1961).

It is convenient to discuss the stratigraphy in terms of three regions— the northeast, the south central, and the western regions. In the northeast a single group (the Pertaoorrta Group) with several formations is recognized. There is no angular unconformity at the base of the Cambrian, and, indeed, it is possible that the boundary of the system lies within the Arumbera Sandstone. This formation is a fine- to medium-grained quartzose sandstone which varies in thickness from 250 to 850 m. The formations above the Arumbera are very variable laterally and exhibit interfingering relationships over relatively short distances (Fig. 2.5). The succession in the east consists almost entirely of carbonates but towards the west the lowest three formations, the Todd River Dolomite, the Chandler Limestone, and the Giles Creek Dolomite pass into the Hugh River Shale (Wells *et al.*, 1965d). Fossils are not abundant, but archaeocyathids have been found in the Todd River Dolomite; Middle Cambrian trilobites and stromatolites are known in the Giles Creek Dolomite and trilobites in the Jay Creek Limestone; and lower Upper Cambrian trilobites in the upper Shannon Formation and the uppermost Jay Creek Limestone (Tomlinson, *in* Wells *et al.*, 1965a). The thickness of this shale-carbonate sequence is about 600 m. Limestones and dolomites form the lower part of the succeeding Goyder Formation (up to 450 m thick), but the bulk of the formation is composed of quartzose sandstones. A few Upper Cambrian trilobites are known from it. Gradually sands spread across the basin, and the system is completed by the lower part of the Pacoota Sandstone.

The southern and western parts of the basin were subjected to orogeny toward the end of the Adelaidean, and consequently there is a marked angular unconformity at the base of the Cambrian succession. In the south central area, however, as much as 1500 m of sediment occur above the basal unconformity though this figure rapidly decreases southwards toward the basin margin (Wells *et al.*, 1963/51; Wells *et al.*, 1965c). Several formations (Fig. 2.5) are recognized in this area, of which only the Goyder can be traced further north. The dominant lithologies are red, purple, and brown micaceous sandstones and siltstones. Occasional dolomites and calcareous sandstones are present, and conglomerates occur in places directly above the unconformity. Cross-stratification and slump rolls are common features, and the sediments are considered to have formed in marine or transitional environments. The oldest known fossils are of early Middle Cambrian age (Tomlinson, *in* Wells *et al.*, 1965*a*).

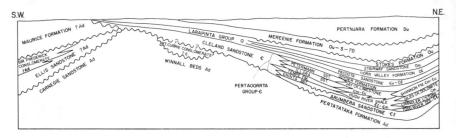

FIG. 2.5. Correlation diagram of the Palaeozoic formations in the Amadeus Basin. Not to Scale. (Modified after A. J. Wells (unpublished).) D = Devonian; Du = Upper Devonian; S = Silurian; O = Ordovician; Ou = Upper; Om = Middle; Ol = Lower Ordovician; C = Cambrian; Cu = Upper; Cm = Middle; Cl = Lower Cambrian; Ad = Adelaidean.

At the southwestern end of the basin there is a thick mass of polymictic conglomerate in the lower part of the sequence. This is a piedmont conglomerate formed as a wedge against the orogenic front along the southern edge of the basin (the Mount Currie Conglomerate) (Forman, 1965). Basinwards the conglomerate tongues out into fine to coarse, pebbly sandstones which are often red in colour, cross-bedded throughout, and contain abundant slump rolls and ripple marks (the Cleland Sandstone and Ayers Rock Arkose, up to 600 m thick). These sandstones are probably of fluviatile and deltaic origin, the rivers emptying into the sea to the northeast. The whole sequence in this western region is unfossiliferous, but the suggested lithological correlations imply the commencement of conglomerate deposition in the Early Cambrian.

Further north in the Ngalia Basin Adelaidean sediments pass up into shales and limestones with a Lower Cambrian fauna (P. J. Cook, pers. comm.).

ADELAIDE GEOSYNCLINE

This geosyncline continued to downwarp and receive marine sediments in the Cambrian, and in most areas there are conformable relations with the Adelaidean Pound Quartzite. At the present time Cambrian rocks outcrop

in several isolated areas separated by Adelaidean sediments, but such isolation is the result of subsequent tectonism (Glaessner and Parkin, eds., 1958).
Most of the sediments are of Early Cambrian age (Dalgarno, 1964), Middle
Cambrian being restricted to the eastern part of the Geosyncline (Daily,
1956).

Throughout the entire area of deposition the earliest Cambrian rocks are
limestones (Kulpara and Wilkawillina Limestones and equivalents). They
have a distribution similar to that of the Pound Quartzite and it is only in
the southeast in the Fleurieu Peninsula that they overlap this formation.
Shallow-water conditions are evident, with oolites, pisolites, intraformational
breccias, dolomites, fossil algae and archaeocyathids. In places these carbonates reach thicknesses of almost 400 m, and most of them are well
bedded. The archaeocyathids do not form reefs.

There followed a period of great uniformity of sedimentary conditions
resulting in the formation of the widespread Parara Limestone, a dark
blue–grey, massive, rubbly limestone which contains *Hyolithes* and the
trilobites *Yorkella* and *Pararaia*. Gradually the sea drained from the western
half of the trough and deposition of the Parara Limestone continued in the
Lake Frome area while thin terrigenous sediments formed along a narrow
western borderland. Apparently the uplift causing this regression was most
intense in the south, because on Kangaroo Island there are Lower Cambrian
polymictic conglomerates (the White Point Conglomerate) containing
limestone clasts with archaeocyathids (Daily, 1956).

Uplift continued, and by the end of the Early Cambrian terrigenous
deposits were accumulating in the Lake Frome depression. The lower
three of these units, the Bunkers Sandstone, the Oraparinna Shale, and the
Narina "Greywacke" are shallow-water marine deposits and aggregate
900 m in thickness; the 1000 m-thick upper unit, the Billy Creek Formation
consists of ripple-marked red beds with thin dolomites in the lower half, and
is probably at least partly terrestrial.

The sea must have entered this depression from the south, and there is
evidence of marine sediments of equivalent age southeast of Adelaide, and
on Kangaroo Island where two facies are represented—shallow-water shales
and sandstones (the Emu Bay Shale) with the trilobites *Redlichia* and
Estaingia (Pocock, 1964), and deep-water greywackes and shales which are
devoid of fossils (the Kanmantoo Group), now strongly metamorphosed
(Fig. 2.6). The relationship of the Kanmantoo Group to the shallow-
water facies has been a problem (Campana and Horwitz, 1956), but it has
recently been shown that in the Fleurieu Peninsula there is a conformable
succession from archaeocyathid limestones up into shales and then phyllites
of this group (Daily, 1963). The eastern edge of the trough remains unknown,
and it is not yet possible to indicate how long it continued to receive

sediments. It is known, however, that during the early Middle Cambrian the
sea again entered the Lake Frome depression depositing the 100-m thick
Wirrealpa Limestone, and that this was succeeded by about 3000 m of
deltaic, fluviatile, and littoral sandstones and shales. The character of this
sequence together with its great thickness and position suggest that this
depression may have been a partly landlocked northern extension along
the axis of the Kanmantoo Trough.

There are Middle Cambrian shelf sediments (the Boxing Day Formation)
along the northern margin of this trough in Kangaroo Island. Neither there

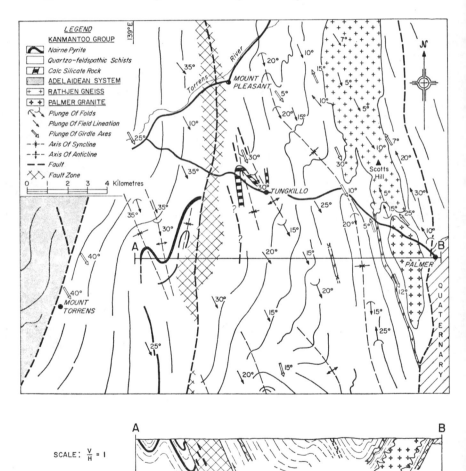

Fig. 2.6. Map and section of part of the Kanmantoo Trough showing the pattern
of deformation. (After Kleeman and White, 1956.)

nor at Lake Frome are there subsequent Cambrian rocks. On this evidence it has been concluded that the deformation of the whole region began late in the Middle Cambrian. However, sedimentation in the Kanmantoo Trough may well have continued on as late as the Ordovician.

TASMAN ORTHOGEOSYNCLINE

Almost nothing is known of the Precambrian history of the area covered by this geosyncline, which encompassed Tasmania, Victoria, most of New South Wales, and most of eastern Queensland. Definite Precambrian rocks outcrop in Tasmania, on the islands in Bass Strait, in western New South Wales where they form the Broken Hill Massif, and in north Queensland where they form the Mount Isa and Georgetown Massifs. It is possible that certain unfossiliferous strata in northeastern New South Wales and in the coastal areas of Queensland as far north as latitude 22°S may be of Precambrian age. The decipherable history of the Tasman Orthogeosyncline began in the Cambrian, but even for this period the data available are meagre, and fossiliferous rocks are restricted to Tasmania, Victoria, and western New South Wales.

The western edge of the structure cannot be precisely defined because so much of it is covered by the Mesozoic and later sediments of the Artesian Basin. However, it is clear that in Queensland it runs east of the Cloncurry–Mount Isa Massif and south of the Georgetown Massif. North from Townsville there is a belt of Palaeozoic rocks some 130–160 km wide separated from the Georgetown Massif by a major crustal dislocation—the Tasman Line. This region has a Palaeozoic history that is distinctly different from that of the areas further south and for that reason, in subsequent chapters, it is treated under the separate heading "North Queensland Basins". In New South Wales the western edge of the geosyncline passed east of the Broken Hill Massif, and then southwards through western Victoria, or alternatively southwestwards through the Fleurieu Peninsula and Kangaroo Island. From the point of view of the latter alternative, the Kanmantoo Trough of South Australia belongs with the Tasman rather than the Adelaide Geosyncline. This has certainly not been proved; but, on the other hand, the position of the eastern margin of the Kanmantoo Trough remains in doubt.

Sequences in different parts of the geosyncline are different in character, but it is not yet possible to divide the mainland part into distinct sub-units as has been done for later periods. However, the prevalence of greenstones, cherts, and greywackes in almost all areas, indicates that in the Cambrian it was a complex structure of eugeosynclinal type. A shelf facies is known only in western New South Wales northeast of Broken Hill and in wells in South Australia at Gidgealpa.

The stratigraphy is discussed below on a regional basis. By the end of the Precambrian the great massif of the Tyennan Geanticline formed the central part of Tasmania, and the smaller Rocky Cape Geanticline occupied the northwestern corner of the island (Spry and Banks, eds., 1962). Between lay the **Dundas Trough.** In a broad belt around the Tyennan Geanticline Cambrian rocks were deposited. Though they are known to occur on its eastern side, their precise distribution cannot be determined owing to the cover of later rocks. At the base of the sequence in the Dundas Trough there are quartzites, slates, dolomites, and tuffs as much as 2500 m thick (the Success Creek and Carbine Groups) which may be latest Adelaidean or Early Cambrian (Spry and Banks, eds, 1962; Campana and King, 1963), the latter age being accepted herein. During the Early Cambrian a volcanic pile (the Mount Read Volcanics, up to 2500 m thick) formed an arc along the western margin of the Tyennan Geanticline. The volcanics thin out rapidly into the Dundas Trough. Flows of keratophyre, rhyolite, and porphyries, pyroclastics including welded tuffs and coarse breccias, together with minor sedimentary units, constitute the formation.

Probably at the end of the Early Cambrian the trough was deformed and Middle Cambrian sediments were then deposited unconformably on the earlier rocks (the Stichtan Unconformity). The Dundas Trough began a period of rapid subsidence, and less profound subsidence occurred around the northern and eastern sides of the Tyennan Geanticline. The presence of Middle Cambrian sediments in the northwestern corner of the island and on King Island indicates similar trough formation on the western side of the Rocky Cape Geanticline.

Within the Dundas Trough, the Dundas Group was deposited during the Middle and Late Cambrian. This group has been interpreted as a synorogenic "flysch" type of deposit, both the trough and its marginal lands being tectonically active throughout its formation (Campana and King, 1963). Rather than treat the numerous named formations in the group separately, it is more convenient to consider the broad lithological changes. The lower part of the section is predominantly argillaceous—slates, mudstones, and shales—with important chert and pyroclastic units. Fossils are rare. These rocks are up to 3500 m thick. They pass upwards, and probably laterally in part, into a greywacke- and conglomerate-rich succession. There appears to be cyclic deposition in this interval, a conglomerate-rich unit being succeeded by greywacke and then argillite units. This lends some credence to the view of tectonic instability. In general, the conglomerates become relatively more abundant towards the top of the group, and they change their character from greywacke breccias to quartzite conglomerates with a quartz-rich matrix. This indicates a shallowing of the basin, and some of the youngest conglomerates have been represented as being of fluviatile origin (Campana and King, 1963). Volcanic rocks of the spilitic suite are interbedded with the deeper-water sediments, but acid types are also present especially towards the geanticline. Fossils are not particularly abundant, but trilobites and brachiopods representative of the upper Middle and lower Upper Cambrian are known. Of particular significance are the trilobites *Ptychagnostus*, *Glyptagnostus*, and *Blackwelderia*.

Most of the sediments outside the Dundas Trough belong to the greywacke–conglomerate association, and have basic volcanics interbedded. They are of late Middle Cambrian and early Late Cambrian age also.

In Victoria, proven Cambrian rocks reach the surface in two linear structurally complex belts—the **Mount William–Heathcote Axis** and the **Mount Wellington Line** (Thomas, 1958) (Fig. 5.11). Similar lithologies are known in structurally similar belts in the valleys of the Glenelg and Hopkins Rivers of western Victoria and at Waratah Bay, but no fossils are known from them (Thomas and Singleton, 1956). The earliest known rocks are "greenstones"— calc-alkaline basic lavas, pyroclastics, and interbedded cherts which are at least 1500 m thick (the Heathcote and Mount Wellington Greenstones). There is a conformable and, in places, gradational passage up into black shales with ash bands as at Heathcote (the Knowsley East Formation, 150 m thick) or into bedded tuffs (the Garvey Gulley Tuffs) as at Mount Wellington. The former formation contains an abundance of the hydroids *Archaeolafoea*, *Mastigograptus*, and *Thallograptus*, and they both contain Middle Cambrian trilobites, including *Dinesus*, *Amphoton*, *Fouchouia*, and *Ptychagnostus*. The unfossiliferous Goldie Shales complete the Cambrian sequence and are overlain with apparent conformity by the Lower Ordovician.

The only fossiliferous Cambrian further north in the geosyncline is the shallow-water sequence in the **Mootwingee Ranges**, 120 km northeast of Broken Hill (Warner and Harrison, 1961; Fletcher, 1964; Öpik, pers. comm.), which is here taken to be a western shelf facies lapping on to the Broken Hill massif, and an occurrence of shallow-water sandstones, marls, and acid volcanics in wells at Gidgealpa.

The section in the Mootwingee Ranges begins with Lower Cambrian volcanics, sandstones, and archaeocyathid limestones. These are followed by shales, marls, and limestones with *Xystridura* and *Pagetia*. The upper Middle Cambrian is missing, but at least some of the Upper Cambrian is represented by coarse conglomerates and feldspathic sandstones with trilobites and orthoid brachiopods. There is a conformable passage into the Ordovician.

In the **eastern part of the geosyncline** there are vast areas of low-grade metamorphic rocks which are probably of Cambrian age, but no fossils have been found in them. Examples of these are (a) the thick cherts, phyllites, greywackes, and pillow lavas of the Wagonga Beds (Brown, 1933) which lie unconformably below Upper Ordovician rocks along the south coast of New South Wales; (b) thick phyllite sequences in the Snowy Mountains region some of which are known to be Ordovician, but which possibly extend down into the Cambrian (Öpik, 1956c); (c) the Black Mountain Sandstone at Canberra, a shallow-water quartzose sandstone, more than 450 m thick, and pre-Middle Ordovician in age (Öpik, 1958a); (d) greywackes and slates near Wellington which are known to be pre-Early Ordovician in age (Packham, 1962); (e) the Girilambone Group near Cobar which is mainly phyllite, sandstone, and quartzite (Rayner, Ph.D. thesis, 1962; Russell and Lewis, 1965); it may be pre-Ordovician in age; (f) the Rocksberg Greenstones, which occur in a narrow belt north of Brisbane, and may be at least partly Cambrian in age. They consist of both completely and partially reconstituted andesitic volcanics, and are over 2500 m thick. Their base is not exposed owing to faulting, and at the top there is a transition zone of interbedded greenstones and phyllite which passes up into the Bunya Phyllites. The dating is insecure (Hill and Denmead, eds., 1960).

New Zealand

Middle Cambrian rocks, first recorded by Benson in 1948 in the Cobb Valley of northwest Nelson, are the oldest accurately dated formations in the Dominion. Associated sequences have also been placed provisionally in the Cambrian System, chiefly on stratigraphical evidence, and, in addition, small areas in the southwest Fiordland have been assigned this age on less substantiated evidence (Fig. 2.7).

Paucity of data on the original extent of the Cambrian deposits of the northwest Nelson area or elsewhere in New Zealand makes it almost impossible to construct a picture of the distribution of land and sea in the New Zealand area at this early time. All that may safely be affirmed is that the Cambrian rocks and their probable correlatives indicate, from their thicknesses and their textures, deposition in a geosynclinal basin with land not far distant.

Igneous activity was strong in the (?) Early Cambrian with eruptives of andesitic and basaltic composition and much pyroclastic material. In Middle Cambrian times, igneous activity slackened and quiet deposition of shallow-water limestones and argillites prevailed, to be interrupted in the Late Cambrian by a resurgence of eruptive activity.

The oldest known fossiliferous rocks in New Zealand occur in the Tasman Formation which outcrops in the **Cobb Valley**. They consist of lenses of grey argillaceous limestone in unfossiliferous grey and green argillites, the whole totalling some 300 m in thickness. At the type locality, there are at least seven of these lenses, all containing fossils, but apparently only a single

zonal assemblage is represented. The fossils have been examined by a number
of specialists (see Benson, 1956) and their affiinities are clear, leading to a
correlation with the upper Middle Cambrian or lower Upper Cambrian.
These authorities have remarked on the affinities of various elements of the
Cobb fauna with those of the Cambrian of eastern Australia. This points to a
lack of any significant provincialism in this earliest known New Zealand
fauna.

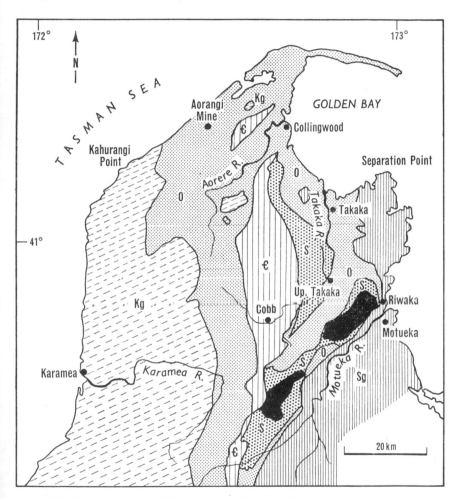

FIG 2.7. Map of northwest Nelson, New Zealand, showing approximate distribution
of Lower Palaeozoic rocks. €1 = Cambrian; O = Ordovician; S = Upper Ordovician
and ? Silurian; Kg = Karamea Granite; Sg = Separation Point Granite; solid
black = rocks of the Riwaka Syncline, including Devonian sediments and metavolcanics, together with younger basic intrusives (After Cooper, 1965.)

The principal constituents of the Cobb Cambrian fauna are agnostid trilobites, e.g. *Peronopsis*, *Hypagnostus*, *Ptychagnostus*, *Phoidagnostus*, and *Oidalagnostus*. Non-agnostid trilobites include *Dorypyge*, *Amphoton* and *Papyriaspis*. Six genera of inarticulate brachiopods have been recorded along with sponges, gastropods, ostracods, worm-tubes, pelmatozoan columnals, and calyx plates. No traces of archaeocyathines have been found.

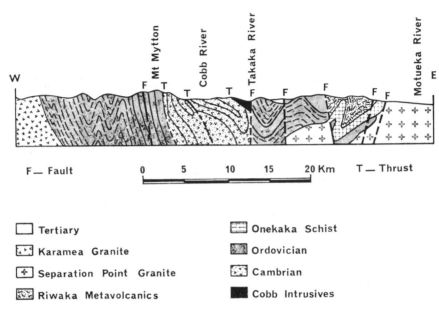

F — Fault   0   5   10   15   20 Km   T — Thrust

☐ Tertiary   ▦ Onekaka Schist

▦ Karamea Granite   ▦ Ordovician

⊞ Separation Point Granite   ▦ Cambrian

▦ Riwaka Metavolcanics   ■ Cobb Intrusives

Fig. 2.8. Section across Cobb Uplift, northwest Nelson, New Zealand. (After Grindley, 1961*a*, Section D–D').

Below this fossiliferous unit, there are apparently conformable thick sequences of volcanics, mostly of andesitic and basaltic type, with pyroclastics and volcanic conglomerates. In the conglomerates of the Devil River Volcanics as it is known, there are pebbles of silicified volcanic rocks, schists, marble, granite, and quartzite. This sequence is probably of Early Cambrian age, but the material in the conglomerates may, in part, be of Precambrian origin.

Above the Tasman Formation, there is a conformable sequence of green volcanic sandstones and interbedded argillites with slaty cleavage, comprising the Anatoki Formation. There are also coarse agglomerates and conglomerates composed of volcanic fragments with an admixture of schist, marble, and quartzite, and, near the top, flows of porphyritic andesites and basalts. The Anatoki rocks, which range in thickness from 1800 to 3000 m, are overlain in places with apparent conformity by fossiliferous Ordovician formations, and are almost certainly of Late Cambrian age. In the Wakamarama Range, west of Collingwood, sandstones and argillites of the Anatoki type grade eastwards into muscovite–chlorite and biotite schists.

The entire sequence described above—Devil River Volcanics, Tasman Formation, and Anatoki Formation—constitutes the major part of the former Haupiri "Series". Further research will undoubtedly introduce finer sub-divisions. Quite recently, coarse conglomerates similar to the Haupiri lithological type, but containing less volcanics and more quartz, have been shown to be Permian in age. They overlie the Golden Bay schists (?Ordo-vician), with slight angular discordance. Much field mapping still remains to be done to delineate the extent of these Permian rocks which may, in fact, occupy a considerable area of outcrop at present mapped as Haupiri Group.

Again, near Collingwood, Grindley and Wodzicki (1960) consider that medium-grained amphibolitic and chloritic schists (Waingaro Schists) are formed from pyroclastics and volcanics similar to those of the Haupiri Group further to the south. They suggest that these schists are thrust over Ordovician slates and that the thrust-plane is the site of extensive mineraliza-tion which probably occurred in the Late Palaeozoic along with nappe-movements and metamorphism.

In the **Fiordland area** in the southwest, Wood (1960) has tentatively placed in the Cambrian System a metamorphic complex of biotite- and amphibolite-schists and gneisses forming the cores of two anticlinal structures in the south-central part of the region. Unconformably above these meta-morphic rocks comes a sequence of quartzose- and calc-schists and gneisses with lenses of marble, in all some 2000 m thick, of which the lower 800 m are provisionally placed in the Cambrian System.

PALAEONTOLOGY

The only region from which substantial numbers of Lower Cambrian fossils are known is the Adelaide Geosyncline, where nine faunal assemblages have been recognized (Daily, 1956). In most of these assemblages there are few genera and most of the material awaits description. Archaeocyathids are particularly abundant in the earliest assemblage, the genera being very numerous and including *Ajacicyathus*, *Archaeocyathus*, *Ethmocyathus*, *Flinder-sicyathus*, *Protopharetra*, and *Syringocnema*. Trilobites and brachiopods are the most significant elements in the later assemblages. The former group con-tains the indigenous genera, *Pararaia*, *Yorkella*, and *Estaingia* together with

Redlichia and *Isoxys*. *Kutorgina* and *Paterina* are the common brachiopods, and *Hyolithes* is ubiquitous.

Middle Cambrian faunas are far more widespread, being known from all basins. The trilobites are by far the most intensively studied group (White-house, 1936, 1939; Öpik, 1958b, 1961a, 1961b, 1963). The earliest beds are characterized by *Redlichia* and then *Xystridura*, but the presence of different species in the Bonaparte Gulf, Ord and Daly River Basins, on the one hand, and in the Georgina Basin, on the other, has led to the suggestion of the existence of eastern and western regions (Öpik, 1956c) which persisted through the Middle Cambrian. In general, the western region has Pacific–Oriental affinities, whereas the eastern is predominantly Acado-Baltic. *Redlichia* indicates oriental affinities; *Xystridura* is endemic. In the Middle Cambrian above the *Xystridura* Zone it is possible to recognize all the Acado-Baltic agnostid zones, and it has become standard practice to use this zonal nomenclature in discussing Australian Cambrian biostratigraphy. In New Zealand fragments of this sequence are known. Agnostids which are particularly significant are *Ptychagnostus*, *Hypagnostus*, *Peronopsis*, and *Lejopyge*. In the lower Middle Cambrian the important polymerid trilobites, in addition to *Redlichia* and *Xystridura*, are *Dinesus*, *Oryctocephalus*, *Fouchouia*, *Lyriaspis*, and *Pagetia*; but in the upper Middle Cambrian these are replaced by *Asthenopsis*, *Amphoton*, *Crepicephalina*, *Papyriaspis*, *Centropleura*, *Mapania*, and *Nepea*. Apart from trilobites, the only fossils yet described are the hyolithoid *Biconulites* which is widespread particularly in the north; the archaeostracans *Svealuta* and *Aristaluta*; a few sponge spicules; the brachiopods *Lingulella*, *Paterina*, and *Acrothele* from Queensland (Öpik, 1961b); and the dendroids from Victoria and Tasmania which have been mentioned above (Thomas and Singleton, 1956; Spry and Banks, eds., 1962). The lower Middle Cambrian assemblages of New Zealand clearly are representative of the eastern Australian region.

Upper Cambrian faunas are more restricted in their distribution and are only now becoming known (Öpik, 1963, 1967). The eastern and western regions persisted—the eastern retaining an Acado-Baltic aspect but with generous admixture of endemic and Oriental genera and an early but brief inruption of an Appalachian *Cedaria* fauna, and the western remaining Pacific. A local zonal sequence for the lower Upper Cambrian has been established (Öpik, 1963), but the upper half has not yet been subdivided. Species of the agnostids *Glyptagnostus*, *Pseudagnostus*, and *Clavagnostus* are associated with the polymerids *Rhodonaspis*, *Blackwelderia*, *Drepanura*, and unnamed cedariids in the basal beds. Above these there is an abrupt faunal break and *Glyptagnostus reticulatus* occurs with *Proceratopyge*, *Eugonocare*, *Eraxinium*, and *Olenus*. Both these faunas are correlated with the American Dresbachian. Franconian and Trempealeauan faunas are known mainly from northwestern Queensland where they include *Paramansuyella, Maladio-della, Kaolishania, Pagodia, Saukia* and *Pseudagnostus*. Brachiopods are much more common than in the Middle Cambrian, and *Eoorthis* and *Billingsella* are widespread.

CLIMATE

The climatological data for the Cambrian in Australia indicates that warm to hot conditions and widespread aridity characterized most of the period. The evidence is as follows:

(a) Palaeomagnetic studies suggest that the equator was directed NW–SE across the centre of the continent (Fig. 2.9), though this needs confirmation (Irving, 1964, and pers. comm.).

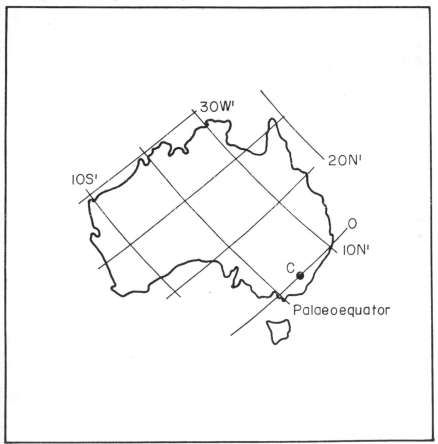

Fig. 2.9. Cambrian palaeolatitudes and palaeomeridians based on Canberra. Reliability C. (After Irving, 1964, by permission of John Wiley & Sons.)

(b) There are widespread limestones, in places oolitic or dolomitic, in the Middle Cambrian of northern and central Australia, and the Lower Cambrian of South Australia. The absence of similar limestones in southeastern Australia is readily explained geotectonically.

(c) Salt pseudomorphs and/or gypsum are known in Middle Cambrian sediments from the Ord, Daly River and Amadeus Basins.

(d) Thick redbed deposits with thin interstratified dolomites occur in the Middle Cambrian in the north of the Adelaide Geosyncline.

(e) Archaeocyathids occur from the Barkly Tableland in the north to the Fleurieu Peninsula in the south. These organisms may now be regarded as warm-water types (Irving, 1964).

(f) There is an association of Acado-Baltic and North American trilobite faunas and both these provinces are tropical to sub-tropical on palaeomagnetic reconstructions. The palaeolatitude of the Oriental Province, which also contributed trilobites, is unknown. The *Centropleura* fauna, which has been used as a cool-water index, in the northern hemisphere lies within 30° of the palaeoequator.

Cool conditions have also been suggested by the Zeehan Tillite of Tasmania and ice crystal casts in both Lower and Upper Cambrian rocks of central and western Australia (Öpik, 1956c). The Zeehan Tillite has been shown to be Permian in age (Spry and Banks, eds., 1962), but the problem of the ice crystals remains unresolved.

TECTONISM

There is no evidence of Cambrian orogenic movements in western or northern Australia. No angular unconformities due to folding have been detected there. There is some evidence of contemporaneous faulting. For example, it is possible that the sub-basins of the Ord Basin were first outlined by normal faults genetically related to the extrusion of the Antrim Plateau Basalts (McWhae *et al.*, 1958). In the Amadeus Basin the after-effects of the Petermann Ranges Folding may have continued on into the early Cambrian, but if so these were relatively minor.

As indicated above, there is good stratigraphic evidence that the deformation of the Adelaide Geosyncline began in the Middle Cambrian, and radiogenic dating of the metamorphism of the Cambrian rocks in the Kanmantoo belt indicates that the deformation continued on into the Ordovician, when indeed it may have reached its climax (see below). For the sake of convenience it will be treated here. The folds in the thin sequences to the west, for example, on Yorke Peninsula, are generally broad and open. Further east, in the Mount Lofty Ranges, that is in and on the

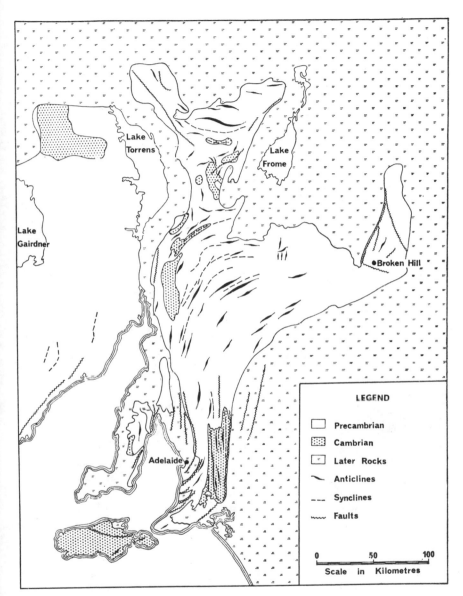

FIG. 2.10. Map showing pattern of major folds and faults in Precambrian and Cambrian rocks of South Australia and western New South Wales. Note in particular the area west and south of Lake Frome.

edge of the Kanmantoo Trough, the anticlines have steeper limbs and are often overturned to the west. Their orientation is meridional in these ranges, but to the south on Kangaroo Island they swing around to east–west, and to the north they swing northeast. Within this belt the folds form a left-handed *en échelon* pattern. The schists and gneisses of the Kanmantoo Group are foliated and lineated, the foliation usually being parallel with the original bedding (Kleeman and White, 1956). The whole belt is one of shearing and thrusting, the faults generally being oriented parallel with the fold axes. The western limbs of the anticlines in some areas have been overthrust.

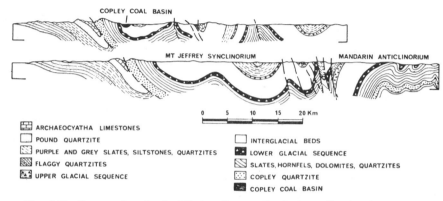

COPLEY COAL BASIN

MT JEFFREY SYNCLINORIUM   MANDARIN ANTICLINORIUM

0   5   10   15   20 Km

⊞ ARCHAEOCYATHA LIMESTONES
☐ POUND QUARTZITE
▨ PURPLE AND GREY SLATES, SILTSTONES, QUARTZITES
▨ FLAGGY QUARTZITES
▨ UPPER GLACIAL SEQUENCE

☐ INTERGLACIAL BEDS
▨ LOWER GLACIAL SEQUENCE
▨ SLATES, HORNFELS, DOLOMITES, QUARTZITES
▨ COPLEY QUARTZITE
▨ COPLEY COAL BASIN

FIG. 2.11. Cross-sections in the Flinders Ranges, South Australia, showing type of deformation in the Cambrian–Ordovician orogeny. (Redrawn after Glaessner and Parkin (eds.), 1958.)

North of Lake Frome and Lake Torrens there is another system of folds forming a broad arc convex to the south. The folds are anticlinal and some have Archaean rocks exposed in the cores. Along the southern edge of the arc there are major thrust and tear faults. In the northern Flinders Ranges, the region between the Mount Lofty–Olary Arc and this northern arc, there is a zone of broad domes and basins, the best known of which are the Blinman Dome and Wilpena Pound.

Little is known of the structural style of the Cambrian deformations in the Tasman Orthogeosyncline. At least in Tasmania orogenic movements were taking place throughout the Middle and Late Cambrian and angular unconformities have been found at various stratigraphic levels, but the main deformation appears to have taken place prior to the late Middle Cambrian (Campana and King, 1963). The whole episode is referred to as the Tyennan Orogeny. It is difficult to disentangle the effects of this orogeny from those of the later ones but it is known that tight folding and rift formation took place.

In Victoria there is no record of movements during the Cambrian, and in the Heathcote and Waratah Bay areas at least, there is apparently conformity between the Cambrian and Ordovician (Thomas, 1939; Lindner, 1953). The Cambrian sequence near Broken Hill is also continuous and overlain conformably by the Ordovician.

IGNEOUS ACTIVITY

EXTRUSIVES

No Cambrian volcanic rocks are known from the Amadeus Basin or from the Adelaide Geosyncline. It is possible to consider those of the other areas under three main headings—the basalts of the non-orogenic northwestern regions, the intermediate and basic rocks of the Tasman Orthogeosyncline, and the intermediate to ultrabasic rocks of the New Zealand Geosyncline.

The Antrim Plateau Basalts and their equivalents occur in the Bonaparte, Ord, Daly River, and western Georgina Basins. They include a variety of types ranging from olivine basalts to quartz basalts, and both flows and pyroclastics are present. They belong to the tholeiitic suite (Edwards and Clarke, 1940).

The Cambrian volcanics of the Tasman Orthogeosyncline can be broadly characterized as belonging to the spilitic suite, but this is not strictly accurate as there are appreciable quantities of rocks belonging to other suites, particularly in Tasmania. Both basic and acidic types occur in the Dundas Group and Mount Read Volcanics in western Tasmania, the acid rocks being more abundant along the edge of the Tyennan Geanticline, and the basic further out in the trough (Spry and Banks, eds., 1962). The bulk of the Mount Read Volcanics consists of flows, pyroclastics, and ignimbrites ranging in composition from andesites, to quartz–feldspar porphyries, keratophyres, and rhyolites. In the Dundas Group and equivalents, spilites, keratophyres and quartz keratophryes are the most common, but potash-rich types such as rhyolites and trachytes have also recently been recognized. Further to the north in Victoria, flows and pyroclastics of the spilite–keratophyre association only are present in the Heathcote Greenstones. These are thought to have been originally normal members of the calc-alkaline suite, mainly basalts and dolerites (Thomas and Singleton, 1956). The Rocksberg Greenstones of southeastern Queensland include several rock types, but are basically divisible into albite–actinolite–epidote rocks with or without augite phenocrysts, and similar rocks in which the abundant feldspar is andesine. The former were probably olivine basalts and the latter possibly sills of porphyrite (Mathews, 1954). More highly metamorphosed equivalents also occur.

On the margins of the geosyncline near Broken Hill there are acid flows and pyroclastics in the Lower Cambrian.

In New Zealand, as stated earlier, the fossiliferous Middle Cambrian rocks of northwest Nelson appear to overlie a thick (4600 m) sequence of andesitic and basaltic volcanics, with green pyroclastics, fine-grained tuffs, coarse agglomerates, and breccias, with interbedded flows or sills of porphyritic basalt and porphyrite, and thick beds of volcanic conglomerate (Grindley, 1961a). This volcanic activity was probably of Early Cambrian age.

After the period of quiescence in the Middle Cambrian, when the Tasman Formation was deposited, volcanism again set in and, in addition to the coarse igneous conglomerates of the Anatoki Formation, there are marked flows of porphyritic andesites and basalts in the upper part of the Cambrian succession.

INTRUSIVES

There is no evidence in Australia of acid intrusives of proven Cambrian age. The granites intruding the Cambrian sediments of the Adelaide Geosyncline have previously been held to be Cambrian (David, 1950), but are now believed to be Ordovician and are dealt with in the next chapter. Apart from the contemporaneous sills intruded into the Heathcote and Rocksberg Greenstones, and minor dykes at various localities, the only intrusions of any consequence are in the ultrabasic masses of western Tasmania and the greenstone belts of Victoria. In Tasmania they are intruded into both the volcanic and sedimentary piles of the Dundas Trough. The commonest rock is a coarse brown pyroxenite, but a whole range of the ultrabasic association is present—gabbros, amphibolites, dunites, peridotites, and serpentinites (Spry and Banks, eds., 1962). Most of these masses are in the form of slightly transgressive sills or of dykes. Some of them have been re-intruded during later movements, e.g. the mass at Anderson's Creek which is in a diapiric structure of Devonian age (Green, 1959). An upper limit to the age of the previous intrusion can be demonstrated locally where the intrusions are in sediments of Cambrian age and the overlying Ordovician sediments contain ultrabasic debris. In Victoria serpentinites and/or pyroxenites and amphibolites are associated with several of the Cambrian greenstone belts (Harris and Thomas, 1954; Wells, 1956).

In New Zealand, an ultramafic intrusive complex, situated between the Cobb and Takaka valleys in northwest Nelson, about 6 km north of Mount Arthur, has been assigned a Middle or Late Cambrian age by Grindley (1961a). This assemblage, which includes serpentinites, peridotites, talc- and quartz-magnesites, gabbros, dolerites, and porphyrites, is believed to have concordant relationships with the Cambrian sediments. These Cobb Intrusives are a valuable source of asbestos fibre and magnesite.

CHAPTER 3

The Ordovician System

WITH the advent of the Ordovician comes a more complete, or at least a more intelligible record, of the history of the Tasman Orthogeosyncline. In this structure it is only in eastern Queensland and northeastern New South Wales that there are extensive occurrences of unfossiliferous rocks of possible Ordovician age. Deposition continued over large parts of the northwestern part of the continent, and in the Amadeus Basin where, except for the uppermost Ordovician, a more or less continuous history may be deciphered. The Adelaide Geosyncline became an area of non-deposition, but fossiliferous Ordovician rocks are of relatively common occurrence throughout southeastern Australia, both in outcrop and in exploration wells put down through the Permian and later rocks of the Murray and Artesian Basins.

Both shelly and graptolitic facies are represented, the graptolitic facies being restricted almost entirely to the Tasman Orthogeosyncline. A few graptolite occurrences have been reported from the Amadeus and Canning Basins. The most extensive shelly facies deposits are in the Amadeus Basin and in a broad belt across northwestern Queensland and the Northern Territory. There are smaller occurrences in the Canning and Bonaparte Gulf Basins of Western Australia, Tasmania, Victoria, and in the central west of New South Wales. In the latter area there are several sections where the two facies interdigitate. The graptolites are relatively well known, but very few of the shelly fossils have been described.

The period was one of relative tectonic stability in most regions, but the Benambran Orogeny at the end of the period caused a reorganization of the trough-and-arch pattern in the Tasman Geosyncline. Volcanism was restricted to the Tasman Orthogeosyncline, apart from some minor activity in the Carnarvon Basin.

In New Zealand, well-defined Ordovician rocks of both the graptolitic and shelly facies are known in the South Island, namely in the northwest Nelson region and in the southwest Fiordland. It is now known that the graptolite-bearing succession of both these localities, though somewhat less complete, corresponds very closely to that in Victoria. The Victorian stratigraphical subdivisions are, in fact, applied directly to the New Zealand sequence.

The boundaries of the system in New Zealand are very indefinite, chiefly because no Upper Cambrian rocks have been identified with certainty on fossil evidence, and the oldest recognized Ordovician rocks (Lancefieldian Substage $2a$ = basal Arenigian) occur in areas far removed from known Cambrian strata. In the same way, the absence of identified Silurian rocks leaves the position of the upper boundary in doubt.

STRATIGRAPHY

Australia

LACHLAN GEOSYNCLINE

Lower Ordovician. By the close of the Cambrian most of the Adelaide Geosyncline had become a land area and was probably providing sediment for the Lachlan Geosyncline, which continued to subside at a relatively rapid rate. The pattern of Ordovician deposition within this geosyncline is much clearer than that of the Cambrian (Figs. 3.1 and 3.2). In western Victoria the Glenelg metamorphic complex could be either Cambrian or Ordovician or both (Wells, 1956), and consequently, in that region it is quite impossible at present to place the position of a shoreline. Further north, Lower Ordovician shelf deposits outcrop in the Broken Hill region of New South Wales, and they have been detected in several exploratory oil wells in the northeastern corner of South Australia, so that the approximate position of the shore can be estimated. In this region also there is some evidence that there was an open seaway between this shelf and the Amadeus Basin. The outcropping sediments to the northeast of Broken Hill near Mootwingee consist of quartzose sandstones with pebble bands, and inter-bedded shales, siltstones, and feldspathic sandstones, the upper part of which is considered to be of Tremadocian age on the basis of the trilobite faunas (Öpik, pers. comm.; Fletcher, 1964). The sediments in the South Australian wells are mainly quartzose sandstones and they contain dichograptids (Pandieburra No. 1 and Dullingari No. 1). Tremadocian calcareous sediments occur at Waratah Bay in southeastern Victoria (Lindner, 1953), and as shown below, Tasmania was the site of extensive shelf deposition. From all this evidence the approximate positions of shorelines to the west and south may be inferred with some confidence.

Within the geosyncline there were several troughs and rising geanticlines. Through western Victoria, to the east of the Glenelg Metamorphics, there was a rapidly subsiding trough here termed the **Ballarat Trough**. As indicated in the previous chapter, the relation of this structure to the Kanmantoo Trough is unknown. The sediments with which it is filled are a monotonous series of quartz-rich greywackes, black and red shales, and black cherts, which reach a maximum thickness of about 4000 m. Their uniformity is reflected by the fact that no satisfactory lithological subdivision has been devised for them and mapping has been based on biostratigraphic units. These are outlined in Table 3.1 (p. 90). Graptolites are known from most areas of outcrop and from this trough one of the most complete sequences

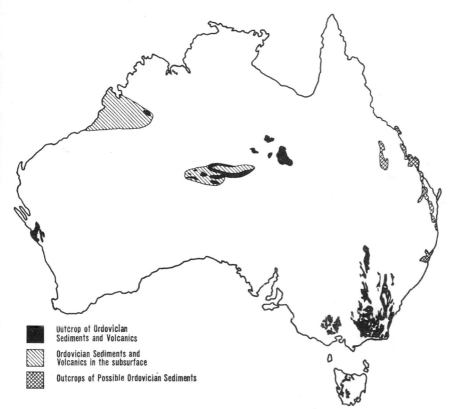

Uutcrop ot Ordovician
Sediments and Volcanics

Ordovician Sediments and
Volcanics in the subsurface

Outcrops of Possible Ordovician Sediments

Fig. 3.1. Distribution of known Ordovician sediments and volcanics. Isolated occurrences near the New South Wales–South Australia border are not shown.

of graptolite faunas in the world has been recovered. The greywackes exhibit the usual structures characteristic of the facies. In particular, they are well graded in both simple and oscillatory styles, and graptolites are more profuse in the fine upper parts of the graded beds than in any other parts of the sequence (Hills and Thomas, 1954). Shelly fossils are extremely rare, but phyllocarids and inarticulate brachiopods are not uncommon in certain beds.

Running through central Victoria is a tract of country, the **Melbourne Trough**, with a distinctive Ordovician and Middle Palaeozoic history. It is bounded on the west by the Mount William–Heathcote Axis, and on the east by the Wellington Line (Fig. 5.11) (Thomas, 1958). Sedimentary thicknesses (Hills and Thomas, 1954) indicate that the former structure was probably a

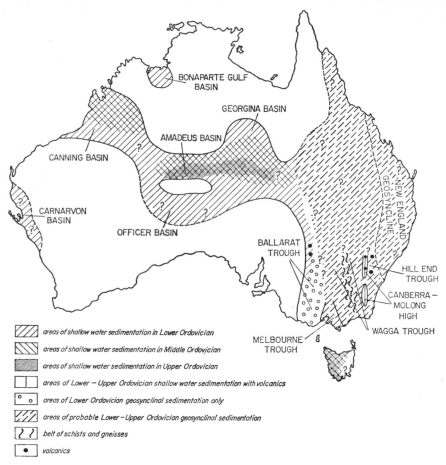

FIG. 3.2. Ordovician palaeogeography.

rising geanticline during Early Ordovician times, and it is not improbable that the latter structure was of a similar type. However, both remained submerged by the sea. The trough they enclose narrowed to the north and may have extended no further than the Murray River. It possibly owes its tectonically stable character and its marginal upthrust areas to an underlying block of Precambrian rocks extending across Bass Strait from

Tasmania. Lower Ordovician sediments do not outcrop extensively, but in the central part of the trough they are greywackes and slates, while on the marginal highs they tend to be more cherty (Hills and Thomas, 1954).

Further east is the **Wagga Trough,** a profound downwarp which extended from southeastern Victoria at least as far as Bourke in New South Wales. It cannot be traced further north because of Mesozoic cover. In this trough most of the sediments were deposited as greywacke shales, but in some places they have been extensively metamorphosed (Joplin, 1947; Vallance, 1953). Graptolites are known at several localities in Victoria and in the Snowy Mountains of New South Wales (Öpik, 1956c; Talent, 1965)a. The occurrence in the Cobar district of cross-stratified quartz-rich sandstone, slate, and chert (Girilambone and Tallebung Groups), may indicate a shallowing of the trough.

The eastern boundary of the Wagga Trough is the **Molong–Canberra High** (Öpik, 1958a; Packham, 1960) along which volcanics and shallow-water sediments accumulated. North of Molong the lower part of the Oakdale Formation (Strusz, 1960), which consists of spilites, quartz keratophyres, tuffs, greywackes, and scattered limestone lenses, contains Lower Ordovician graptolites. In the vicinity of Canberra no definite Lower Ordovician rocks are known, but the shallow-water Black Mountain Sandstone may be of this age. The Molong–Canberra High is not a continuous structure. There was a wide passage through it south of Mandurama, and another one south of Canberra.

In the **Hill End Trough** (Packham, 1960, 1962) to the east of this high there are thick successions of black shales, and silicified siltstones and shales below graptolite-bearing Upper Ordovician sediments. These may be of Early Ordovician age. Because of the cover of Late Palaeozoic and Mesozoic sediments of the Sydney Basin, little evidence bearing on the problem of the eastern edge of this trough is available, but the inferred unconformity between Upper Ordovician shales and the Wagonga beds on the New South Wales south coast (Brown, 1933), suggests that there was a "high" in that position.

Middle Ordovician (Darriwilian). During Middle Ordovician times the western shoreline of the Victorian end of the Lachlan Geosyncline moved well to the east of its former position, and the **Ballarat Trough** was gradually restricted. Consequently the thickest known sections west of the Mount William–Heathcote axis are only of the order of 500 m thick. No rocks of this age are known in the **Mootwingee Region**, but they are present in the exploratory wells of northeastern South Australia, suggesting that a connexion with the Amadeus Basin was maintained. Quartz-rich greywackes and slates of Darriwilian age are widespread in the **Melbourne** and **Wagga Troughs**. During the Darriwilian, the **Molong–Canberra High** became the site of shallow-water sedimentation, presumably as a result of subsidence related to the movements further west. Volcanic activity continued along the structure, though probably with a lesser intensity than previously, and in the south around Canberra, it is entirely absent. The sediments in the Orange–Wellington area are calcareous, and in many places contain a large bioclastic element. They are widespread and are known under various names. Perhaps the best-known occurrence is between Cowra and Orange, where the Cliefden Caves Limestone is over 800 m thick and consists of both fine and coarse-bedded limestones and shales. Small biohermal masses are also known. The fauna is profuse, and predominant in it are the brachiopods *Rhynchotrema*, *Spanodonta*, and *Rafinesquina*, the trilobites *Lichas*, *Trinucleus* and undescribed asaphids and pliomerids, the gastropods *Lophospira*, *Raphistoma*, and *Maclurites*, and the corals *Propora*, *Nyctopora*, and *Billingsaria* (Stevens, 1952; Hill, 1957a). The Cliefden Caves Limestone is succeeded in places by the Malongulli Formation, a unit made up of thin-bedded shales, siltstones, and sandstones showing structures of the greywacke suite, but in some areas the two units can be shown to be facies equivalents. Graptolites in the Malongulli Formation are *Glyptograptus*, *Climacograptus*, and *Dicellograptus*, and these indicate a late Darriwilian and early Gisbornian age. The Cliefden Caves Limestone also grades laterally into volcanics to the north (Walker, 1959; Strusz, 1960). To the south, in the Canberra–Queanbeyan district, the Darriwilian equivalents are only 200–300 m thick and are composed entirely of terrigenous materials.

At the northern end of the **Hill End Trough**, volcanics near Sofala extend down into the Darriwilian (Packham, pers. comm.), and this is probably also true of the lower part of the Triangle Group of shales and greywackes which outcrops further south (Stanton, 1956).

Upper Ordovician (Gisbornian–Bolindian). The coming of the Late Ordovician brought little change in the depositional pattern. A maximum of about 800 m of greywackes and shales lie conformably on the Darriwilian in the **Ballarat Trough** west of the Mount William–Heathcote axis, but by the end of the period, rudites, coarse sandstones, and mudstones (the Riddel Grits) with a shelly fauna, heralded the cessation of deposition. There is a conformable succession of greywackes and shales in both the **Melbourne** and **Wagga Troughs**, in Victoria. They are up to 400 m thick in the former, but perhaps as much as several thousand metres in the latter. These rocks, like those of the Lower Ordovician, are not subdivided into lithostratigraphic units. Graptolites are of frequent occurrence, and have been found in the Wagga Trough at localities as far north as Cobar (Tallebung Group). It is probable that some of the metamorphic rocks in this belt are of Late Ordovician age.

Along the northern half of the **Molong–Canberra High** there is an interdigitating complex of andesites, andesitic tuffs, keratophyres, bedded limestones and sandstones, and shales largely of volcanic derivation known as the Malongulli Tuff and Angullong Formation (Stevens, 1952; Stevens and Packham, 1953; Packham and Stevens, 1955; Stevens, 1957; Walker, 1959; Strusz, 1960). Maximum thicknesses are about 1000 m. Facies changes are rapid in both east–west and north–south directions, and graptolite and shelly faunas are represented in most sections. Graptolites representative of the Gisbornian, Eastonian, and Bolindian Stages are known. The shelly faunas include the corals *Palaeophyllum, Tryplasma, Heliolites, Schedohalysites, Halysites* and *Favosites,* the polyzoans *Batostoma, Homotrypa,* and *Stictopora,* the trilobites *Trinucleus, Dionide,* and *Remopleurides,* and brachiopods.

On the western edge of the high near Cargo the Cargo Andesite is the correlative of the Walli Andesite, but the higher part of the sequence is less tuffaceous than at Cliefden Caves and consists of various limestones followed by thick arenites, siltstones, and some interbedded andesitic tuffs (the Millambri Formation), are over 1500 m thick. They probably extend up into the Silurian.

As was the case earlier in the period, the volcanic rocks disappear to the south, and in the Canberra district the Upper Ordovician is encompassed in less than 100 m of black graptolite-bearing shale (the Acton Shale) which contains graptolites of all three stages. There are few data on the existence of the arch south of Canberra, but it appears to extend as far south as the Cooma district where some very clean orthoquartzites are known (Lambert and White, 1965).

Great thicknesses of volcanics, slates, and cherts occupy the **Hill End Trough**. At the northern end volcanics predominate. Near Sofala there are about 2000 m of volcanics which are mainly andesitic, though more acid types also occur. South of Bathurst the upper part of the Triangle Group and the Rockley Volcanics, which together total about 4500 m, cover a wide area. Andesitic pyroclastics predominate here also. Still further south the volcanic component is greatly reduced, and graptolitic slates are the most common rocks. This fact is to be correlated with the absence of volcanic rocks at the Canberra end of the Molong–Canberra High. Graptolitic slates are also found on the east of the Hill End Trough.

Provenance of the Ordovician Greywackes. Most of the Ordovician greywackes in the Lachlan Geosyncline are quartz-rich. The only known sources for the quartz in the Lower Ordovician rocks are the Precambrian and Cambrian of South Australia, western New South Wales, and Tasmania. In the Late

Ordovician it is probable that the Lower Ordovician sediments in the western part of the Ballarat Trough were themselves being eroded. These sources are adequate to account for the origin of the sediments of the Ballarat, Melbourne, and perhaps Wagga Troughs, but not the Hill End Trough. Rocks on and derived from the Molong High should not be quartz-rich, since it was the site of andesitic volcanism, and there are no known Cambrian or older granites in the area. The presence of quartz-rich rocks on the high in the Canberra area suggests that granites were exposed in this area but have been covered by later deposits.

TASMANIAN SHELF (Fig. 3.3)

Movements that began during the latter part of the Cambrian culminated in an extensive phase of faulting and uplift, the Jukesian Movement, during the earliest Ordovician. Several geanticlinal areas forming an arcuate belt in the west and northwestern parts of the island became prominent. The largest of these was the Tyennan Geanticline, along the outer edges of which a series of fault troughs, or more probably fault angle depressions, developed (Spry and Banks, eds., 1962; Campana and King, 1963). Within the geanticlinal areas similar structures were also formed, as in the vicinity of Adamsfield. In these depressions the earliest rocks of the Junee Group, the Jukes and Owen Conglomerates and their correlatives, were deposited. Away from the areas of major uplift these rocks are conformable on the Cambrian Dundas Group, but elsewhere they rest with disconformity or angular unconformity on the Cambrian or Precambrian. The earliest units of the sequence are very coarse in places and contain angular to sub-rounded blocks up to 1 m in diameter. Stratification is poor and the rock bodies thin rapidly, suggesting that they are fanglomerates. Higher in the sequence sandstones are interbedded and the conglomerates become finer grained, more regularly bedded, less lenticular, and more siliceous, these features indicating a reduction in the topography of the Tyennan Geanticline, a decrease in the rate of subsidence of the troughs, and an increase in the efficiency of the transporting agents working parallel to its length. Consequently the later units exhibit successive overlap. Some workers have favoured a marine origin for the sequence, but recent opinion favours a terrestrial environment for all except some thin members near the top of Owen Conglomerate. No fossils, apart from a few tracks, have been found, but in all areas the conglomerates lie conformably below Arenigian rocks, and at certain localities lie unconformably on Dresbachian and Franconian rocks. It is concluded that they are penecontemporaneous and of earliest Ordovician age. Their thickness varies considerably from place to place. The maximum figure is about 2000 m, but 200–500 m is general.

By the early Arenigian the highlands formed during the Jukesian movement had been greatly reduced. The sea had occupied the areas in which
the Early Ordovician conglomerates had been deposited, and had begun to
transgress the remnants of the former geanticlines. In these shallow seas
the well-washed quartzose sandstones and siltstones of the Caroline Creek
Formation were laid down. They vary in colour from white to brown and
red depending on the nature of the cement and the degree of weathering.
In some areas these rocks are followed by a finer phase of calcareous siltstones
and mudstones which have been separated off as the Florentine Valley
Mudstones. Palaeontological evidence indicates that these two formations
were deposited during the Arenigian, but there is evidence that the Caroline
Creek Formation is diachronous within this interval (Spry and Banks,
eds., 1962). The commonest fossils are the brachiopods *Tritoechia* and
Syntrophopsis; the trilobites *Asaphellus, Asaphopsis, Tasmanocephalus, Tasmanas-
pis, Etheridgeaspis, Carolinites,* and *Pliomerops*: the graptolites *Dictyonema,
Tetragraptus,* and *Didymograptus*; and the worm tube *Skolithos*. Together they
are up to 2000 m thick, but the average figure is 300–700 m.

Most of the remainder of the Ordovician was occupied by deposition of
the Gordon Limestone, a sequence of bedded calcilutites with some calcarenites and occasional calcirudites. The average calcium carbonate
content of the rock is over 90 per cent, the main impurities being dolomite
and silica. However, terrigenous material increases in proportion towards
the northwestern corner of the island, in which direction the unit also
gradually thins out. The greatest thicknesses (1800 m) occur in the south
and east where the limestones are covered by Permian or Jurassic rocks,
and hence it is probable that they extended considerably further east than
the present outcrops. Presumably a shallow basin occupied most of the
central and western parts of the island at this time.

The Gordon Limestone is well-bedded, the beds ranging in thickness
from a few millimetres to a few metres. Oolites have been recorded. The
silica impurities are usually present as chert nodules which are strung out
parallel to the bedding planes. No reefs have been discovered.

Fossils are present in abundance at certain localities, but the limestones
are not continuously fossiliferous. The oldest known fossils are of late Canadian age (late Arenigian), and it is probable therefore that deposition of
limestone began in some areas while the terrigenous facies of the Florentine
Valley Mudstone was being deposited towards the western shoreline. The
youngest fossils are probably Cincinnatian (Late Ordovician). In the early
faunas (Canadian) the common fossils are the graptolite *Phyllograptus*, the
brachiopod *Tritoechia*, and the nautiloids *Manchuroceras* and *Piloceras*. Towards
the middle of the sequence (Chazyan and Blackriveran) the corals *Tetradium,
Lichenaria, Nyctopora* and *Saffordophyllum* are of importance, along with the

gastropod *Maclurites* and the alga *Girvanella*. The upper sequence (Trentonian and Cincinnatian) contains the corals *Streptelasma, Tryplasma, Favistella, Eofletcheria, Palaeofavosites, Catenipora*, and *Tetradium*, undescribed brachiopods and trilobites, and the nautiloids *Beloitoceras, Anaspyroceras*, and *Trocholitoceras*.

Towards the end of the period limestone deposition ceased and shales and sandstones followed. Some of these are probably of latest Ordovician age.

New England Geosyncline

As noted in the previous chapter, the thick sequence of low-grade metamorphic rocks, mainly phyllites and slates, of this region was possibly deposited in part during the Ordovician. In southeast Queensland these rocks are known as the Bunya Phyllites and are thought to be several thousand metres thick. The characteristic rock type is phyllite, which has fine micaceous layers attenuating with coarse quartzose layers. They are strongly deformed and are laced by quartz veins and, according to Bryan and Jones (1954), they show evidence of having been subjected to two periods of regional metamorphism. Some parts of the sequence are more highly deformed than others owing to extensive horizontal thrusting. Nothing is known of their age apart from the fact that they lie unconformably beneath the Neranleigh–Fernvale Group. Similar rocks outcrop in northern New South Wales where they have been referred to as the Woolomin Beds, and contain a poor fauna of *Halysites* and *Favosites* at two localities. On this very tenuous evidence an Ordovician age has been assigned to part of the sequence.

Rocks similar to the Bunya Phyllites occur along the coast north to Rockhampton, and south to Kempsey. In the latter area they are known as the Nambucca Beds (Voisey, 1958*a*).

As was the position in the Cambrian, the relationship of these rocks to those of the Lachlan Geosyncline is obscured by the Permian–Mesozoic sediments of the Sydney Basin.

North Queensland Basins

The oldest sediments in these basins are unfossiliferous, but are believed to be Ordovician on grounds of superposition. They consist of greywackes and argillites, and form the lower part of the sequence of the **Greys Creek Shelf.**

Georgina Basin

There was no apparent break in sedimentation in this basin at the end of the Cambrian. In the Toko Range which spans the Queensland–Northern Territory boundary, and in the Boulia region, most of the Ninmaroo Formation belongs to the Ordovician. It consists of units of dolomite interbedded with calcilutites, calcarenites, and dolomitic quartzose sandstones. Some of the limestones are oolitic. Approximately 500 m of this formation belong to the Tremadocian and the remainder to the Upper Cambrian. Fossils are abundant but most are undescribed; nautiloids, gastropods, and ribeirioids are among the most common, but asaphid trilobites and syntrophioid and orthoid brachiopods are also present (Hill and Denmead, eds., 1960; Tomlinson, pers. comm.). To the west and northwest the Ninmaroo Formation thins out and is replaced laterally by the upper part of the Tomahawk Beds, which are largely quartzose sandstones with abundant glauconite in places. The Ordovician part reaches a maximum thickness of about 200 m. Fossils again are common, but have not been described (Smith, 1960/73, Smith and Milligan, 1963/46).

Towards the end of Tremadocian times sedimentation ceased over at least the eastern part of the basin and lower Arenigian sandy rocks were laid down with slight angular unconformity on the Ninmaroo Formation. These sandstones and shales (known as the Kelly Creek Formation and Swift Beds) are only of the order of 150 m maximum thickness and contain trilobites, brachiopods, gastropods, and nautiloids (Smith and Vine, 1960/71). Further west it is probable that the upper (lower Arenigian) parts of the Tomahawk Beds are conformable with the lower (Tremadocian) parts.

Only in the Toko Range did subsidence continue through the Arenigian and into the Llanvirnian (or perhaps the Llandeilian), and a very shallow basin was formed in which the Toko Group was deposited. The four formations comprising this group are all thin (from 50 to 150 m) and apparently conformable. They consist of quartz sandstones, siltstones, calcilutites, calcarenites, cherts, and coquinites in varying proportions. Most units are thin-bedded, and some are gypsiferous. Shelly fossils are very abundant in the calcareous beds, brachiopods, nautiloids, gastropods, trilobites, and ribeirioids being particularly common. The Nora Formation is the only one of these four formations known outside the Toko area, but it is widespread to the west and northwest, where it lies disconformably on the Tomahawk Beds.

No Upper Ordovician deposits are known in the region, and it has been concluded that gentle deformation occurred at that time.

OFFICER, AMADEUS, AND NGALIA BASINS

In the Ordovician, as in the Cambrian, seas probably covered these three basins and at least some of the intervening areas. In the Officer Basin probable Ordovician rocks are known along the northern edge, where they dip basinward but little is yet known of their extent (Sprigg and Woolley, 1963). They are thick sandstones, coarsely cross-stratified, and containing abundant *Skolithos* tubes.

The presence of Ordovician sediments in the Ngalia Basin has not yet been demonstrated. Fortunately, our knowledge of the Ordovician rocks of the Amadeus Basin has recently been greatly increased and an integrated interpretation can be attempted. The rocks are all shallow-water marine sediments and belong to four apparently conformable formations which together make up the Larapinta Group. All of the formations are thickest along the present northern edge of the basin, though their areas of greatest thickness are not coincident. In general, the greatest thicknesses are in the northeast and each formation overlaps the previous one to the south and west (Wells *et al.*, 1963/51).

At the base is the Pacoota Sandstone, a poorly cemented, cross-stratified, ripple-marked, silty, quartz sandstone with occasional pebble beds, the basal part of which is of Cambrian age. It rests conformably on the Goyder Formation. The trace fossil *Skolithos* occurs throughout, but is exceedingly common in the middle part of the unit, in some beds as high as 32,000 per sq m having been recorded, but this is exceptional (Stelck and Hopkins, 1962). It is the thickest of the Ordovician formations and reaches a maximum (including the Cambrian part) of 1000 m. Shelly fossils are found in thin bands in a predominantly unfossiliferous sequence, but asaphid and other trilobites, ribeirioids, nautiloids, bivalves, and gastropods indicate that the formation ranges from Late Cambrian to early Arenigian in age (Prichard and Quinlan, 1962; Wells *et al.*, 1965a). The succeeding Horn Valley Siltstone is much thinner (up to 470 m), and contains several thin limestones, and is in places glauconitic. Fossils are abundant and many reach a large size. The most conspicuous are the brachiopods "*Orthis*" *dichotomalis* and lingulids, the gastropods *Raphistomina* and ?*Helicotoma*, the trilobites *Trinodus*, *Carolinites* and asaphids, nautiloids including *Madiganella*, single-cusped conodonts, and the graptolite *Didymograptus* (Crespin, 1943; Thomas, 1960; Tomlinson, in Wells *et al.*, 1965b, 1963/51). The bulk of the evidence indicates an Arenigian age. Cross-stratified quartz sandstones with interbedded laminated siltstones form the bulk of the Stairway Sandstone (maximum thickness 600 m). Although all the Larapinta Group sediments contain phosphorites, by far the highest concentration of them is in the Stairway, where they occur as pellet beds averaging about 5 cm thick and in places numbering 4 per 10 m (Wells *et al.*, 1963/51). The fauna is rich, and contains a large percentage of endemic species. Several species of the bivalve "*Isoarca*" have been described.

In the Stokes Formation there are limestones and sandstones in the lower half, but siltstone is the predominant lithology. Some of the siltstones are gypsiferous and also contain salt casts. The distribution of the Stokes Formation has been limited by a period of erosion prior to the deposition of the Mereenie Sandstone, which lies unconformably on it or earlier formations over much of the eastern part of the basin. The age of the Stokes Formation has not been definitely determined but it is probably Caradocian. Its most characteristic fossils are the brachiopod *"Orthis" leviensis* and the bivalve *"Isoarca" etheridgei*, though in addition to these there is a large undescribed fauna of brachiopods, bivalves, gastropods, nautiloids and trilobites.

The continuous marine deposition, the very rich faunas, the occurrence of gypsum and salt pseudomorphs, and the prevalence of phosphorites, pose palaeogeographical problems. Clearly these sediments were all deposited under shallow-water marine conditions, and circulation over at least parts of the area must have been restricted at certain times. The considerable thickness of the sediments at the present eastern end suggests continuity of access to the open sea in this direction. The general thinning of the sequence to the west suggests that the high basement between the Amadeus and Canning Basins may have acted as a partial barrier. It is possible that the features mentioned above may be explained by continuous access of the sea over a threshold in the east and periodic access to the Canning Basin in the west.

WEST COAST BASINS

Outcropping Ordovician rocks are known only from the Fitzroy Depression along the northern edge of the **Canning Basin**, but they have been identified also in the subsurface as far south as the Samphire Depression (Veevers and Wells, 1961). Their extent over the central and eastern parts of the basin remains unknown.

Two conformable (or possibly disconformable) formations are recognized in outcrop, the Emanuel and the overlying Gap Creek, which together form the Prices Creek Group (up to 1000 m thick). Both of these are highly calcareous and contain dolomite and interbedded siltstones and sandstones, but in the Gap Creek Formation the dolomites are more common, alternation of sedimentary types more marked, and the resistance to erosion greater. Outside the main area of outcrop, conglomerates and interbedded quartz sandstones equivalent to the lower part of the Emanuel Formation are known. Both formations contain rich trilobite, brachiopod, and molluscan faunas, only a small part of which has been described. The trilobite *Xenostegium*, asaphids and agnostids, the nautiloids *Eothinoceras*, *Cyrtendoceras*, *Proterocameroceras* among others, and the graptolites *Tetragraptus*, *Didymograptus*, and *Clonograptus* are known from the Emanuel Formation (Teichert and Glenister, 1953; Thomas, 1960), while the trilobites *Bumastus* and *Isotelus* and the brachiopod *Spanodonta* are common in the Gap Creek Formation. The former unit is considered to cover the Canadian and perhaps

Chazyan (Tremadocian–Arenigian), while the latter is Trentonian (Lower Caradocian). This indicates a disconformity between the two formations.

Deep wells in the Fitzroy Depression and on the La Grange Platform and the Samphire Depression have intersected limestone–dolomite–shale sequences of Early and Middle Ordovician age, though the base of the sequence is missing in places, presumably owing to irregularities in the basement topography. The section on the La Grange Platform begins with the Arenigian Thangoo Limestone which lies unconformably on Precambrian. It contains plectambonitid brachiopods and the gastropod *Helicotoma,* and the graptolites *Tetragraptus* and *Didymograptus* and *Amplexograptus* (Tomlinson, 1961). It is upper Arenigian and Llanvirnian. On the northern flank of the platform 120 m of dolomite (previously known as the Roebuck Dolomite) forms the basal part of the Thangoo Limestone. It contains the conodonts *Drepanodus, Acontiodus, Paltodus,* and *Gothodus* (Glenister and Glenister, 1958). Further south on the Wallal Platform the sequence thins out and the Llanvirnian part of the section is missing. It is concluded that during the Early and Middle Ordovician the Canning Basin was a shallow downwarp, with only slight topographical relief on its floor. In it shallow-water well-aerated sediments were deposited. In the Late Ordovician subsidence ceased and no further deposition took place until the Devonian.

In the **Bonaparte Gulf Basin** deposition of the Carlton Group continued conformably from the Cambrian into the Ordovician. The Pander Greensand, its uppermost formation, consists of about 170 m of medium grained, cross-bedded, friable glauconitic sandstone. The Lower Ordovician conodonts *Drepanodus* and *Acontiodus* have been recorded, but there is also a rich undescribed shelly fauna.

On the eastern margin of the **Carnarvon and Perth Basins** an unfossiliferous clastic sequence known as the Tumblagooda Sandstone outcrops. This unit, which is more than 1800 m thick, consists mainly of quartz sandstone, with some conglomerate and siltstone. It contains the trace fossils *Protichnites* and *Skolithos* and a tentative Middle Cambrian–Early Ordovician age has been suggested on this evidence (Öpik, 1959), though the presence of rocks of similar lithology below Middle Silurian limestones on Dirk Hartogs Island has given rise to the suggestion that the upper part of the unit could be Early Silurian in age (McWhae *et al.*, 1958).

Despite this lack of accurate data for correlation, it seems reasonable to infer that the Perth and Carnarvon Basins were both active regions of subsidence in the Early Palaeozoic.

New Zealand

The geosynclinal nature of the Ordovician deposits is clearly recognizable even though they are sparsely distributed. In the northwest Nelson area, the Lower and Middle Ordovician is composed mainly of graptolitic shales deposited in a marine basin under poorly aerated conditions. The trend of this basin is roughly meridional. In the upper part of the sequence throughout the basin, there is a rather marked change to a more calcareous facies of probable shallow-water origin. In contrast to the Cambrian sequence, eruptive activity appears to have been much reduced and there is considerably less evidence of conglomerates and coarse sediments in this area. This suggests that the marginal lands were no longer rising and that erosion had largely reduced them to areas of gentle relief.

A consideration of the Ordovician sequence in the Fiordland area at first sight, leads to the conclusion, on somewhat scanty evidence, that a meridional graptolitic facies there is bordered on the east by a calcareous facies (the Long Sound calc-schists, gneisses, and marbles), arranged in a basin parallel to that of the northwest Nelson area. It should be pointed out however, that the latter area of Lower Palaeozoic rocks and the southwest Fiordland area are on opposite sides of the Alpine Fault, along which a relative horizontal displacement of some 480 km has been postulated. Restoration to a former position based on a movement of this magnitude could result in a rough alignment of the respective facies as part of a single depositional basin.

The striking similarities between the New Zealand Ordovician sequence and that in the classical Victorian areas clearly suggests direct or close connexion between the basins of deposition.

Nelson Region

The Ordovician rocks here occupy two roughly meridional belts to the southwest of Golden Bay. The rocks are folded, in places isoclinally, in a north–south direction and the effects of later oblique fold movements are also visible.

The **western belt** includes the fossiliferous (graptolitic) localities in the Slaty Creek area, about 22 km west of Collingwood, and the Cobb River area, Mount Peel and Leslie River, southwest of Takaka. The graptolite-bearing horizons occur in a sequence of carbonaceous shales and slates, quartzites, contact schists, and phyllites—the Aorangi Mine Formation—some 1200–1800 m thick. The graptolite faunas in the Slaty Creek area include substantial portions of the Lancefieldian, Bendigonian, Chewtonian, and Castlemainian Stages (= Arenigian). The upper part of the

GD

sequence comprises the Aorere Formation of green and grey semischist, green phyllite and greywacke, 1800–2400 m thick. It is unfossiliferous (except possibly for a cobble from Paturau River containing *Ogygites* (*Basiliella*) and is probably late Early to Middle Ordovician in age (?Llanvirnian and Llandeilian). The two formations mentioned constitute the Aorere Group and where its rocks are in contact with the "Karamea Granite" (= Kahurangi Point to Ahaura River Granite of Reed, 1958), hornfelses and spotted schists with "lit-par-lit" injections of granite are developed (Fig. 6.3).

In the southerly part of the westerly belt near Lake Cobb, Leslie River and Mount Peel,* beds containing Gisbornian (= Llandeilian) graptolites have been found. In this area also, a species of the trilobite *Triarthrus* has recently been discovered, together with a new variety of *Nemagraptus gracilis* in lower Gisbornian rocks (Skwarko, 1962).

The **eastern belt**, which is separated from the western belt by the main area of Haupiri-type rocks (see Fig. 2.7) extends from south of Collingwood in a somewhat sinuous pattern southwards to Mount Arthur. In this area, the two Ordovician belts coalesce and continue southwards as far as Mount Owen. In the easterly belt, the rocks consist of graptolite-bearing argillaceous sediments associated with thick lenses of limestone or marble (Mount Arthur Group).

The lowest formation in the Mount Arthur Group (Patriarch Formation) apparently rests conformably on Haupiri rocks in a steep anticlinal fold in the Wangapeka Valley. The beds, 150–950 m thick, consist of thin-bedded shales and sandstones and dark argillites, frequently showing graded-bedding, cross-stratification and slump structures. Some volcanics and limestones are also present. From these rocks, the Lower Ordovician trilobite *Taihungshania* has been obtained.

Stratigraphically above the Patriarch Formation, though nowhere apparently in contact with it, comes the Flora Formation (600–1500 m) of dark, graphitic argillites with interbedded bands of black limestone and some volcanics. At Lodestone Peak and Flora Track, about 40 km south of Takaka, the graptolites are characteristic of the Gisbornian Stage.

The sequence in the eastern belt is capped by 300–1000 m of cream to grey to black marble (Mount Arthur Marble). To the north and west the marble becomes muddy and to the south, sandy. At a few places, the marble contains corals and in Takaka River, about 3 km west of Upper Takaka, graptolitic shales are probably interbedded with a limestone breccia containing crinoids, corals, sponges and stromatoporoids. The corals are regarded as Upper Ordovician forms, and this is confirmed by the recent

*Note: the Leslie, Douglas, and Peel Formations, consisting of graptolitic shales, 1800–2400 m thick, are included in the Mount Arthur Group, which is chiefly developed in the easterly belt (see Grindley, 1961*a*).

discovery of Upper Ordovician (?Eastonian) graptolites in slates of the overlying Wangapeka Formation near Mount Owen (Johnston *et al.*, 1965).

In the Pikikiruna Range, the widespread Mount Arthur Marble overlies biotite–garnet and biotite–garnet–sillimanite schists commonly containing chloritoid and staurolite. These schists are tentatively correlated with the Middle Ordovician.

Under this regional heading, we shall also include the recent discovery by Wellman (1962) of a graptolite locality at Alfred River, near Springs Junction, south Nelson. Wellman suggests that the Lower Palaeozoic rocks of northwest Nelson extend south as a narrowing belt partly hidden by Cainozoic rocks of the Murchison Depression, and that they are cut off by the Alpine Fault.

SOUTHWEST FIORDLAND REGION

At the extreme southwest of the South Island, about Preservation Inlet, Cape Providence, and Edwardson and Cunaris Sounds, there is a sequence of greywackes, argillites, and slates with a graptolite assemblage representing the majority of sub-stages of the Lancefieldian–Castlemainian succession of Victoria (Benson and Keble, 1935; Skwarko, 1958). This succession, the Preservation Formation, about 1200 m thick, is involved in a series of tight north–south folds. It passes eastwards into regionally metamorphosed schists of the biotite and chlorite zones and is thermally altered and intruded lit-par-lit by the Kakapo Granite (?Late Palaeozoic).

At Cape Providence and Preservation Inlet, the greywackes and quartzites, which are interbedded with phyllites and graptolitic slates, show cross-stratification and ripple-marks (Wood, 1960). In addition to the graptolites, the slates of Preservation Inlet and Cape Providence have yielded small inarticulate brachiopods, sponges, and phyllocarids.

In contrast, in the head of Long Sound and about Dusky, Breaksea, Doubtful, and Caswell Sounds, there are considerable areas of calc-gneisses, calc-silicate schists, and hornfelses, interbedded with bands of marble containing graphite and phlogopite (the Long Sound Formation), which have been correlated almost exclusively on lithological grounds with the Upper Ordovician Mount Arthur Marble of the Nelson Region. It is believed that the Long Sound Formation is underlain by a series of hornblende–plagioclase gneisses and schists, garnet–augite- and garnet–hypersthene-gneisses and amphibolites of the Wet Jacket Formation. Large areas of hornblende–plagioclase, para- and orthogneisses with many concordant apophyses of granite and diorite (the Bradshaw gneisses and the Mount Solitary metamorphics) together with the upper part of the Seaview Formation of massive quartzo-feldspathic schists and siliceous metagreywackes with some marble bands, are correlated on stratigraphical grounds with the Lower and Middle Ordovician (Wood, 1960).

About 10–25 km northeast of the mouth of Milford Sound, Wellman and Wilson (1964) have reported the occurrence of a marble, faulted against the Alpine Fault, which they tentatively correlate, in the absence of fossils, with the Ordovician rocks of southwest Fiordland.

PALAEONTOLOGY AND CLIMATE

The graptolite faunas of Australasia are particularly comprehensive and abundant. The most complete successions occur in Victoria and New Zealand (Table 3.1), but graptolite-bearing rocks are now known from all States (except Queensland), and from the Northern Territory. In Victoria the sequence up to the zone of *Nemagraptus gracilis* is as complete, perhaps more complete, than any other in the world, and it has certain distinctive features; for example, the absence of *Dichograptus* in the Lancefieldian, the long-continued evolution of four- and three-branched forms of *Tetragraptus fruticosus*, and the abundance of *Oncograptus* and *Cardiograptus* in the Yapeenian. The absence of this latter stage is the only significant gap in the New Zealand Lower Ordovician sequence.* In the pre-*Nemagraptus gracilis* interval the affinities of the faunas are more with western and central North America (Thomas, 1960; Ross and Berry, 1963; Skevington, 1963) than with western Europe, though it is possible to establish general correlations between all regions at certain points by widespread species or assemblages, such as the *Dictyonema*-anisograptid assemblage of the Tremadocian, the *Tetragraptus approximatus* assemblage and the first appearance of *Isograptus* in the Arenigian, and the *Glyptograptus teretiusculus* assemblage in the Llandeilan. Provincialism seems to disappear with the *Nemagraptus gracilis* zone, since it and all subsequent zones can be recognized throughout the world.

In contrast to the graptolites, the shelly faunas are limited in their distribution, and have not been comprehensively studied. They are best discussed on a regional basis. The Canadian–lower Trentonian rocks of the Canning Basin are remarkable for the similarity of their nautiloid faunas to those of North America. For example, of the 24 genera of nautiloids described, 11 are indigenous, 2 are also known from Europe, and 10 are known elsewhere only from North America. The nautiloids of the Georgina and Amadeus Basins which cover much the same time range are, however, clearly boreal in type, while the trilobites and brachiopods of the Amadeus Basin include a strong indigenous element along with others with cosmopolitan, Asian, and American affinities (Tomlinson, pers. comm.). The nautiloids of the Tasmanian *Manchuroceras-Piloceras* fauna are of east Asian

---

* *Oncograptus* has since been reported in northwest Nelson (Smith, 1966).

type, but the brachiopods *Tritoechia* and *Syntrophopsis* have American affinities. In addition there is a prominent endemic trilobite fauna. The post-Canadian faunas of Tasmania and New South Wales have much in common, particularly the corals *Eofletcheria*, *Tetradium*, *Lichenaria*, *Nyctopora*, *Calapoecia*, and *Coccoseris*, which are not known elsewhere in the continent, but are widely distributed in other parts of the world (Hill, 1955, 1957*a*). Polyzoans are abundant in New South Wales (Phillips-Ross, 1961), and species of *Austrophylloporina*, *Batostoma*, *Homotrypa*, and *Stictopora* show resemblances to North American forms. The occurrence in the Cliefden Caves Limestone of the brachiopod *Spanodonta* provides a link with the Canning Basin, and the trilobite *Encrinurella* is a link with east Asia. It seems then that this region received migrants from most other provinces during the middle and late parts of the period.

The extensive limestone and dolomite deposition which took place during the latter half of the period from as far north as the Canning Basin to as far south as Tasmania, indicates a warm climate for the continent during that interval. Similar deposits were formed in the Canning and Georgina Basins in the earlier half of the period while coralline limestones formed during the Middle Ordovician in central New South Wales, so that there is reason to believe that similar temperatures also prevailed at these times. Supporting evidence for this interpretation is to be found in the occurrence of salt crystal casts in the Georgina and Amadeus Basins, the occurrence of massive calcareous algae and rugose coral colonies in New South Wales and Tasmania, the diversity of the faunas as a whole, and the affinities of the faunas with known warm-water faunas overseas. There is no clear evidence of wide climatic fluctuation over the continent during this period.

The shelly faunas of the New Zealand Ordovician are quite insignificant, and apart from corals such as *Plasmoporella*, *Proheliolites*, and *Favistella* (Cooper, 1965), there are only a few scattered trilobite remains, e.g. *Taihungshania*, *Ogygites* (*Basiliella*), and *Triarthrus*.

TECTONISM

Over most of the continent only epeiric movements occurred during the Ordovician. Gentle subsidence with intervals of equilibrium or perhaps mild uplift, prevailed in the Canning, Amadeus, and Georgina Basins. Disconformities, overlaps, and slight angular unconformities have been recorded in these depositional areas. There are also belts of high dips such as the Toomba Structure in the Georgina Basin, but these are due to deep-seated vertical movements. Nowhere in these basins is there evidence of orogeny.

Almost nothing is known of movements in the New England Geosyncline, but a relatively clear picture is emerging for the Lachlan Geosyncline. Th' movements during the Early Ordovician which culminated in the restriction of the Ballarat Trough, probably caused extensive folding in western Victoria. At the present time the Lower Ordovician rocks of this area are steeply folded into a series of doubly plunging anticlinoria and synclinoria which have meridional trends (Belt of Brachydomes, Thomas, 1958) (Fig. 3.4). It is not known how much of this folding took place in the early part of the Ordovician, but it seems probable that at least the pattern was set at that time. Accompanying the fold movements there was extensive reverse strike faulting. In the Late Ordovician began the deformation which has become known as the Benambran Orogeny. Fold movements affected a relatively limited area and caused unconformities in the region shown on Fig. 4.3 (p. 100). Locally within this region deformation was intense, and there are strong angular unconformities between Upper Ordovician and Lower to Middle Silurian rocks in the Mitta Mitta Valley, near Delegate, and at Canberra (Öpik, 1958a; Talent, 1959; Packham, 1960). Insufficient work has been done to disentangle the effects of this orogeny from those of the Late Silurian Bowning Orogeny. Although the Benambran movements began in the Late Ordovician they continued into the Early Silurian. The oldest known Silurian rocks above the unconformity are the Llandoverian Panuara Formation near Orange and the upper Llandoverian Camp Hill Sandstone at Canberra. This, of course, does not mean that folding had ceased over the whole region by late Llandoverian times, but it does indicate that by this time marine transgression across the upfolded area was beginning.

Pursuing another line of evidence, Hills and Thomas (1954) consider the increase in grain size and colour intensity of the early Llandoverian sediments of the Melbourne Trough indicate an Early Silurian age for the orogeny in that area. However, in view of the abundance of Eastonian faunas over eastern Victoria and New South Wales, and the general absence of Bolindian faunas, it seems reasonable to conclude that many parts of these areas were being uplifted in the Late Ordovician.

There is considerable evidence that the Bunya Phyllites in Queensland (and their equivalents) were deformed prior to the deposition of the Neranleigh–Fernvale Group. This deformation involved the formation of great northnorthwesterly trending folds and extensive thrusting from the northeast (Bryan and Jones, 1954). Some of these movements may be of Ordovician age.

In the Amadeus Basin the Mereenie Sandstone in places rests with slight angular unconformity on the Larapinta Group, which was being eroded during the intervening period. It is thought that shallow anticlines were being developed parallel to the edge of the Arunta Block at this time. Precise dating is not yet possible, but a Late Ordovician age is thought most probable.

Tectonic activity in the New Zealand area during the Ordovician appears to have been confined to the gentle sinking of a shallow basin, the axis

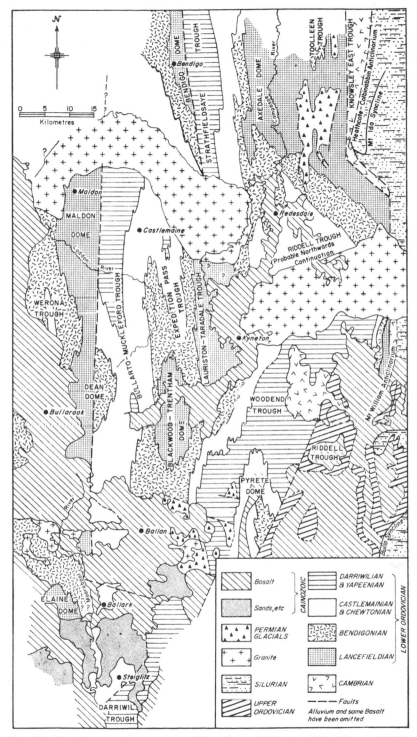

FIG. 3.4. Sketch map of the structures of West Central Victoria. (After Thomas, 1939.)

of which was located to the west of the present South Island area. The tight folding of the Ordovician sediments was probably accomplished in later Palaeozoic times.

IGNEOUS ACTIVITY

EXTRUSIVES

Apart from some trachytes and trachytic tuffs of doubtful Ordovician age in the Perth Basin, the only known Ordovician volcanic rocks in Australasia occur in the Lachlan Geosyncline. Within this structure the bulk of them are found along the Molong–Canberra High, though they do occur also in the troughs on either side, for example the Rockley Volcanics near Bathurst. No detailed work has been published on the Molong rocks, but they are known to include members of the calc-alkaline and spilitic suites—augite andesites, spilites, keratophyres, quartz keratophyres, some dacite and spilite (Walker, 1959; Strusz, 1960). The volcanics of the troughs are dominantly of the same character, though rhyolites have also been recorded in this environment (Joplin, 1962).

INTRUSIVES

No plutonic rocks of Ordovician age are known from the western half of the continent or from New Zealand. Until recently (for summaries see David and Browne, 1950; Joplin, 1962) the Benambran Orogeny in the Tasman Orthogeosyncline at the end of the Ordovician was considered to have been accompanied by the emplacement of banded (or in places gneissic) fine-grained, two-mica granites with numerous inclusions. The dating of these plutons was not based, however, on conclusive stratigraphic evidence but rather on the fact that they form a petrographic group, are known to cut Upper Ordovician sediments at some localities, and in turn are cut by plutons of foliated granite considered to be Late Silurian in age. Also there is ample evidence from many areas in the Cowra Trough and further east (see next chapter), that the Ordovician rocks were metamorphosed prior to the deposition of the Silurian. It seems not unreasonable to suppose that this metamorphism was accompanied by granitic intrusion. This latter view has been supported recently by Talent (1965a) who, in the Mitta Mitta area of Victoria, has found granite boulders in Middle Silurian sediments which unconformably overlie the Upper Ordovician. Furthermore, in the Nymagee district of New South Wales the Erimeran Granite is known to intrude the Tallebung Group and is overlain unconformably by the Lower Silurian Cobar Group (Russell and Lewis, 1965).

However, radiometric dating (Evernden and Richards, 1962) indicates that these banded and gneissic granites range in age from Silurian to Middle

Devonian, and hence it has been suggested that rock type is not a reliable guide to age determination. It is possible that some of the radiometric dates are too young, owing to the loss of argon during subsequent deformation and intrusion. In one case, that of the Cooma Gneiss, dating by the Rb/Sr method gives a value of 412 ± 12 m.y. as opposed to 382 m.y. for the K/Ar method, indicating that the argon loss has been relatively small (Pidgeon and Compston, 1965). At the present time, the nature and extent of Late Ordovician plutons can only be regarded as a matter for further study; but that there was some plutonic activity seems to have been established beyond reasonable doubt.

Many of the granites intruded into the Adelaidean and Cambrian rocks of the Adelaide Geosyncline have been radiogenically dated as Ordovician on the Kulp Scale (Compston *et al.*, 1966), and the granites of the Glenelg River of western Victoria are also probably of the same age. They are of two types —the contact-aureole granites which are found in the western shelf (Flinders Range) and the regional-aureole granites of the Kanmantoo Trough and western Victoria. Bodies of the former type are large, massive, rather acid biotite granites or adamellites (Mirams, 1961) : those of the latter are smaller, gneissic or foliated, often porphyritic, and generally adamellite (Kleeman and White, 1956; Wells, 1956).

CHAPTER 4

The Silurian System

APART from relatively minor occurrences in the northern part of the Perth Basin and in the Carnarvon Basin, in Western Australia, and rather more widespread occurrences in the Amadeus Basin, the only Silurian rocks on the continent are to be found in the Tasman Orthogeosyncline. The bulk of these outcrop in the southeastern States, though their presence in the subsurface beneath the Mesozoic sediments of the Artesian Basin has been proved by deep exploratory wells in some areas.

The sediments in the two Western Australian Basins are limestones, dolomites, and cross-stratified quartzose sandstones, products of deposition in broad shallow-water basins with margins of low relief. The Amadeus Basin was receiving only terrestrial sediments. In the Lachlan Geosyncline the pattern of arches and troughs had been greatly modified during the Benambran Orogeny, the only structures which retained their characters being the Molong–Canberra High and the Melbourne Trough. Following this deformation there was extensive acid and intermediate volcanism which seems to have been largely restricted to the deformed areas. Sediments containing probable Silurian fossils have been found in the New England Geosyncline, but most of the sediments from this region treated in this chapter cannot be accurately dated at present, and have been placed in the Silurian on the dubious grounds of lithological similarity. The volcanic rocks of the New England Geosyncline are spilites. In the North Queensland Basins there was further subsidence, but shelf limestone successions were formed for the first time along their western edges. The volcanic rocks of this region were basaltic.

Towards the end of the period over most of the Tasman Orthogeosyncline, but particularly in the Lachlan Geosyncline, there began another tectonic episode which continued on into the Early Devonian. Associated with this was the large-scale intrusion of granodiorite into the central New South Wales–eastern Victorian sector, and probably the injection of serpentinites into a narrow northnorthwesterly trending zone through central New South Wales.

In the eastern states shelly faunas are more prolific and widespread than they are in older systems, and graptolites are locally abundant.

There are no rocks of undoubted Silurian age in New Zealand, though in Nelson there are limited occurrences of sediments which are thought to be Silurian on grounds of superposition.

STRATIGRAPHY

Australia

LACHLAN GEOSYNCLINE

As a result of deformation and uplift during the Benambran Orogeny, the Silurian geography of this geosyncline was very different from that of the Ordovician. The Ballarat Trough, which had been shrinking since the end of the Early Ordovician, probably received no sediment in the Silurian, or if it did, sedimentation was restricted to its eastern edge. Growing geanticlines and subsidiary troughs appeared within the Melbourne Trough, and to a greater extent in the Wagga Trough. It is probably best to regard

Fig. 4.1. Distribution of Silurian strata.

the Wagga Trough as having ceased to function as a unit, and as having been superseded by a complex system of troughs, arches, and shelves. The geology of the Silurian rocks in Victoria and southeastern New South Wales is relatively well known, but the vast area elsewhere covered by sediments

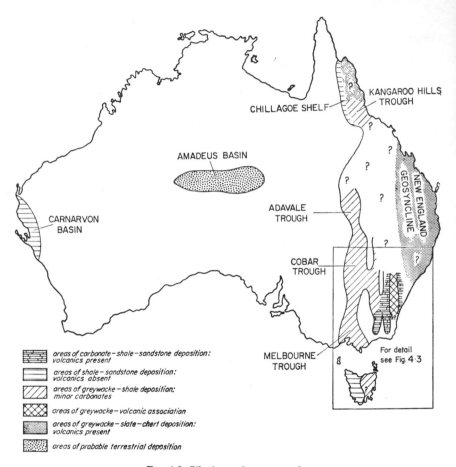

FIG. 4.2. Silurian palaeogeography.

of this age has received only cursory treatment, and the literature on it is very small. Consequently any attempt at a synthesis must be highly speculative. A large part of Victoria east of the Wellington Highlands, and the southeastern corner of New South Wales, formed a land area, but extending into it there were relatively shallow gulfs. Northwards, in the vicinity of Yass this mass was submerged, and on it a vast, rather flat shelf (the Yass Shelf) was formed by the accumulation of acid tuffs. Still further north this shelf extended out into two troughs, the Cowra on the east and the Trundle on the west. These were separated by a narrow arch which may not have been land. On its western side the Trundle Trough was partly bounded by the land area extending north from Victoria, but through it there were passages into the Cobar Trough. The Molong–Canberra High remained a positive area, but a new uplift, the Capertee High, developed to form the eastern boundary of the Hill End Trough.

In the **Melbourne Trough** the Silurian sediments are conformable on the Upper Ordovician at most localities, though there is some evidence of disconformable relationships in the east. No shelf deposits are known on the west, but offshore Silurian sediments are over 5000 m thick near the western limit of present outcrop in Victoria, and this suggests either that the shelf sediments have been subsequently stripped, or that the slope into the trough was steep and no shelf was present. The latter alternative seems to be more satisfactory in view of the known uplift of western Victoria during the Ordovician.

In the past it has been customary to describe the stratigraphy of this region in terms of time-rock units, and these have had a long and chequered history (Philip, 1960). For this reason they are avoided herein where possible. It is convenient to consider the deposits in terms of three typical areas where the sequences have been most thoroughly studied Heathcote in the west, Melbourne–Kinglake in the centre, and Walhalla Eildon in the east. At Heathcote the sequence, which is about 4500 m thick, begins with the Costerfield Formation of green mudstones, the base of which is not exposed. The Wapentake Formation which follows consists of mudstones and interbedded thick greywackes. The so-called "*Illaenus* band" at its base contains a Llandoverian assemblage of fossils including *Monograptus* and *Climacograptus*, the brachiopods *Leangella*, *Sowerbyella*, and *Leptaena*, the trilobites *Thomastus*, *Phacops*, and *Dalmanites*, and the ostracods *Aechmina*, *Kayatia*, and *Gillatia* (Öpik, 1953). The Dargile Formation has a similar lithology, but its lower part contains an early Ludlovian monograptid fauna, and its upper part a rich Ludlovian shelly fauna. With the succeeding McIvor Formation the evidences of shallowing are manifest and quartz sandstones with brachiopods, trilobites and molluscs become common (Talent, 1965a). The unit probably contains the Siluro–Devonian boundary.

In the Melbourne district the Silurian is spanned by the "Keilorian" below and the "Melbournian" above, the former having a clearly defined base at the incoming of monograptids but not being defined at the top; the latter being defined at neither the top nor the bottom but corresponding to at least the lower part of the European Ludlovian. There are unnamed unfossiliferous sediments between these units. Recently the equivalents of the Ludlovian north of Melbourne have been divided lithologically into the

Yan Yean Formation below, and part of the Humevale Formation above (Williams, 1964). The whole Silurian sequence is relatively homogeneous, consisting of massive and thin-bedded mudstones and greywackes, with

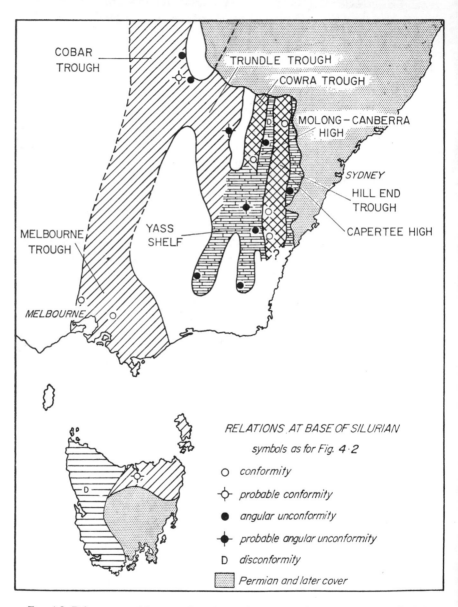

Fɪɢ. 4.3. Palaeogeographic map of southeastern Australia during the Silurian Period.

minor lenticular polymictic conglomerates, slump breccias, and ripple-marked quartzose sandstones, which sometimes contain shelly fossils. Graded-bedding, ripple cross-stratification, and sole markings are not uncommon. Monograptids are common throughout the lower Keilorian, where they are accompanied by *Climacograptus*, *Glyptograptus*, and *Stomatograptus*. In the Melbournian various species of *Monograptus*, including *M. chimaera*, *M. roemeri*, *M. bohemicus*, and *M. dubius*, have been recorded. These indicate an early Ludlovian age. Shelly fossils are most common in the upper parts of the succession. Similar sediments have been described from further north in this central part of the trough (Schleiger, 1964a, 1964b; Moore, 1965). Throughout the region the major sedimentary source direction was from the southwest quadrant, though growing anticlines within the trough itself may have been subsidiary sources.

In the Walhalla–Wellington–Eildon region of central eastern Victoria a subsidiary trough developed within the main Melbourne Trough during Early Silurian times. Within it the oldest rocks are the green, yellow, and purple slates (in places phyllites) of the Mount Useful Beds, which contain no fossils apart from fucoid markings and worm tracks. They are considered to be Lower Silurian on grounds of superposition and they have a maximum thickness of about 1700 m. They are overlain conformably by the Jordan River Group which overlaps them on the west. The lithology of this group varies with its position in the sub-trough. Along the western side mudstones, shales with interbedded sandstones, and conglomerates predominate, but the coarser units wedge out to the east, presumably into the sub-trough. Graptolites are found throughout the sequence and indicate ages from the Wenlockian to the Early Devonian (Harris and Thomas, 1954; Jaeger, 1962).

Further north, at Eildon, the Jordan River Group is more finely divided (Thomas, 1953; Berry, 1965). The lowest unit is as yet unnamed, but it consists of shales and interbedded greywackes. The Eildon Beds which are next in the sequence are largely greywacke sandstone, with some interbedded shales and patches of limestone. The lower parts of this unit are of Ludlovian age, but its upper levels contain graptolites and shelly fossils indicating that it extends into the Lower Devonian.

It seems probable that the southern end of this eastern sub-trough extended down to the northeast corner of Tasmania, where the Mathinna Beds outcrop. The base of this unit is not exposed except near the western edge of its distribution near Beaconsfield. There it is said to be disconformable on the Gordon Limestone. The dominant lithologies are mudstones or graded sandstone–mudstone associations, and the thickness of these rocks is in excess of 2000 m. The source area was in the southwest. The plant *Hostimella*, and unidentifiable tabulate corals, polyzoans, and brachiopods, are the only fossils. Because of this, precise dating has not been possible, but the general stratigraphy suggests that most of the Silurian and part of the Devonian are represented.

Six formations collectively known as the Eldon Group were deposited in western Tasmania, which appears to have been the southwestern shelf of the Melbourne Trough. They range in age from Llandoverian to Early Devonian (probably Siegenian), the Silurian section reaching a maximum thickness of only 900–1000 m. Within the Silurian part of the sequence there are probably some disconformities, but their positions and magnitudes have not yet been determined. Gradational conformable, abruptly conformable, and disconformable contacts between this group and the Gordon Limestone have all been recorded. The basal formation is coarser than the succeeding ones, and in places it contains fragments of Ordovician limestone. Also, the distribution of the group is more restricted than the Gordon Limestone. It is concluded therefore that, apart from some shallowing and uplift in the marginal geanticlinal areas, the Benambran Orogeny left this area largely unaffected.

At the base of the Eldon Group is the Crotty Quartzite, a well-sorted cross-bedded quartzite with some pebbly bands and siltstones. It contains brachiopods, and rare graptolites of the *Monograptus halli* type. The overlying Amber Slate has beds crowded with tentaculitids and ostracods, including *Gillatia*, which is known elsewhere only from the upper Llandoverian of Victoria. A specimen of *Cyrtograptus* is also known. The Keel Quartzite and Austral Creek Siltstone are both thin units almost devoid of fossils, but the lower Ludlovian *Monograptus colonus* has been found in rocks thought to be equivalent to the latter unit.

The Silurian geology of the **Trundle and Cobar Troughs** is poorly understood, partly because of the very indifferent character of the exposures and partly because almost the only systematic work has been done in the neighbourhood of deposits of economic minerals. The Silurian deposits in the two troughs are separated by outcrops of Ordovician rocks intruded by granite. These Ordovician rocks may have formed a ridge during the Silurian, though there is a belt of Silurian rocks across the Ordovician southeast of Cobar. Little is known about the behaviour of this ridge as a divide during the Silurian, but recent work has shown that the Silurian rocks of the Cobar Trough are unconformable on it over a distance of more than 100 km, and so it must have been at least a positive structure at the end of the Ordovician.

Along the eastern edge of the Trundle Trough shales with interbedded sandstones and limestones, from which abundant shelly faunas have been obtained, have been recorded at several localities, for example the Parkes–Forbes and Cootamundra districts. The only records of sediments toward the

axis of this trough are of slates and greywackes, for example in the Condobolin–Trundle District (Raggatt, 1936).

The Cobar sequence is the subject of major conflict of opinion (Thomson,
1953; Rayner, Ph.D. Thesis, 1962; Russell and Lewis, 1965). Several
formational and group names have been used for bodies of strata the
relationships of which have not been satisfactorily determined because of
poor outcrop, structural isolation, differing degrees of metamorphism, and
sedimentary facies changes. Most work has been done along or near the
eastern edge of the trough, and there are hints that the stratigraphic record
there is probably more broken than it is further west. Even the sequence is in
dispute. It can be said, however, that the Silurian rocks include thick
sequences of greywacke, quartzite, conglomerate, and slate with minor
limestones interbedded toward the top. These limestones have been interpreted as discontinuous reef masses. Fossils are relatively abundant locally
in both the limestones and the quartzite, but they have not been studied in
detail. There are also minor developments of "porphyries" which have been
assigned to the Silurian.

In the **Adavale Trough**, approximately 400 m of grey shales and
siltstones, tuffs, and thin basalt flows at the base of the Etonvale Formation,
to date known only in the subsurface, have been referred to the uppermost
Silurian on the basis of a small bivalve-brachiopod fauna (*Oil and Gas*, 1964,
p. 27). It is probable that this structure, like the Cobar Trough, was initiated
in the Silurian, and that further drilling will reveal an extensive Middle
and Upper Silurian sequence.

During the Llandoverian, acid volcanism prevailed on the **Yass Shelf
and southwards**, and the submarine relief was gradually obliterated.
Two volcanic units, the Hawkins and Douro Formations of unknown thickness, are separated by one of tuffs, sandstones, shales, and occasional limestones—the Bango Formation. The limestones contain, *inter alia*, specimens
of *Halysites*. Following upon these are the Yass and Laidlaw Formations
(500 m thick) with varying amounts of water-laid tuffs, tuffaceous sandstones, mudstones, and thin limestones with a sparse fauna. All these rocks
appear to have accumulated in relatively shallow water. The presence of
washouts, cross-stratification, mudcracks, chemically deposited limestone,
and some limestone breccia all support this view. Among the fossils are the
corals *Rhizophyllum* and *Phaulactis*, the brachiopod *Spirinella*, and the trilobite
Encrinurus. Interbedded in the volcanics south of Yass are limestones and
quartz sandstones with the brachiopods *Conchidium*, *Molongia*, and *Atrypoidea*.
They are considered to be Wenlockian.

Lying conformably on this sequence is a succession of shales and mudstones with two prominent limestones, the whole being about 200 m thick.
It is known as the Hume "Series". The shales are generally well-bedded,

dark coloured, carbonate-rich, and in places concretionary. They vary little over their outcrop, the changes being limited to variations in the sand content and thickness. Fossils are particularly abundant and are useful in zonation. In the Barrandella Shales the brachiopods *Barrandina*, *Atrypa*, and *Atrypoidea*, the trilobites *Calymene* and *Encrinurus*, and the corals *Phaulactis* and *Rhizophyllum* are common. In the Hume Shales trilobites and brachiopods are particularly abundant in several thin units, and graptolites in others. Among the trilobites, *Dalmanites*, *Calymene*, *Scutellum*, *Encrinurus*, *Sphaerexochus*, cheirurids, and harpids are the most important, and among the brachiopods dalmanellids, strophomenids, plectodontids and eospiriferids are particularly common. The graptolites are found at several levels in the Hume Shales and correlation with the British graptolite sequence in the upper Wenlockian–upper Ludlovian interval has proved possible. The two limestone units are extensive in their distribution, outcropping over more than 130 sq km, though they are only a few metres thick. The lower, or Bowspring Limestone, varies in character from a highly nodular, thin-bedded black limestone–shale unit almost barren of fossils, to a bioclastic limestone with a rich coral fauna. The upper or Hume Limestone is a typical biostrome composed of beautifully preserved corals, many in their position of growth, set in a calcareous muddy matrix. Many of the coral genera are common to both limestones. Examples are *Fletcheria*, *Phaulactis*, *Tryplasma*, *Mucophyllum*, *Favosites*, and *Heliolites*. They indicate a Wenlockian–early Ludlovian age.

There were at least two gulfs to the south of the Yass Shelf, the eastern one running through Cooma to Delegate and Bombala, and the western one through Yarrangobilly to the Mitta Mitta River in Victoria. The margins of these depositional areas have not been preserved, the existing remnants being fault bounded. It is possible that they covered wide areas and that the divide between them was much narrower than it is at present. Volcanics are the oldest Silurian rocks in these gulfs in several places, and they rest unconformably on steeply dipping Ordovician sediments. They are followed by sediments which sometimes overlap them, to lie on the Ordovician. At least in the heads of the gulfs the marginal relief was considerable. For example, in the Mitta Mitta area the earliest rocks are the acid Mitta Mitta Volcanics, and these are followed by the Wombat Creek Group at the base of which is about 1000 m of conglomerates, representing the products of the rapid erosion of the borderlands. However, by the late Wenlockian all areas had become the sites of deposition of well-bedded shales, sandstones, and limestones with rich coral, brachiopod, mollusc, and trilobite faunas. Further east, around the headwaters of the Murray River, the Cowombat Group, which is apparently in excess of 4000 m thick, outcrops. The base is not exposed, and no volcanics are known, but low in the sequence the sandstones and quartzites of the Towanga Formation enclose enormous lenticular masses of conglomerate, and higher up the Cowombat Formation consists of siltstones and minor limestones. Fossils in these limestones include the corals *Mazaphyllum, Fletcheria, Phaulactis,* and *Propora,* and the brachiopods *Atrypoidea* and *Protatrypa* (Talent, 1965*a,* and pers. comm.). A similar type of succession has been reported from further north in the gulf at Cooleman Caves (Stevens, 1958; Walpole, 1962*a*).

The only area within the **Cowra Trough** for which published information is available is in the vicinity of Cargo, near its southeastern end. There the upper part of the Millambri Formation may extend into the Llando-verian. It is followed with apparent conformity by the Cudal Shale which is correlated with the lower part of the Panuara Formation (Stevens, 1957). The upper part of the Silurian, however, is largely occupied with volcanics— mainly coarse dacite breccias and tuffs, and rhyolites, with some interbedded shales and sandstones (Packham, pers. comm.).

Along the **Molong–Canberra High** to the east and north of the Yass Shelf the Benambran Orogeny had only minor effects on the sedimentary regime, and there is a notable deficiency in volcanic rocks as compared with the underlying Ordovician and the Silurian of the Yass Shelf. At both Canberra and Orange shallow-water Llandoverian sediments rest with unconformity on the Ordovician. In general, the sediments are similar to those of the Yass Shelf, and apart from temporarily disruptive bursts of volcanic activity, sedimentary conditions must have been uniform along much of the arch (Packham and Stevens, 1955; Stevens, 1954; Walker, 1959; Strusz, 1960). For example, near Orange and near Molong respectively, the Panuara and the Mumbil Formations are widely developed. Both range from the upper Llandoverian to the lower Ludlovian, contain only minor amounts of tuffaceous material, include shelly and graptolite faunas, and are in the vicinity of 700 m thick. Within these formations there are rapid changes in the proportions of sandstone, shale, and limestone in sections east–west across the arch. The Silurian sequence is completed by the tuffaceous Wallace Shale, which may be partly Devonian. However, there are sectors between Wellington and Orange where volcanic rocks occupy most of the Lower and Middle Silurian. On the flank of the arch in the Can-berra district a similar environment is reflected by the tuffs, shales, sand-stones, and sporadic limestone lenses which have been subdivided into thirteen formations (Öpik, 1958*a*). Volcanics are present only in the Middle and Upper Silurian part. The succession reaches a thickness of about 1500 m, though only a few kilometres away at Queanbeyan a similar sequence is reported to be only about 500 m thick (Phillips, 1956). The sandstones are largely orthoquartzites but in places they are calcareous; the shales also are frequently carbonate-rich, and at certain levels have rhythmically interbedded limestones only a few centimetres thick; the volcanics are acid crystal tuffs and acid flows, usually in units a few metres thick. Sedimentary structures and faunas both indicate shallow water. Shelly fossils, particularly brachiopods, corals, and trilobites are common, and a thin bed containing graptolites occurs in the Lower Silurian. No detailed work has been done on the faunas, but many of the brachiopod, trilobite, and solitary coral genera also occur at Yass.

Thick sections of a Silurian greywacke–volcanic facies are known from the **Hill End Trough** over a north–south distance of some 250 km, but most of them are highly deformed and little is known of the detailed stratigraphic successions. From near Bathurst, Stanton (1956) has described about 6000 m of greywackes, shales, and conglomerates with some prominent bioclastic limestones, which he refers to as the Campbell's, Kildrummie, and Burraga Groups. The two former are probably at least partly facies equivalents and are correlated with the Panuara Formation on the Molong High (Packham, pers. comm.). Both the greywackes and shales contain considerable amounts of andesitic volcanic material. The limestones have a patchy distribution and presumably indicate the presence of local "highs" within the trough. The tabulate corals *Halysites*, *Heliolites*, and *Favosites*, together with the brachiopod *Conchidium*, are locally abundant. Such a lithological and palaeontological assemblage is apparently typical of the trough, and the limestones, in particular, have been recorded from several localities. Where the base is exposed it is usually conformable on the Ordovician and, in fact, the boundary cannot be satisfactorily placed. Accurate dating of the upper parts of the section is not yet possible, but the Burraga Group is at least partly Lower Devonian.

Towards the northern end of the exposed part of the trough, in the Hill End area itself, a succession of shales, greywackes, tuffs, and andesites has been recorded (Packham, 1962, and pers. comm.). The stratigraphic succession is more finely subdivided than that near Bathurst, and it also reveals several minor breaks in the sequence, indicating considerable mobility during the Silurian. Graptolites are relatively abundant.

The sediments of the Hill End Trough thin out to the east onto the **Capertee High**, which must have begun to rise in Late Ordovician or Early Silurian times, since on it in some places, for example east of Goulburn, Llandoverian rocks lie unconformably on Upper Ordovician. Little of this structure is at present exposed because of the overlap of Permian sediments from the east, but thick lenticular limestones interbedded with graptolite slates, conglomerates, tuffs, and andesitic flows have been recorded in the north near Mudgee. Massive limestones and graptolite slates occur east of Goulburn; and at Jenolan, limestones 150 m thick containing abundant specimens of *Conchidium*, *Favosites*, and *Heliolites*, rest on mudstones with interbedded acid tuffs and lavas, and spilites.

The existence of another trough between the Capertee High and the New England Geosyncline is still a matter for conjecture.

NEW ENGLAND GEOSYNCLINE

As was the case with the Ordovician, the amount of accurate information on the dating of the rocks of the Silurian System in this geosyncline is almost negligible. In the New England area of New South Wales several thousands of square kilometres are occupied by the highly deformed greywackes, slates, cherts, and jaspers of the Woolomin Beds. The greywackes and slates form a very monotonous section which is broken only by occasional thick beds of coarse greywacke breccia, jasper, or chert. Quartz usually makes up less than 20 per cent of the greywackes, and intermediate and basic volcanic fragments form the bulk of the lithic fraction (Voisey, 1958a). At two localities small patches of limestones have been found to contain rugose and tabulate corals (Whiting, 1954; Chappell, 1961)—one with *Tryplasma* and *Favosites*, the other with *Favosites*, *Halysites*, and *Plasmoporella*. These are considered to be of Silurian age, but their position within the sequence is unknown.

Rocks of Woolomin type continue north of the border where they are known as the Neranleigh–Fernvale Group near the coast, or the Bald Mountain Jaspers and Thanes Creek Slate further west. Apart from the radiolarians that abound in the jaspers (and probably in the other rocks also), the only recognizable fossils are the tabulate corals *Alveolites* and *Heliolites* from limestones within the Thanes Creek Slate. Outcrops of comparable rocks are found at intervals along the Queensland coast to beyond the Tropic of Capricorn. A feature of the group is the widespread occurrence of low-grade manganese deposits, notably of psilomelane, and of thin phosphatic beds. Volcanic rocks are rare, the only records being of sodic intermediate lava, and lapilli tuff in the Thanes Creek Slate, and occasional flows of spilite in the Woolomin Beds and Neranleigh–Fernvale Group. So far, structural complications have frustrated attempts to determine the thickness of all these stratigraphic units, but in their thickest parts they must be at least 5000 m.

NORTH QUEENSLAND BASINS

During the Ordovician—or perhaps even in the Cambrian—the area east of the Georgetown Massif began to subside. The boundary between these two units, the Tasman Line, is known to be a fault, in part at least, and is probably a fault throughout. Along the northern part of its length it is known as the Palmerville Fault (De Keyser, 1963; Amos and De Keyser, 1964), a fundamental structure or lineament which has continued to be a major factor in the geography of the area to the present time. South of Mount Garnet this fault is joined by the Burdekin River Fault to form a deep embayment in the Tasman Line (Fig. 4.4). This embayment has a complex Middle Palaeozoic sedimentary and tectonic history. The Tasman Line remained as an important structural feature throughout the Palaeozoic, and as will be seen in later chapters, it played a dominant role in the geological evolution of this region. It clearly separates the rocks of the region from those of the main Tasman Orthogeosyncline to the south, and forms a sharply defined province which has such a distinctive tectonic and sedimentary history, that it could be considered as an entirely separate entity. The reconstruction of the geological evolution is made difficult by widespread faulting and intrusion, and by the absence of fossils, so that sedimentary relationships are often obscure. White (1961) has prepared a synthesis which forms the basis of the interpretation given herein.

The oldest fossiliferous beds lie along the western edge of the basin and are earliest Silurian or possibly latest Ordovician. There are conformable sediments exposed beneath them, but basement is not exposed. Further out from the shoreline, however, upper Wenlockian or lower Ludlovian fossils are known from near the top of a 14,000 m pile of sediments, which in turn lies unconformably on about 1000 m of greywacke facies sediments. Presumably these latter must extend well down into the Ordovician, if not further, and it must be concluded therefore that the basin is at least as old as the Ordovician.

During the Llandoverian a shallow-water sequence, the Wairuna Formation, began to accumulate in a re-entrant known as the **Greys Creek Shelf.** About 1700 m of quartzose siltstone and sandstone, with a calcareous and a volcanic member near the base, form the unit. The sedimentary structures are of shallow-water types. The carbonate member is massively bedded, and contains occasional reefs and oolitic units. The corals from this member include *Propora, Plasmopora, Heliolites, Schedohalysites, Paliphyllum,* and *Tryplasma,* which are of early Llandoverian or late Ordovician age. Higher in the sequence the trilobites *Encrinurus* and *Proetus,* and a graptolite *Monograptus* sp. (probably of the *griestoniensis* zone) occur.

The succeeding Graveyard Creek Formation transgresses beyond the western boundary of the Wairuna Formation, and around its margin the basal beds are pebble and boulder conglomerates which lie directly on the Precambrian. The two Silurian formations are unconformable, and White (1961) indicates that a major redistribution of land and basinal areas took place during the interval between them. The Graveyard Creek Formation consists of 2600–4000 m of greywacke siltstones and sandstones with occasional limestone lenses which increase in prominence toward the top. One of these, the Jack Limestone Member, contains a rich upper Wenlockian–Ludlovian coral fauna including *Entelophyllum, Phaulactis, Tryplasma,*

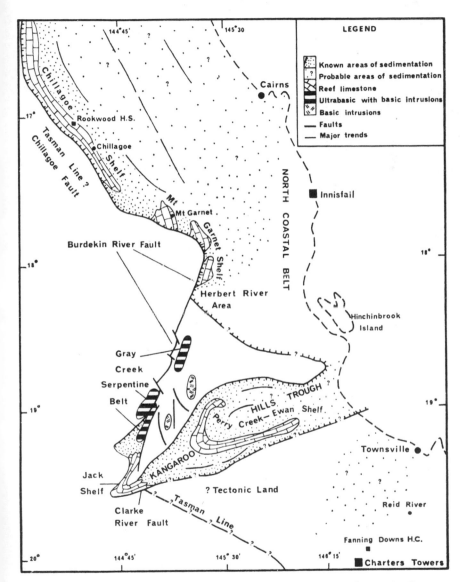

FIG. 4.4. Depositional pattern in the North Queensland Basins during the Late Silurian and the Early Devonian. (Modified after White, 1961.)

Cystiphyllum, *Rhizophyllum*, *Favosites*, *Heliolites*, *Propora*, and halysitids. Still higher members may possibly be of Early Devonian age, the small faunas they contain being diagnostic of neither the Silurian nor Devonian. Graded beds, load casts, slumps, and micro-cross-stratification occur in the formation.

During the Ludlovian a new shallow-water depositional area, the **Chillagoe Shelf**, developed astride the Tasman Line further north. Here limestones, feldspathic sandstones, and bedded cherts with minor amounts of volcanics, lie on Precambrian metamorphics. To the east these sediments grade into bedded cherts, quartz greywackes and siltstones, conglomerates, and stringers of limestones. The shelf limestones contain a coral fauna which suggests a correlation with the Ludlovian limestones of the Graveyard Creek Formation. On an extension of the shelf about 100 km southeast of Chillagoe, quartzites, conglomerates, cherts, and thin limestones are present at Mount Garnet. These are either Upper Silurian or Devonian, and are known as the Herberton Beds (see next chapter).

Away from the shelves the above stratigraphic units cannot be recognized. The lowest unit exposed is the unfossiliferous Greenvale Formation, which comprises some 9000 m of quartz greywackes and greywacke siltstones. It is overlain unconformably by rhythmically alternating impure quartz sandstones and siltstones, with some greywackes, known as the Kangaroo Hills Formation, which thickens to about 12,000 m to the east. These are limited to the area of the **Kangaroo Hills Trough**. The occasional fossils are too poorly preserved to be positively identified. However, the conformably overlying Perry Creek Formation, which is composed of about 1200 m of shallow-water calcareous sandstones and bedded limestones, contains a fauna comparable with that of the upper part of the Graveyard Creek Formation. Taking this into account, together with the thicknesses involved and the presence of the unconformity at the base of the Kangaroo Hills Formation, the Greenvale Formation is unlikely to be younger than Early Silurian, and is possibly older. This would mean that the unconformity between the Wairuna and Graveyard Creek Formations in the west is probably represented in the deeper parts of the trough by that between the Greenvale and Kangaroo Hills Formations.

Still further east these Silurian rocks possibly pass into the Barron River Metamorphics but the relationships are not clear.

AMADEUS BASIN

The history of the Amadeus Basin area subsequent to the deposition of the Stokes Formation cannot be accurately interpreted since at present the formations cannot be satisfactorily dated. Only trace fossils are available and these offer no evidence of age. The Mereenie Sandstone is up to 700 m thick and is unconformable on the Stokes Formation in the central northern part of the basin, but towards the west and the south there is conformity (Wells *et al.*, 1963/51). Presumably, therefore, it ranges in age from latest Ordovician into Silurian, and may even extend into the Devonian. It is made up largely of quartz sandstones, which occur in medium to thick beds, often cross-stratified and ripple marked, and not uncommonly slumped. In places the cross-stratified beds are as much as 16 m thick and are very extensive, suggesting an aeolian origin. This is supported by petrological studies of the quartz. The overall environment is considered to be fluviatile and aeolian, but locally it may be shallow marine (Prichard and Quinlan, 1962; Ranford *et al.*, 1965).

PERTH AND CARNARVON BASINS

The only known Silurian rocks in Western Australia occur in the northern part of the Perth and in the Carnarvon Basin. Their outcrop is very limited but they have been detected over several thousands of square kilometres in the subsurface, particularly in the western half of the Carnarvon Basin. Two units have been recognized—the older a quartzo-feldspathic, fine- to coarse-grained, cross-stratified sandstone, and the younger, an interbedded sequence of dolomites, limestones, siltstones, and occasional thin anhydrites. Their contact is probably gradational. The lower unit has been referred to as the Tumblagooda Sandstone (though it is some 300 km north of Tumblagooda, see previous chapter), and the upper unit is the Dirk Hartogs Limestone. Species of the conodont genera *Acontiodus*, *Paltodus*, *Spathognathodus*, *Ozarkodina*, and *Euprioniodina* and the brachiopod genus *Conchidium* indicate a probable Wenlockian age for the Dirk Hartogs Limestone, and the underlying unit may be at least partly Llandoverian.

Deep wells in the eastern part of the Carnarvon Basin have failed to encounter these units and the Permian lies directly on the Precambrian. It seems probable then that in the Silurian the basin was of limited size and consisted of a broad carbonate platform lying off a coast of low relief.

New Zealand

In spite of diligent search, no positively identified Silurian fossils have yet been discovered in New Zealand. On stratigraphical grounds, however, there is good reason to suppose that formations of this age are present, at least in northwest Nelson. For instance, in the Wangapeka and Baton valleys, south of Mount Arthur, the Lower Devonian calcareous argillites and quartzites of the Baton Formation are believed by Willis (1965) to overlie conformably a sequence of massive quartzites and quartzites with interbedded argillites (Ellis Formation). Graptolites have been found quite close to the top of this formation and its age is probably Silurian.

Below the Ellis Formation and above the Mount Arthur Marble of Late Ordovician age, comes a series of dark slates, quartzitic sandstones, schists, and rare limestones (600–1500 m) of the Wangapeka Formation. This sequence may possibly be Silurian in part, but the recent find of Upper Ordovician (?Eastonian) graptolites at Mount Owen in the Wangapeka slates 15 m stratigraphically above the top of the Mount Arthur Marble, leaves little room for a Silurian component (Johnston *et al.*, 1965).

PALAEONTOLOGY AND CLIMATE

The only faunas of any size to be discovered to date are restricted to the southeastern corner of the continent and to north Queensland. The most striking elements in these faunas are the corals, the brachiopods, the trilobites, and the graptolites. Ostracods are profuse at many localities but they have not been systematically studied. Bivalves and gastropods are of minor significance.

The corals have been used for stratigraphical correlation (Hill, 1940, 1954, 1958; Strusz, 1961) and have received more attention than any group apart from the graptolites. Certain of them, for example the tabulate corals *Acanthohalysites* and *Schedohalysites*, and the rugose coral *Nipponophyllum*, suggest that there may have been a weakly defined Australo-East Asian province in the Llandoverian and Wenlockian. However, the evidence for the cosmopolitan character of the faunas as a whole is considered to be overwhelming (Hill, 1958). Recent summaries of the graptolite faunas (Sherrard, 1953; Thomas, 1960) have shown that they span the entire period, that the great majority of species are of European type, and that there is no difficulty in recognizing the sequence of European zones. One feature noted is that the burst of *Cyrtograpti* characteristic of the Middle Silurian in Europe, is much subdued in Australia. The brachiopods and the trilobites are both in urgent need of revision, but from what is known at present there is little to suggest that the faunas are provincial. The brachiopods *Isorthis*, *Leptostrophia*, *Amphistrophia*, *Plectodonta*, *Strophomena*, *Schuchertella*, *Chonetes*, *Conchidium*, *Barrandina*, *Sieberella*, *Atrypoidea*, *Nucleospira*, and *Janius* are among the most common, and the trilobites *Gravicalymene*, *Dalmanites*, *Cheirurus*, *Encrinurus*, *Sphaerexochus*, *Phacops*, and *Thomastus* are also important. The bivalves (Talent, 1965*b*; Sherrard, 1959) include no genera unknown from Europe or North America. On the other hand, the only group of ostracods yet studied in detail by modern standards, that from the Costerfield Formation (Öpik, 1953), includes two genera unknown in the northern hemisphere; and most of the species are distinctive.

As would be expected from the above there appears to be little evidence of latitudinal zonation of the Australian faunas though they are known to extend over 25° of present latitude. The only feature of significance is the rarity of compound rugose corals from Tasmania. This could be due to the absence of the appropriate sedimentary facies rather than latitudinal zonation, though it is of interest to note that on the palaeolatitude maps of Irving, Tasmania would lie at about 20°S'.

There are several lines of evidence which, when taken together, suggest that most of the continent lay in a warm to tropical climatic belt during this period. In the first place evaporites have been recorded interbedded with the calcareous marine rocks of the Carnarvon Basin. Then, although actual bioherms are known only from Northern Queensland, extensive coral bio-stromes are common as far south as Victoria. And finally, in the Mereenie Sandstone of the Amadeus Basin there are aeolian sandstones (which could be considered to be coastal dunes, though the sand grains have been inter-preted as having formed under desert conditions), and in places the forma-tion contains halite pseudomorphs.

TECTONISM

Towards the end of the Silurian the Lachlan Geosyncline was again deformed during the Bowning Orogeny. The Melbourne Trough again remained relatively undisturbed, as probably did the Cobar and Adavale Troughs. The structures further east suffered disruption to varying degrees. The most deformed belt extends from eastern Victoria north to the Yass Shelf and along the Trundle Trough. Much of this area was uplifted to such an extent that no further deposition took place on it until the Late Devonian; but such uplift is probably as much the result of granite intrusion as of folding. There is evidence that the northern ends of the Canberra–Molong High and the Cowra Trough were only mildly affected, and that the Hill End Trough was almost undisturbed.

In only a few areas does the folding at this time appear to have been in-tense. In the Cowombat Group of northeastern Victoria dips of 50–60° are common, but broad open folds with flank dips often as low as 20° are quite common in Silurian rocks at Delegate, Cooleman Caves, and Yass. In the Trundle Trough similar structures have been observed. However, in a meridional belt through and to the east of Canberra, recumbent folds have been observed in Silurian rocks, and this has been attributed to the Bowning Orogeny (Stauffer and Rickard, *J. geol. Soc. Aust.* 13, 419–438 (1966).)

In Victoria it has been concluded that the Bowning movements took place at the end of the Late Silurian or perhaps in the earlier part of the Early Devonian (Talent, 1959). At Canberra two phases have been recognized, one during the early Ludlovian and the other in the late Ludlovian–Early Devonian (Öpik, 1958a).

The New England Geosyncline must have suffered profound deformation during the Silurian, since at numerous localities there are relatively unde-formed Lower Devonian rocks in contact with more highly deformed and altered Lower Palaeozoic rocks. Nowhere has an unconformity between these two sets of rocks been described. Wherever it has been observed, the contact is faulted. However, both structural and stratigraphic data suggest a major unconformity. In the Brisbane area these movements emphasized the structures formed during the preceding deformation, and produced further major low-angle thrusts (Bryan and Jones, 1954).

There were no movements at the end of the Silurian in the North Queens-land Basins, but during the Middle Silurian the sediments of the Burdekin River area were folded along generally northeast-trending axes, and there was widespread uplift resulting in angular unconformity between Lower and Upper Silurian sediments. Faulting along lines parallel to the border faults of the basin, also took place at this time. Movement along these faults was predominantly vertical, but some minor horizontal movement also has been noted.

The mild folding movements initiated in pre-Mereenie Sandstone times in the Amadeus Basin probably continued during the deposition of that unit, for the succeeding Pertnjara Formation in places lies on the eroded edges of the Mereenie, and elsewhere transgresses across units as old as the Jay Creek Limestone (Prichard and Quinlan, 1962). These movements therefore may have begun during the Silurian, and continued into the Devonian. The rise of the Arunta Block to the north of the basin probably began during this time.

IGNEOUS ACTIVITY

EXTRUSIVES

Volcanic rocks of Silurian age are restricted to the eastern part of the Tasman Orthogeosyncline. Coarse crystal tuffs and flows of rhyolitic and dacitic composition characterize the Yass Shelf and the area southwards into northeastern Victoria. They are frequently intruded by sills of acid porphyries which are thought to be contemporaneous. Andesites are developed locally, as for example at Yarrangobilly. Similar associations of acid volcanics also occur in the Cobar Trough where they are known under various names. Here also they are intruded by sills of acid porphyries.

Although rhyolites and dacites are known on the arches and in the troughs east of the Trundle Trough, andesites bulk larger in this province. Along the eastern edge of the Trundle Trough near Parkes and Forbes, andesites are well developed in association with shales and limestones; augite andesites, trachyandesites, amygdaloidal basalts and andesitic tuffs and breccias occur in the Cowra Trough near Canowindra; andesitic debris, which presumably has been stripped from the Molong and Capertee Highs, forms a large part of the detritus in the Hill End Trough, and andesitic flows, tuffs, and breccias are interbedded with shallow-water sediments along the northern end of the Capertee High.

In the North Queensland basins volcanics of an entirely different type are common, presumably because in this region basin formation resulted from fundamentally different tectonic processes—block subsidence rather than trough and arch formation. The Everetts Creek Volcanics, which reach a maximum thickness of about 1000 m are mainly albitized basalt, basaltic agglomerate, and tuff. They have a limited distribution along the western edge of the basins in the Burdekin River valley.

The New England Geosyncline forms a third volcanic province in which spilites are the characteristic rocks.

INTRUSIVES

As mentioned in the previous chapter, there is still some doubt as to the dating of many of the batholiths in the Lachlan Geosyncline. Be that as it may, it is clear that the Late Silurian–Early Devonian was a period of very active plutonism, and that the main belt of activity extended from eastern Victoria northwards to the Yass Shelf and along the Trundle Trough and the Cobar Trough. Its northern extension is unknown, but no doubt it runs into the Adavale Basin and its eastern and southern flanks (Evernden and Richards, 1962; Joplin, 1962). One remarkable feature of this distribution is that in its exposed part at least, it is co-extensive with the distribution of the acid flows, tuffs, and sills mentioned in the previous section. Insufficient work has been done to confirm the view that the plutonic and volcanic rocks represent different phases of the one protracted igneous episode; but it must be pointed out that the volcanism began in the Llandoverian and the batholiths were still being emplaced in the Early Devonian, a period covering some 30 m.y.

The acid plutonic rocks intruded at this time are both foliated and massive types. Where cross-cutting relationships have been observed the massive types are the later. Detailed petrological work has been done in a few areas only (Snelling, 1960), but the dominant rock type throughout is apparently a biotite granodiorite.

Though precise dating is not at present possible the best available evidence suggests that serpentinites, gabbros, and amphibolites were intruded at the end of the Silurian or in the Early Devonian. However, a late Middle

TABLE 4.1. CORRELATION TABLE FOR SILURIAN SYSTEM

EUROPEAN STAGE	NORTH QUEENSLAND BASINS — Kangaroo Hills Trough	NORTH QUEENSLAND BASINS — Greys Creek Shelf	CANBERRA–MOLONG HIGH — Wellington Area	CANBERRA–MOLONG HIGH — Orange Area	CANBERRA–MOLONG HIGH — Canberra Area	HILL END TROUGH	COWRA TROUGH	YASS SHELF AND — Yass Area	YASS SHELF AND — Mitta Mitta Area	SOUTH — Cooleman Caves Area	MELBOURNE — Heathcote Area	MELBOURNE — Melbourne Area	MELBOURNE TROUGH — Walhalla-Eildon Area	WESTERN TASMANIA
LUDLOVIAN	? Tribute Hills Sandstone; Perry Creek Formation	GRAVEYARD CREEK FORMATION; Jack Creek Limestone Member	Basal Cuga Burga Volcanics; Barnaby Hills Shale Member (MUMBIL)	Wallace Shale	Red Hill Group	Basal Burraga Group	Rhyolites; Sandstone and Shale; Dacitic Pyroclastics	Unnamed sediments and tuffs; Hume Shales (HUME "SERIES")	? Shale (WOMBAT CREEK GROUP)	Mary's Hill Formation; Wilkinson Cliff Limestone (COOLEMAN GROUP)	Basal McIvor Formation; Dargile Formation	Melbournian	Unnamed (JORDAN RIVER GROUP)	? Austral Creek Siltstone (ELDON GROUP)
WENLOCKIAN	Kangaroo Hills Formation	Crooked Creek Cgl. Member	Narragal Limestone Member		Fairbairn Group	CAMPBELL'S GROUP	? ; Cudal Shale	Hume Limestone; Barrandella Shales; Bowspring Limestone; Laidlaw "Series"	Limestone; Shale; Limestone; Sandstone; Conglomerate	Mount Murray Branch Formation; Peppercorn Beds; Tantangara Beds	Wapentake Formation		Formation	Keel Quartzite
LLANDOVERIAN	Greenvale Formation	WAIRUNA FORMATION; Everetts Creek Volcanic Member; Carriers Well Limestone Member	Rosyth Limestone Member (PANUARA FORMATION)		St. John's Church Beds; Canberra Gp.; State Circle Sh.; Camp Hill Sst.	KILDRUMMIE GROUP	Millambi Formation (upper part)	Yass "Series"; Douro "Series"; Bango "Series"; Hawkins "Series"	Mitta Mitta Volcanics		Costerfield Formation; (Illaenus Band)	Keilorian	Selma Sandstones; Mount Useful Beds	Amber Slate; Crotty Quartzite

Devonian age is yet possible. The serpentinites are best developed in three parallel northnorthwesterly-striking belts east and southeast of Gundagai. Small isolated outcrops occur along the strike of these belts as far north as Nyngan. It seems reasonable to regard these as forming a single injection zone which cuts across the Trundle Trough at a very oblique angle. It lies to the east of, and almost parallel to, the great belt of Silurian–Early Devonian granodiorites that trends across central New South Wales; but in the south, where the granodiorites alter trend sharply to the northeast, the serpentinites terminate. This is a critical area for the geological interpretation of southeastern Australia, but little has been written on it. It is significant that the elongate basic plutonics (gabbros and amphibolites) that parallel the southern end of the serpentine belt, here abruptly change to a northeast trend.

It was during the Late Silurian–Early Devonian that ultrabasic rocks were emplaced into the Greys Creek Shelf of the North Queensland Basins. These rocks are serpentinized dunite, peridotite, pyroxenite, gabbro, and microdiorite, and in places they intrude the Everetts Creek Volcanics with which they are considered to be co-magmatic (White, 1961).

CHAPTER 5

The Devonian System

FEW systems have as much to offer the student of geology in Australia as the Devonian. The variety of its sedimentary records embraces all environments from arid terrestrial basins to reef limestone platforms and deep-water troughs. Its record of life ranges from an abundance of freshwater vertebrates and primitive land plants to finely preserved shallow-water marine invertebrates. It began with tectonism and intrusion, and during its middle history one of the greatest orogenies ever to affect the eastern States produced structures which are now well exposed over wide areas. Deposits of economic minerals formed during the Devonian have been exploited for many years.

Over much of eastern Australia the Lower and Middle Devonian rocks form a natural unit separated from later rocks by major unconformities. A great deal of work has been done on rocks of this age in central New South Wales, Victoria, and Tasmania, where the sequences are generally continuous. There was considerable modification of the depositional patterns in the Lachlan Geosyncline as a result of the Bowning Orogeny, and new geotectonic elements appeared. A new phase of sedimentation was initiated in the New England Geosyncline, but the outcrops there are limited and more difficult to interpret. The North Queensland Basins continued to evolve and develop their own distinctive characteristics. After the late Middle Devonian Tabberabberan Orogeny large areas of all the eastern States except Tasmania became the sites of terrestrial deposition.

The history of the Western Australian basins was very different from that of the eastern troughs. Following the recession of the Early Palaeozoic seas, deposition did not resume until late in the Middle Devonian, and marine sediments accumulated during the remainder of the period. Though both volcanic and plutonic rocks are of major importance in eastern Australia, no igneous rocks are known from Western Australia.

In New Zealand, Devonian rocks are restricted to two very small areas in the South Island, one near Reefton in north Westland, and the other at Baton River in central Nelson (Fig. 5.1). The early discovery of both these small exposures resulted from their close association with auriferous deposits.

Areas of Outcrop of Devonian
Sediments and Volcanics

Devonian Sediments and
Volcanics in the Subsurface

Fig. 5.1. Distribution of Devonian strata.

STRATIGRAPHY

Eastern Australia

A. LOWER AND MIDDLE DEVONIAN

LACHLAN GEOSYNCLINE

As noted in the previous chapter, the Bowning Orogeny caused widespread uplift in many parts of the Lachlan Geosyncline. While conditions in the Melbourne Trough were largely unaffected, the Trundle and Cowra Troughs were completely disrupted and probably most of central New South Wales rose above sealevel to form what is here called the Condobolin High. The persistent Hill End Trough and the Capertee High remained as geotectonic entities. To the south and east the Condobolin High was partly submerged, and the marine Buchan and Taemas–Molong Platforms, areas of extensive carbonate sedimentation, were formed. The only remaining sea in the west was in the Cobar Trough, which seems to have had a history similar to that of the Melbourne Trough.

The Condobolin High passes north under the Artesian Basin sediments, forming the Nebine Ridge, and its eastern flank emerges in central Queensland where it is known as the Anakie High (Fig. 5.2). Off its western flank the Adavale Trough continued to evolve in a fashion comparable with the analogous Cobar Trough further south. The Drummond Basin developed

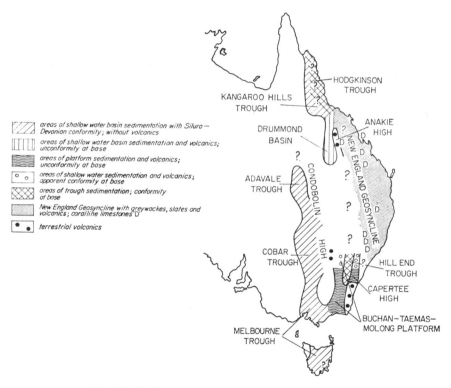

FIG. 5.2. Early and Middle Devonian palaeogeography.

early in the Devonian as the result of sag on the western side of the Anakie High. So far as is known it was separate from the Adavale Trough.

In the **Melbourne Trough**, to the north and east of Melbourne there was continuity of sedimentation from the Silurian into the Devonian. The boundary between the two systems lies in an unfossiliferous part of the sequence and cannot be precisely fixed. In the Heathcote area, on the western edge of the trough, the upper part of the McIvor and Mount Ida Formations, both of which are shallow-water sandstones and mudstones, have been referred to the Devonian. Together they reach a thickness of over 2500 m, and contain several beds in which brachiopods, bivalves, and trilobites occur. Prominent among the fossils are the Lower Devonian brachiopods *Fimbrispirifer, Maoristrophia* and *Notoconchidium,* and the tabulate coral *Pleurodictyum* (Talent, pers. comm.).

In the central area the thick Yering Group (4000 + m) consists of the Ruddock Siltstone sandstones in the lower part passing up into mudstones, and coralline Lilydale Limestone near the top. It is capped by the thin Cave Hill Sandstone, the whole succession being of shallow-water origin. The sandstones and shales contain a rich fauna characterized by the tabulate coral *Pleurodictyum,* the brachiopods *Chonetes, Leptaena, Plectodonta, Maoristrophia, Isorthis, Hysterolites,* and *Atrypa,* the bivalves *Actinopteria* and *Ctenodonta,* and the trilobite *Gravicalymene.* The limestones also are very fossiliferous, the most abundant forms being species of the tabulate corals *Favosites* and *Thamnopora,* the rugose corals *Phillipsastraea, Disphyllum, Tipheophyllum, Acanthophyllum, Tryplasma,* and *Xystriphyllum,* the stromatoporoids *Anostylostroma* and *Stromatoporella,* and a rich gastropod fauna. The age of these faunas is Early Devonian.

Along the eastern side of the Melbourne Trough there are sequences of sediments of disputed age, some authors claiming them to be Devonian only, but others Silurian and Devonian (Philip, 1960). The succession is best known at the northern end of the belt in the vicinity of Eildon. Here the uppermost part of the Eildon Beds (see previous chapter) contains specimens of *Monograptus aequabilis* together with a few tabulate corals and the brachiopod *Notanoplia* (Thomas, 1947, 1953; Berry, 1964, 1965; Philip, 1964a), which together suggest a post-Ludlovian age (Jaeger, 1962). The succeeding Wilsons Creek Shale (500 + m) has *Monograptus* sp. cf. *M. praehercynicus* associated with the plant *Baragwanathia,* and conformably above this is the Nortons Creek Sandstone (300 m) with shales containing the bivalve *Panenka* and the tentaculitoid *Styliolina.* These are possibly as young as Siegenian (Talent, 1965a). Impersistent conglomerates, varying in stratigraphical position, occur near the base of the apparently conformable Walhalla Group. The associated sandstones are similar to those below but they rarely contain recognizable fossils. Higher units are finer grained. Further south in the Walhalla Synclinorium, the Jordan River Group spans the Siluro–Devonian boundary; its upper part is comparable with the Devonian sequence at Eildon. The Walhalla Group in this area is a complex of slates, coarse sandstones and grits with some lenses of limestone. Marine fossils, mainly brachiopods, occur in the sandy units. The group reaches a thickness of 3000 + m. Marine shales, known as the Centennial Beds, complete the sequence. They contain the land plants *Zosterophyllum* and *Hostimella,* and are probably of Emsian to Eifelian age (Talent, 1965a).

Lateral equivalents of the upper Jordan River Group and basal Walhalla Group are the Tanjil Formation, and the Boola Beds and Coopers Creek Formation of the Tyers area. The Tanjil Formation contains the bivalves *Panenka* and *Actinopteria*, the tentaculitoids *Nowakia* and *Styliolina* (Talent, pers. comm.), and occasional nautiloids, together with *Monograptus* sp. cf. *M. praehercynicus*, and the land plant *Baragwanathia*.

The faunas of the Boola Beds and Coopers Creek Formation have been described in detail (Philip, 1962, 1965). The corals include *Favosites*, *Pleurodictyum*, *Pseudamplexus*, *Phillipsastraea*, *Thamnophyllum*, and *Tipheophyllum*, and among the brachiopods *Tyersella*, *Plectodonta*, *Notanoplia*, and *Howellella* are important. Thirty-four species of conodonts belonging, *inter alia*, to the genera *Eognathodus*, *Hindeodella*, *Icriodus*, *Plectospathodus*, *Ozarkodina*, *Spathognathodus*, and *Trichonodella*, together with the above macrofauna, indicate a Siegenian age (Philip, 1965; Talent, 1965a).

The presence of these limestones at Tyers and Lilydale and abundant land plants in the Centennial Beds in the Walhalla Synclinorium indicates that the Melbourne Trough was subsiding only slowly at the end of the Early Devonian and in the early Middle Devonian. No late Middle Devonian rocks are known from the area.

In the Tabberabbera Synclinorium on the eastern shelf of the Melbourne Trough, sedimentation continued through the Early Devonian well on into the Middle Devonian. Even so the deposits are thinner than those further west. They reach a maximum of 2300 m, and contain a higher proportion of coarse clastics. The base of the succession rests with angular unconformity on Ordovician slates, indicating onlap to the east. The rocks are collectively known as the Wentworth Group, and consist of the lower conglomeratic Wild Horse Formation, and the upper sandy and shaly Tabberabbera Formation. The fauna of the latter formation is profuse, the brachiopods *Isorthis*, *Phragmophora*, *Plectodonta*, *Nadiastrophia*, *Leptostrophia*, *Hysterolites*, *Adolphia*, *Atrypa*, *Megakozlowskiella*, and *Chonetes*: the bivalves *Actinopteria*, *Ctenodonta*, and *Cypricardinia*: the gastropods *Straparollus* and *Loxonema*, being most common. A Siegenian to Eifelian age has been suggested (Talent, 1963).

Almost the whole of the Tasmanian area lay within the Melbourne Trough. On the western part of the island the two uppermost formations of the Eldon Group—the Florence Sandstone (500 m) and the Bell Shale (500 m)—are Early Devonian in age. Both units consist of shallow-water sediments, quartzose sandstones, and calcareous shales in varying proportions. They contain a rich brachiopod fauna—*Maoristrophia*, *Mesodouvillina?*, and *Notoconchidium* in the lower unit, and these together with *Australocoelia* in the upper. A small and separate basin was initiated at Spero Bay on the west coast in the Early Devonian. In it coralline limestones, conglomerates, and sandstones were deposited. It persisted till the Middle Devonian. A deeper-water facies outcrops in the northeastern corner of the island in the upper parts of the Mathinna Beds. The only marine fossils are indeterminable, but the land plant *Hostimella* has been recognized.

A succession of about 1500 m of shallow-water, flaggy mudstones, silt-stones, sandstones, and quartzites in the **Cobar Trough** forms the Amphi-theatre Group. They contain an abundant shelly fauna which indicates an Early to Middle Devonian age (Russell and Lewis, 1965). The unit is wide-spread and in most places only gently deformed. The structural and sedi-mentational history of this basin invites a comparison with the Melbourne Trough and its eastern margins. Although deep wells in the intermediate area have not penetrated rocks of known Siluro-Devonian age, and the shape of the Melbourne Trough suggests that it narrowed to the north, a marine connexion between the two troughs seems probable. However, this connecting sea probably remained very shallow and its floor subsided only slowly in comparison with the floors of the adjacent troughs. The sea probably also gained access to the trough across the Condobolin High at various times.

The history of the **Adavale Trough** extends back into the Silurian, but no details are yet available. Mesozoic sediments cover it entirely, and the deep wells provide the only data on the Palaeozoic section. The earliest Devonian rocks yet discovered belong to the upper Etonvale Formation, and consist of sandstones and shales with carbonates (including dolomite), and some salt. They have been dated as Early Devonian on the shelly fossils (*Aust. Oil and Gas*, 1964, p. 26). To the south the trough appears to shallow against a structure in the position occupied at present by the Eulo Ridge. However, it seems probable that the sea gained access to the trough through the Cobar Trough rather than through the Drummond Basin, in view of the very incomplete sequence in the latter. The presence of evaporites suggests that the Eulo Ridge area may have acted as a partial barrier to marine circulation. Along the southeastern edge of the Condobolin High there developed in the Early Devonian a marine platform (the **Taemas–Molong Platform**) which increased in width to the south in the area of the upper Murrumbidgee River. Further south, in Victoria, similar conditions obtained over a wide area around and to the north and east of Buchan and Bindi (the **Buchan Platform**). Probably there was a connecting seaway between the two areas, and their histories are so similar that they are most satisfactorily treated together. The platforms originated partly as a result of erosion, and partly as a result of the rapid accumulation of acid volcanic rocks. The earliest Devonian rocks are conglomerates and sandstones with plant frag-ments. These are of limited extent. Lying unconformably on them are acid volcanics, which are very widespread and at most localities can be shown to transgress Silurian or older formations (Teichert and Talent, 1958; Ringwood, 1955). They are best known in eastern Victoria (the Snowy

River Volcanics), on the Murrumbidgee and Goodradigbee Rivers (the
Black Range Group), near Orange (the Bulls Camp Rhyolite), and near
Wellington (the Cuga Burga Volcanics). Thicknesses are difficult to determine
but the Snowy River Volcanics are probably up to 4000 m. Interbedded in
the Black Range Group in the Goodradigbee area is a shale unit (the
Kirawin Shale) over 500 m thick, indicating that the time of deposition of
the group may have been quite considerable. The sequence continues with
apparent conformity into interbedded limestones and shales at most localities,
but at the southern end of the emergent Canberra Welt (Noakes and Öpik,
1954), reefs were formed in the neighbourhood of Buchan. In the Buchan
area the Snowy River Volcanics are overlain by thin units of bedded tuffs
and limestones, and then by the well-bedded bioclastic Buchan Caves

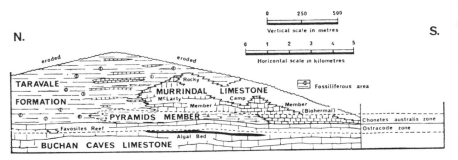

FIG. 5.3. Reconstructed section of the Buchan Devonian sequence showing the
relations of the Buchan Caves Limestone and superposed reef and basin deposits.
(Redrawn from Teichert and Talent, 1958.)

Limestone (Fig. 5.3). Occasional reef patches are present. On this limestone
platform a reef complex developed, the details of which are shown in Fig. 5.3.
The land mass to the north was probably low, and there was open sea to
the south. All the units are fossiliferous. Corals and stromatoporoids are
abundant throughout the limestones and many of the species have restricted
ranges. The common genera are *Favosites, Thamnopora, Syringopora, Acanthophyllum, Lyrielasma, Breviphyllum, Zelolasma, Spongophyllum,* and *Xystriphyllum.*
Brachiopods (especially rhynchonelloids) are particularly abundant in the
Murrindal Limestone, though they occur in all the more calcareous sediments. The spiriferoid *Spinella* is characteristic of the Buchan Caves Limestones and *Chonetes* of the overlying sediments. In the basinal Taravale
Mudstone the tentaculitoids *Nowakia* and *Styliolina* occur in profusion. From
the point of view of correlation the occurrence of the cephalopods *Bactrites,
Lobobactrites,* and *Teicherticeras* in the Taravale Mudstone is of considerable
importance. Other common fossils are calcareous algae, trilobites, and ostracods. The Buchan Caves Limestone is probably late Early Devonian, and the

remainder of the sequence early Middle Devonian (Talent, 1956; Teichert and Talent, 1958), though an attempt has been made to show that the entire section is Lower Devonian (Philip and Pedder, 1964).

Outcrops of Lower and Middle Devonian rocks occur at intervals along the length of the northern platform, but they are best known around Taemas and Wee Jasper, and between Molong and Wellington. In the former area the platform was at least 40 km wide and probably much wider. It was almost devoid of relief. On it bioclastic carbonates accumulated with only a small terrigenous contribution. The sedimentary units are thinly bedded, persistent

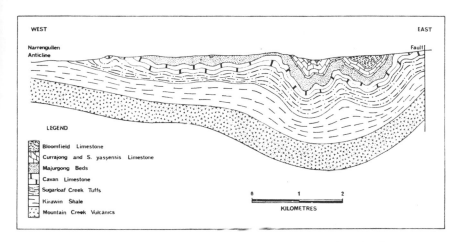

FIG. 5.4. Cross-section through the Taemas Syncline continued to depth to show possible décollement on the Kirawin Shale and on the Sugarloaf Creek Tuffs. (Modified after Browne, 1958.) Attitude of fault on eastern margin unknown.

over wide areas, and relatively uniform in thickness (Browne, 1958). Many of the limestones are black and fetid. Algae are important contributors to the sediments, and are present as comminuted detritus, pisolites, and as thick stromatolite-like units. Crinoidal debris also forms the bulk of the carbonate detritus at certain levels, one such unit being 180 m thick. No trace of reefs has been found. Shales occur both as thin beds within the limestones and as larger mappable units up to 140 m thick. This Devonian sedimentary succession is known as the Murrumbidgee "Series" and reaches a maximum thickness of 1200 m (Fig. 5.4). Fossils are abundant in most rocks, and the succession can be readily zoned on the basis of both the corals and the brachiopods. The most abundant corals are those listed above for the limestones at Buchan. The brachiopods *Spinella* and *Chonetes* occur in profusion in some of the shales, and stropheodontids, atrypoids, and rhynchonelloids in the limestones. Of considerable palaeontological interest are the large specimens of the spongiomorph *Receptaculites* which are abundant at one horizon, the arthrodires *Buchanosteus* and *Taemasosteus*, and the dipnoan *Dipnorhynchus*.

The Garra Formation of the Wellington–Molong area is of a similar type to the Murrumbidgee "Series" and appears to be the product of a similar environment (Strusz, 1964, 1965). The faunas of the two sequences also have much in common. In this area, however, the eastern margin of the shelf where it joins the Hill End Trough, has been preserved. A chain of islands, formed from the underlying andesitic volcanic rocks (the Cuga Burga Volcanics) marked this line, and around them a complex of calcareous shales, biostromes, and small bioherms (the Tolga and Nubrigyn Formations) accumulated (Strusz, 1960; Wolf, 1965). Algae formed the bulk of the carbonate rocks, and in places formed rings of small bioherms around the islands.

The Garra Formation has also been mapped further south than Molong, and in the vicinity of Borenore (west of Orange) there is a much higher percentage of terrigenous sediments in the sequence than there is further north (Walker, 1959). Coarse sandstones interbedded with shales occur at the base, and these are overlain by about 300 m of shales with plant fragments and occasional marine fossils, and then by about 200 m of interbedded shales and limestones with abundant brachiopods and corals. This succession is interpreted as indicating the emergence of the platform above sealevel in the area to the south.

Along the western edge of the **Anakie High** the earliest Devonian formation is the Silver Hills Formation, which consists of andesitic and rhyolitic pyroclastics and flows, with some interbedded slates. It lies unconformably on a metamorphic basement. Southwards, the volcanics probably merge in part into marine sediments (the Dunstable Formation), which are up to 1100 m thick and have a large volcanic component. Intercalated thin limestone lenses contain an Eifelian coral fauna. Eastwards where the volcanics transgress on to the Anakie Metamorphics, they are strongly deformed and stratigraphical relations are difficult to determine. Small outcrops of Eifelian coralline limestone are also known on the Anakie High, where they are associated with slates (Veevers *et al.*, 1964*a*, *b*).

At the northern extremity of the **Drummond Basin** there are the well-bedded, shallow-water, marine sandstones, siltstones, shales, and limestones of the Ukalunda Beds. Their relationship to the underlying rocks is unknown. They contain abundant brachiopods, molluscs, polyzoans, and corals, including *Atrypa*, *Mesophyllum*, and *Calceola*, indicating a Middle Devonian age, but the lower parts of the sequence possibly extend down to the Lower Devonian. Occasional thin volcanics are interbedded (Malone *et al.*, 1962/72; Reynolds, 1963/159).

The **Hill End Trough** was not deformed by the Bowning orogenic movements and the Devonian is conformable on the Silurian. The carbonate sediments of the Molong–Wellington area grade rapidly eastwards into volcanics, greywackes and slates up to 8000 m thick. The volcanics are concentrated in the lower part of the sequence and are predominantly dacitic (Packham, pers. comm.). Presumably they are equivalents of the Cuga Burga Volcanics to the west. The upper unit is the Cunningham Formation, composed of shales and siltstones (Strusz, 1960; Wolf, 1965).

The extent of Lower and Middle Devonian sedimentation on the **Capertee High** is unknown. It is possible that much of the sediment laid down was subsequently stripped prior to the deposition of the Upper Devonian. The only sediments remaining on the exposed sector is a sequence of shales, tuffs, limestones, and limestone breccias near its northern end. In the vicinity of Mudgee limestones low in the sequence contain *Zelolasma*, *Pachyphyllum*, *Endophyllum*, and *Stringophyllum* (Pedder, 1963; Wright, 1965) indicating a Middle Devonian age. There is no apparent break between the limestones and the overlying Upper Devonian sandstones in this area.

Acid volcanics, however, are very widely distributed. They are best known on the southern end of the structure where they are referred to as the Eden Rhyolites.

The width of this arch cannot be determined on present knowledge, but what evidence there is from exploratory wells and the provenance of Carboniferous sediments, suggests that it was a broad structure and extended well to the east into the area now occupied by the Permian sediments of the Newcastle Geosyncline.

New England Geosyncline

Only small segments of the Devonian rocks laid down in this mobile downwarp have been recognized as such, and in almost every case recognition has been dependent on the existence of coralline limestones. These are invariably associated with thick sequences of bedded siliceous rocks, slates, acid tuffs, and andesitic flows and tuffs. Without the limestones the age of these rocks would not have been determinable by palaeontological means and they would have been classed with the ubiquitous "undifferentiated lower Palaeozoics". This, together with the considerable thickness of known Lower and Middle Devonian rocks at certain localities (over 5500 m at Warwick), suggests that deposition may have been widespread throughout the structure. Its floor must have been mobile, and although sediments characteristic of deep quiet water are common, the occurrence of the relatively thin coralline limestones mentioned above indicates the presence of temporarily upwarped areas.

Outcrops are known from near Barrington in the south to beyond Rockhampton in the north. However, since they occur in areas that have been extensively faulted and intruded by granitic rocks, the stratigraphic successions are not well understood. Two exceptions to this are the linear outcrops along the Great Serpentine Belt from the north of Tamworth to south of Murrurundi, and the fault block outcrops near Warwick.

At Warwick the Silverwood Group is divisible into two clear (but unnamed) units—a basal sequence (2000 m thick) of andesites and spilites with lenses of coralline limestone at one horizon, and an upper sequence (1700 m thick) of finely banded radiolarian cherts and fissile shales. The limestone lenses contain the rugose corals *Pseudamplexus*, *Hexagonaria*, *Xystriphyllum*, *Spongophyllum*, and *Chlamydophyllum*, various tabulates, and stromatoporoids, and are considered to be Eifelian. The banding in the cherts is due to the presence of quantities of fine tuffaceous material in the light-coloured layers, and the abundance of fine siliceous material and radiolarians in the darker layers. Slumps, microfaults, and intraformational breccias are common in this unit. The indications are that it was deposited in relatively deep water well away from land.

In the Tamworth area approximately 3000 m (base not known) of cherty radiolarian argillites, greywackes, greywacke breccias, limestone lenses and breccias, keratophyres, and spilites (the Tamworth Group) have been divided into several formations (Crook, 1961a). The terrigenous rocks are fine-grained and display sedimentary structures of turbidity current type while the volcanic rocks are coarse-grained. A relatively deep-water environment at a distance from the source is indicated. On the other hand, the interbedded limestones, which are apparently restricted to three main levels and are associated with coarse red limestone breccias at several localities, indicate very shallow-water conditions. The greywackes are composed largely of andesitic debris with minor rhyolite, granite and sedimentary components. The argillites are black- and white-banded owing to the predominance of radiolarian and volcanic detritus in alternate layers. The terrigenous material was derived predominantly from the southwest, but was distributed in part by currents along the axis of the trough (Crook, 1964). The limestones are either thickly bedded with masses of corals and stromatoporoids or coarse breccias with a red clastic matrix. The latter probably developed either on reef aprons or marginally to limestone banks. Three distinct faunas occur in the limestones. The lowest or Ningha Limestone has an abundance of *Xystriphyllum insigne* and is probably Emsian, the Sulcor Limestone has *Phillipsastraea*, *Tipheophyllum*, and *Pseudamplexus* and is Eifelian, while the top or Moore Creek Limestone has *Dohmophyllum*, *Phacellophyllum*, *Sanidophyllum*, the stromatoporoid *Amphipora* and the stringocephalid brachiopod *Bornhardtina*, and is Givetian.

The contiguous occurrence of shallow-water limestones and apparently deep-water turbidites probably indicates that the floor of the trough was in a highly mobile state and that deeper-water sediments were being arched up penecontemporaneously. Where the arches reached the zone in which corals and stromatoporoids could become established, limestones developed. Under these circumstances slight angular unconformities would be expected at the base of the limestones.

NORTH QUEENSLAND BASINS

The palaeogeographical regime of the Silurian continued into the Early Devonian throughout these basins (White, 1961), and as has been noted in the previous chapter some formations cross the boundary between two systems. During the Early Devonian, however, a series of block-faulting movements with associated folding caused the redistribution of land and sea shown in Fig. 5.5. Middle Devonian sediments transgressed over Lower Palaeozoic metamorphic and plutonic rocks to the south, and show angularly unconformable relationships with Silurian sediments at several localities. On the site of the old **Chillagoe Shelf** in the Hodgkinson Trough there may have been thin limestones of Middle Devonian age, and there are conglomerates thought to be of the same age out in the trough, but by and large sedimentation in this structure was probably at a minimum. Only the western end of the **Kangaroo Hills Trough** remained below the sea, but it continued to subside rapidly and received up to 5700 m of shallow-water sediments, mainly siltstones and limestones (the Broken River Formation), during the Emsian and Middle Devonian. The broad **Burdekin River Shelf** developed to the south of the site of the Kangaroo Hills Trough, and on it a thinner sequence of carbonates, known as the Burdekin Formation, accumulated. They are up to 2500 m thick, and contain several true reefs and their accompanying breccias. The corals are the only organisms from these formations that have been examined in detail, and these indicate the presence of Emsian to Givetian, and at one locality, Frasnian rocks. The genera are too numerous to list, but the most significant ones are *Pseudamplexus*, *Acanthophyllum*, *Spongophylloides*, and *Tryplasma* in the Emsian and *Endophyllum*, *Stringophyllum*, *Phacellophyllum*, *Mesophyllum*, and *Calceola* in the Givetian. Stromatoporoids, particularly *Amphipora*, and the large brachiopod *Stringocephalus* are also common with the latter faunas.

Further north the **Hodgkinson Trough** was probably receiving sediments during the Lower and Middle Devonian. Along the western edge of the trough there is a monotonous thick sequence of greywackes, shales, and basic volcanics, with occasional thin limestones known as the Hodgkinson Formation. These are difficult to date but are thought to range in age from

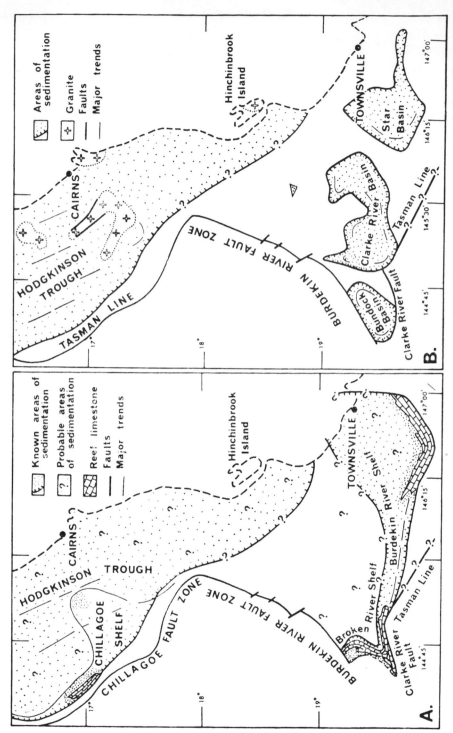

FIG. 5.5. Depositional pattern in the North Queensland Basins during A, the Middle Devonian; and B, the Late Devonian to Early Carboniferous.

Middle to Upper Devonian (De Keyser, 1964, 1965). Eastwards they become progressively more strongly metamorphosed, and on the coast they are known as the Barron River Metamorphics or the Barnard Metamorphics, the latter being only a higher metamorphic grade of the former. In addition to equivalents of the Hodgkinson Formation, these metamorphics may include time equivalents of rocks as old as the Chillagoe Formation.

B. UPPER DEVONIAN

The Tabberabberan Orogeny profoundly modified the palaeogeography of eastern Australia. In the Lachlan Geosyncline the old troughs were disrupted, and across and beyond them a new sedimentary regime involving the deposition of widespread terrestrial and, in part, paralic deposits, was initiated. Almost the only structure in this region to retain its individuality was the Molong–Taemas–Buchan Platform, which in the south rose above depositional level, but in the north after forming an effective barrier to the sea in the early part of the epoch, was finally inundated. At the Queensland end of this geosyncline there were extensive modifications, which are at present becoming apparent as data from deep wells become available. The North Queensland Basins also were disrupted and new structures receiving sediments similar to those deposited earlier were formed. In the New England Geosyncline, too, there were modifications in the conformation of the depositional area, but marine sedimentation continued. There are no known Upper Devonian rocks in Tasmania.

LAMBIAN BASINS

Along the whole area previously occupied by the Lachlan Geosyncline quartzose and lithic sandstones predominantly of terrestrial origin, but in places marine, began to accumulate. Rocks of this facies outcrop from Victoria to north Queensland, and from Lithgow in the east to the western part of the Georgina Basin in the west, and they therefore form one of the most widespread lithological types of the Australian Palaeozoic. In the eastern states they occupy meridionally trending belts. It is not definitely known whether these belts represent depositional basins, or the preserved parts of a far more extensive sheet. In New South Wales there is some evidence, from facies relationships and current directions, of sedimentary interconnexion between these now isolated belts, and the rocks are thought to have been deposited mainly from an extensive river system, or systems, which discharged into a shallow sea in the east. However, the limited thickness data available (Conolly, 1963) suggest that differential subsidence must have been going on in meridional belts throughout this time. As Fig. 5.7 shows, there is a marine facies in the lower part of the Lambie and Catombal Groups, which form an Eastern Province (Mackay, 1961) and in the northern part of the Hervey Group in the Central Province. These rocks vary from volcanic lithic sandstones to protoquartzites. Thick cross-stratified units are common. In places they contain masses of the brachiopods *Cyrtospirifer*

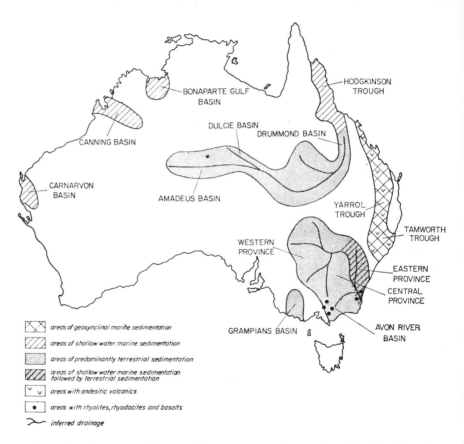

Fig. 5.6. Palaeogeographic map of Australia during the Late Devonian. The inferred drainage pattern for the areas of terrestrial deposition is indicated. It is possible that the Amadeus and Dulcie Basins at various times drained southwards through New South Wales rather than through the Drummond Basin.

and *Camarotoechia* piled into shell banks. Over most of the Central Province, however, the basal beds are mainly arkosic or lithic red sandstones which contain the fish *Bothriolepis* and the plant *Leptophloeum*; and in the entire Western Province they are coarse conglomerates which have the characters of river gravels. In all provinces these basal rocks are followed conformably

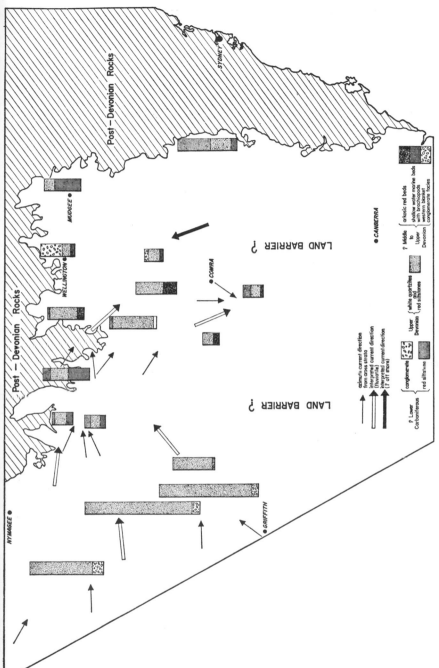

FIG. 5.7. Map showing variations in thickness, lithology, and direction of depositional currents in the Upper Devonian and ?Lower Carboniferous rocks of central and western New South Wales. Directional data refer to the brachiopod-bearing sandstones in the east and the fish-bearing sandstones further west. (Redrawn and modified after J. R. Conolly.) Column scale, 1 cm = 1800 m.

by a sequence of alternating red and white siltstones, lithic sandstones, and protoquartzites (Conolly, 1965, and pers. comm.). The environment of deposition probably alternated between lacustrine and fluvial. In the Catombal Group these rocks are capped by a sequence of the same type but with numerous interbedded massive red oligomictic conglomerates. In the Hervey and Mulga Downs Groups the conglomerates are replaced by red siltstones. The upper parts of these groups contain plants referable to *Archaeopteris*, and may be as young as Early Carboniferous.

In Victoria there are two large basins containing rocks of this facies, an eastern one in the Avon River area, and a western one in the Grampian Mountains. In addition there are small outliers scattered over a wide area to the east. The axis of the **Avon River Basin** is more or less collinear with that of the Central Province basin of New South Wales, and there may well have been a connexion between the two. In it the sequence begins with a variable thickness of terrestrial conglomerates, purple sandstones, and red mudstones, and these are followed by acid volcanics. On the western side of the basin these formed in cauldron subsidences (Hills, 1959) where they reached thicknesses of over 1000 m and interbedded sedimentary rocks were absent. Over wider areas they were much thinner and occurred as flows and tuffs separated by thicker sedimentary units. The volcanics were probably not completely contemporaneous. The sediments contain the fishes *Dipterus*, *Bothriolepis*, and *Phyllolepis* together with the plants *Archaeopteris*, *Sphenopteris*, and *Cordaites*. Above the volcanics, near the northern end of the basin, are red sandstones and conglomerates with plant remains and fish of Carboniferous age. In the south there are quartzose and lithic sandstones, conglomerates and some claystones, which are possibly Upper Devonian.

In the **Grampians Basin** there are 7000 m of well-bedded coarse to fine-grained quartzose sandstones and micaceous siltstones. Many of these rocks are red coloured, and cross-stratification is common. Four formations are recognized in the Grampians Group on the basis of the varying proportions of the above rock types (Spencer-Jones, 1965). No definite volcanic rocks have been recorded. Many geologists have considered the group to be mainly, or possibly entirely, Carboniferous. The only palaeontological evidence for this is the occurrence of a species of *Lingula*, elasmobranch remains, and the fish *?Physonemus* in the Silverband Formation near the middle of the group. It has been pointed out (Talent and Spencer-Jones, 1963) that these fossils give no precise indication of age, and there seems to be no good reason why at least the lower part of the group should not be Upper Devonian. The fossils do indicate that some of the sequence is marine. No work has been done on current directions, but the existence of these marine rocks and the current directions in the Western Province of New South Wales, combine to suggest that the Grampians Basin was a separate structure. The extent of the basin is unknown as it is entirely surrounded by Cainozoic rocks, but it must have been much larger than the present area of outcrop.

The **Drummond Basin** of central Queensland lies immediately to the west of the Anakie High and is the analogue of the Central Province of New South Wales. The Upper Devonian Telemon Formation (up to 2300 m thick) lies unconformably or disconformably on the underlying Middle Devonian rocks. It is mainly terrestrial in origin, but the presence of small branchiopods, doubtful crinoid remains, and a few bivalves, may indicate that it is partly estuarine (Hill, 1957*b*). Against the Anakie High it contains a large amount of volcanic material, including tuffs, thin andesite, basalt, and rhyolite flows and some volcanic lithic sandstones, the last having been derived from the Silver Hills Formation. The volcanic content decreases to the west where conglomerates, flaggy and ashy sandstones, and thin limestones composed of freshwater algae occur (Veevers *et al.*, 1964*a*).

At the northern end of the basin, the Mount Wyatt Beds overlie the Ukalunda Beds unconformably. The siltstones and lithic sandstones of which they are composed are the only marine Upper Devonian rocks in the basin, and probably indicate an opening to the sea northwards through the Star Basin. Presumably, then, the Drummond Basin at this time was a subsiding drainage basin, the streams in general running from south to north. Fossils in the Mount Wyatt Beds include the plant *Leptophloeum* and the brachiopod *Cyrtospirifer*.

Still further west, about 1000 m of red sandstones and siltstones, the Buckabie Formation, have been penetrated in wells in the **Adavale Trough**. They are probably Late Devonian and Early Carboniferous in age, and are the analogues of the rocks of the Western Province in New South Wales. Their relationship to the underlying Etonvale Formation is probably one of unconformity.

In the Northern Territory the western **Georgina Basin** contains the clean white Dulcie Sandstone (up to 700 m thick) which has a fauna of *Bothriolepis* and *Phyllolepis* (Smith, 1967/61; Smith *et al.*, 1961/65, 1963/46; Hills, 1958*b*, 1959).

AMADEUS BASIN

The Pertnjara Formation which forms the top unit in much of the Amadeus Basin is at least partly of Late Devonian age. It lies unconformably and disconformably above the Mereenie Formation and unconformably below Permian glacials. It is over 7000 m thick and is made up of calcareous lithic sandstones and conglomerates, two of the latter units each being up to 2700 m thick. The boulders are derived from the north and northeast, and are representative of all the earlier formations in the basin. It probably represents a series of coalescing fans emanating from the rising Arunta Massif (Stelck and Hopkins, 1962; Wells *et al.*, 1965*b*; Ranford *et al.*, 1965). Upper Devonian fish remains have recently been discovered in the formation (Tomlinson, 1967).

NEW ENGLAND GEOSYNCLINE

The effects of the Tabberabberan Orogeny were of much more limited extent in this than in the Lachlan Geosyncline. The supply of andesitic detritus for the sediments of the early Upper Devonian was maintained, presumably from volcanoes within the geosyncline; but unlike the Middle Devonian sequences there is an almost complete lack of limestone. In the Yarrol Trough (Maxwell, 1953) and the Tamworth Trough (Voisey, 1957; Crook, 1961*b*; White, 1964), massive graded units composed largely of andesitic debris, together with interbedded shales, were deposited as a greywacke facies. They are known as the Thomson Clastics in the north and the Baldwin Formation in the south. Since wherever their base is exposed they are known to be in contact with Middle Devonian rocks, any unconformity which exists must be relatively minor. There is practically no quartz or chert in any of these rocks, indicating the presence of an effective barrier to the west and the absence of emergent siliceous rocks within the geosyncline (Chappell, 1961). In New South Wales there are few fossils at this level, but in Queensland the characteristic Upper Devonian *Cyrtospirifer–Camarotoechia–Productella* assemblages are present.

Volcanism continued until the latest Devonian in places (the Boulder Creek Grits near Rockhampton), but in most areas there is a tendency for the coarse green volcanics and greywackes to pass up into finely bedded siltstones and sandstones, the coarser units being graded (the Mandowa Mudstone, Tangaratta Formation of the Tamworth Trough, (Crook, 1961*b*; White, 1964)). That the geosyncline was mobile during this period is demonstrated by the presence of coarse polymictic conglomerates and minor angular unconformities caused by movements that failed to bring the area above sealevel (Crook, 1959; White, 1964). By the end of the period the sediments show evidence of a shallow-water depositional environment in most areas except along the east coast of New South Wales.

Cyrtospirifer, *Sulcatospirifer*, and *Camarotoechia* occur in the Yarrol Trough, and though fossils are much rarer in the Tamworth Trough the stratigraphically important *Platyclymenia* and *Cymaclymenia* have been found. As is the case elsewhere in Australia, *Leptophloeum* is present.

NORTH QUEENSLAND BASINS

The changes in shapes of these basins are shown in Fig. 5.5 (White, 1961). In the Bundock and Clarke River Basins there are probably no Upper Devonian rocks, and Tournaisian sediments rest unconformably on Middle Devonian and older rocks. In the Star Basin and Hodgkinson Trough however, sedimentation continued, and a small downfaulted block at Gilberton indicates the presence of a short-lived terrestrial basin in that area.

In the **Star Basin** the rocks overlying the Burdekin Formation are the coarse conglomerates, feldspathic and arkosic sandstones, red siltstones, and acid volcanics of the Dotswood Formation. These are of terrestrial origin and are the result of the uplift within the basin and in the surrounding areas. The sea then re-entered the basin to deposit the Star Beds, a unit of about 400 m of hard calcareous sandstones, shales, and numerous beds of conglomerate. The Upper Devonian plant, *Leptophloeum australe*, is found in both formations, but in the Star the rich brachiopod, molluscan, and trilobite faunas prove that the unit spans the Devono-Carboniferous boundary. To the north this basin must have opened into an extension of the **Hodgkinson Trough** (De Keyser, 1964), in which turbidite deposits of rhythmically bedded siltstones and greywackes comprise the bulk of the sequence (upper parts of the Hodgkinson Formation and Barron River Metamorphics). They contain *Leptophloeum australe* in abundance on certain levels.

Western Australia

CANNING BASIN

Devonian rocks are restricted to the northern sector of this structure. They are relatively thin in outcrop along the Napier Platform in the north, but exploratory wells have shown that they thicken considerably towards the axis of the Fitzroy Depression and thin out again to the south on the flank of the Broome Swell. Despite their limited outcrop in relation to their total extent, these rocks form one of the finest exposures of Devonian rocks in Australia and possibly in the world. They are variable in character, relatively undisturbed, and highly fossiliferous.

Sedimentation began in the Givetian with the deposition of the calcarenites, biostromes, and bioherms of the Pillara Formation, a unit which oversteps Precambrian–Ordovician rocks along the basin edge (Guppy *et al.*, 1958; Veevers and Wells, 1961). These carbonates give place to clastic sediments in some places, but details are not available. The lithological types are uniform over wide areas, and they are interpreted as indicating the presence of a platform (the Napier Platform) with low relief covered with clear, circulating water, and largely free from terrigenous material. The faunas of the bioherms are predominantly stromatoporoids (*Amphipora, Actinostroma*) but compound corals are also present (*Hexagonaria, Disphyllum, Temnophyllum,* and *Thamnopora*). Three brachiopod zones are present in the formation, the lowest (STRINGOCEPHALUS FONTANUS) being of Givetian age, and the upper two (CRURITHYRIS APENA and LADJIA SALTICA) being Frasnian. In these latter zones brachiopods are prolific, the most important forms being *Douvillina, Nervostrophia, Hypothyridina, Gypidula, Devonoproductus,* and *Atrypa.* The MANTICOCERAS ZONE ammonoids *Manticoceras, Ponticeras, Beloceras,* and *Tornoceras* occur in the same units.

During the Frasnian, block-faulting movements and minor associated folding caused the remoulding of the sedimentary pattern along the whole outcrop. In places there are marked angular unconformities at the base of the late Frasnian deposits, whereas elsewhere there is conformity. The sedimentary pattern was diversified and continued to be so until the end of the Devonian. Shorelines were continually migrating, and in places Famennian limestones rest directly on the Precambrian. Uptilted edges of blocks became the sites for bioherms which are far more numerous than in the Pillara Formation. Coarse conglomerates and breccias, which were presumably laid down as fanglomerates in the fault angle depressions, are of common occurrence. The clasts include quartzites, acid igneous rocks, and metamorphics indicating a source area in the Precambrian to the north. Among the bedded rocks calcarenites and calcilutites are by far the most common, but the contribution of quartz sand is important, and in some units it is predominant. Extensive bedded limestones developed during periods of stability. The total thickness at any one place along the length of the outcrop is rarely more than 600 m, and is usually less. Out in the deeper parts of the basin however, sections of 1000 m have been penetrated.

The interrelationships of all these rock types are not clearly understood. Attempts have been made at a reconstruction, but the data are as yet adequate for a broad interpretation only. Part of one such interpretation is given in Fig. 5.8 (Veevers and Wells, 1961, pp. 28–29).

Fossils are again abundant. Compound rugose corals are, however, absent, and only a few genera of small solitary corals remain. Three more brachiopod zones are recognized in the upper Frasnian and Famennian; the EMANUELLA TORRIDA ZONE dominated by *Emanuella, Plicochonetes, Atrypa, Uncinulus* and *Schizophoria;* the NYEGE SCOPIMUS ZONE with only one other form, *Pugnax hullensis;* and the AVONIA PROTEUS ZONE with *Avonia, Schuchertella, Leptaena, Schizophoria, Uncinulus,* and *Cyrtospirifer.* In addition, ammonoids representative of the MANTICOCERAS ZONE (*Manticoceras, Ponticeras, Probeloceras,* and *Hoeninghausia*); the CHEILOCERAS ZONE (*Cheiloceras, Imitoceras, Tornoceras,* and *Dimeroceras*); the LOWER PLATYCLYMENIA ZONE (*Sporadoceras, Tornoceras,*

Dimeroceras, Pseudoclymenia, and *Platyclymenia*); and possibly the UPPER PLATYCLYMENIA ZONE (*Cyrtoclymenia* and *Platyclymenia*) have been found (Teichert, 1943; Glenister, 1958). These represent the four lowest of the six STUFEN in the German Upper Devonian succession. Nautiloids also are relatively common, though not nearly as common as the ammonoids. More recently ostracod and conodont assemblages have been identified, but they have not been described.

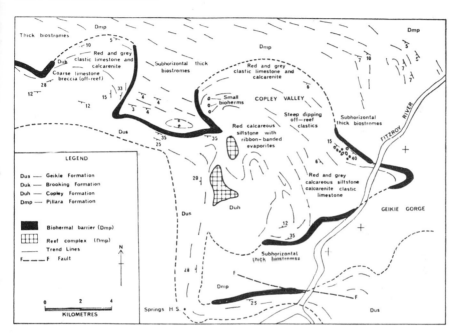

Fig. 5.8. Sketch map of a small sector of the Devonian sediments on the Napier Platform, Canning Basin, showing the arrangement of the reef deposits. (Modified after Veevers and Wells, 1961.)

CARNARVON BASIN

The late Givetian or early Frasnian saw further sedimentation in this basin. Rocks of this age outcrop only along the eastern edge of the basin, but they have been identified in exploratory wells sunk near the present coast line, so they probably have a continuous distribution across the basin. At the base of the sequence are thin arkosic and lithic sandstones which rest unconformably on Precambrian gneisses. Approximately 500 m of shallow-water sandstones, calcarenites, fossiliferous limestones, and dolomites (the Gneudna Formation) follow. They contain *Disphyllum, Hexagonaria, Austrospirifer, Cyrtospirifer, Polygnathus,* and *Icriodus,* which probably indicate a

Frasnian age. The Munabia Sandstone and the Willaraddie Formation which complete the Devonian succession, are lithic and quartz sandstones and siltstones with some conglomerates. They total about 900 m, and are shallow-water, cross-stratified units devoid of fossils apart from a few lepidodendroid fragments.

BONAPARTE GULF BASIN

In this basin there was probably a depositional hiatus between the Lower Ordovician and the Upper Devonian. When sedimentation recommenced, about 1300 m of shallow-water, cross-stratified, quartz sandstones with pebble beds, and occasional dense limestones were deposited around the margins of the basin. They are known as the Cockatoo Sandstone. At least in the south they overlap the Lower Palaeozoic rocks and lie directly on the Precambrian. Parts of the sequence are possibly deltaic and parts definitely marine, and both plants (*Leptophloeum*) and bivalves (*Palaeoneilo, Modiomorpha* and *Leiopteria*) are known. Overlying these sandstones is a sequence of bedded marine calcarenites and quartzose sandstones (the Burt Range Formation), the very basal part of which may be of Devonian age, but the upper parts are definitely Carboniferous (Glenister, 1960; Veevers *et al.*, 1964c).

New Zealand

The nature of the Lower Devonian sediments, limited though their outcrops are, clearly indicates a change in the character of the sources of supply from that responsible for the Ordovician sequence. The presence of quartz sandstones and coral limestones with rich brachiopod assemblages shows that the neighbouring lands had ceased to rise and were reduced substantially to low relief. The Reefton Mudstone (lower Emsian) and the overlying Reefton Limestone (uppermost Emsian or basal Eifelian) are part of an inshore facies of the Rhenish Devonian type, while the Baton River sequence (upper Gedinnian), some 110 km to the northnortheast, is of the Bohemian (off-shore) facies. Apart from this there is little evidence bearing upon the problem of the shape of the depositional area (Gill, 1952; Suggate, 1957).

NELSON REGION

South of Mount Arthur and extending for a short distance south of the Wangapeka River, is a narrow belt of thick-bedded quartzites and argillites with a fairly rich fauna of brachiopods, corals, bivalves, sponges, polyzoans, trilobites. This sequence is terminated both in the north and south by the underlying Mount Arthur Marble and is in fault contact on both east and west sides with older and younger rocks.

As mentioned under the Silurian System, the massive quartzites and quartzites with interbedded argillites of the Ellis Formation lying above the Mount Arthur Marble, are probably Ordovician or Silurian in age (Willis, 1965). Unconformably above comes a faulted sequence of moderately to steeply dipping calcareous mudstones and shales, marbles, and sandstones, of the Baton Formation, at least 2400 m thick. Some of the members of this formation have extremely rich faunas. It is intruded by post-Devonian igneous rocks.

The fossiliferous nature of the Baton River rocks was well known in the late nineteenth century, when McKay (1879) identified them as Silurian in age. However, Shirley (1938) revised the faunas of what is now Member No. 3 of the Baton Formation (Willis, 1965) and showed them clearly to be of Early Devonian age. A recent examination of the faunas (Boucot *et al.*, 1963) suggests that, from "The absence of acrospiriferids . . . as well as the abundance of *Howellella* and a number of Devonian-type genera such as *Cyrtina, Fascicostella*, and *Mutationella*", a late Gedinnian age is most likely.

Willis (1965) also suggests the probability of a Devonian transgression across the whole of the Nelson region, especially in view of his discovery of an unconformity at the base of the Baton Formation and the occurrence of a major unconformity at the base of the Devonian sequence at Reefton.

There are also reasons for believing that certain groups of metamorphic rocks in the Nelson Province such as the Riwaka amphibolites, hornblende-schists, porphyrites, meta-basalts and serpentinites, and the Onekaka schists, are, in part at least, of Devonian age (Cooper, 1965).

WESTLAND REGION

Devonian rocks occupy small lensoid (in plan) areas, totalling about 4 sq km, southeast and east of Reefton Township. These small areas are downfaulted blocks, with their long axes aligned almost north and south, surrounded by greywackes of the Waiuta Group (?Precambrian), and comprise an apparently conformable sequence of quartzites, mudstones, and limestones.

The sequence, which is steeply tilted and sometimes overturned, begins with a series of quartzites, often ferruginous (the Lower Quartzite), at least 750 m thick. The unit has a rich fauna of brachiopods and polyzoans at the top, a fauna which is indistinguishable from that in the overlying Reefton Mudstone (190 m), except for the presence, in addition, of many other organisms in the latter. Boucot *et al.*, (1963), in their revision of the brachiopod faunas, have concluded that the presence of large spiriferids and the terebratuloid *Pleurothyrella*, make correlation with the upper Siegenian and lower Emsian substages of Europe most likely.

Above the Reefton Mudstone is the thin sequence (25 m) of the Reefton Limestone, with an abundant coral and polyzoan fauna, correlated by Hill (1956) with the basal Eifelian or uppermost Emsian. Stromatoporoids have also recently been noted as common by Cockbain (1965). The affinities of the Reefton coral faunas to those of eastern Australian Devonian formations (Sulcor Limestone and Cavan "Stage", New South Wales) had already been recognized by Gill (1952) in his reconstruction of the palaeogeography of the Australasian region.

The sequence closes with sandstones and quartzites (the Upper Quartzite) exceeding 180 m in thickness.

PALAEONTOLOGY

Australia

From a palaeobotanical point of view, the occurrence of the land plants *Baragwanathia*, *Yarravia*, *Hostimella*, and *Zosterophyllum* in the earliest Devonian rocks of Victoria is of particular interest. However, plant fossils are not common in the Australian Lower or Middle Devonian. In contrast the spread of the Upper Devonian plant *Leptophloeum australe* from the Bonaparte Gulf Basin to Victoria, and its profusion in both terrestrial and marine rocks, is noteworthy. Two Upper Devonian spore assemblages are known from Western Australia—a Frasnian one dominated by *Geminospora* and a Famennian one dominated by *Leiozonotriletes* (Balme, 1964; Balme and Hassell, 1962).

Tabulate and colonial rugose corals are abundant in all areas where Lower or Middle Devonian rocks are known, but the coral faunas of the Upper Devonian are very meagre and consist mainly of a few solitary genera. There is evidence in the eastern states of the provincial distribution of some of the species during the Early and Middle Devonian, but in general they are widely distributed geographically. Stratigraphically they have proved to be of great value, and up to the present they have been one of the most widely used groups for purposes of correlation. Among the other coelenterates the stromatoporoids are the most abundant, but they have not been extensively studied. Brachiopods also are widespread and abundant and have recently begun to receive the attention that they deserve (Gill, 1949, 1950, 1951; Philip, 1962; Talent, 1963, 1965b; Veevers, 1959). Important conclusions from this work are the similarity of the faunas at any given time throughout eastern Australia and the provincialism of the Upper Devonian faunas of northwestern Australia. Ammonoids are rare in the east, being found only in the lower Middle (and possibly Lower) Devonian at Buchan and in the Upper Devonian in New England, but they are profuse in the Upper

Devonian of the Canning Basin in the west. Trilobites and ostracods (Krömmelbein, 1954) are relatively common but have received little attention. Two fine carpoids, *Victoriacystis* and *Rutroclypeus*, have been described by Gill and Caster (1960) from the Lower Devonian of Victoria. The conodonts *Spathognathodus*, *Hindeodella*, *Ozarkodina*, *Trichondella*, and *Plectospathodus*, *inter alia*, have been recorded (Philip, 1965; Philip and Pedder, 1964). Though there certainly are several endemic genera (e.g., *Australophyllum*, *Sanidophyllum*, and *Eddastraea* among the corals, and *Notoconchidium*, *Notanoplia*, *Tyersella*, and *Teichertina* among the brachiopods), in general the coelenterate, brachiopod, bivalve, gastropod, ammonoid, trilobite, carpoid, and conodont faunas have pronounced Eurasian affinities.

Vertebrate fossils are known from both the Middle and Upper Devonian. The Middle Devonian limestones on the southern part of the Taemas–Molong Platform have yielded the arthrodires *Buchanosteus*, *Williamsaspis*, and *Taemasosteus* together with the dipnoan *Dipnorhynchus*. Upper Devonian vertebrates are known from almost all basins. The antiarchs *Bothriolepis* and *Remigolepis* are particularly widespread, and the phyllolepid *Phyllolepis* and tooth plates of the dipnoan *Dipterus* are also relatively common. These occurrences reinforce the Eurasian affinities of the faunas alluded to above.

New Zealand

The Baton Formation in northwest Nelson was clearly shown by Shirley (1938) to be Early Devonian in age and was regarded by him as similar in facies to that of the Koněprusy Limestone of Czechoslovakia (Bohemian facies). A recent examination of the faunas (Boucot *et al.*, 1963) suggests that a late Gedinnian age is most likely. The principal generic elements in the Baton River fauna are the spongiomorph *Receptaculites*; the tabulate coral *Pleurodictyum*, the brachiopods (in addition to the four mentioned above) *Kozlowskiellina*, *Gypidula*, *Eospirifer*, *Cymostrophia?*, *Leptaenisca*, *Isorthis*, and *Mesodouvillina?*; the bivalves *Actinopteria*, *Cypricardinia*, *Nuculites*, and *Pterinea*; and fragments of trilobites such as *Gravicalymene*.

In the Devonian sequence at Reefton, there are two principal fossiliferous horizons. The Reefton Mudstone contains the brachiopods *Maoristrophia*, *Mesodouvillina?*, *Stropheodonta*, numerous large spiriferids, *Tanerhynchia*, *Reeftonia*, *Chonetes*, *Reeftonella*, and *Pleurothyrella*; the bivalves *Paleodora*, *Actinopteria*, *Pterinopecten*, and *Goniophora*; the gastropod *Platyceras*; the trilobite *Digonus*; and a mitrate carpoid (placocystitid). Boucot *et al.* (1963) consider correlation with the upper Siegenian and lower Emsian substages of Europe most likely.

The overlying Reefton Limestone has a rich fauna of corals including the rugose genera *Hexagonaria* and *Tipheophyllum* and the tabulates *Favosites*,

Emmonsia?, and *Thamnopora*. The polyzoans *Fistulipora*, *Lioclema?*, and *Fenestella* are also present. This fauna has been correlated by Hill (1956) with the uppermost Emsian or basal Eifelian. Cockbain (1965) has recently recorded the presence of the stromatoporoids *Anostylostroma* and *Stromatopora* corresponding specifically to those known in southeast Australia at Buchan and Lilydale (Ripper, 1938).

Many of these genera from both the Baton River and Reefton areas are common to both sides of the Tasman. In turn, many of these, e.g. the brachiopods *Gypidula*, *Howellella*, *Kozlowskiellina*, *Cyrtina*, *Mesodouvillina?*, *Cymostrophia*, *Schizophoria*, *Fascicostella*, *Isorthis*, and *Mutationella*, the spongiomorph *Receptaculites*, the tabulate corals *Favosites* and *Pleurodictyum*, and the trilobite *Gravicalymene*, are cosmopolitan in their distribution. There is some evidence, however, in favour of an Australasian sub-province in that the brachiopod *Maoristrophia* and the rugose coral *Tipheophyllum* appear to be restricted to this area. The only elements yet described that suggest Austral affinities are the Lower Devonian brachiopods *Australocoelia* and *Pleurothyrella*, though current faunal revisions are likely to augment these.

CLIMATE

Both faunas and floras suggest an equable and warm climate over the whole Australasian region during the Devonian. The large areas of Australia covered by terrestrial sands in the Upper Devonian suggest desert conditions, but the fact that *Leptophloeum* is so common indicates that succulent plants could exist not only around the continental margins but also in what is now the interior. These data are consistent with the pole positions given by Irving (1964) (Fig. 5.9).

TECTONISM

There was no major folding in Western Australia during the Devonian. Block faulting in the Canning Basin during the Late Devonian was associated with mild folding (Veevers and Wells, 1961), and there must have been marginal uplifts during the same epoch in the Bonaparte Gulf Basin to produce the thick conglomerate units in the Cockatoo Sandstone. Apart from this, all the basins of the west coast show only regional subsidence from the Middle Devonian onwards.

In eastern Australia, however, the tectonic history is much more complex, and both geosynclines and the North Queensland Basins evolve their own distinctive patterns. The Lachlan Geosyncline was disrupted during the Middle Devonian by the Tabberabberan Orogeny, which appears to have been most intense in the southern part of the continent. In Tasmania

(Spry and Banks eds., 1962) the older structures, such as the Tyennan Geanticline, have exercised an important control on the pattern of deformation (Fig. 5.10). On the western side of the island, at least, both concentric and similar folds are known, slaty cleavage is common in the mudstones, and there are numerous associated thrusts. In central Victoria, on the other

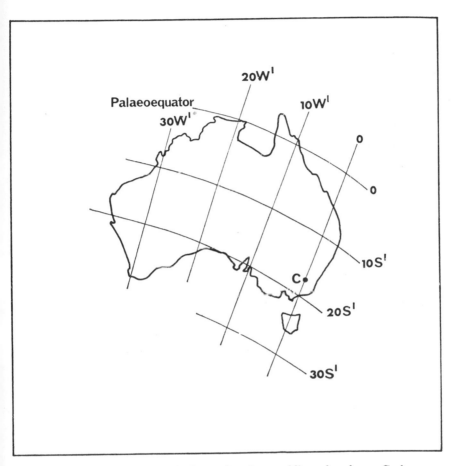

Fig. 5.9. Devonian palaeolatitudes and palaeomeridians based on Canberra. Reliability C. (After Irving, 1964, by permission of John Wiley & Sons Inc.)

hand, the folding is of concentric type, cleavage is generally absent, the folds are long and arcuate, and large-scale faulting is at a minimum (Williams, 1964) (Fig. 5.11). In eastern Victoria the deformation was probably more intense, but little is known about the regional picture. Northwards along the Taemas–Molong Platform the degree of deformation decreases, until

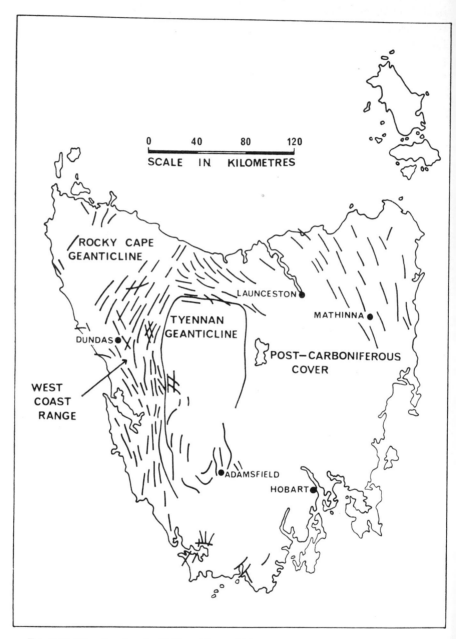

FIG. 5.10. Map showing the Tabberabberan fold trends in Tasmania. (After Solomon *in* Spry and Banks, 1962.)

near Wellington there are areas where the Upper Devonian and Eifelian rocks are almost parallel. At Taemas the limestones and shales are strongly folded, but there is evidence that the folding is disharmonic and has taken place by a décollement between the sediments and the underlying acid volcanics. Both to the west (in the Cobar Trough) and to the east (in the Hill End Trough) the deformation was stronger. However, it is noted that along the Capertee High the degree of deformation decreases northwards, and near Mudgee there is apparent conformity between Middle and Upper Devonian rocks (Wright, 1965).

Little is known of the structural picture in the Lachlan Geosyncline in Queensland apart from the eastern half of the Drummond Basin. There the deformation was only mild, and was comparable with that of the Wellington area of New South Wales.

The Tabberabberan movements took place during the Middle Devonian. It is significant that nowhere in the Lachlan Geosyncline are there any proven Givetian sediments, the only known Middle Devonian rocks being of Eifelian age. Possibly exceptional in this respect are certain limestones and shales at the northern end of the Capertee High near Mudgee (Wright, 1965). The oldest known rocks above the unconformity are Frasnian. Presumably, therefore, the deformation began during the Eifelian, and was complete, at least in some areas, by the early Late Devonian. The great extent and the character of the Upper Devonian sediments, and the nature of the folds themselves suggest that the Tabberabberan Orogeny was not a great mountain-building movement. It had the effect of producing wide land areas where previously there had been sea, but there is no evidence of the formation of high topographical relief except perhaps in Tasmania where the deformation was intense and sedimentation did not resume until the Permian.

Throughout the New England Geosyncline there is no indication of the relation between the Lower Devonian and the Silurian, and in fact there is no clear evidence of the presence of basal Devonian rocks. Consequently the early tectonic history of the period is quite unknown. The Tabberabberan Orogeny had only relatively minor effects, there being Eifelian and Givetian sediments in several areas, and no unconformities between Upper Devonian and earlier sediments have been recognized. That there was regional mobility during the Middle Devonian is shown by the presence of coralline limestones interbedded in turbidite sequences, but such mobility was on a different scale from that in the Lachlan Geosyncline. Similar conditions continued into the Late Devonian when local unconformities, such as the Bective Unconformity of the Tamworth Trough (White, 1964), was formed.

In the North Queensland Basins during the Early Devonian, fold and fault movements disrupted the Kangaroo Hills Trough, producing structures that are obviously related to the shape of the Precambrian borderlands. At the

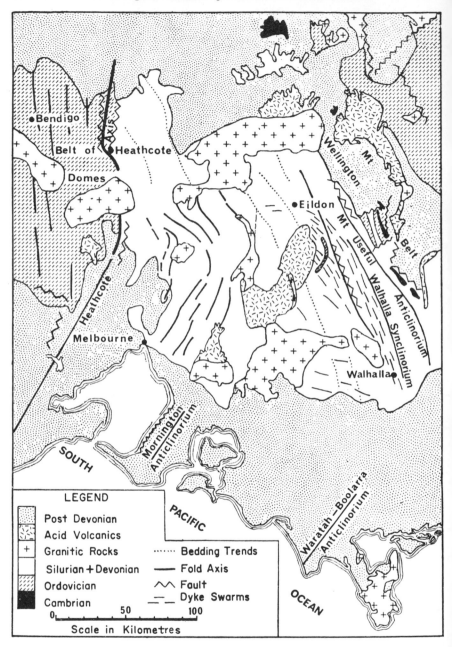

Fig. 5.11. Map showing the generalized structure of the Cambrian–Devonian rocks of central Victoria. (Modified after Williams, 1964.)

present time the folds in the Upper Silurian–Lower Devonian rocks are broad and open and plunge to the southwest at angles of up to 50° (Hill and Denmead, eds., 1960), but some of this shape could be due to subsequent movement. Marginal faults, along which the movement has been mainly vertical, are common. At the end of the Middle Devonian there was regional warping of the area and minor unconformities are found between the Middle and Upper Devonian.

The Amadeus Basin was deformed between the deposition of the Mereenie and Pertnjara Formations, and again after the deposition of the Pertnjara, but before the Early Permian glaciations. The first of these deformations is possibly of Devonian age, and the second is most probably Carboniferous.

The dating of the deformation of the Devonian rocks in New Zealand is uncertain, and is masked by the very much younger movements along the present alpine axis. The apparent absence of any Upper Devonian or Lower Carboniferous rocks from the New Zealand area may well be explained by the onset of tectonic movements at this time, but other agencies, such as the Late Jurassic–Early Cretaceous Rangitata Orogeny and its accompanying metamorphism, may be responsible for this phenomenon.

IGNEOUS ACTIVITY

Australia

There are no igneous rocks of Devonian age reported from Western Australia. In the Tasman Orthogeosyncline, however, the profusion of volcanic rocks is one of the features of the period, and granites and possibly ultrabasics were intruded during the various phases of deformation.

EXTRUSIVES

Lower and Middle Devonian. Volcanism was a feature of the Early Devonian along the Capertee High, the Taemas–Molong and Buchan Platforms, and probably the Condobolin High. Most of the rocks were acid, but andesites were also present. They are known to occur from eastern Victoria in the south, to just north of the Tropic of Capricorn. One interesting point is that the North Queensland Basins were remarkably free of volcanics at that time.

The petrology is best known at the Victorian end of the belt. The Snowy River Volcanics consist mainly of rhyodacites which are usually porphyritic in texture. Pyroclastics and incandescent tuff flows predominate. Relatively small amounts of latite, quartz andesite, rhyolite, and basalt occur as thin flows (Cochrane and Samson, 1947; Ringwood, 1955). The Eden Rhyolite of southern New South Wales consists largely of pyroclastics and is a potash rhyolite. On the Taemas–Molong Platform, and on its western land mass, there are rhyolites and dacites, but on its eastern side, adjacent to the Hill End Trough, keratophyres and quartz keratophyres alone occur. At Clermont in Queensland, andesites (sometimes carrying free quartz) predominate over rhyolites and dacites, though the acid rocks are still abundant.

In the southern half of the New England Geosyncline the most abundant volcanics are andesites and andesitic pyroclastics which in places reach a thickness of over 2000 m. Keratophyres and quartz keratophyres are also common, for example near Tamworth. However, in the northern half, rhyolites (probably ignimbrites) are also important contributors, and in places near Rockhampton they form the entire volcanic sequence.

Upper Devonian. Throughout most of the area occupied by the Lambian facies, volcanic rocks are present and in some structures they are almost as thick as the accompanying sediments. In most districts they are predominantly acidic in character—dacites (often with hypersthene), rhyodacites, toscanites, and rhyolites some of these rocks at least are ignimbrites. Basalts, however, are not infrequently present, and at some localities, for example the Lochiel Formation in the southeast corner of New South Wales, they predominate. There is a particularly fine display of rhyodacites, toscanites, rhyolites, and basalts (the Cerberean and Dandenong Volcanics) associated with cauldron subsidences in central Victoria and east and northeast of Melbourne (Hills, 1959). Many of the acid members are ignimbrites.

In the New England Geosyncline pyroclastics probably provided the detritus for a large part of the Upper Devonian sediments. The Baldwin Formation in the Tamworth Trough, and the Thomson Clastics and Boulder Creek Grits and their equivalents of the Yarrol Basin contain large quantities of water-laid andesitic debris, and the latter units also include flows of the same composition. They have all been albitized.

Thus, during the Late Devonian there were two distinct volcanic provinces in eastern Australia—a rhyodacite–rhyolite–basalt province associated with sediments of the Lambian Basins and an andesite province with the deeper water marine facies. This division cannot be extended back to the Early and Middle Devonian, presumably because prior to the Tabberabberan Orogeny conditions within the crust were more uniform over the entire region.

INTRUSIVES

Following the Late Silurian to Early Devonian period of injection there appears to have been no active plutonism until late in the Middle Devonian. At that time discordant batholiths were intruded into the Taemas–Molong

GF

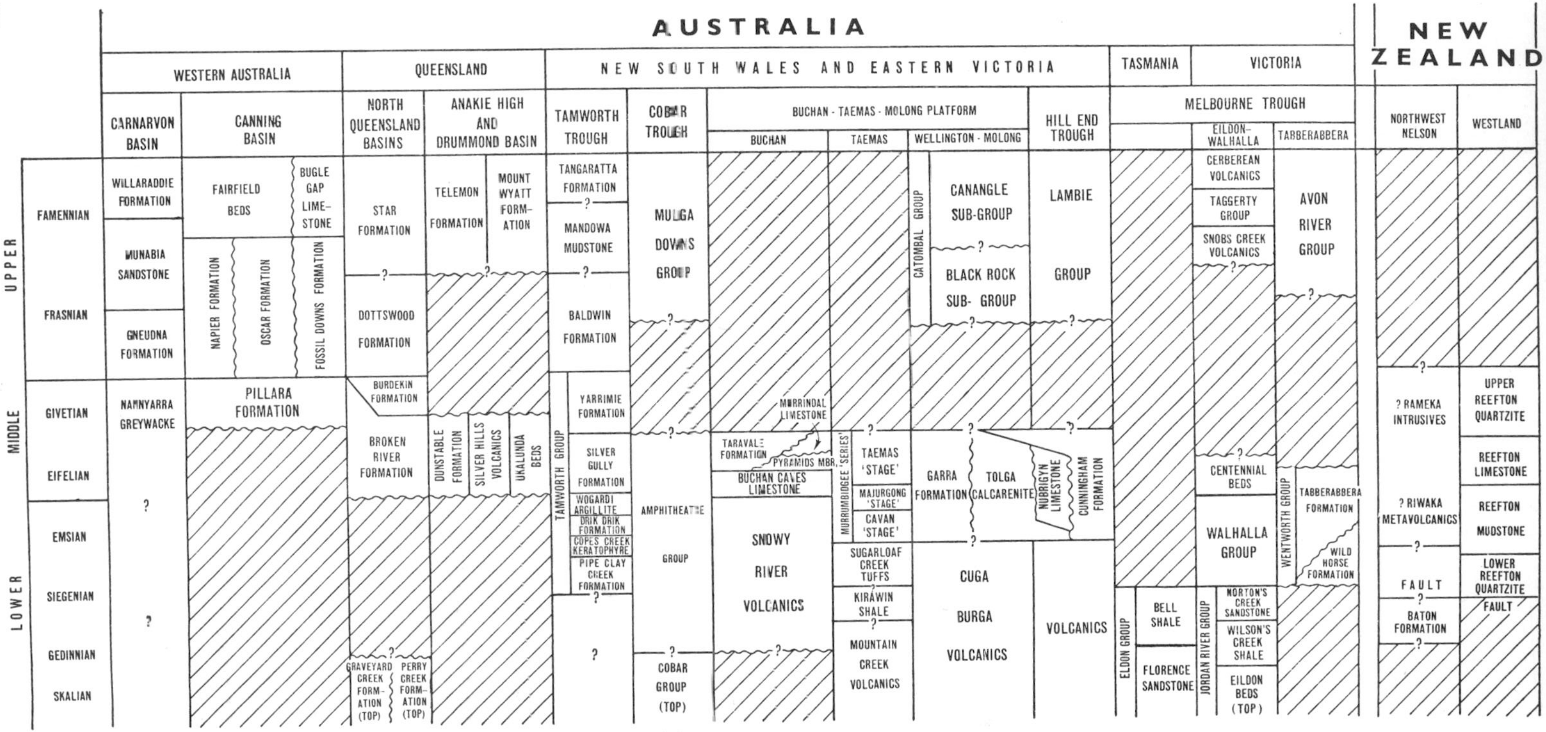
AUSTRALIA
NEW ZEALAND
WESTERN AUSTRALIA
QUEENSLAND
NEW SOUTH WALES AND EASTERN VICTORIA
TASMANIA
VICTORIA
CARNARVON BASIN
CANNING BASIN
NORTH QUEENSLAND BASINS
ANAKIE HIGH AND DRUMMOND BASIN
TAMWORTH TROUGH
COBAR TROUGH
BUCHAN - TAEMAS - MOLONG PLATFORM
BUCHAN
TAEMAS
WELLINGTON - MOLONG
HILL END TROUGH
MELBOURNE TROUGH
EILDON-WALHALLA
TABBERABBERA
NORTHWEST NELSON
WESTLAND
UPPER
MIDDLE
LOWER
FAMENNIAN
FRASNIAN
GIVETIAN
EIFELIAN
EMSIAN
SIEGENIAN
GEDINNIAN
SKALIAN
WILLARADDIE FORMATION
MUNABIA SANDSTONE
GNEUDNA FORMATION
NANNYARRA GREYWACKE
FAIRFIELD BEDS
BUGLE GAP LIME-STONE
NAPIER FORMATION
OSCAR FORMATION
FOSSIL DOWNS FORMATION
PILLARA FORMATION
STAR FORMATION
DOTTSWOOD FORMATION
BURDEKIN FORMATION
BROKEN RIVER FORMATION
GRAVEYARD CREEK FORM-ATION (TOP)
PERRY CREEK FORM-ATION (TOP)
TELEMON FORMATION
MOUNT WYATT FORM-ATION
DUNSTABLE FORMATION
SILVER HILLS VOLCANICS
UKALUNDA BEDS
TANGARATTA FORMATION
MANDOWA MUDSTONE
BALDWIN FORMATION
YARRIMIE FORMATION
SILVER GULLY FORMATION
WOGARDI ARGILLITE
DRIK DRIK FORMATION
COPES CREEK KERATOPHYRE
PIPE CLAY CREEK FORMATION
TAMWORTH GROUP
MULGA DOWNS GROUP
AMPHITHEATRE GROUP
COBAR GROUP (TOP)
MURRINDAL LIMESTONE
TARAVALE FORMATION
PYRAMIDS MBR.
BUCHAN CAVES LIMESTONE
SNOWY RIVER VOLCANICS
TAEMAS 'STAGE'
MAJURGONG 'STAGE'
CAVAN 'STAGE'
MURRUMBIDGEE 'SERIES'
SUGARLOAF CREEK TUFFS
KIRAWIN SHALE
MOUNTAIN CREEK VOLCANICS
CANANGLE SUB-GROUP
BLACK ROCK SUB- GROUP
CATOMBAL GROUP
GARRA FORMATION
TOLGA CALCARENITE
CUGA BURGA VOLCANICS
LAMBIE GROUP
NUBRIGYN LIMESTONE
CUNNINGHAM FORMATION
VOLCANICS
BELL SHALE
FLORENCE SANDSTONE
ELDON GROUP
CERBEREAN VOLCANICS
TAGGERTY GROUP
SNOBS CREEK VOLCANICS
CENTENNIAL BEDS
WALHALLA GROUP
NORTON'S CREEK SANDSTONE
WILSON'S CREEK SHALE
EILDON BEDS (TOP)
JORDAN RIVER GROUP
AVON RIVER GROUP
TABBERABBERA FORMATION
WILD HORSE FORMATION
WENTWORTH GROUP
? RAMEKA INTRUSIVES
? RIWAKA METAVOLCANICS
FAULT
BATON FORMATION
UPPER REEFTON QUARTZITE
REEFTON LIMESTONE
REEFTON MUDSTONE
LOWER REEFTON QUARTZITE
FAULT

TABLE 5.1. CORRELATICN TABLE FOR THE DEVONIAN SYSTEM

Platform and the Condobolin High at intervals over their entire length, into the Melbourne and Cobar Troughs, and into the southern part of the Capertee High. For the most part these rocks are massive adamellites, but quartz–mica–diorites and granodiorites are also common. It is important to note that no plutons of this age have been recorded in the New England Geosyncline.

A feature of this period is the abundance of hypabyssals, particularly in eastern Victoria. At Tabberabbera (Talent, 1963), there are several sets of dykes some of which may possibly be post-Givetian, and may have been feeders for the overlying Upper Devonian volcanics. However, the main swarm of quartz diorite, hornblende porphyrite, and quartz–feldspar–porphyrite dykes, is intruded roughly parallel with the strikes of the Wentworth Group, and is of Tabberabberan age. In the Snowy River and Eildon areas also, there are numerous lamprophyre dykes of this age.

During the late Late Devonian (or perhaps Early Carboniferous) there was another period of intrusion in central Victoria associated with the volcanic rocks mentioned above. In this region there are several large cauldron subsidences (Hills, 1959) within which calc-alkaline volcanic piles have been preserved. Some of these structures are up to 40 km across, but most of them are much smaller. Ring dykes of porphyritic granodiorite and quartz porphyry fill their boundary faults. In the Dandenong and Strathbogie Ranges granodiorite plutons are intruded into the Upper Devonian volcanic piles. These intrusives have been regarded as the final phase of the evolution of a granodiorite magma which was differentiating at a shallow depth in the crust and periodically bursting through to produce the effusive rocks (Edwards, 1956; White, 1954).

Some workers believe that serpentines were first intruded at this time in the eastern part of the New England Geosyncline at Baryulgil, Pine Mountain (Ipswich), and in the Mary River Valley. There is no direct evidence in support of this age, and these rocks will be considered in the next chapter. In North Queensland, however, there are two small basic to ultrabasic complexes of probable Early Devonian age, intruded along the Burdekin River Fault. They consist mainly of serpentinite, pyroxenite and gabbro with some diorite, granodiorite and amphibolite.

New Zealand

Little is known of the igneous activity of the Devonian in New Zealand, but some of the porphyrites, meta-basalts, and serpentinites of Nelson are possibly of this age.

CHAPTER 6

The Carboniferous System

THE Carboniferous rocks of eastern Australia were brought forcibly to the attention of the geological world in 1914 when T. W. E. David led the British Association excursion to observe the evidence of glaciation in the neighbourhood of Seaham in the Hunter Valley. Prior to this date the only systematic work on this system in New South Wales was that of Benson on the Great Serpentine Belt further to the north, and that of Etheridge and Dun on collections of fossils from various localities, while in Queensland the monumental investigations of Jack and Etheridge provided almost the only studies of regional scope. Subsequently stratigraphical, structural, and petrographical studies have been completed in both these States and in Victoria also. Recognition of Carboniferous rocks in Western Australia came much later than in the east, though erroneous records are numerous and date back to the turn of the century. Matheson and Teichert made the first authentic discovery in 1945, and later work has revealed widespread and varied sequences which have yielded rich faunal and floral assemblages.

The definition of the system in Australia is a matter which has occasioned much difficulty and many disputes. In most areas there is continuity of deposition from the Devonian into the Carboniferous with a lack of fossils in the region of the boundary, and the choice of the base of the system is thus often arbitrary. Its separation from the Permian is vexed not only by the lack of unanimity in the definition of the type Permian, but also by the lack of adequate palaeontological criteria for the establishment of Late Carboniferous correlations with Europe or America. The situation at present is quite unsatisfactory and it will not be resolved without much more palaeontological study.

The Carboniferous history of New Zealand remains to be elucidated, since no rocks that can be positively identified as belonging to this period have yet been discovered.

STRATIGRAPHY

Australia

LAMBIAN BASINS

During the Late Devonian there was uplift in the **Drummond Basin**, causing a pause in deposition. There appears to have been little or no deformation, for the earliest formation of the Carboniferous Snake Range Group lies with disconformity on the Telemon Formation, and is known to overlap it only slightly at one locality (Veevers *et al.*, 1964*b*). These sediments are oligomictic conglomerates with some interbedded quartz sandstones indicating a change in environment and provenance from that of the Telemon Formation. The sedimentary units are all lenticular and the whole formation, which reaches a maximum thickness of about 900 m, is itself highly irregular in distribution. It was presumably deposited from a stream system which flowed through the basin from south to north. The upper part of the Snake Range Group consists of flaggy feldspathic and lithic sandstones with interbedded siltstones and greenish to purplish mudstones in varying proportions. Along the edge of the Anakie High there are also interbedded basalt flows. The Ducabrook Formation, which conformably overlies the Snake Range Group, varies in thickness from 2000 to 3000 m and consists of interbedded, micaceous, lithic, feldspathic and quartzose sandstones, siltstones, and mudstones. Individual sandstone beds are commonly only 1–2 m thick, and oscillation ripple marks are common. A terrestrial to estuarine environment has been postulated for the formation. The only fossils are plants (*Lepidodendron*) and fish (*Gyracanthides* and *Elonichthys*), indicating an Early Carboniferous age.

At this time the Drummond Basin was confined along its northeastern side by the Anakie High and along its northwestern side by an unnamed structure formed by Lower Palaeozoic sediments, revealed by drilling. However, along its southwestern edge it was probably in connexion with the **Adavale Trough** within which the red and grey sandstones and shales of the Buckabie Formation accumulated. These are known only in the subsurface, but are lithologically very similar to the Ducabrook Formation. The southern limit of the Drummond Basin and Adavale Trough in the Early Carboniferous has not yet been proved but it was probably in the vicinity of the Nebine–Eulo Ridge.

Unconformably overlying the Ducabrook Formation in the Drummond Basin is the 800 m thick terrestrial Joe Joe Formation, most of which is probably Late Carboniferous in age. It would probably be best to regard the Drummond Basin as having become extinct as a result of the deformation after the deposition of the Ducabrook Formation, and to consider the Joe Joe Formation as initiating deposition on a much broader and more stable geotectonic entity, the **Springsure–Corfield Shelf***. This structure will be discussed in more detail in the next chapter. The formation contains no specimens of *Glossopteris*, but there are numerous well-preserved specimens of *Cardiopteris*, and the spores indicate that the unit is older than the Undivided Freshwater Beds at the base of the Springsure Permian sequence. The lower part of the formation consists of conglomerates, conglomeratic mudstone, and quartz-lithic sandstone. Cobbles and boulders are common, some of

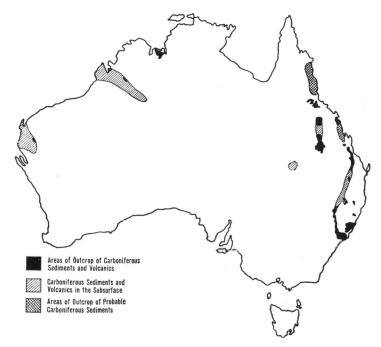

FIG. 6.1. Distribution of Carboniferous strata.

them faceted and striated by ice action. The upper part is fine- to medium-grained, quartz, lithic sandstone, and carbonaceous shale with coaly beds. Some of the finely bedded units have been interpreted as varves. In any case there is ample evidence of shallow-water deposition, and local erosional unconformities are common (Mollan *et al.*, 1964/27; Evans, pers. comm.).

The volcanics on the **Anakie High** in the Douglas Creek area, mentioned in the previous chapter, probably span the Devono-Carboniferous boundary. On the northeastern flank of the high in what is in fact the northwestern corner of the Bowen Basin, there is a thickness of up to 6000 m of acid to intermediate volcanics and thin interbedded tuffaceous sandstones, as yet

*Now generally referred to as the Galilee Basin.

unnamed, outcropping over some 2000–3000 sq km. They unconforrᴉably overlie the rocks of the Anakie High and are possibly conformable on the Mount Wyatt Beds. Probable Upper Devonian plants occur near the base and Lower Carboniferous plants near the top (Malone *el al.*, 1962/72).

FIG. 6.2. Early Carboniferous palaeogeography.

Resting on these volcanics and on the Drummond Beds and the Mount Wyatt and Ukalunda Beds with unconformity, are the Bulgonunna Volcanics. These are a mass of acid flows and pyroclastics, the most common rock type being porphyritic rhyolite. They are unconformably overlain by Permian Middle Bowen sediments, and hence are probably Upper Carboniferous (Malone *et al.*, 1962/72).

As mentioned in the previous chapter the sediments in some of the **Lambian Basins in New South Wales** probably extend into the Lower Carboniferous, but there is insufficient palaeontological evidence to permit the placing of a boundary between the two systems, and there is no lithological break in the sequence.

In the **Grampians Basin** the Grampians Group cannot be accurately dated at the present time, and though part of it is probably Carboniferous, the whole group has been discussed in the previous chapter for the sake of convenience. At the northern end of the **Avon River Basin** near Mansfield there is a sequence of red conglomerates and sandstones of continental origin in which a Lower Carboniferous fish fauna, including *Gyracanthides, Acanthodes, Eupleurogmus, Strepsodus,* and *Elonichthys,* has been found. The extent of the Carboniferous portion of the Avon River Group remains unknown.

NEW ENGLAND GEOSYNCLINE

The known Carboniferous rocks within this structure are largely confined to the Yarrol–Tamworth Trough, though they are also widely distributed along the east coast of New South Wales in the Manning and Macleay Valleys. Opinion is divided on the problem of existence of a structural high bounding the eastern side of Yarrol Basin, but there is agreement that the Tamworth Trough was at least partially confined in the east during a large part of the Carboniferous by the rising New England High. It is convenient, therefore, to treat the rocks of this period in terms of the Yarrol–Tamworth Trough, and basins further east.

At the present time it is not possible to demonstrate that the **Yarrol** and **Tamworth Troughs** united to form a single depression during the Carboniferous, but structural, sedimentary, faunal, and geophysical evidence supports this view. Both western and eastern boundaries of the troughs are faults which were active at least until the Late Mesozoic, and this makes reconstruction of the trough shapes difficult. On the western side the fault is known as the Mulgildie Fault in the north and the Hunter–Mooki Fault in the south, whereas on the eastern side the corresponding structures are the Yarrol and Peel Faults.

It is convenient to divide the **Tamworth Trough** into a northern sector lying north of the Liverpool Range, and a southern sector in the Hunter Valley. There is evidence of uplift along the western margins of the trough at the end of the Devonian. This caused a slight restriction of the area of sedimentation, and on the western edge of the northern sector there is an unconformity (the Onus Creek Unconformity, White, 1965) between the Upper Devonian Baldwin and Tangaratta Formations and the Lower Carboniferous Tulcumba Sandstone. The latter is a cross-stratified feldspathic sandstone with persistent oolitic limestones (Voisey and Williams, 1964). The base of the Carboniferous is not exposed elsewhere on the west, but in the deeper parts of the trough some workers believe that there is a conformable succession from the Devonian into the Carboniferous within the Goonoo Goonoo Mudstone (Crook, 1961*b*); whereas others, dividing the sequence into different units, claim that the Onus Creek Unconformity can be recognized here also, though it does not involve the loss of nearly as much section as further west (White, 1964, 1965). These Lower Carboniferous marine sediments thicken considerably towards the Peel Fault where they reach a maximum of 4500 m, but still further east only scattered, thin, shallow-water Carboniferous successions are known, and nowhere are their bases known to be exposed. In the southern sector the western shoreline is unknown, and relationships to Devonian rocks have not been determined.

In general the rocks of the Tournaisian and lower to middle Viséan are dark green to brown mudstones—the Namoi Formation in the north and the Bingleburra Formation in the south. Interbedded along the western side of the trough are lenticular polymictic conglomerates and crinoidal and oolitic limestones, but further east there are extensive conglomerate, greywacke, and arenite members. The bulk of the detritus was probably derived from the western land mass (Crook, 1964). Fossils are abundant in the coarser detritals and the limestones. The Tulcumba Sandstone contains the brachiopods *Spirifer* and *Quadratia*, the bivalves *Euchondria* and *Palaeoneilo*, and the ammonoids *Protocanites* and *Prionoceras* (*Imitoceras*) indicating a Tournaisian age (Campbell and Engel, 1963). The lower parts of the Namoi and Bingleburra Formations also contain Late Tournaisian to Early Viséan faunas with the brachiopods *Productina*, *Antiquatonia*, *Schuchertella*, *Unispirifer*, *Syringothyris*, and "*Thomasaria*". Middle to upper Viséan faunas including the brachiopods *Werriea*, *Waagenoconcha*, *Echinoconchus*, *Unispirifer*, *Brachythyris*, *Asyrinxia*, *Kitakamithyris*, and *Schizophoria*, the gastropods *Loxonema* and *Straparollus*, and in places the ammonoids *Prolecanites* and *Beyrichoceras* occur near the top of the Namoi and Bingleburra Formations (Campbell, 1957; Roberts, 1965; Brown *et al.*, 1965).

At this time the seas were shallowing over most of the central and southern parts of the trough, and during the late Viséan these areas became the sites of deposition of very coarse terrestrial sediments up to 2500 m thick. Polymictic conglomerates and coarse, pink, cross-bedded lithic sandstones containing a high percentage of volcanic detritus are widespread and rest with apparent conformity, disconformity, or slight angular unconformity on the underlying mudstones (Roberts, 1965). In the north they are known as the Merlewood Formation and in the south as the Wallaringa Formation. They show evidence of terrestrial deposition and of having been derived from contemporaneous volcanic rocks poured out on the relatively high landmass to the west and on the New England High as well as in the trough itself. Many of these andesites, toscanites, and tuffs have been preserved as interbedded members, and around certain centres in the Hunter Valley they form enormous piles up to 2000 m thick, as, for example, in the Gilmore

Volcanics which overlie the Wallaringa Formation. Northwards the incidence of volcanics within the trough decreases, though judging from the related sediments there must have been an extensive volcanic source in the north.

Marine conditions persisted for a longer period in the northern sector, where there is ample evidence of advancing and retreating shorelines with calcareous banks and heavy mineral sands in the Caroda Formation on the western side of the trough, and reef knolls containing the corals *Aphrophyllum*, *Amygdalophyllum*, *Lithostrotion*, and *Syringopora* in the east against the Peel Fault. There were occasional marine transgressions across the Merlewood Formation to the south giving rise to sandstone beds containing small coralline mound reefs.

Probably by the end of Namurian times the whole trough was above sealevel and coarse clastics were everywhere being deposited. Cyclic deposition has been described, and thin coal seams recorded (Rattigan, 1964). Plants, particularly *Lepidodendron* and *Rhacopteris*, are common. Minor occurrences of varved shales and tillites have been recorded in the Mount Johnstone Formation in the south, and in the Spion Kop Conglomerate in the north (White, 1965). However, glacial rocks occupy a progressively greater proportion of all subsequent deposits. Fluvio-glacial conglomerates are the most abundant of these, but tillites and varved shales are also very important rock types. They are known as the Seaham, Currabubula, and Rocky Creek Formations in different areas. There may have been two or more ice advances, but this has not been proved. Contemporaneous volcanicity was widespread. Areas of volcanic eruption and of ice accumulation are thought to have existed in highlands on both east and west of the trough (Voisey, 1957).

As in the Tamworth Trough the earliest Carboniferous sediments in the **Yarrol Trough** are black and dark blue–grey mudstones and shales in most areas, though in the west there are extensive conglomerates (Hill and Denmead, eds., 1960). Many of the mudstones are very hard and siliceous. Wherever the Devono-Carboniferous boundary has been observed, it is conformable. Étroeungtian faunas are more abundant than they are in New South Wales, and in the Rockhampton Group, the Pond Argillites, and the Tellebang Formation, important genera are the brachiopods *Tenticospirifer*, *Sinospirifer*, *Avonia*, and *Megachonetes*, and the ammonoids *Protocanites* and *Pseudarietites*. Later faunas of these formations are essentially similar to those of the Namoi Formation listed above.

As might have been expected from the persistence of marine conditions in the north of the Tamworth Trough, the Viséan uplifts that caused the change from marine to terrestrial conditions at the base of the Merlewood Formation in the Tamworth Trough left most of the Yarrol Trough beneath the sea. Along the western side of the basin, as in the Baywulla Formation near Yarrol and the Mundowran Group near Mundubbera, oolitic and bioclastic limestones, reefs, muddy calcarenites, and conglomerates form the bulk of sediments and reach a maximum thickness of 600 m. In the limestones the corals *Lithostrotion*, *Amygdalophyllum*, *Symplectophyllum*, *Aphrophyllum*, *Michelinia*, and *Syringopora*, and the brachiopods *Delepinea*, *Martinia*, *Unispirifer*, *Inflatia*, *Eomarginifera*, *Marginirugus*, *Schellwienella*, *Rhipidomella*, and *Schizophoria*, and the gastropods *Loxonema*, *Straparollus*, and *Yunnanella* are abundant, and it has been possible to zone the sequence in some detail (Driscoll, 1960; Maxwell, 1961*a*, *b*, 1964). Eastwards in the trough the limestones and coarse terrigenous sediments wedge out and are replaced by olive to grey mudstones with lenses of sandstone and chert as is illustrated by relations within the Mundowran Group (Driscoll, 1960). In this part of the section there is an absence of volcanic flows and tuffs, a feature which accords well with the northerly decrease in volcanism in the Tamworth Trough.

At the end of the Viséan and perhaps during part of the Namurian there was a period of general uplift, as a result of which the area around and north of Rockhampton became land, and the western margin of the trough migrated eastwards. In the Rockhampton–Mount Morgan district coarse (possibly partly terrestrial) conglomerates composed of well-rounded boulders of plutonic and volcanic rocks, spread disconformably across the Viséan marine sediments. They are known as the Neerkol and Turner Creek Conglomerates. In the trough at Yarrol, marine sedimentation continued, but the sediments of the Branch Creek Formation are much coarser in general than are the underlying rocks. A little further west at Cania the corresponding conglomerates are massive. All of these rudites are attributed to tectonic activity. There is no evidence of glaciation.

Following this episode marine mudstones were deposited across the conglomerates—the Neerkol Mudstones and the Poperima Formation. They contain the distinctive brachiopod *Levipustula* and several distinctive species of the polyzoan genera *Polypora*, *Fenestella*, and *Fistulamina*. The age is probably Westphalian. Near Yarrol the Poperima Formation thickens from about 250 m in the west to 400 m in the east. To complete the period, there was uplift in the north and the Neerkol shales are disconformably overlain by the terrestrial Dinner Creek Conglomerate which contain *Glossopteris* whereas around Yarrol conditions remained marine and the Rands Formation of shales, cherts, arkoses, and muddy arenites, in all 1600 m thick, was deposited. Bivalves, particularly *Oriocrassatella*, *Limipecten*, and *Schizodus*, are abundant. No volcanics or glacial deposits are known. The absence of the latter could be due either to latitude or to the moderating effects of the sea which had been completely excluded from the Tamworth Trough at this time, or both of these factors together.

The Tamworth Trough was partly constricted where it passed through the southern end of the New England High, but it was in communication with the great Manning–Macleay Basin to the east. In this area of confluence, the **East Coast Trough**, which covers approximately the area east of the meridian of Maitland, the southern margin of the basin had a similar history to the area west of the New England High, but to the northeast, that is further out in the basin, a different pattern of events has been recorded. (It must be emphasized that there was no break in deposition between this area and that of the Tamworth Trough to the west, and that no sharp boundary can be drawn between them. In fact many stratigraphic units are common to both areas.) Throughout most of the eastern area the Tournaisian and lower Viséan sediments are dark argillites, including many turbidites, which attain a thickness of 8000–10,000 m in the east (for example the Wootton Beds), but are generally much thinner. In most areas similar sediments continued to accumulate throughout the Viséan, but on the Girvan Platform volcanic lithic sandstones and conglomerates with some oolitic limestones and acid lavas began to accumulate during the latter part of the Viséan. They are known as the Conger and McRae Formations. On the eastern side of the platform toscanites and andesites form a massive unit, the Nerong Volcanics, which is up to 800 m thick (Engel, 1962). Important faunas in this interval are successively characterized by the brachiopods *Delepinea*, *Rhipidomella*, *Fluctuaria*, and *Marginirugus*. The trilobite *Linguaphillipsia* and the ammonoid *Beyrichoceras* are associated with the *Rhipidomella* fauna. Similar faunas are known in the mudstones off the margins of the platform where there are no volcanic flows.

During the Namurian there was a general increase in the coarseness of the sediments over the whole basin. In places some of the conglomerates were terrestrial, but generally they were marine. All contain large quantities of volcanic detritus. On the Girvan Platform they are known as the Karuah and lower Crawford Formations which are about 300 m thick, and in the Manning and Macleay Valleys they form the lower parts of the Kullatine "Series". Although it is not yet proved, it is probable that this part of the section contains several disconformities. The bivalve *Oriocrassatella* is especially abundant, and the ammonoid *Cravenoceras* is known. At about this time also a trough began to develop northwards through Drake to Mount Barney in Queensland.

The pattern of sedimentation during the Westphalian and part of the Stephanian was a diversified one. Across the Girvan Platform there were large areas receiving only muds (the Booral Formation), and others receiving lithic sands and muds alternately (the upper Crawford Formation and Isaacs Formations). In the Manning and Macleay Valleys, the Kullatine "Series" with coarse sandstones, conglomerates, tillites, and some mudstones was accumulating. The so-called tillites are marine, in some instances at least, and are thought to be an inshore deposit beneath sea ice. The Kullatine "Series" is up to 2000 m thick. In the Drake Trough up to 2000 m of mudstones, muddy sandstones, tuffaceous sandstones, and conglomerates were deposited (Hill and Denmead, eds., 1960). They are all marine. Two important faunas make their appearance—the lower (Westphalian) dominated by the brachiopods *Levipustula, Spinuliplica, Neospirifer, Alispirifer,* and *Kitakamithyris,* and the upper (probably Stephanian) dominated by *Syringothyris* and *Kitakamithyris.* The former is very widespread, being known over the whole region, while the latter is restricted to the south.

Deposition of the Kullatine "Series" persisted to the end of the period, and it is overlain with apparent conformity by the *Eurydesma*-bearing Yessabah Limestone and its equivalents. The sediments of the Drake Trough also pass conformably up into the Permian. On the Girvan Platform, however, the period ended with enormous outpourings of basalts and fluidal rhyolites (the Gloucester and Alum Mountain Volcanics) which reach thicknesses of more than 1000 m. The Permian on this structure is non-marine and is unconformable on the volcanics.

North Queensland Basins

The geological pattern of the Late Devonian probably persisted into the Early Carboniferous in the Hodgkinson Trough, but there were several significant modifications in the basins along the old Burdekin Shelf. In the **Star Basin**, the uppermost parts of the Star Beds may be of Tournaisian age, but there is no evidence of later deposition. Early in the Carboniferous, however, the **Clarke River** and **Bundock Basins** began to subside and in each great thicknesses of shallow-water marine and terrestrial sediments accumulated. These show regional overlap, with disconformity on the Middle Devonian, and angular unconformity on the Lower Devonian and older rocks. The sequence in the two basins is similar, though the Bundock Creek Formation with almost 7000 m of sediment reaches three times the thickness of the Clarke River Formation. At the base of each sequence there are micaceous siltstones, quartzose sandstones, and arkoses, with minor fossiliferous calcarenites. The brachiopods *Brachythyris* and *Avonia*, the bivalves *Crenipecten* and *Leiopteria*, and euomphalid and turreted gastropods indicate a Tournaisian age. The higher parts of these units are thought to be entirely terrestrial in origin and consist of quartzose, lithic, and feldspathic arenites, the coarser beds of which are current-bedded on a large scale, polymictic conglomerates and micaceous siltstones, together with some tuffs and occasional basic lavas. In the Clarke River Basin the plants *Calamites, Rhacopteris, Sigillaria, Stigmaria,* and *Lepidodendron* are common. It is possible that some of these rocks are as young as Namurian.

WEST COAST BASINS

The **Bonaparte Gulf Basin** is divided into two structures, the small Burt Range Sub-Basin in the southeast, and the much larger Carlton Sub-Basin in the north and northwest. They are separated by the Precambrian rocks of the Pincombe Range. Along most of its eastern boundary the Carboniferous is downfaulted against the Precambrian, though in places there is possibly some onlap. The lowest outcropping Carboniferous unit is the Burt Range Formation, a shallow-water sequence of calcarenites and minor well-sorted quartz sandstones, up to 700 m thick, which is known only from the Burt Range Sub-Basin. It contains Lower Carboniferous shelly faunas, and species of the conodonts *Ozarkodina, Ligonodina, Lonchodina,* and *Pseudopolygnathus* (Glenister, 1960; Thomas, 1962b; Veevers *et al.,* 1964c). In the Burt Range Sub-Basin this is followed by the clean quartzose sandstones of the Enga Sandstone, and then by the richly fossiliferous Septimus Limestone. The latter unit also consists of calcarenites and quartzose sandstones, and it contains the brachiopods *Rhipidomella, Leptagonia, Unispirifer, Punctospirifer, Pustula,* and *Schellwienella;* the gastropods *Straparollus* and *Baylea;* the conodonts *Cavusgnathus, Spathognathodus,* and *Hindeodella;* and the ostracods *Bairdia, Paraparchites,* and *Macrocypris* (Thomas, 1962a, b). A late Osagean (Viséan) age has been suggested for these faunas. Then follow the black shales of the Milligans Beds and the arenites of the Point Spring Sandstone (Veevers *et al.,* 1964c).

In the Carlton Sub-Basin there is a major unconformity below an unnamed unit of sandstone, siltstone, shale, and dolomite. This is followed conformably by the Point Spring Sandstone which covers most of this sub-basin and extends as a tongue down into the Burt Range Sub-Basin. The sediments are predominantly cross-bedded coarse- to fine-grained sandstones with some siltstones and thin detrital limestones. The fauna includes the brachiopods *Dictyoclostus, Schellwienella, Syringothyris,* and *Spirifer* sp. aff. *S. bisulcatus,* and the ostracods *Carboprimitia, Paraparchites, Macronotella,* and *Cryptophyllus.* It is probably Namurian.

Recent drilling in the deeper parts of the sub-basin (Bonaparte Nos. 1 and 2) has shown that below the Point Spring Sandstone there is a section of about 1800 m of black shales with some thin sandstones and dolomites towards the top. These show no apparent break in deposition and are probably offshore correlatives of the carbonate-quartzose sandstone succession in the Burt Range area. Unconformably below them are shales with interbedded sandstones and carbonates.

The Lower Carboniferous of the **Canning Basin** is restricted to the Fitzroy Depression, along the northern edge of which it is approximately 500 m thick. It probably rests with slight unconformity on the Upper Devonian.

Towards the axis of the trough thicknesses in excess of 700 m have been observed. Shallow-water siltstones and sandy calcarenites are the dominant sediments forming the only unit recognized, the Laurel Formation. Brachiopods (*Unispirifer, Pustula, Linoproductus, Schuchertella, Eomartiniopsis,* and *Cleiothyridina*), ostracods (*Bairdia, Cavellina, Knoxiella, Paraparchites, Acratia, Glyptopleurites,* and *Graphiadactyllis*), conodonts (*Prionodina, Hindeodella, Gnathodus, Ligonodina,* and *Cavusgnathus*), and an ammonoid (*Imitoceras*) occur, the brachiopods and ostracods being the most abundant. It is thought that the upper Tournaisian and lower Viséan are represented but that the lower Tournaisian is everywhere absent.

Later Carboniferous sediments do not outcrop, but 1500–2000 m of alternating sandstone, siltstone, and shale, with some dolomite and anhydrite (the Anderson Formation), are known from bores in the Fitzroy Trough. These rocks are thought to have accumulated at least partly under estuarine conditions. Fossils include the non-marine bivalves *Naiadites* and *Anthracosia,* the conchostracan *Leaia* (*Hemicycloleaia*), the brachiopod *Lingula,* the plants *Bothrodendron* and *Protolepidodendron,* and spores of the "Lycosporoid"-Microflora (Balme, 1960a, 1964). A Westphalian age is generally accepted. The Grant Formation unconformably overlies them. Its lower part contains the "Lycosporoid"-Microflora also, and may therefore be Stephanian in age.

Shallow-water sediments of Early Carboniferous age conformably overlie the Upper Devonian which outcrops along the eastern edge of the **Carnarvon Basin.** The sequence consists of 300–400 m of poorly sorted, cross-stratified micaceous sandstones, siltstones, and conglomerates laid down under deltaic conditions, sandwiched between two much thinner units composed dominantly of limestone. The lowest formation, the Moogooree Limestone, is well bedded in units of 2–60 cm thick, and includes both detrital and chemically precipitated layers. Silicified specimens of the brachiopods *Syringothyris, Unispirifer, Streptorhynchus, Rhipidomella,* and *Camarotoechia,* and the polyzoan *Fenestella* are common, and indicate an Early Carboniferous age (Thomas, 1962a). With the partial withdrawal of the seas, delta deposits of lesser extent than the underlying rocks were laid down. These belong to the Williambury Formation, a suite of friable, cross-bedded lithic sandstones, with conglomerates and reddish siltstones. Fossils are absent.

The upper limestone-bearing unit, the Yindagindy Formation, consists of thin beds of hard oolitic limestone interbedded with quartz sandstones and occasional conglomerates. There is a transition between it and the underlying formation. The unit is slightly transgressive to the south indicating submergence of the Williambury delta. Fossils are not particularly abundant but include brachiopods, crinoids, gastropods, and ostracods, thought to indicate a Dinantian age though details are not yet available. The total thickness of all outcropping Carboniferous formations is 800 m.

Rocks of the same age are known to occur at depth within the basin, but few details of their character and distribution have been discovered apart from the fact that they, too, are siltstones and sandstones, probably of shallow-water origin. The available evidence is consistent with the view that the basin was a shallow-water shelf area at this time, sediments being received from relatively stable land to the east.

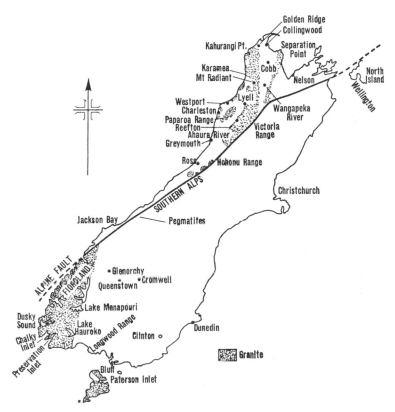

FIG. 6.3. Distribution of granitic rocks in the South Island of New Zealand. (After Reed, 1958.)

New Zealand

In spite of the relatively large size of this system in terms of absolute time and its widespread distribution throughout the world, no rocks of this age have been positively identified in the Dominion. The very considerable thickness of the volcanic–sedimentary sequence below the Upper Permian sediments in the Takitimu Ranges of Southland has been regarded by many geologists as extending downwards into the Carboniferous System, but Waterhouse (1958*b*) has shown that, even well down in this sequence, the fossils present are still of Permian age (early Sakmarian).

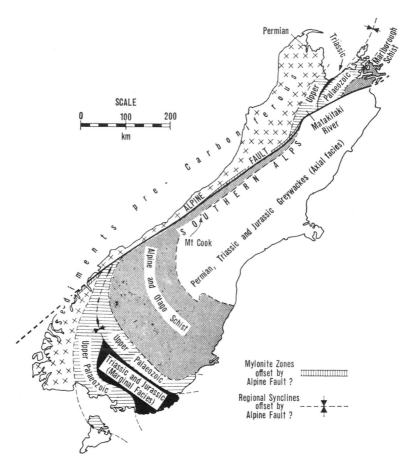

Fig. 6.4. Structural trends in the pre-Cretaceous sediments of the New Zealand Geosyncline. (After Grindley, *N.Z.J. Geol. Geophys.* **6**, 872–930, 1963.)

It is very probable also that Carboniferous formations, the diagnostic characters of which have been obliterated by later tectonic movements, are present in the metamorphic belts of the South Island (see below under Alpine Metamorphics).

A number of igneous bodies has been correlated on somewhat tenuous grounds with the Carboniferous System. For instance, the Separation Point Granite of the northwestern part of the South Island is believed to transect

Devonian formations, and pebbles of a similar rock type occur in the Lower Permian sediments of east Nelson. Reed (1958, p. 61), however, suggests that this granite probably intrudes Permian volcanics and he includes it in his post-Permian group. Some of the Fiordland intrusions (Deas Cove Granite, Cameron Granodiorite) are probably also of Carboniferous age and the Longwood Complex of basic and ultramafic intrusives in Southland is most probably in part, at least, Late Carboniferous (see Fig. 6.3).

ALPINE METAMORPHICS (Figs. 6.4, 6.6)

In discussing this very important and extensive group of rocks at this point it is not meant to imply that they are necessarily of Carboniferous age, and it is, in fact, known that they include sediments containing Permian, Triassic, and Jurassic fossils. For the purposes of this discussion the term "metamorphics" is taken to include the rocks of the Chlorite 1 subzone of Hutton and Turner, namely the "Alpine Greywackes" (Turner, 1938; Hutton, 1940; Mason, 1962).

As pointed out by Suggate (1961), these rocks constitute a major portion of the outcrops in the South Island and ". . . form three main belts, non-schistose sediments lying both to the east and discontinuously to the west of a schist belt". To the non-schistose sediments of the eastern belt he applied the term "Torlesse Group", and to the schistose rocks of the New Zealand Geosyncline in which this deposition took place, he gave the name "Haast Schist Group".

It appears likely that in Carboniferous times a geosynclinal trough (the precursor of the New Zealand Geosyncline) lay with its axis to the west of the present New Zealand area (cf. Fig. 8.5 (p. 232)). Through the period from Early Permian to Late Jurassic, this geosynclinal axis lay approximately along the line of the present mountain axis or, if the transcurrent nature of the Alpine Fault is real, to the east of its former position. It is probable, therefore, that during the evolution and eventual collapse of the geosyncline during the Late Jurassic–Early Cretaceous Rangitata Orogeny, the oldest sediments in the trough were converted to the various grades of schists in the Haast Schist Group. These are high-stress, low-temperature metamorphic rocks of original greywacke composition now altered to chlorite–muscovite–quartz–albite schists, biotite–quartz–albite schists and biotite–garnet–quartz–oligoclase gneisses, divided into three main zones on the basis of index minerals, namely chlorite, biotite, and garnet or oligoclase (see Hutton, 1940; Fyfe *et al.*, 1958).

Waterhouse (1964a) also supports the view that some of the less metamorphosed, unfossiliferous sedimentary sequences underlying known Lower Permian rocks in the Nelson, Waipahi, and Eglinton regions are probably of

168   *The Geological Evolution of Australia and New Zealand*

Carboniferous age. In the Nelson region, the Pelorus Group of Chlorite 1 semischists lies between the Haast (Marlborough) Schists and the Lower Permian Lee River Group. The Tuapeka Group in the Waipahi District occupies the same position between the Otago Schists and the Waipahi Group, and in the Eglinton region of northwest Otago, the Caples Group of semischists appears to separate the main Haast Schist belt from the Humboldt Group. In every case, however, the relations between these various units are by no means conformable, and a good deal of tectonic disturbance is frequently involved. Much structural work remains to be done before the complex stratigraphical relations of the Alpine Metamorphics can be deciphered.

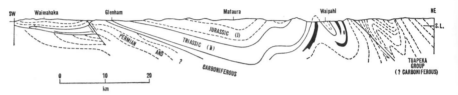

FIG. 6.5. Geological section across the Southland Syncline, New Zealand.
(After Wood, 1952.)

PALAEONTOLOGY AND CLIMATE

No biostratigraphic subdivision of the Carboniferous of Western Australia has yet been published, but in both Queensland and New South Wales it is becoming possible to recognize a sequence of widespread faunal assemblages. It is not possible to recognize these assemblages in all areas—for example the basal Tournaisian zones are known only from the northern part of the Yarrol Basin. Most of the biostratigraphic work has been based on brachiopods and corals, but bivalves have also been used in recent works. Currently known ranges of the most important species are given in Table 6.1. Particularly in the Stephanian, they are not precise.

The most striking feature of the Dinantian biotas of Australia is their large cosmopolitan element. Among the invertebrates, the corals *Lithostrotion, Michelinia,* and *Syringopora;* the brachiopods *Inflatia, Eomarginifera, Productina, Echinoconchus, Pustula, Schizophoria, Rhipidomella, Unispirifer,* and *Delepinea;* the polyzoans *Polypora* and *Fenestella;* the bivalves *Euchondria, Palaeoneilo, Panenka,* and *Polidevcia;* the gastropods *Yunnanella, Retispira, Loxonema,* and *Straparollus;* the ammonoids *Prionoceras (Imitoceras), Protocanites, Prolecanites,* and *Beyrichoceras;* the conodonts *Hindeodella,* "*Ctenognathus*", *Ozarkodina,* and *Lonchodina;* and the ostracods *Bairdia, Glyptopleura, Paraparchites,* and *Cryptophyllus,* to mention only a few genera, contribute to this cosmopolitan group. Although there are several endemic genera, and others

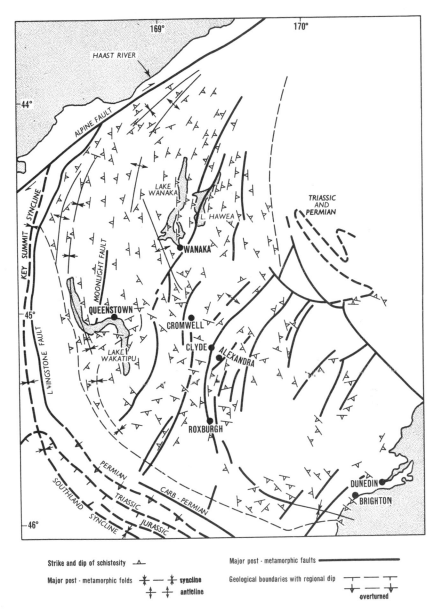

Strike and dip of schistosity

Major post - metamorphic folds — syncline

anticline

Major post - metamorphic faults

Geological boundaries with regional dip

overturned

FIG. 6.6. Post-metamorphic faults and folds in the Otago schists, New Zealand. (After Wood, 1963.)

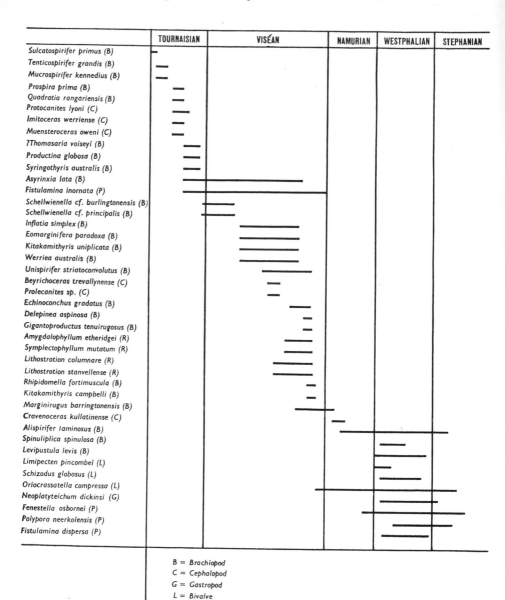

TABLE 6.1. SPECIES-RANGE TABLE FOR AUSTRALIAN CARBONIFEROUS FOSSILS.
(ÉTROEUNGTIAN FAUNAS ARE INCLUDED IN BASAL TOURNAISIAN).

which indicate provincial relationships with southeast and east Asia (the coral *Amygdalophyllum*, and the brachiopod *Asyrinxia*) or America (the brachiopod *Marginirugus*), there is much evidence to suggest open migration routes to Europe, Asia, and America for the whole of the Dinantian and at least part of the Namurian Epoch. Both shelly faunas and corals have been successfully used in zonation.

Lower Carboniferous vertebrate fossils are rare but are known from both Victoria and Queensland. The acanthodians *Gyracanthides* and *Acanthodes* and the actinopterygian *Elonichthys* are the commonest genera, and the faunas as a whole are quite comparable with those of Europe and North America except that they are less varied (Hills, 1958a).

In Westphalian times new and markedly provincial faunas developed in eastern Australia. They are completely lacking in compound corals, fusulinids, ammonoids, and other groups common in the northern continents at this time. The range of genera present is very small, though the faunas in themselves are rich in specimens. Relationships are with Argentina where almost identical assemblages occur (Amos, 1958, 1961). The most abundant genera are the brachiopods *Levipustula* (also known from Europe), *Spinuliplica*, *Spiriferellina*, *Neospirifer*, *Kitakamithyris*, *Alispirifer*, and *Booralia*, and the polyzoans *Fenestella*, *Polypora*, and *Fistulamina*. No faunas of this type are yet known from Western Australia where only a few specimens of *Leaia* and *Naiadites* are recorded.

The Dinantian, and perhaps part of the Namurian, are characterized by the *Lepidodendron veltheimianum* flora which is dominated by species of *Lepidodendron*, but also includes *Ulodendron*, *Stigmaria*, and *Pitys*. The succeeding *Rhacopteris* flora, which to date is recorded only from eastern Australia, is richer in genera and species, but species of *Rhacopteris* and the related *Cardiopteris* are by far the most abundant. A few elements such as *Clepsydropsis* are common to both floras. Recent work suggests that the *Rhacopteris* flora is of Namurian to Late Carboniferous age. One feature is the absence of *Neuropteris*, *Pecopteris*, and *Alethopteris* which are so common in the northern hemisphere floras of this age.

Spores are known from both Western Australia and Queensland (Balme, 1960a, 1964; Evans, pers. comm.). In the Lower Carboniferous, *Auroraspora Punctatisporites*, *Cyclogranisporites*, *Endosporites*, and *Leiotriletes* occur among others and indicate relationships with the U.S.A. and U.S.S.R. Spores of Late Carboniferous age are known from the Anderson Formation in Western Australia and the Joe Joe Formation in Queensland. The Anderson Formation is dominated by cf. *Lycospora* which is absent from the earlier assemblages, and the Joe Joe contains the first occurrence of the *Nuskoisporites* flora (it occurs with abundant *Cardiopteris*), and is younger than the Anderson (Evans, pers. comm.). It seems probable that the Australian post-Tournaisian microfloras indicate the existence of a flora different from any existing contemporaneously in the Northern Hemisphere (Balme, 1964).

Both the widespread invertebrate fauna alluded to above and the extensive occurrences of limestones of chemical origin indicate that most of the continent enjoyed a warm climate until the Namurian. The earliest evidences of glaciation are those in the Namurian Spion Kop Conglomerate of northeastern New South Wales (White, 1965), and it is probable that at this time the ice was restricted to this region. The evidence of glacial marine deposits in the Manning and Macleay valleys indicates the presence of ice at sealevel even at this early date, and makes an explanation in terms of a small mountain glaciation difficult. This abrupt climatic change may be related to the

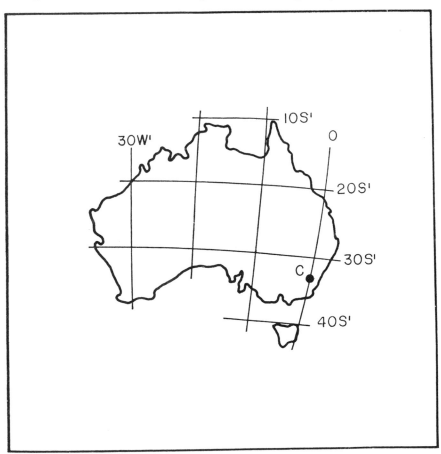

Fig. 6.7. Carboniferous (Lower Kuttung) palaeolatitudes and palaeomeridians based on Canberra. Reliability C. (After Irving, 1964, by permission of John Wiley & Sons Inc.)

sudden change in position of the pole relative to the Australian continent shown in Figs. 6.7–6.9 (Irving, 1964). Glaciation continued through the Westphalian and into the Stephanian in northeastern New South Wales; and if the basal parts of the so-called Permian glacials (which are discussed

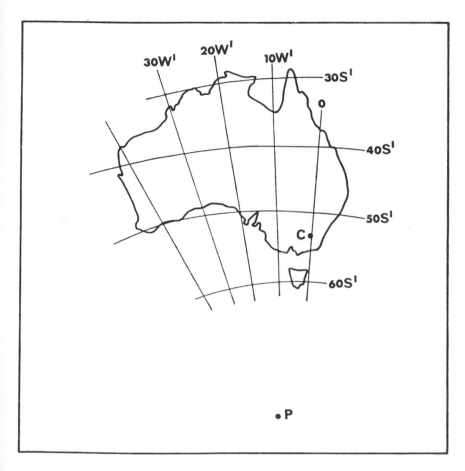

Fɪɢ. 6.8. Carboniferous (Paterson toscanite) palaeolatitudes. Reliability C. (After Irving, 1964, by permission of John Wiley & Sons Inc.)

in the next chapter) are proved to be uppermost Carboniferous, as seems quite possible, all the continent except the northeastern corner must have been affected by ice by the end of the Stephanian. Whether this glaciation was continuous or periodic cannot at present be decided definitely, though there is some evidence of interglacial deposits in New South Wales.

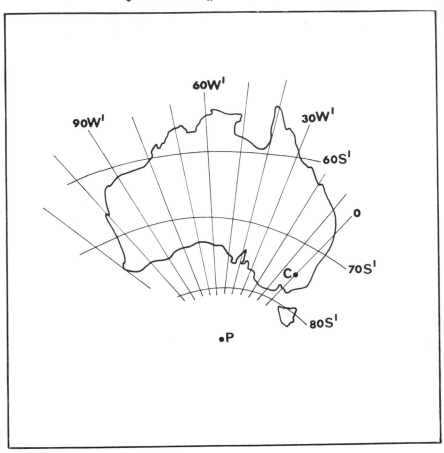

FIG. 6.9. Carboniferous (Glacial Stage) palaeolatitudes. Reliability B. (After Irving, 1964, by permission of John Wiley & Sons Inc.)

TECTONISM AND IGNEOUS ACTIVITY

The continent, except for the Tasman geosynclinal zone, was relatively stable tectonically and free from igneous activity during the Carboniferous. In Western Australia there are disconformities or low-angle unconformities between Lower Permian and Lower Carboniferous rocks in the Carnarvon and Canning Basins, and there are minor angular unconformities, disconformities, and onlaps within the Lower Carboniferous sequence around the margins of the Bonaparte Gulf Basin (Veevers *et al.*, 1964*c*). Much of the movement appears to have been epeirogenic, but in the Fitzroy Trough and on the Derby Ramp of the Canning Basin, and along the eastern margin of the Carnarvon Basin, gentle folds and fairly extensive faults were developed

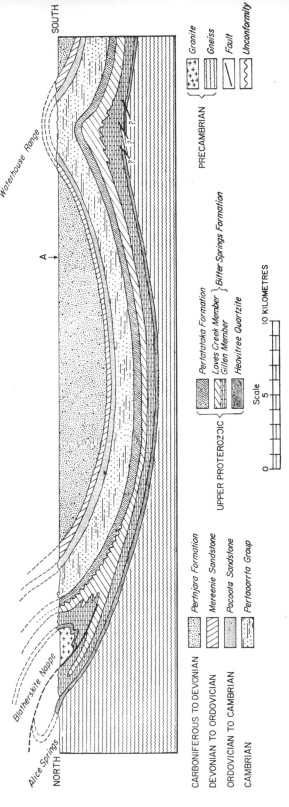

Fig. 6.10. Cross-section through the Amadeus Basin from Alice Springs to the Waterhouse Range, showing the structure of the Blatherskite Nappe and the Waterhouse Anticline. At Point A, an offset of 22·5 km has been made to enable both structures to be shown in the one diagram. Vertical and horizontal scales are equal. (After A. J. Stewart, unpubl.)

after Early Carboniferous and before Sakmarian times. No Carboniferous plutonics are known from Western Australia.

Diastrophic movements affected most of the Tasman Orthogeosyncline at intervals throughout the Carboniferous, and both volcanic and plutonic rocks were associated with them. These movements are together referred to as the **Kanimblan Orogeny**. As yet the accuracy of dating does not permit the recognition of phases, if, indeed, such exist.

The Lambian Basins and the New England Geosyncline have markedly different tectonic and magmatic histories during the Carboniferous. It is probable that by the end of the Devonian the Lambian Basins were becoming disrupted by both faulting and folding. This was certainly the case in the Avon River Basin and in the small downfaulted basins in the deformed Melbourne Trough, where there was extensive volcanism accompanying the faulting, and also in the Drummond Basin where uplift produced changes in the provenance of the sediments. At this time also the western edge of the Tamworth–Yarrol Trough was becoming deformed and the erosion of Upper Devonian rocks was proceeding. Further out in the trough there was shallowing, and in places minor structural breaks occurred, though nowhere was there subaerial erosion.

During the Early Carboniferous all the Lambian Basins were deformed to such an extent that deposition in them had effectively ceased before the Namurian. The folds formed were meridionally oriented, elongate, open synclines and anticlines, usually with the flanks dipping at less than 45°. Higher dips are generally associated with faults. There was little contemporaneous volcanism over most of the region, but along the more mobile area between the Lambian Basins and the Tamworth–Yarrol Trough volcanic rocks were erupted in quantity. Many of these were eroded and redeposited in the trough, and most of those that remain are now covered by Permian and Mesozoic sediments. However, they are known near the northern end of the Drummond and Bowen Basins and in the Sydney Basin near Rylstone, as well as in the Tamworth Trough itself. More volcanics were extruded along the New England High which was rising at this time. The predominant rock types are toscanites, dellenites, hornblende and augite andesites, and some rhyolites forming a typical calc-alkaline suite. Ignimbrites and tuffs of various kinds are common. Into this same area at about the same time were intruded granodiorites, the edges of which now appear from beneath the Permian sediments along the western edge of the Sydney Basin, and are known in the subsurface near Roma and further west in Queensland (Webb *et al.*, 1963). However, not all the Lower Carboniferous granites were restricted to this site. In the areas occupied by the Lambian Basins there are many plutonic masses. For example, stocks of granodiorite intrude the Grampians Group (Spencer-Jones, 1965); batholiths, which are mainly granodiorite, cut across

Table 6.2. Correlation Table for Carboniferous System.

Stage	WESTERN AUSTRALIA			North Queensland Basins	QUEENSLAND			Tamworth Trough		NEW SOUTH WALES		
	Bonaparte Gulf Basin	Canning Basin	Carnarvon Basin		Drummond Basin	Yarrol Trough — Mount Morgan	Yarrol Trough — Yarrol	Rocky Creek Syncline	Werrie Syncline — Nundle	Hunter Valley	Manning–Macleay Rivers	Myall Valley
STEPHANIAN		Anderson Formation	Harris Sandstone		Joe Joe Formation	Dinner Creek Conglomerate	Rands Formation	Lark Hill Formation	Currabubula Formation	Seaham Formation	Kullatine "Series"	Crawford Formation / Conger Formation / Nerong Volcanics / Basal Crawford Fm.
WESTPHALIAN						Neerkol Beds	Poperima Formation	Rocky Creek Conglomerate / Clifden Formation / Ermelo Andesitic Tuff / Spion Kop Conglomerate	Doeypoly Conglomerate	Paterson Volcanics / Mount Johnstone Formation		Wootton Beds
NAMURIAN	Point Spring Sandstone		Yindagindy Formation	Bundock Formation	Ducabrook Sandstone	Turner Creek Conglomerate / Branch Creek Formation		Caroda Formation	Merlewood Formation / Goonoo Goonoo Mudstone (upper part)	Gilmore Volcanics / Wallaringa Formation / Wiragulla Beds	Boonanghi "Series"	
VISÉAN	Septimus Limestone / Enga Sandstone	Laurel Formation	Williambury Formation	Clarke River Formation	Mount Hall Conglomerate / Raymond Sandstone (Snake Range Group)	Neils Creek Clastics	Baywulla Formation	Namoi Formation	Namoi Formation / Tulcumba Sandstone	Formation		
TOURNAISIAN	Burt Range Limestone		Moogooree Limestone			Pond Argillites	Tellebang Formation	Luton Formation		Bingleburra Formation		

KUTTUNG GROUP

the Tabberabberan structures of the Melbourne Trough; and adamellite bosses are known in the Raymond Sandstone, and granite, diorite and gabbro masses are known in the Drummond Beds and the Bulgonunna Volcanics of the Drummond Basin (Malone *et al.*, 1962/72; Veevers *et al.*, 1964*b*). It is also possible that granites were being intruded into the rising New England High at this time, for example, the Hillgrove Granite.

The duration of the movements in the Lambian area has not yet been determined, but in the New England Geosyncline, where there was no major diastrophism, they continued on into the Late Carboniferous as is shown by the continuing change in basin and platform development. Volcanics were extruded over wide areas of New South Wales, and they probably originated from the New England High as well as from the western margin of the geosyncline. Fluidal rhyolites and basalts are found in all areas.

Finally, some authors have suggested that during the movements at the end of the Early Carboniferous the first ultrabasic intrusions associated with the Great Serpentine Belt of New South Wales were emplaced (Benson, 1913; Carey and Browne, 1938), though a Permian age is now considered to be more likely.

The North Queensland Basins continued their independent evolution. The rocks of the Hodgkinson Trough were probably uplifted, folded, metamorphosed, and thrust against the Georgetown Block during the Carboniferous, the Palmerville fault becoming reversed (De Keyser, 1963). In the Broken River Embayment there was continued subsidence of the Bundock Basin along marginal faults, and possibly similar movements occurred around the other basins. It is thought that the barrier between the Bundock, Clarke River, and Star Basins was formed during the Early Carboniferous (White, 1961); and it is probable that the folding of the Devono–Carboniferous sediments into domes and basins, which in general are related to the orientation of the marginal faults, took place in the Late Carboniferous.

During the deposition of the Pertnjarra Formation the deformation of the Amadeus Basin and the uplift of the Arunta Massif continued. The folding reached a climax in the Carboniferous when the entire basin was affected, and some complex structures were formed (Fig. 6.10). In general the folds are broad and open in the north-central part of the basin where the greatest thickness of Pertnjarra Formation occurs, but to the south and along the northern margin dips are steep and many structures have steeply overturned limbs. The general trend of the folds is between east and eastsoutheast. Rapid changes of plunge are common. Some of the complication in the folding is probably due to further development of the décollement on the Bitter Springs Formation (Wells *et al.*, 1965*c*). At this time there was also strong strike thrust-faulting, and throws of the order of 4000 m have been estimated. Minor oblique reverse faulting also occurred.

CHAPTER 7

The Permian System

THE Permian rocks of Australia have long excited interest for four main reasons. In the first place, they are an important source of coal, and recently they have been extensively explored for petroleum; then, on a continent-wide scale they contain evidences of glaciation which are among the best preserved of their age in the world; third, they cover a vast area of the country; and, finally, the faunas and floras are of characteristic Gondwana type and are very profuse.

In New Zealand, on the other hand, Permian rocks have been known for a much shorter period of time than those in Australia. It is true that, to date, they have produced no clear evidence of glacial activity, but within the extraordinarily complete marine faunal sequence recently revealed, it is possible to match the climatic variations observed in the Australian sequence quite closely. The New Zealand marine Permian, moreover, promises on present indications to provide a sorely needed reference section for Gondwana and Indo-Pacific correlations.

This problem of correlation with northern hemisphere sequences has bedevilled Australian investigations since the earliest days, and as a result the rocks dealt with in the Australian section have been variously referred to the Carboniferous, Permian, Permo-Carboniferous, and even to a locally defined system, the Kamilaroi. As is indicated below, the boundaries of the Permian System in both countries cannot yet be precisely defined, but it is now possible to make closer approximations than previously as a result of work in the fields of palynology and invertebrate palaeontology.

The Permian is also notable for the marked deepening of the New Zealand Geosyncline, a structural trough which may be termed the birthplace of the country and in the axial portions of which there continued to accumulate, until Jurassic times, those sediments now represented by the so-called "Alpine Greywackes". These rocks now outcrop over an area exceeding 20 per cent of the total surface.

STRATIGRAPHY

Australia

NEWCASTLE GEOSYNCLINE

The Newcastle Geosyncline (Voisey, 1959*a*, *b*) is a broad downwarp extending through eastern Australia from latitudes 20°–35°S. At its northern end it is known locally as the Bowen Basin and at its southern end as the Sydney Basin. Between these two basins it is covered by Mesozoic and later

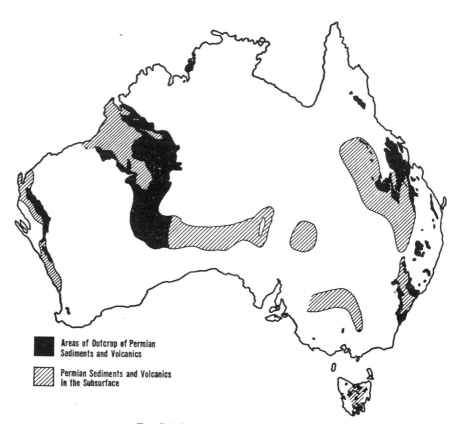

Areas of Outcrop of Permian
Sediments and Volcanics

Permian Sediments and Volcanics
In the Subsurface

FIG. 7.1. Distribution of Permian strata.

deposits and sedimentary continuity in Permian times has not been established. However, although the Permian sequence is known to be thinning out towards the State border from both north and south, both geophysical and drilling evidence supports the view that there was a sedimentary connexion between the basins at least during part of the period.

The **Bowen Basin** is a complex structure in which several well-defined tectonic elements have in a large measure controlled the deposition. The main outlines of the basin have been given (Hill and Denmead, eds., 1960, pp. 184–212), but many subsequent modifications have resulted from the work

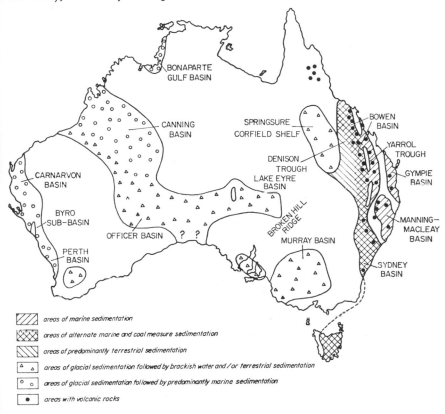

areas of marine sedimentation

areas of alternate marine and coal measure sedimentation

areas of predominantly terrestrial sedimentation

areas of glacial sedimentation followed by brackish water and / or terrestrial sedimentation

areas of glacial sedimentation followed by predominantly marine sedimentation

areas with volcanic rocks

FIG. 7.2. Permian palaeogeography.

of the Bureau of Mineral Resources and several oil companies (Malone, 1964; Malone *et al.*, 1964; Veevers *et al.*, 1964*b*; Dickins *et al.*, 1964). Within the basin proper the area of thickest sedimentation lies in the region of the Mimosa Syncline. It is bounded to the east by the Eungella–Gogango High, which may have been partly land in the Permian, and to the west by the relatively stable Comet Ridge on which Permian sediments are relatively thin (Fig. 7.3). Still further west is the deep elongate Denison Trough which has a very distinctive early history, and this is followed to the west by the extensive Springsure–Corfield Shelf (see p. 155, footnote) which forms a great lobe toward the northwest across the Middle Palaeozoic Adavale Trough.

In the eastern belt and along the north and northwestern margins of the basin the beginning of the Permian saw the accumulation of thick volcanic deposits, both pyroclastics and flows. They are unconformable on rocks as young as Carboniferous (the Bulgonunna Volcanics). Andesitic and rhyolitic material predominates in the east and basaltic in the north. Lithic, feldspathic, and quartz sandstones, polymictic conglomerates and well-bedded siltstones and shales are interbedded, and at the northern end of the basin coal measures are developed locally. These rocks are collectively known as the Lower Bowen Volcanics. The only fossils, apart from a few marine forms (Fauna I of Dickins, 1964/96) at the very top of the unit, are silicified wood and *Glossopteris* leaves. In thickness the unit is locally in excess of 6000 m, and sections of 3000 m are not uncommon.

It is believed that the source was in the Eungella–Gogango High, which was, in fact, an active volcanic arc shedding debris into the Bowen Basin to the west and the Yarrol Basin to the east. Within the Bowen Basin conditions were partly marine and partly freshwater, indicating that the supply of debris was adequate to balance subsidence. This arc was not a continuous structure but had passages through it into the Yarrol Basin, as is shown by the presence of marine Permian sediments in and to the north of the Eungella–Gogango High.

Dating of the Lower Bowen Volcanics and their equivalents remains a problem. Since they lie conformably below fossiliferous Artinskian sediments they are commonly held to be mainly Sakmarian, but they may well extend down into the Stephanian.

The Lower Bowen Volcanics wedge out on to the Comet Ridge, particularly in the south central part of the basin where this structure was probably above depositional level. In the Denison Trough at the same time volcanics were negligible contributors to the deposits, which were dark-coloured mudstones and siltstones known as the Undivided Freshwater Beds. In places these are as much as 3000 m thick. No definite marine fossils are known, but *Glossopteris* is abundant at several levels and a predominantly non-marine environment is postulated. On the Springsure–Corfield Shelf there was slight deformation after the deposition of the Joe Joe Formation, and then followed a period of non-deposition except in a few areas where there are thin shales and sandstones with *Glossopteris*. These have been correlated with the Undivided Freshwater beds (Mollan *et al.*, 1964/27).

Following this phase there was a period of complex marine transgression and regression during which the Middle Bowen Beds and their equivalents were deposited. They are considered to span the Artinskian–Kungurian interval and perhaps part of the Kazanian. Again the site of maximum deposition was in the central eastern sector (the Mimosa Syncline) where thicknesses in excess of 2500 m have been recorded (Fig. 7.4), and the

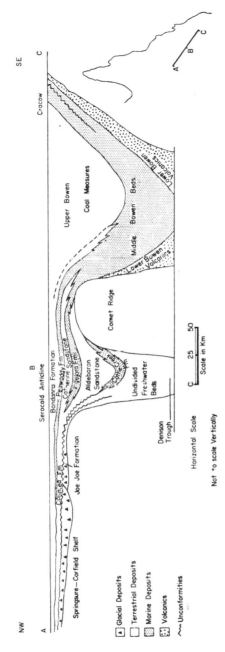

Fig. 7.3. Correlation diagram showing the relationships between the Permian stratigraphic units in the Bowen Basin, Denison Trough, and Springsure–Corfield Shelf (see p. 155, footnote).

sequence is probably entirely of marine origin. It consists of shales, calcareous quartzose, volcanic lithic and feldspathic sandstones, and occasional thin detrital limestones, most of which accumulated under shallow-water conditions. The occurrence of occasional large erratic blocks up to several tons weight at intervals through the entire sequence, indicates the presence of sea ice. Marine fossils occur in abundance at several levels, and three broad distinctive faunal associations, labelled Faunas II–IV, have been recognized (Dickins *et al.*, 1962/87). Each contains a large number of restricted species, and there are also some restricted genera. Some of the fossiliferous units are very persistent and easily recognizable, for example the *Eurydesma-Taeniothaerus* beds of Fauna II, and the Big *Strophalosia* Zone, the Mantuan *Productus* Bed, and the *Streptorhynchus pelicanensis* Bed of Fauna IV.

Towards the northern end of the basin there is a gradual decrease in the thickness of the Middle Bowen Beds, and near the present northern extremity the units below those containing Fauna IV pass northwards into the Collinsville Coal Measures (Fig. 7.5). These are the product of sedimentation in a large delta which was able to maintain itself during periods of widespread subsidence; and though there is evidence that it was occasionally submerged by the sea (for example the marine Glendoo Member which contains Fauna III), it was not finally destroyed until the transgression associated with Fauna IV which inundated vast areas of central Queensland.

During the early part of Middle Bowen time large sectors of the Comet Ridge stood above sealevel, and later sediments are much thinner than their equivalents in the troughs on either side. This structure formed a partial barrier between the Bowen Basin proper to the east and the Denison Trough on the west. In the latter there is a threefold alternation of marine shales and limestones, and terrestrial quartzose lithic sandstones. The three faunas listed above can be readily recognized in the Dilly, Cattle Creek, Ingelara, and Peawaddy Formations respectively. The maximum thickness of the Middle Bowen equivalents here is about 3000 m. On the Springsure–Corfield Shelf there are no equivalents of the lower part of the Middle Bowen, but the upper part is represented by the terrestrial quartz conglomerates and sandstones of the Colinlea Formation. These lie unconformably on the Joe Joe Formation, and contain fossil plants including *Glossopteris* and *Gangamopteris*. The marine transgression of Fauna IV time crossed the eastern part of the shelf and deposited the Peawaddy Formation conformably on the Colinlea (Mollan *et al.*, 1964).

Clearly this transgression was the most widespread of all, but following it the seas rapidly receded and coal measure conditions were gradually established over the entire basin. These were initiated first across the Springsure–Corfield Shelf and the Denison Trough, where the Lower Bandanna Formation began to accumulate while marine conditions persisted

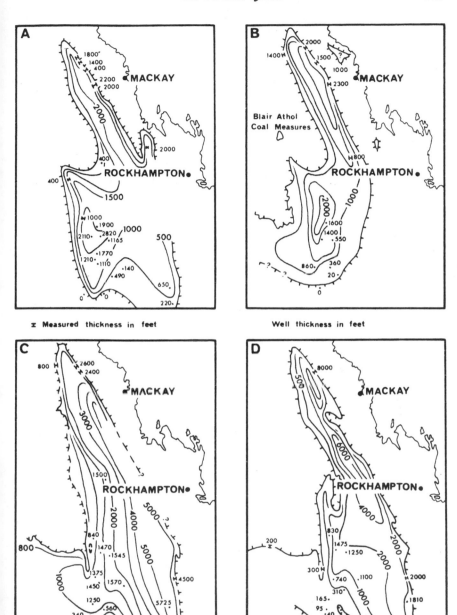

FIG. 7.4. Isopach maps showing the distribution of Permian units in the Bowen Basin.
A, Middle Bowen Beds Unit A. B, Middle Bowen Beds Unit B. C, Middle Bowen Beds
Unit C. D, Upper Bowen Coal Measures. (After Malone, 1964.)

in the basin east of the Comet Ridge. The basin proper was still sinking at a relatively rapid rate, and as much as 2500 m of lithic and feldspathic sandstones, black shales, and coal formed the Upper Bowen Coal Measures and its equivalents. The coal is of high volatile bituminous type, but is increased in rank to semi-anthracite in the more highly deformed areas.

The southern sector of the Bowen Basin which lies beneath the Mesozoic rocks of the Surat Basin is being actively explored for petroleum, and there are Permian troughs and ridges present south of the Denison Trough and Comet Ridge. Details of the stratigraphy are not yet available, but in general the thickness of the Permian decreases toward the New South Wales border.

The **Sydney Basin** began its history as a narrow deep trough about 50–60 km wide oriented in a northwesterly direction through the Hunter Valley. In it marine sediments of the Dalwood Group were laid down. It was bounded on the northeast by the tectonically active New England region against which the sediments wedge out rapidly, and on the west by the stable landmass formed after the Kanimblan Orogeny. At the present time most of the contacts between these rocks and the Carboniferous rocks are faults. However, at a few localities apparently conformable contacts are known over small areas, and within the trough it is known that Carboniferous rocks formed some islands against which the sediments of the Dalwood Group were deposited. These data, together with the variable thickness of Dalwood sediments, suggest that at the beginning of the Permian the Carboniferous rocks were being gently deformed, no doubt as a result of the rising of the New England High.

The sediments of the Dalwood Group are of shallow-water type and reach a thickness of over 1800 m. The dominant rock types are dark brown to grey shales which are often calcareous, well-bedded lithic sandstones with large quantities of volcanic detritus, polymictic conglomerates and water-laid tuffs. Thin impure limestones occur locally. Rapid lateral changes of facies are a common feature of the group as a whole. Large erratic blocks are scattered through the sediments but are particularly numerous at certain levels. Interbedded basaltic flows are of frequent occurrence, and in places they occur in such abundance that they form an almost continuous pile. Rhyolites and tuffs also occur. Benthonic fossils are common, the bivalves *Eurydesma* (represented by two species), *Deltopecten*, and *Aviculopecten*, the gastropods *Keeneia*, *Ptychomphalina*, and *Warthia*, the brachiopods *Terrakea*, *Strophalosia*, *Trigonotreta*, and *Ingelarella*, and forams being among the most abundant. The upper Sakmarian–lower Artinskian ammonoid *Uraloceras pokolbinense* occurs near the top of the group (Farley Formation), and the plant *Gangamopteris* near its base (Lochinvar Formation). Though little recent work has been done, the Allandale and Farley faunas are tentatively correlated

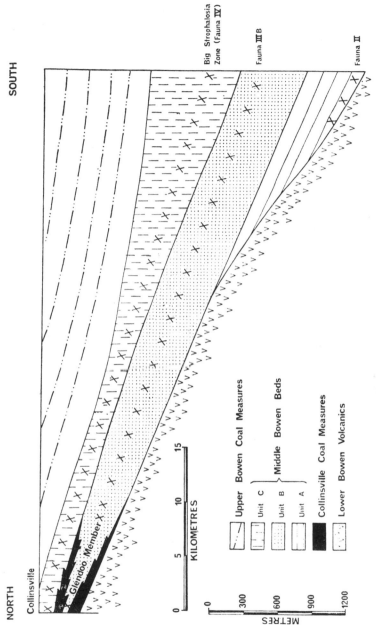

Fig. 7.5. Diagrammatic north–south section through the Bowen Basin at Collinsville showing the thickening of the marine units to the south, the position of the various faunal units, and the relationships of the Collinsville Coal Measures.

with Faunas I and II of the Bowen Basin, and it is concluded that the lower formations are equivalents of the Lower Bowen Volcanics.

Traced along the trough to the northwest the Dalwood Group sediments rapidly thin. Locally, however, basalts of the same age form piles up to 1500 m thick as in the Werrie Basin. The Dalwood Group has been considered to thin out rapidly to the south and west of the Hunter Valley, but recent work suggests the possibility of representatives of the group appearing in the lower part of the Conjola Formation at the southern extremity of the basin near Batemans Bay (Runnegar, 1965).

During the period of widespread terrestrial conditions that followed, the Greta Coal Measures were formed. They occupy an area more or less coincident with the Dalwood Group except that they overlap it slightly to the south and west. There is little evidence to suggest that the unit is contemporaneous over its entire outcrop, and, indeed, one would not expect it to be. It is usually between 30 and 90 m thick, but on the coast north of Newcastle it contains about 300 m of basaltic flows and tuffs. Sedimentation is cyclic, a complete cycle consisting of conglomerates, then sandstone, siltstone, shale, and finally coal (Booker, 1960). There are no seat earths, and occasionally thick seams rest directly on sandstones or even conglomerates. The coal is thought to be allochthonous in origin. It reaches a maximum thickness in the Cessnock area which was apparently the site of maximum subsidence. Splitting of the seams and distribution of the conglomerates suggests that there were source areas in both the northeast and the west. The coal is good quality bituminous in type, and has played a major part in the development of the Hunter Valley as one of the largest industrial areas in Australia.

In the northwestern extension of the basin there are no coals and the interval is thought to be represented by thin shales with *Glossopteris*. Small isolated basins in which coal was formed developed on the southern platform, for example the Clyde Coal Measures on the south coast (Fig. 7.6), but these are possibly somewhat older.

There was extensive overlapping on to Devonian and earlier rocks to the south and west during the ensuing return to shallow-water marine conditions. The sediments of this interval, known as the Maitland Group, are similar to those of the Dalwood Group. On certain horizons they contain massive concretions up to 5·5 m in diameter. In the Hunter Valley the volcanic contribution to the sediments is small, but on the south coast (where the equivalent rocks are called the Shoalhaven Group and the Gerringong Volcanics), it is very much greater, and tuffs and flows are also common (McElroy and Rose, 1962). Erratics and glendonites occur abundantly, and in places there are thick unsorted masses of sediment containing large angular blocks and numerous fossils, many of which still have delicate structures preserved. Such a rock type is widespread in the Muree Formation,

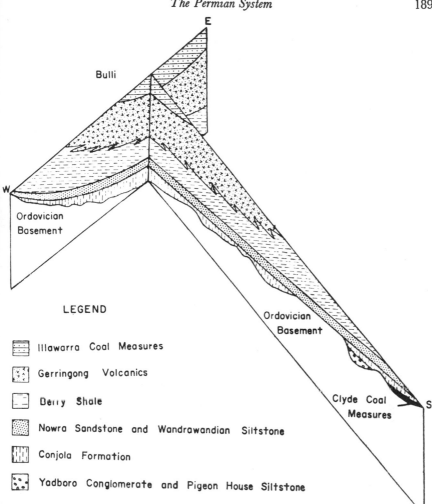

E

Bulli

W

Ordovician
Basement

LEGEND

Ordovician
Basement

☰ Illawarra Coal Measures

⟦⟧ Gerringong Volcanics

⟦⟧ Derry Shale

▦ Nowra Sandstone and Wandrawandian Siltstone

⟦⟧ Conjola Formation

⟦⟧ Yadboro Conglomerate and Pigeon House Siltstone

Clyde Coal
Measures

S

FIG. 7.6. Diagrammatic representation of the relationships between the Permian units in the southern part of the Sydney Basin. (Data from C. T. McElroy and G. Rose.)

and it is not inappropriately referred to as a marine tillite. Embryonic folds had begun to develop along the site of initial Permian deposition, and already these sediments were being cannibalized. Towards the end of this period there appears to have been a withdrawal of the sea to the Hunter region. As would be expected, rapid facies changes are again conspicuous. The fossil assemblages contain the same genera as the Dalwood Group, but many new species have evolved. Of particular interest are the massive colonies of *Stenopora crinita* which are up to 0·5 m in diameter, the profusion of fenestellids forming the so-called *Fenestella* Shales, and the presence of a single specimen of the Artinskian ammonoid *Neocrimites meridionalis* probably in the Elderslie Formation. The faunas of the Elderslie Formation and *Fenestella* Shales are compared with those of Fauna III, and those of the Muree and Mulbring Formations with Fauna IV of the Bowen Basin, though it is noted that some workers consider the Elderslie faunas to be of Fauna II type (Dickins, 1964/96).

West of the main Permian outcrops of the Sydney Basin in the general vicinity of Mudgee there are terrestrial sediments, at present up to 100 m thick, occupying the floors of rather steep-walled valleys. These are correlated with the upper part of the Maitland Group, and consist mainly of conglomerates, sandstones, and siltstones containing *Glossopteris* and *Gangamopteris*. Striated and soled cobbles are relatively common, and varves have been found (Dulhunty and Packham, 1962; Dulhunty, 1964). It is thought that in this region an ice-moulded terrain is at present being exhumed.

As a result of the recession at the end of the Maitland Group time the area occupied by the succeeding Tomago Coal Measures was limited to a very small but rapidly subsiding basin in the Lower Hunter Valley in which over 900 m of sediment accumulated (Booker, 1960). Coal-measure environments spread rapidly, however, and the Newcastle Coal Measures and their equivalents were probably the most extensive of all the Permian units in New South Wales. From a landmass in the northeast huge deltas built out depositing great shoestrings of conglomerates and sandstones with intervening coal swamps. The grainsize of the sediments decreases to the southwest. Along the southern and western areas of deposition conditions were more uniform, and the coal seams are very extensive. The Lithgow seam has been traced over 160 km without reaching its limits. Cycles similar to those of the Greta Coal Measures are found everywhere.

YARROL BASIN

In Queensland there was a partial divide between the Bowen Basin and the old Devono-Carboniferous Yarrol Basin during Permian times, but in New South Wales no comparable divide existed. As a result the Permian rocks in a belt from south of Mundubbera to the north of Rockhampton are unlike those of the Newcastle Geosyncline. In the axial parts of this belt there is conformity between the Carboniferous and Permian, though there is unconformity along the margins (Hill and Denmead, eds., 1960). In the Yarrol area, near the central part of the basin, the period began with extensive shale, lithic sandstone, and bioclastic limestone deposits and interbeds of tuff, known as the Burnett and Yarrol Formations. In these the characteristic elements of the Bowen Faunas I and II occur. They are overlain by the andesites of the Owl Gully Volcanics, and the remainder of the sequence is missing. In the vicinity of Rockhampton the lowest Permian unit is the upper part of the Dinner Creek Conglomerate which is thought to be of terrestrial origin and contains *Glossopteris*. It is followed disconformably by the possibly Upper Permian Rookwood Volcanics (Malone, pers. comm.). The trough did not persist and at the end of the Early Permian it began to deform. Accompanying this deformation was the eruption of extensive volcanic rocks, mainly basalts and andesites.

EASTERN BASINS

To the east of the Yarrol Basin and extending south almost to Newcastle was a broad barrier of Lower Palaeozoic rocks (the New England High), which was not very high topographically but which, nevertheless, effectively divided off an eastern depositional area. Much of it is now intruded by granite so that it is not possible to determine the extent of Permian sedimentation upon it, but it is clear that there were several deep embayments into the barrier, for example, the Esk Rift, the Texas–Drake and the Armidale Embayments, and at times it must have been almost entirely submerged. Sediments laid down on the eastern flank of the structure are also preserved in the Gympie Basin of Queensland, and the Manning–Macleay Basin of New South Wales. The sediments of the flanks and the embayments are almost entirely marine, and at many localities contain abundant volcanic detritus. Owing to structural dislocation, areas of outcrop are now limited, but the main outlines of the sequence are clear enough. Dark-coloured indurated shales and muddy lithic and calcareous sandstones form the bulk of the sediments, but biogenic limestones also make a significant contribution. Although it is clear that shallow-water conditions must have prevailed for most of the time, there are sufficiently numerous occurrences of graded beds, minor slumps, and ripple cross-stratification to suggest that subsidence to relatively deep water was not uncommon. Rhyolites and andesites appear at different levels in different areas, and in places they are up to 1500 m thick. There is a striking difference between these sediments and those of the Newcastle Geosyncline. These are much darker in colour, less well sorted and more indurated, and show closer affinities with the rocks of the Yarrol Basin. They also lack the interbedded coal measures. Fossils are present on several horizons and are representative of Faunas I to III.

TASMANIA BASIN

Permian deposits are widespread in Tasmania and originally must have covered most of the island apart from the West Coast Range (Spry and Banks, eds., 1962). The total thickness of Permian rocks in any one section rarely exceeds 600 m, and the individual stratigraphic units are thin and sheet-like in character. Thus, though there was considerable topographic relief at the beginning of the period, this must have been quickly reduced to produce extensive lowlands which were subject to marine transgression and regression. One important feature is the close comparison between the Tasmanian and Hunter Valley sedimentary successions, though the latter is many times thicker. This is taken to indicate that Tasmania was structurally part of the western shelf of the Newcastle Geosyncline.

At the beginning of the Permian, ice was present in most regions of Tasmania, and was generally moving in northerly to southeasterly directions from areas of accumulation in high lands along or beyond the present position of the west coast. The deposits of this ice, the Wynyard Tillite, everywhere have an unconformable base. At least nine tillites and four varved shale units have been recognized, and these are interstratified with sandstones and conglomerates. Marine fossils are occasionally present in the tillites, but are not well preserved. The ice must therefore have reached sealevel in some areas.

After the melting of the ice, mudstones, siltstones, and thin limestones of the Quamby and Golden Valley Groups developed in a broadly transgressive sea. Abundant large erratic blocks testify to the presence of floating ice, and the presence of glendonites is further evidence of very cold conditions. Tasmanite, a marine oil shale, accumulated in the shallower water around islands. Fossils are numerous, and among the most important are species of the foram *Calcitornella*; the polyzoans *Stenopora* and *Fenestella*; the brachiopods *Ingelarella* and *Strophalosia*; the bivalves *Deltopecten*, *Eurydesma* and *Chaenomya*; the gastropod *Keeneia*; and the crinoid *Calceolispongia*, indicating a Fauna II assemblage associated with some Western Australian elements.

Regional warping brought almost the whole of the Tasmanian area out of the sea in late Artinskian times, and wide areas were covered with sediments apparently formed in a series of coalescing deltas. There are widespread conglomerates at the base, and ripple-marked, cross-stratified sandstones with seams of bituminous coal predominate in the upper part of the Mersey Group. The plants *Glossopteris*, *Gangamopteris*, and *Noeggerathiopsis* are found, and spores including, *inter alia*, species of *Nuskoisporites*, *Punctatisporites*, and *Verrucosporites*, indicate a correlation with the Greta Coal Measures of New South Wales.

During the deposition of the succeeding shallow-water marine sediments of the Cascades, Malbina, and Ferntree Groups, warping of the sea floor produced local transgression and regression along with variously oriented shallow troughs. Dark siltstones, calcareous sandstones, and limestones form the bulk of these units. In places there is rhythmic alternation of calcarenites and siltstones suggesting slow cyclic changes in sealevel. Elsewhere there is evidence of graded bedding. Fossils are abundant and are closely related to those of the Maitland and Shoalhaven Groups of the Sydney Basin.

The sequence is completed by the Cygnet Coal Measures.

WEST COAST BASINS

In each of these basins sedimentation was extensive, and the sedimentary sequence follows a generally similar pattern. Widespread glacials were formed in Stephanian to Sakmarian times, and were followed by shallow-water marine sandstones and limestones alternating with terrestrial or brackish water deposits. Sedimentation had ceased by the Kazanian in all basins except the Canning where it continued on a restricted scale till the Tatarian.

In the **Bonaparte Gulf Basin** marine glacial rocks lie with probable unconformity on Carboniferous sandstones. They are thought to be of Sakmarian age. Later Permian sediments are known only from the Port Keats area where approximately 300–400 m of ferruginous sandstones and siltstones lie unconformably on the Weaber Group (Thomas, 1957). These beds contain abundant fossils including the Upper Permian *Leptodus nobilis*.

In the **Canning Basin** late Stephanian and Sakmarian sedimentation was rather closely controlled by the intra-basinal structures noted in earlier chapters.

The Grant Formation which is partly glacigene, reaches almost 3000 m in the Fitzroy Trough, but it is much thinner on the platforms to the south. Its lowest members are often calcareous sandstones and detrital limestones, but the bulk of the formation consists of well-bedded and well-washed sandstone. Intercalated at several levels are outwash conglomerates, tillites, and varved shales. Most of these rocks accumulated under marine conditions, but the presence of varves and pavements suggest that the area was above sealevel for part of the time. Vestiges of the action of terrestrial ice also remain along the southern edge of the basin where, from the Braeside Tillite and Paterson Formation fluvioglacial conglomerates, tillites, and striated pavements have been described, the latter indicating movement of the ice to the north and northwest. Apart from long-ranging smaller forams, the only fossils in the Grant Formation are spores. The "Lycosporoid" Microflora (known also from the Anderson Formation) occurs in the lower part of the formation, and the *Nuskoisporites* assemblage in the upper (Veevers and Wells, 1961), indicating that part of the Stephanian as well as the Sakmarian may be represented.

In the main parts of the basin the succeeding Permian sediments were deposited under alternating shallow-water marine and terrestrial conditions. The areas of deposition were widely fluctuating, and as a result the sequences vary considerably from place to place. The most complete succession is in the northwest of the Fitzroy Trough, but even there most of the Kazanian seems to be missing. There were extensive marine transgressions over almost the entire basin in earliest Artinskian and late Artinskian–Kungurian times resulting in the formation of the Poole Sandstone, Lower Liveringa, and Noonkanbah Formations; and the Upper Liveringa was deposited in a more limited transgression in the Fitzroy Trough during the Tatarian. In the intervening periods freshwater deposits were formed only in the Fitzroy Trough. The marine sediments are predominantly fine- to coarse-quartzose sandstones, which are often highly ferruginous, calcareous sandstones, and shale. Cross-stratification is very common, and in places there are sequences of finely bedded shale and sandstone. Relatively thin limestones and occasional thin oolitic iron ores occur, the former often being abundantly fossiliferous. The Nura Nura Member at the base of the Poole Sandstone contains the Stage B assemblage of Dickins (1963), which contains a profusion of brachiopods, bivalves, gastropods, polyzoans, and some ammonoids. It is probably of Sakmarian age (Glenister and Furnish, 1961). The Noonkanbah Formation and the Lightjack Member of the Liveringa Formation contain Stage D faunas in which the same groups of fossils occur though represented by different species. In addition the crinoid *Calceolispongia* makes a striking contribution to the fauna. A middle to late Artinskian age is indicated. And, finally, the Tatarian Hardman Member of the Upper Liveringa Formation contains the Stage F fauna.

The terrestrial deposits consist of cross-bedded sandstones with shales and thin coal seams abounding with remains of the *Glossopteris* flora.

The total thickness of Permian deposits in the Fitzroy Trough is in excess of 2500 m, but elsewhere it is much thinner, and along the southwestern edge of the basin a thickness of only 200 m is recorded (Fig. 7.7).

Permian sediments outcrop in the eastern part of the **Carnarvon Basin**; to the west they are covered by Mesozoic sediments. They thicken considerably to the west, but both drilling and geophysical surveys have indicated the presence of a ridge approximately in the position of the present coast line during Permian times, so that the basin was in the nature of an elongated trough (Fig. 7.8). Internally it contains several graben structures which form subsidiary basins. It is divisible into the Carnarvon Basin proper, and the shallower embayment of the Byro Sub-Basin to the south, partly separated off by a large Precambrian inlier. In the former, Permian sediments are in the vicinity of 3600 m thick, but in the latter the maximum is estimated at only 1350 m. Each sub-basin has its own stratigraphic nomenclature, but the sedimentary sequence in each is much the same (Fig. 7.9).

A patchy development of clean quartz sandstone, the Harris Sandstone, begins the sequence. It rests with disconformity on the Lower Carboniferous

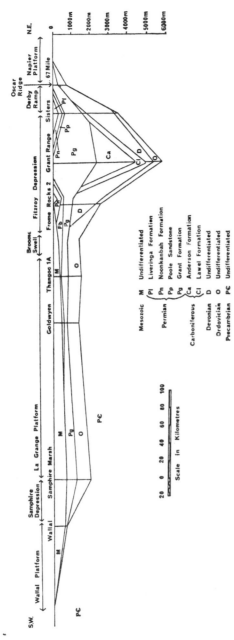

Fig. 7.7. Diagrammatic section across the Canning Basin from northeast to southwest through certain exploratory wells. The distribution of the rocks of the various systems is shown. (Modified after Veevers and Wells, 1961.)

or with angular unconformity on the Precambrian. Though it is sometimes stated to be of Permian age, the poorly preserved plant remains more probably indicate that it is Carboniferous (Kräusel, 1961). The disconformably overlying Lyons Group is considered to be almost entirely of marine origin, and consists of at least five tillites interbedded with quartz-rich lithic sandstones and finely laminated siltstone and shale. The tillites have either a silty or sandy matrix and a coarse fraction of cobbles and boulders up to 6 m in diameter. Striated and faceted boulders have been observed. Parts of the tillite sequences contain hard, well-bedded carbonate cemented sandstones, and these are not infrequently fossiliferous. The non-tillitic rocks are usually soft, porous, and have a small amount of kaolinitic matrix, but units with a calcareous cement also occur. Macro- and micro-fossils occur on several horizons. In the Byro Sub-Basin, marine fossils are not so numerous as further north, and this, together with the evidence of a striated pavement, the presence of varvoid rocks, and the general thinning of the unit to the southeast, suggests that land ice was probably present in this region. Maximum thickness is approximately 1500 m. The main fossils are the brachiopods *Neospirifer*, *Cancrinella*, *Streptorhynchus* and *Permorthotetes*; the bivalves *Eurydesma*, *Deltopecten*, and *Schizodus*; and the gastropod *Keeneia*, contituting Stage A of Dickins.

Subsequently the whole basin was covered by a shallow sea in which up to 270 m of well-bedded calcarenites and calcilutites of the Callytharra Formation were deposited. Fossils are numerous, over 100 species being recorded. They are comparable with the Nura Nura fauna Stage B above.

Shallow-water marine conditions persisted in the Carnarvon Basin proper, while the deltaic rocks of the Wooramel Group were accumulating in the Byro Sub-Basin (Konecki *et al.*, 1958). In both regions arenaceous rocks predominate and cross-stratification is common. Faunas are not well developed, and where present are often stunted. They belong to Stage C. *Glossopteris* is known from the delta deposits.

Following this came the Byro Group which is subdivided into different formations in the two sub-basins. In the Carnarvon Sub-Basin it is composed of shallow-water marine arenites, siltstones, and shales with some thin detrital limestones which have rich benthonic faunas. Occasional units contain quantities of carbonaceous matter, and the faunas are thought to be dwarfed, indicating that the deltaic conditions, which persisted in the Byro Sub-Basin, temporarily advanced northwestwards. Gradual uplift caused cessation of deposition in the Byro area earlier than in the Carnarvon Sub-Basin. In the latter structure the type of deposition appears to have been only slightly modified by this uplift, and the succeeding Kennedy Group is composed of similar lithologies to the underlying rocks. Towards the top of the Kennedy Group, however, there are some sandstones which have been

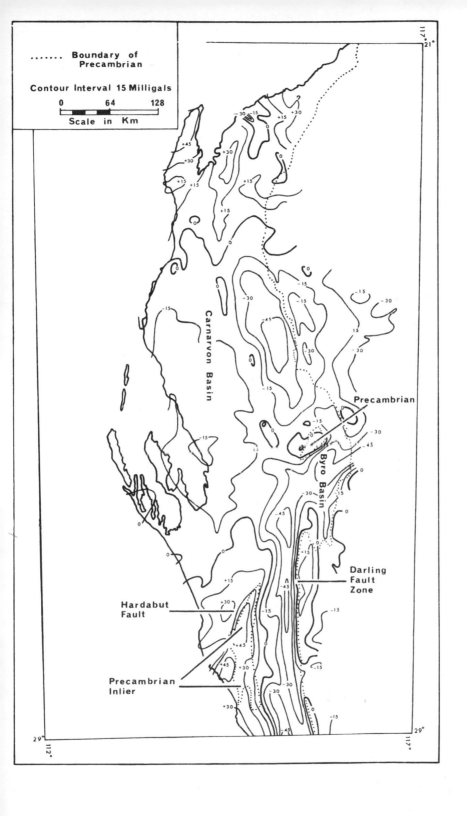

interpreted as probably continental, reflecting the final filling of the basin. The faunas of these two groups belong to Stages D and E. One of the most remarkable features is the profusion of the crinoid *Calceolispongia* in Stage D.

There was continuity of sedimentation between the **Byro Sub-Basin** and the **Perth Basin**. The base of the Permian is rarely exposed, but where it is there is unconformity on the Precambrian. The eastern boundary of the basin is at present formed by the Darling Fault, a major structure over 950 km long and with a downthrow of over 9000 m on the west. In Permian times the boundary must have been further to the east since Permian sediments aggregate more than 900 m in areas adjacent to the fault, but it is unlikely that it was any further east than was the edge of the Byro Sub-Basin. Geophysical evidence suggests that the basin was only of the order of 80 km wide.

At the base of the sequence are the Nangetty Glacials, probably mainly terrestrial in origin. They consist of boulder beds and tillites which are not well cemented, and readily erode. Varved shales are known but are rare. Spores indicate that at least the upper parts of the formation are Sakmarian in age.

Three marine formations—The Holmwood, Fossil Cliff and High Cliff— follow conformably. Parts of these were deposited under conditions of restricted circulation in a barred basin, but normal shallow-water conditions must have existed for considerable periods. Dark-coloured clayey siltstones with beds of gypsum and limestones predominate, but there are also cross-stratified sandstones with some conglomerates. Macrofossils are particularly abundant on certain restricted horizons.

The onset of emergence, already apparent in the upper High Cliff Sandstone, was completed by the development of a coal-measure environment over wide areas. The Irwin River Coal Measures reach a maximum of over 120 m in thickness and are characterized by rapid lateral and vertical changes of lithology and by thin lenticular coals. The *Glossopteris* flora is well represented. In a brief marine interlude the Carynginya Formation was deposited in a barred basin, and then the terrestrial succession is completed by the thick quartz-rich Wagina Sandstone.

OFFICER, LAKE EYRE, AND MURRAY BASINS

In the Early Permian there appears to have been an extensive shallow basin, approximately oval in outline and with its major axis east–west, extending across the Officer–Lake Eyre region. A similar type of structure occupied the Lower Murray area. The great extent of these basins has been revealed only recently as a result of deep drilling, since the Permian sediments are covered by Mesozoic and later deposits. However, in the Wilkinson

Range area of the Officer Basin a thin veneer of flat-lying soft boulder clay, sandstones, and shales has been known for some time, as have smaller areas of similar rocks to the south of Alice Springs. In the deeper parts of the Lake Eyre Basin the basal units consist of coarse ill-sorted rudites which are generally considered to be glacigenes (Ludbrook, 1961c; Freeman, 1964). Towards the basin margins they become coarser and contain less interstratified material. Overlying these there are dark-coloured siltstones and shales containing forams, which probably indicate a brackish environment, and the sequence is topped by interbedded siltstones and sandstones with coals. The total thickness in the Lake Eyre region is about 1000 m, and this is maintained almost to the New South Wales border where most of the units rapidly wedge out against the Broken Hill Ridge. This structure clearly was a divide separating the Lake Eyre and Murray Basins in Permian times. The sequences in the Murray Basin are very similar to those described above, but are thinner.

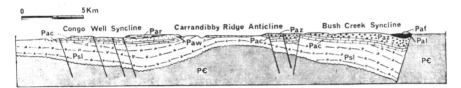

Fig. 7.9. Cross-section through the Permian and Precambrian rocks on the eastern side of the Carnarvon Basin showing the simple structure characteristic of this basin. (Redrawn after Konecki, Dickins, and Quinlan, 1958.) Psl = Lyons Group; Pac = Callytharra Formation; Paz = Congo Formation; Paw = Moogooloo Sandstone; Par = Coyrie Formation; Paf = Bogadi Greywacke; Pal = Madeline Formation; PC = Precambrian.

Spores have been obtained from both the Lake Eyre and Murray Basins and suggest a correlation of the lower glacigenic part of the sequence with the Sakmarian glacials of Western Australia, whereas the coal-bearing parts of the sections range as high as the Newcastle Coal Measures (Evans, 1963; Balme, 1964).

The occurrence of glacials in this environment over such a wide area is of great palaeogeographical significance since it indicates the presence of ice at sealevel over most of the south central part of the continent. The deposits of the valleys down which the ice moved into these basins have been preserved at several localities. Some are exposed at the surface, as for example, those of the Fleurieu Peninsula in South Australia where a Permian landscape is being revealed by present erosion, and it has been possible to recognize details such as glacial amphitheatres and bars (Campana and Wilson, 1955). At several well-separated localities in central and western

Victoria there are excellently exposed sequences of glacials; the best known is near Bacchus Marsh, where fifty-one tillite beds, ranging in thickness from a few centimetres to a few metres, have been recorded (Wanless, 1960). A thin marine band with *Conularia* occurs near the top of this sequence (Singleton, 1965).

New Zealand

Permian rocks have been recorded widely over the South Island, and are the oldest known formations in the North Island. Recent work by Waterhouse (1963*d*) indicates that the Permian marine succession in the New Zealand area is not only the thickest (up to 20,000 m) but is also the most complete in the world.

In general terms it may be divided into two major sections: (a) a Lower Permian sequence (Sakmarian–Kungurian) consisting of volcanics and volcanic-derived sediments, possibly including Carboniferous units at the base, underlying (b) an Upper Permian sequence (Kazanian–Tatarian) of limestones overlain by finely banded, grey, green and red argillites, and massive green sandstones and conglomerates.

By the beginning of the Permian the sedimentational picture of the New Zealand region had changed considerably from that of the Devonian Period, as interpreted from the small outcrops of Devonian rocks on the west coast of the South Island (q.v.). To the east and northeast of a foreland of older rocks (now represented by coastal Westland and the Fiordland areas), a trough began to develop, later to become a geosyncline of very considerable proportions. This, the **New Zealand Geosyncline**, extended over the remaining parts of the South Island and the whole of the North Island (Fig. 7.10 and see Fig. 8.5).

In the Permian, and continuing through the Triassic and Jurassic periods, the geosyncline received deposits of different facies. Along its western, southern, and probably southeastern flanks, a *marginal sequence* developed (= Hokonui facies of Wellman). This consisted of shelf deposits with abundant corals and brachiopods on the west side of the Southland Syncline, the sediments being only a few hundred metres thick and comprising mainly limestones and conglomerates. Volcanic rocks are common. Here also may be included what Wellman (1956) refers to as transitional deposits located on the east flank of the Nelson Syncline from D'Urville Island to Tophouse, and on the east side of the Southland Syncline from north of Milford Sound to the east coast, south of Dunedin; the sediments here are argillaceous limestones, grey-, red-, and green-banded mudstones, fossiliferous limestones, and conglomerate and sandstone bands, with a total thickness of about 6000 m.

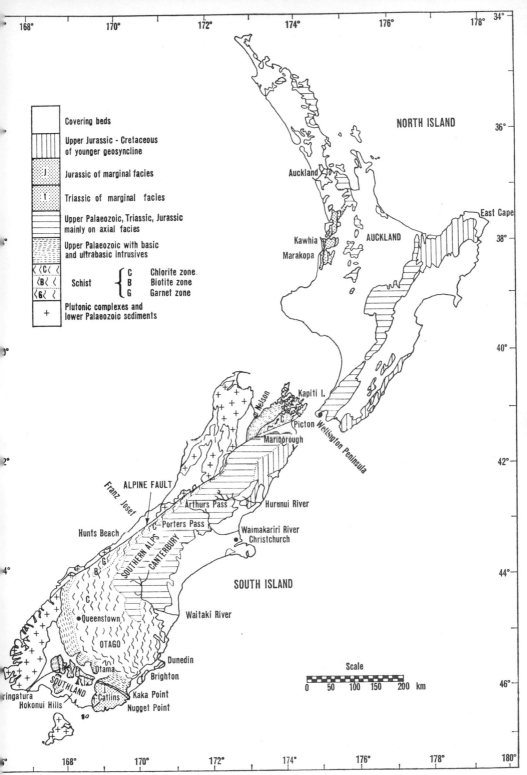

FIG. 7.10. Geological sketch map showing rocks of New Zealand Geosyncline. (After Coombs *et al.*, 1959.)

In the early part of the Permian, the folding of the New Zealand Geosyncline was accompanied in the marginal areas by intense volcanism and intrusion. Thus in the Nelson and Southland synclines there are thick sheets of augite-rich basalts (up to 15,000 m thick in the Southland Syncline) slightly preceding or probably contemporaneous with large ultramafic intrusions (Dun Mountain, Nelson, and Red Hill, western Otago). Mainly in the south (Takitimu Mountains), the basalt sheets have numerous fossiliferous marine intercalations and, on the eastern limbs of the above synclines, there are spilites with serpentinites and volcanic greywacke formations.

In the most rapidly sinking portion of the geosyncline, an *axial sequence* (= Alpine facies of Wellman) was laid down. This consisted of poorly fossiliferous, redeposited greywackes, limestones, shales, and quartzites, together with some spilites, now more indurated, metamorphosed, and deformed, located on the east side of the schist axis in Waitaki Valley and near Fairlie in Canterbury. This facies also occurs in eastern Northland and contains the only Palaeozoic fossils known in the North Island.

The accumulating sediments were subjected to deep burial in the geosyncline, and the oldest of them (probably Carboniferous in age) are now represented by part of the Haast Schist Group, a term adopted by Suggate (1961) to embrace all the schists formed by the regional metamorphism of the rocks of the New Zealand Geosyncline. (See above under Alpine Metamorphics, p. 167.)

Permian rocks also form part of the Torlesse Group of non-schistose sediments (greywacke–argillite facies) lying both to the east and discontinuously to the west of the Haast schist belt. The rocks are texturally less altered than the low-grade (Chlorite subzone 2) schists into which they commonly grade to the south and west. According to Campbell and Warren (1965), who have made a detailed review of the fossil occurrences in the Torlesse Group, it includes strata representing part of Permian, Middle and Late Triassic, Late Jurassic and Early Cretaceous time.

Northland Region

Along the east coast of Northland Peninsula is a sequence of rather well-bedded, jointed, indurated, locally deformed, and highly contorted siltstones and sandstones (Waipapa Group) arranged in two roughly parallel belts, separated by a belt of chert- and manganese-bearing greywackes and volcanic rocks. On the east side of Whangaroa Bay, the volcanic rocks in the form of pillow-lavas are associated with the underlying limestones which have yielded specimens of the rugose corals *Waagenophyllum* and *Wentzelella*, and the fusulinids *Yabeina*, *Verbeekina*, and *Neoschwagerina* of Tethyan and American affinities, clearly warm-water in origin and correlated with the

Kazanian and Guadalupian Stages. Thicknesses are unknown owing to the high degree of folding.

NELSON REGION

The marginal facies of the Permian is well represented in the north-easterly-trending syncline east of Nelson City, especially in its eastern limb at Dun Mountain and Red Hills. The Lower Permian here consists mainly of spilites and serpentinites, dunites and harzburgites with intercalations of volcanic greywackes (e.g. the Rai Sandstone), about 2400 m thick, forming the Lee River Group (Lauder, 1965*a, b*; Challis, 1965). On the overturned western limb of the syncline, volcanic rocks dominate comprising augite-rich sheet basalts with rare fossiliferous marine intercalations (Brook Street Volcanics). Included here are basic volcanics at Pepin Island which are intruded by a granodiorite and extensively metasomatized (Lauder, 1964).

Recently, extensive outcrops of Permian rocks with rich fossiliferous horizons have been found in the Onekaka District of northwest Nelson corresponding in age and lithology to the Mangarewa Formation of the Takitimu Mountains in Southland (see below) (Fig. 7.11). This sequence, known as the Parapara Group, begins with unfossiliferous conglomerates (30 m) resting unconformably on the Golden Bay Schists (?Ordovician) followed by about 120 m of quartz sandstones and conglomerates with a rich fauna of Kungurian fossils. (Flowers Formation and Pupu Conglomerate). The Upper Permian is represented by two formations of sandstones and conglomerates, some 300 m thick, the lower unit with siltstone members rich in spessartine garnet and with a porphyrite intrusion at the top (Waterhouse and Vella, 1965). This discovery has considerably changed the palaeogeographical picture of the New Zealand area in the Permian Period as the northwest Nelson area was formerly regarded as a source area for much of the Permian sediments.

The folding of the New Zealand Geosyncline, marked by the intrusion of ultramafics and much volcanic activity, preceded and accompanied the rapid sinking of the trough. This igneous activity ceased quite abruptly at the close of the Early Permian in the Nelson Region, and in the eastern limb of the Nelson syncline there began the deposition of a marine sedimentary sequence (Maitai Group) some 5400 m thick.

In common with other parts of the New Zealand Geosyncline, the sediments begin with a calcareous unit, the Wooded Peak Limestone, forming lensoid masses, mostly recrystallized, from 15 to 600 m thick. In its lower part, it is a light- to dark-grey stone interbedded with green sandstone and fine conglomerate, and in the upper part, a finely banded, pink and green limestone, with beds of green sandstone and calcareous mudstone (Lensen,

1963; Beck, 1964). It is devoid of fossils, except for fragments of the bivalve *Atomodesma* and frequent animal trails. Conformably overlying the limestone is a laminated calcareous green and grey sandstone and siltstone, the Tramway Sandstone, 450–600 m thick. Then follow grey argillites and slates of the Greville Formation (1200–1500 m) and siltstones, sandstones, and

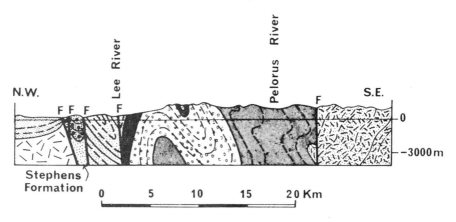

FIG. 7.11. Section south of Nelson, New Zealand. (After Beck, 1964, Sections A–B.)

mudstones of pink and green colour of the Waiua Formation (300–600 m). In the Greville Formation at D'Urville Island the ammonoid *Xenaspis* has been found (Waterhouse, 1964*a*), suggesting a correlation with the upper Kazanian. *Atomodesma* is virtually unknown from the Greville Formation, and completely absent from the Waiua Formation.

The Permian sequence in the Nelson Syncline concludes with the Stephens Formation (2100 m), consisting of green sandstones, dark argillites and conglomerates, and lenses of fossiliferous limestone near the base, from which a brachiopod–mollusc–coral fauna has been described.

The clastic sediments of the Upper Permian here were probably produced by the rapid erosion of a broad anticlinal arch elevated along the zone of Palaeozoic volcanism during the Late Palaeozoic and Early Mesozoic. Grindley (1961*b*) has suggested that the Palaeozoic volcanic belt was the precursor of the New Zealand Geanticline, and has thus played a fundamental part in the growth and development of present-day New Zealand.

OTAGO AND SOUTHLAND REGION

Permian rocks form the limbs of the Southland Syncline which is a broad structure plunging to the southeast. They extend northwards and northwestwards through the Eglinton and Hollyford valleys. By far the most complete sequence is that observed in the Takitimu Mountains of Southland where the Lower Permian rocks are at least 15,000 m thick and the Upper Permian, although incomplete near the top, range in thickness from 3000 to 4500 m in the Hollyford Valley to the north (Fig. 6.5).

The sequence of events begins, possibly in Late Carboniferous times, with the Longwood–Bluff intrusives, chiefly laccolithic masses differentiated into peridotite, pyroxenite, gabbro, and norite, with minor amounts of albite granite, granophyre, and pegmatite. These rocks intrude tuffaceous greywackes, tuffs, and spilitic lavas containing prismatic fragments of *Atomodesma*. The upper age limit of the intrusives is defined by the presence of pebbles of the same lithological type in the basal conglomerates of the Maitai Group (Upper Permian) in eastern Southland. These intrusives and their country rocks are believed to be part of a marginal eruptive assemblage that lay close to the southwestern shore of the New Zealand Geosyncline during the Late Palaeozoic.

Following this intrusive complex comes the Takitimu Group, consisting of about 15,000 m of pyroclastic breccias, spilitic and andesitic tuffs, spilitic pillow lavas, andesite flows and sills, and red and green mudstone and sandstone. Low down in this sequence, in the bluffs at Wairaki Gorge, there is a brachiopod–mollusc–coral fauna with well-defined Sakmarian affinities. There is a striking similarity between this fauna and those of the Lower Permian of eastern Australia (the Cattle Creek Shale of the Springsure region of Queensland; the Dalwood Group of the Hunter Valley, New South Wales), with one notable exception, namely the absence of the bivalve *Eurydesma*. The presence of the brachiopods *Strophalosia*, *Ingelarella*, and *Plekonella* indicates a cold-water regime coincident with a "Gondwana" climate. Other important genera reminiscent of the Permian of eastern Australia are the brachiopods *Cancrinella* and *Terrakea* and the gastropod *Cycloscena*. The brachiopods *Psilocamara* and *Martinia* provide reliable correlations with the Sakmarian Stage of Europe and Asia. Higher up in the Takitimu Group, there are marine intercalations of rather warmer-water affinities containing the brachiopods *Aulosteges* and *Attenuatella*, indicating a lower Artinskian (Aktastinian) age.

In the southwestern and eastern parts of the Southland Syncline, volcanic activity apparently ceased earlier than in other Permian areas in New Zealand. Thus, the volcanic formations of the Takitimu Group are succeeded by sandstones and mudstones of the Productus Creek Group, about 300 m thick, derived from volcanic sources. The lower portion, the Letham Formation, contains a rich fauna of brachiopods (*Strophalosia*, *Wyndhamia*, *Cancrinella*, *Plekonella*, and *Ingelarella*), gastropods (*Warthia*, *Mourlonopsis*, *Platyteichum*, and *Peruvispira*), bivalves (*Stutchburia* and *Streblochondria*), poorly preserved rugose corals referred to the genera *Rotiphyllum*, *Stereostylus*, and *Euryphyllum*, and the tabulates *Thamnopora* and *Cladochonus*. These are correlated with the upper Artinskian. The upper portion of the volcanic sedimentary sequence, the Mangarewa Formation, contains the most fossiliferous horizons in the New Zealand Permian sequence. The key forms are species of the brachiopods *Streptorhynchus*, *Strophalosia*, *Terrakea*, and *Ingelarella*, and are fairly reliably correlated with the Kungurian Stage and possibly the basal Kazanian.

Then came the submergence at the beginning of the Late Permian and the deposition of the Elsdun Formation, including the Glendale Limestone member, followed by a clastic sequence greatly condensed in thickness ending with the coarse Wairaki Breccia similar in texture to the sandstones and grits of the Stephens Formation in the Nelson region.

The northeastern limb of the Southland Syncline is formed of a sequence of red and green pyroclastic breccias, black-banded argillites, purple and green tuffaceous sandstones, lithic tuffs, spilitic pillow lavas, sills of dolerites and keratophyres, and intrusions of gabbro. Through this sequence, known as the Waipahi Group, some 4500 m thick, fragments of *Atomodesma* are common, and an Early Permian age is suggested. Below the Waipahi Group and probably conformable with it, is the Tuapeka Group, consisting of sub-schists, green feldspathic, and tuffaceous greywackes—a typical geosynclinal sequence without any known fossils.

Although eruptive activity ceased somewhat earlier in the Southland Syncline than elsewhere in New Zealand, the Upper Permian is initiated, as in all other localities, by marine limestones. In common with the Waipapa Limestone of Northland and in marked contrast to the Wooded Peak and Howden Limestones of Nelson and northwest Otaga, the Elsdun, Waimahaka and Arthurton Limestones are fairly rich in fossils.

The most complete Upper Permian section in the Southland Syncline, comparable with the Maitai Group of Nelson, is the Bryneira Group in the northeastern limb. Here the Howden limestones and associated green and blue–green sandstones form a narrow meridional belt thickening northwards to 1500 m towards the Alpine Fault where they are abruptly cut off along with other Permian formations. Throughout its length the Howden Formation abuts directly against the volcanic assemblages of spilites, albite dolerites and gabbros, breccias, and tuffs of the Livingstone Formation which, in its turn, is associated closely with the Red Mountain Ultramafics of serpentines and altered dolerites. Stratigraphically above the Howden Formation, the sequence consists chiefly of argillites, sandstones, and conglomerates, with a maximum thickness of 5400 m.

A similar Upper Permian sequence is seen in the eastern limb of the syncline where the Waipahi Group is overlain by 900 m of limestones, sandstones, and argillites of the Arthurton Group. It is of interest to note that the latter contain remains of the plants *Noeggerathiopsis*, *Sphenopteris*, and *Cladophlebis*, usually associated with the *Glossopteris* Flora, as well as a rich brachiopod and molluscan fauna.

Recently a limestone in the Torlesse Group near Benmore Dam in the Waitaki Valley yielded fusuline forams and polycoeliid rugose corals (Hornibrook and Shu, 1965).

PALAEONTOLOGY

The faunas of Australia may be characterized as Gondwana in type in that the distinctive elements *Eurydesma*, *Sanguinolites*, *Atomodesma* (Bivalvia), *Warthia* (Gastropoda), and *Ingelarella* and *Taeniothaerus* (Brachiopoda) occur in all regions. But simply to do this is to obscure the important fact that the western Australian and eastern Australian areas each formed distinct faunal provinces, to say nothing of their constituent sub-provinces. One remarkable feature is the complete absence of the warm-water fusulinid forams, compound rugose corals and enteletid, richthofeniid and notothyrid brachiopods from the Australian continent.

There is a strong Tethyan and Uralian element in the western Australian faunas. This is particularly evident in the large number of ammonoids (*Juresanites*, *Metalegoceras*, *Propinacoceras*, *Uraloceras*, and *Thalassoceras*), the brachiopods (*Aulosteges*, *Dictyoclostus*, *Marginifera*, *Leptodus*, *Neospirifer*, *Spiriferella*, and *Hoskingia*), the polyzoans (*Fistulipora*, *Hexagonella*, *Stenopora*, and *Dyscritella*), many of which are specifically identical with Timor and Salt Range forms, and the bradyodont shark *Helicoprion*. In addition there are strikingly abundant indigenous forms such as the crinoid *Calceolispongia*. This influence is absent from eastern Australia which was dominated by an indigenous fauna. The solitary coral *Euryphyllum*, the brachiopods *Ingelarella*, *Notospirifer*, *Grantonia*, *Trigonotreta*, *Strophalosia*, and *Terrakea* are profuse, as also are the bivalves *Etheripecten*, *Deltopecten*, *Stutchburia*, *Eurydesma*, and

Glyptoleda, the gastropods *Platyteichum* and *Warthia*, and the polyzoans *Fenestella*, and *Stenopora*. Ammonoids are represented by only a handful of specimens, and *Calceolispongia* is known from rare occurrences in Tasmania, New South Wales, and Queensland. A large number of smaller forams including *Calcitornella*, *Hyperammina*, *Ammodiscus*, *Nodosaria*, and *Frondicularia* is found in both east and west (Crespin, 1958). And, finally, insects are common at certain horizons in the Newcastle Coal Measures. A few species of these show similarity to Lower and Upper Permian forms from Russia, and to Lower Permian species from Kansas, but in general there is little evidence of a close relationship with Permian faunas elsewhere in the world.

There appears to have been no marked floral differentiation within the continent, the *Glossopteris–Gangamopteris* flora and the *Striatites* Microflora being ubiquitous (Balme, 1960*b*).

In the New Zealand Permian biota, the most important element for local correlation and general identification of the system is the bivalve *Atomodesma* and its various species, several as yet undescribed. Their shells occur, most commonly as comminuted fragments, from the Lower Permian (?Upper Carboniferous) Longwood Complex to the uppermost Permian Stephens Formation and its correlatives (Waterhouse, 1958*a*).

There is a considerable degree of similarity between the faunal successions of the Lower Permian in eastern Australia and New Zealand. Of particular interest is the occurrence in common of such peculiarly Australasian genera as the brachiopods *Fletcherithyris* and *Terrakea*; the gastropods *Platyteichum* and *Keeneia*; and the bivalves *Etheripecten* and *Glyptoleda*, along with a host of other genera of wider distribution. The New Zealand sequence, on the other hand, includes fusulinids and compound corals, but lacks such characteristic Australian genera as the bivalve *Eurydesma*, the brachiopod *Trigonotreta*, and the crinoid *Calceolispongia*, a feature which suggests that the New Zealand waters were somewhat warmer than those of eastern Australia. Moreover, a link with Tethys is indicated by the presence not only of the fusulinids and compound corals but also by that of the brachiopods *Spiriferella* and *Martiniopsis*, which are absent from the eastern Australian Permian.

With regard to stratigraphical palaeontology the invertebrate sequences of both eastern and western Australia have been subdivided into the informal units indicated above—Faunas I–IV in the east and Stages A–E in the west (Dickins, 1963, 1964/96). Faunas I and II are very similar and are dominated by the brachiopods *Ingelarella ovata*, *Notospirifer hillae*, *Neospirifer* spp., *Strophalosia preovalis*, *Terrakea pollex*, and *Anidanthus springsurensis*; the bivalves *Eurydesma cordatum*, *E. hobartense*, *Megadesmus nobilissimus*, and *Deltopecten limaeformis*; and the gastropod *Keeneia platyschismoides*. These faunas are recognizable in New Zealand in the lower part of the Takitimu Group (Waterhouse, 1963*a–d*, 1964*a*). They are considered to span the late

Sakmarian and early Artinskian. Fauna III contains the same group of genera save *Deltopecten*. The distinctive brachiopods are *Ingelarella ingelarensis*, *Neospirifer wairakiensis*, *Strophalosia dalwoodensis*, *Terrakea elongata*, *Cancrinella magniplica*, and *Plekonella acuta*; the polyzoans *Polypora woodsi* and *Fenestella alticarinata*; the bivalves *Stutchburia costata*, *Glyptoleda glomerata*, and *Atomodesma exaratum*; and the gastropods *Platyteichum costatum* and *Mourlonopsis strzeleckiana*. It is considered to be late Artinskian and Kungurian. Again, this fauna is easily recognizable in New Zealand, this time in the Letham Formation. However, the upper part of the Takitimu Group has a fauna intermediate between Faunas II and III, containing the brachiopods *Aulosteges* sp. cf. *A. ingens* and *Attenuatella* sp. Fauna IV contains the distinctive brachiopods *Strophalosia clarkei*, *Terrakea solida*, *Ingelarella mantuanensis*, *Neospirifer* sp., and *Streptorhynchus pelicanensis*; the bivalves *Chaenomya etheridgei*, *Aviculopecten multicostatus*, and *Myonia carinata*; and the gastropods *Keeneia ocula* and *Walnichollsia subcancellata*. It is Kungurian to Kazanian in age. In New Zealand it occurs in the Mangarewa Formation and its equivalent in the Onekaka District of Nelson.

No later faunas are found in eastern Australia, but in New Zealand two distinct Kazanian faunas and a Tatarian one are known. In the South Island the Kazanian brachiopods *Lissochonetes brevisulcus*, *Horridonia* sp., *Attenuatella incurvata*, *Martinia* sp. aff. *M. mongolica*, and *Stenoscisma papilio* occur in the Arthurton Group, while in the North Island the corals *Waagenophyllum novaezelandiae* and *W. texanum* occur with the fusulinids *Yabeina multiseptata*, *Neoschwagerina margaritae*, and *Verbeekina* sp. in the Waipapa Limestone. The occurrence of the ammonite *Xenaspis* sp. aff. *X. carbonarius* (upper Kazanian) has already been noted in the Greville Formation in the Nelson area. The Tatarian faunas include *Strophalosia planata*, *Neospirifer nelsonensis*, and *Notospirifer microstriatus* (Waterhouse, 1964a, b). A small brachiopod fauna from breccias and sandstones in Southland, correlated with the upper part of the Stephens Formation, is provisionally assigned to the upper Tatarian (Waterhouse, pers. comm.).

Correlations between eastern and western Australia are not strong, being based on a few bivalves, crinoids, polyzoans, and brachiopods (Coleman, 1957; Crockford, 1957; Thomas, 1958; Dickins and Thomas, 1959). The fauna of Stage A is sparse and is characterized by the bivalves *Eurydesma playfordi*, *Deltopecten lyonsensis*; the gastropod *Peruvispira umariensis*; and the brachiopods *Permorthotetes crespinae* and *Linoproductus lyoni*. There is a proliferation of forms in Stage B which is characterized by the crinoid *Calceolispongia digitata*; the brachiopods *Streptorhynchus plicatilis* and *Dictyoclostus callytharrensis*; the polyzoan *Dyscritella spinigera*; the bivalves *Atomodesma mytiloides* and *Euchondria callytharrensis*; and the ammonoids *Juresanites jacksoni* and *Propopanoceras ruzhencevi* (Glenister and Furnish, 1961). Stages A and B are of Sakmarian age. Stage C has few fossils, but Stage D again

The Geological Evolution of Australia and New Zealand

has a rich assemblage prominent among which are the crinoid *Calceolispongia abundans*; the brachiopods *Strophalosia kimberleyensis, Spiriferella australasica,* and *Streptorhynchus hoskingae*; the polyzoan *Dybowskiella arborescens*; the bivalves *Atomodesma exaratum* and *Oriocrassatella stokesi*; the ammonoids *Propinacoceras australe* and *Paragastrioceras wandageense*. It is late Artinskian–Kungurian. Stage E has no marine fossils and only a few plants, and Stage F, which is known only from the Canning and Bonaparte Gulf Basins, has the distinctive brachiopods *Streptorhynchus luluigui* and *Aulosteges fairbridgei* and the bivalves *Atomodesma* sp. nov. It is thought to be Tatarian.

There is a further biostratigraphic subdivision of the Permian rocks of the continent based on microfloras. In the east this has four units labelled P_1–P_4, the basis of which is shown in Table 7.1 (Evans, 1963). More work

	Nuskoisporites Assemblage	*Vittatina* Assemblage		*Dulhuntyispora* Assemblage	
	P_1	P_2	P_3	P_4	R_1
Microreticulatisporites bitriangularis			—		
Thymospora hamatus			– –		
Dulhuntyispora parvitholus			——————		
Marsupipollenites sinuosus			——————		
"Cirratriradites" splendens		– –			
Lunatisporites limpidus	——————				
Thymospora cicatricosus		————			
Verrucosisporites pseudoreticulatus	————————				
"Cirratriradites" sp.	———				
Vestigisporites sp.	———				
Nuskoisporites triangularis	———				

TABLE 7.1. PLANT MICROFOSSIL ASSEMBLAGES FROM THE AUSTRALIAN PERMIAN

is needed to establish the exact relationship of these zones to the Western Australian sequences in which three assemblages have been recognized (Balme, 1964), though sufficient has been done to show a general similarity.

Finally, in regard to the New Zealand Permian faunas, it is important to note that knowledge of these has been gleaned largely from a study of the marginal facies of the New Zealand Geosyncline. Permian fossils, chiefly fragments of *Atomodesma*, have also been identified in the axial facies, the so-called "Alpine Greywackes" (Waterhouse, 1958a) or Torlesse Group (Campbell and Warren, 1965). The indurated greywackes of south Canterbury and north Otago have a sparse occurrence of these fossils, but because of the complex deformation of these rocks, it is almost impossible to delineate the boundaries of the various components of this axial sequence which range in age from Permian to Jurassic. It is possible that the lithologically similar greywackes that form the mountain axis of the North Island, may in future also yield Permian fossils.

CLIMATE

The distribution of tillites and varves of Sakmarian age leaves no doubt that large parts of the southwestern two-thirds of the continent were under ice at that time. Attempts to explain these glacials as the result of small mountain ice caps have proved unsatisfactory since such bodies of ice could not produce the extensive sheets of debris found in the Canning, Carnarvon, Officer, Lake Eyre, and Sydney Basins, or Tasmania, and many glacial deposits are found in areas where there must have been little relief in Permian times. The evidence of glacial pavements, the orientation of overdeepened basins and other glacial topographical features, and the study of provenance of glacial detritus, indicates ice movements as shown in Fig. 7.12. It is interesting to note that these data require areas of ice accumulation in the regions now covered by the sea from the Great Australian Bight to Western Tasmania.

During the Artinskian the climate became warmer, particularly in Western Australia where there is little evidence of very cold conditions. Presumably the accumulation of coal measures at this time in the eastern States indicates a sub-glacial or warmer climate at least for part of the time. The presence of dropped boulders in abundance as far north as northern Queensland and of marine glacials and terrestrial varves and tillites in late Artinskian or Kungurian times in New South Wales and Tasmania argues the presence of land ice in these regions again at this time. There were probably several advances and retreats of the ice cap, but attempts to document these in detail have not yet been successful. Extensive coal-measure conditions during the Kazanian and Tatarian indicate another warmer period.

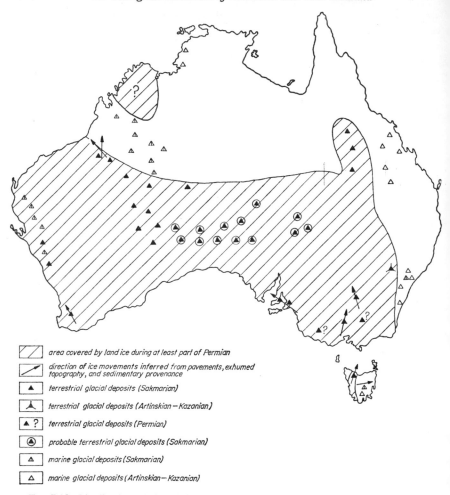

Fɪɢ. 7.12. Distribution of glacial deposits of Permian age in Australia. The area is considered to have been covered by ice during at least part of the period, and the inferred directions of ice movement, are also shown.

Until recently it has generally been considered that the Permian marine deposits of New Zealand show no evidence of the refrigeration that affected the southern hemisphere lands at this time. However, some New Zealand geologists are now inclined to believe that certain Lower Permian formations in Southland and Nelson, with their wide variety of bouldery and angular clastics, especially those recently discovered in the Onekaka District of northwest Nelson, may be deposits from floating ice similar to those forming at present below the Ross Ice Sheet. They are similar also to some of the

Permian glacial rocks of eastern Australia. The main evidence for climatic variation, however, is palaeontological. As is shown above, the lower Takitimu faunas are of eastern Australian type and indicate cold conditions, while those of the upper Takitimu include the warmer-water genera *Aulosteges* and *Attenuatella*. It is significant that this part of the section is correlated with the Greta Coal Measures (Waterhouse, 1963*d*). This then gives place to another cold episode represented by the Letham and Mangarewa Formations of Southland and their partial equivalents in northwest Nelson.

In the succeeding limestones of both islands there is clear evidence of warm-water Tethyan faunas—corals and fusulinids in the north and brachiopods, molluscs, and fusulinids in the south—flourishing while the

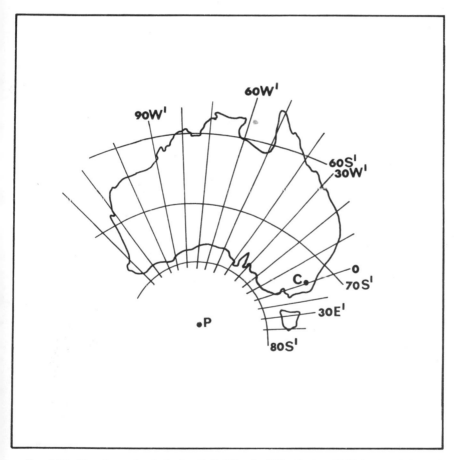

FIG. 7.13. Permian palaeolatitudes, Reliability A. (After Irving, 1964, by permission of John Wiley & Sons Inc.)

Tomago Coal Measures and their equivalents were being deposited in eastern Australia. The cycle is completed by a brief return to cold conditions in the uppermost Permian, the faunas being dominated by *Strophalosia*, *Plekonella*, and *Ingelarella*.

From palaeomagnetic observations of well-dated igneous rocks in Australia, Irving and Parry (1963) have estimated that the mean position of the Permian South Pole with respect to present coordinates was at approximately 45°S, 128°E (Fig. 7.13).

TECTONISM

Australia

The Permian Period in Western Australia was one of only minor activity. Movements were almost entirely vertical along pre-existing faults or were regional downwarps. The transgressions and regressions noted above may possibly have been partly due to eustatic changes as well as to crustal movements.

By contrast the Newcastle Geosyncline and the basins to the east of it were tectonically active, the movements increasing in intensity and reaching a climax towards the end of the period. Collectively they are referred to as the Hunter–Bowen Orogeny. As noted above, folds were developing in the floor of the Newcastle Geosyncline while active sedimentation was occurring, and some of these folds were being eroded as they formed. Downwarping was very rapid in narrow belts in other parts of this structure, as, for example, the Denison Trough. Along the eastern margin of the Newcastle Geosyncline a series of faults (the Hunter–Bowen thrust system) developed, along which Carboniferous and older rocks were thrust over the Permian. Further east, the old Great Serpentine fault belt and its analogue in Queensland, the Yarrol thrust zone, were re-activated. At least in New South Wales this appears to be mainly a wrench fault. Still further east there was extensive block faulting (Fig. 7.14).

Concurrent with this faulting there was widespread folding. In the Newcastle Geosyncline the degree of deformation is closely related to the nature of the basement and to proximity to the marginal faults. In the zone immediately to the west of the Hunter–Bowen thrust system the rocks are in places strongly deformed, as, for example, along the eastern edge of the Bowen Basin to the west of Rockhampton where isoclinal folding and over-turning are common. This, however, is unusual even for this zone, and open domes and anticlines are the rule elsewhere. In general the degree of deformation decreases to the west of the faults. Basement platforms exercised an important role both as buttresses against which the rocks of the neighbouring troughs were folded, and as stable blocks on which only minor folding took

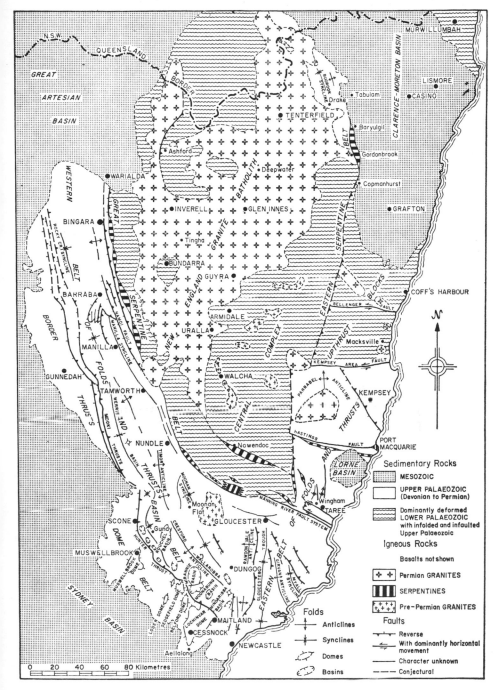

FIG. 7.14. Tectonic map of northeastern New South Wales. (Modified from Voisey, 1959*b*.)

place. On the Comet Ridge, for example, the Permian folds are shallow and apparently due to vertical movement in the basement.

The Carboniferous rocks of the old Tamworth and Yarrol Troughs were deformed at this time into a series of elongate synclines and anticlines, though in many cases the anticlines yielded by thrusting and only the synclines separated by thrust faults now remain (Fig. 7.15). Of particular interest is the folding pattern in the Hunter Valley where the Hunter Thrust System

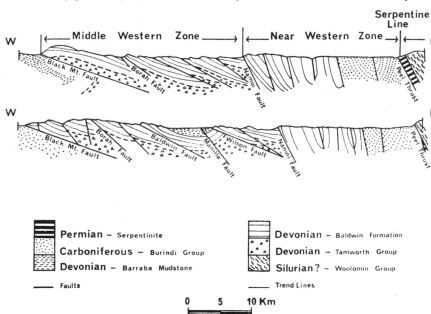

Permian – Serpentinite

Carboniferous – Burindi Group

Devonian – Barraba Mudstone

Devonian – Baldwin Formation

Devonian – Tamworth Group

Silurian? – Woolomin Group

——— Faults

——— Trend Lines

0   5   10 Km

FIG. 7.15. Sections through the Devonian and Carboniferous rocks of the Tamworth Trough west of the Peel Fault, north of Tamworth. Note the repetition of the competent Baldwin Formation by thrusting. (After Voisey, 1957.)

separates Carboniferous rocks in the northeast from Permian rocks to the southwest. Shear stresses in this region have thrown the Carboniferous rocks into a series of small shallow basins, and the Permian into domes of the same scale.

To the east of this region deformation is generally greater, but part of this could be due to Mesozoic movement.

New Zealand

The prime importance of the tectonically active New Zealand Geosyncline in Permian sedimentation has already been stressed. The deepening trough received very thick and mainly eugeosynclinal deposits in the Early Permian at the close of which volcanism appears to have ceased along the margins. The trough, however, continued to receive deposits, initially of a calcareous facies, through most of the Late Permian with a distinct shift of the locus of maximum accumulation towards the Nelson region. The marked similarity between the various Permian formations on either side of the Alpine Fault at points now separated by a distance of about 480 km, forms part of the evidence for a major transcurrent movement along this fracture, probably having taken place largely during the Upper Jurassic–Lower Cretaceous Rangitata Orogeny (cf. Beck, 1964).

IGNEOUS ACTIVITY

Australia

Permian igneous rocks are restricted to the eastern geosynclinal region where both volcanics and plutonics are abundant (Table 7.2).

EXTRUSIVES

Four volcanic units can be recognized. (1) The North Queensland Province in which felsites, rhyolites, and ignimbrites cover several thousands of square kilometres and lie unconformably on the middle Palaeozoics of the Hodgkinson and Bundock Basins, across the Tasman Line, and on to the Precambrian of the Georgetown Massif. In most places these rocks are undated, but at a few localities they have been found conformably overlying sandstones with a *Glossopteris* flora (Hill and Denmead, eds., 1960). (2) In the Newcastle Geosyncline there is a predominance of volcanics in the Lower Permian. Local volcanic sequences may be almost entirely basaltic as in the Hunter Valley or on the northwestern edge of the Bowen Basin, basaltic and rhyolitic in northern New South Wales, andesites as in the Dawson Valley, or interstratified andesites, rhyolites, and trachytes as along most of the northeastern edge of the Bowen Basin. Many of the lithic sandstones in this structure contain material of volcanic origin which is often stated to be tuffaceous but which may equally be due to the degradation of a pre-existing volcanic terrain. Extensive Late Permian volcanism was present only on the south coast of New South Wales. (3) The Yarrol Trough has a long volcanic history, and in places there are thousands of metres of Upper Permian andesites and basalts. The equivalents of the Lower Bowen Volcanics are developed only locally. (4) Volcanic rocks were extruded at various times during the Permian on and in basins along the eastern flanks of the South Coastal–New England High. Rhyolites and acid porphyries together with acid tuffs form the bulk of these rocks, but andesite and andesitic tuff is also particularly abundant in some areas, for instance the Maryborough Basin.

TABLE 7.2. CORRELATION TABLE FOR PERMIAN SYSTEM IN AUSTRALIA.

EUROPEAN STAGE	WEST AUSTRALIAN STAGE	PERTH BASIN	CARNARVON BASIN	CANNING BASIN	BOWEN BASIN FAUNAS	SPRINGSURE–CORFIELD SHELF	DENISON TROUGH	NORTHERN BOWEN BASIN	SOUTH EASTERN BOWEN BASIN	SYDNEY BASIN (HUNTER VALLEY)	SYDNEY BASIN (SOUTH COAST)	TASMANIA	ESK BASIN	YARROL BASIN
TATARIAN ?–?	F		BINTHALYA FORMATION	UPPER LIVERINGA FORMATION (INCL. HARDMAN MEMBER)	?–?–?	UPPER BANDANNA FORMATION	UPPER BANDANNA FORMATION	UPPER BOWEN COAL MEASURES	BARALABA COAL MEASURES / GYRANDA FORMATION	NEWCASTLE COAL MEASURES / TOMAGO COAL MEASURES	ILLAWARRA COAL MEASURES	CYGNET COAL MEASURES		OWL GULLY VOLCANICS
KAZANIAN	E		MUNGADAN SANDSTONE	MIDDLE LIVERINGA FORMATION	IV ?–?–?	LOWER BANDANNA FORMATION	LOWER BANDANNA FORMATION	UNIT C	FLAT TOP FORMATION	MULBRING FORMATION	GERRINGONG VOLCANICS	FERNTREE GROUP	BOX GULLY FORMATION ?–?–?	
KUNGURIAN	2	WAGINA SANDSTONE / MINGENEW FORMATION	COOLKILYA GW. / BAKER FORMATION / MALBIA GW. / WANDAGEE FM. / CUNDLEGO SH. / BULGADO SH. / MALLENS GW. / COYRIE FM.	LOWER LIVERINGA FORMATION (INCL. LIGHT JACK MEMBER)	III	PEAWADDY FM. (MANTHAN PRODUCTUS BED AT TOP)	CATHERINE SANDSTONE	UNIT B	BARFIELD FORMATION / BLACK ALLEY SH.(?)	MUREE FORMATION / BELFORD FORMATION / FENESTELLA SHALE / ELDERSLIE FORMATION	BERRY SHALE(?) / NOWRA SANDSTONE / WANDRA-WANDIAN SILTSTONE	MALBINA FORMATION	BIARRAVILLE FORMATION	YARROL FORMATION
	1	CARYNGINIA FORMATION		NOONKANBAH FORMATION	?–?–?	COLINLEA FORMATION	INGELARA FORMATION						HAMPTON ROAD RHYOLITES	
ARTINSKIAN	D / C	IRWIN RIVER COAL MEASURES	WOORAMEL GROUP	POOLE SANDSTONE (UPPER PART)	II		ALDEBARAN SANDSTONE / SIRIUS SHALE / STAIRCASE SANDSTONE / STANLEIGH FORMATION	UNIT A	BUFFEL FORMATION	GRETA COAL MEASURES / FARLEY FORMATION / RUTHERFORD FORMATION	CONJOLA FORMATION / YADBORO CGL. / PIGEON HOUSE SILTSTONE / CLYDE COAL MEASURES(?)	CASCADES GROUP	?–?–? / PINECLIFF FORMATION	BURNETT FORMATION (UPPER PART)
SAKMARIAN	B	HIGH CLIFF SANDSTONE / FOSSIL CLIFF FORMATION	CALLYTHARA FORMATION	POOLE SANDSTONE (NURA NURA MEMBER)	I	UNNAMED PLANT BEDS	UNDIVIDED FRESHWATER BEDS (INCLUDING ORION FORMATION)	LOWER BOWEN VOLCANICS	CAMBOON ANDESITE	ALLANDALE FORMATION	MERSEY GROUP / GOLDEN VALLEY GROUP	FORMATION	
SAKMARIAN	A	HOLMWOOD SHALE / NANGETTY GLACIAL FORMATION	LYONS GROUP	GRANT FORMATION		JOE JOE FM. (UPPER PART)	CATTLE CREEK FORMATION			LOCHINVAR FORMATION		QUAMBY GROUP / WYNYARD TILLITE	?–?–?	

TABLE 7.3. CORRELATION TABLE FOR PERMIAN SYSTEM IN NEW ZEALAND.

European Stages	Correlations with Eastern Australia — Denison Trough	Hunter Valley	Northland Region	Nelson Syncline — West	Nelson Syncline — East	Southland Syncline — Taktimu Mountains South Limb	Southland Syncline — South Otago North-east Limb	Southland Syncline — Mataura Island South-east Limb	Western Region Area — Hollyford and NE Limb	Western Region Area — Eglinton / Valleys NW Limb
TATARIAN	UPPER BANDANNA FORMATION	NEWCASTLE COAL MEASURES	Sandstone		Stephens Formation Greenish greywacke, rare limestone 1200 m; Waiua Fmn. Grey and marine siltstone 600 m	Wairaki Breccia; Hawtel Formation Tuffs (sequence condensed)	Red argillite; Grey banded argillite 650 m		Countess Formation Green and variegated sandstones 1700 m; Winton Formation Argillites and sandstones 300 m; Tapara Formation Argillites and sandstones 1600 m	
?										
KAZANIAN	LOWER BANDANNA FORMATION	TOMAGO COAL MEASURES	Limestone with fusulinids and corals		Greville Fmn. Sandstones 460 m; Tramway Fmn. Sandstones 400 m; Wooded Peak Formation Limestones 330 m	Eisdun Limestone	Argillite, limestone sandstone; AG4 Limestone 200 m	Titiroa Limestone 55 m; Pine Bush Sandstone 375 m; Waimahaka Limestone 100 m	Annear Formation sandstones 500 m; Howden Formation Limestones, green and blue sandstones 1000 m	Eglinton Volcanics and McKay Intrusives
KUNGURIAN	PEAWADDY FORMATION; CATHERINE SANDSTONE; INGELARA FORMATION	MAITLAND GROUP	lava chert	Green Creek Formation Tuffs 750 m	Breccias spilites gabbros; Dun Mountain ultramafics	Mangarewa Formation; Letham Formation Argillites	Sandstone Argillite Conglomerate 450 m		Livingstone Volcanics; Red Mountain Ultramafics	
ARTINSKIAN	ALDEBARAN SANDSTONE	GRETA COAL MEASURES		Koka basalts 1500 m	Patuki Volcanics 950 m; Rai Sandstone 2400 m	Takitimu Group Pyroclastics, tuffs, sandstones, mudstones, spilites, andesites ? 1500 m	Otama Intrusives; Wajohi Group Sandstones Conglomerates Spilites Greywackes 3500 m		Faulted Section	? Skippers Volcanics
	SIRIUS SHALE; STAIRCASE SANDSTONE; STAMLEIGH FORMATION	DALWOOD GROUP		Grampian Formation Argillites 750 m; Botanical Hill Formation Tuffs 510 m						
SAKMARIAN	UNDIVIDED FRESHWATER				Caesilles Volcanics 120-900 m				? Routeburn Formation	

FAULT (Nelson Syncline)

Group labels (vertical): WAIPAPA GROUP; MAITAI GROUP; BROOK STREET GROUP; PRODUCTUS GROUP; ARTHURTON GROUP; KURAROU GROUP; BYNIRA GROUP; HOLLYFORD GROUP

INTRUSIVES

The Permian–Early Triassic was a period of intense plutonic activity in northeastern New South Wales and eastern and northeastern Queensland. No plutons of proven Permian age are found outside this region. Most of the rocks are acid, mainly adamellites, but there are also other acid and intermediate types. Most have been intruded into rocks of the Tasman Orthogeosyncline, though in north Queensland they also intrude the Precambrian Georgetown Massif. The bulk of them were intruded into the New England High or the Eungella–Gogango High, but it is probable that small bodies were also intruded into the Bowen Basin sediments themselves at this time. All are structurally discordant, intruded at a high level in the crust, and produce only narrow contact aureoles. In New England and southern Queensland the New England Batholith has been shown to be composite. The sequence of intrusions does *not* follow the acid to basic pattern, and on the contrary some are exactly the opposite. This is considered to be the result of progressive hybridization (Chappell, pers. comm.).

Of particular interest are several stocks of granite in north Queensland which were intruded to very high levels in the crust, and in places broke the surface to form rhyolites. The base of these extrusives was then intruded by the granite. Elsewhere the granites are "hooded" by flow-banded porphyry (Hill and Denmead, eds., 1960).

Little is known of the time relations of these rocks since most of them are dated in the most general way only. An upper limit is set in some places to the north of Brisbane where granites are faulted against Lower Triassic rocks and are overlain by Jurassic sandstones. Radiogenic dates from New England and from the eastern side of the Bowen Basin suggest that the period of intrusion ranged from Early to Late Permian. Some plutons, for example, in the Hillgrove district, may be Carboniferous in age (Cooper *et al.*, 1963).

Serpentinites are found in contact with Permian rocks in the Great Serpentine Belt of New South Wales and its continuation into Queensland (the Yarrol thrust zone), as well as in the area near Taree. At one locality near Taree the serpentinites occupy a fault zone between Upper Carboniferous and Permian sediments. It is thought possible that these relationships are the result of re-intrusion of earlier serpentinite, but this is not proved.

New Zealand

The nature of the intense igneous activity associated with the development and extreme deepening of the New Zealand Geosyncline in the Early Permian has already been noted in the stratigraphical section of this chapter and in Table 7.3. Some of the acid intrusions of the Fiordland region (Kakapo, Pomona, and Deas Cove Granites) are also probably of this age, as well as the granitic and dioritic intrusions at Pepin Island, Nelson.

CHAPTER 8

The Triassic System

ROCKS of this system are widely distributed in both islands of New Zealand and, apart from some formations at the top of the sequence that have been correlated with the Rhaetian Stage of Europe, they are entirely marine in origin. In eastern Australia, Triassic sedimentation was widespread in the exogeosynclinal and intramontane basins associated with the Hunter–Bowen mountain chain (Hill and Denmead, eds., 1960; McElroy, 1963). In contrast to those in New Zealand these Triassic sediments are terrestrial—predominantly fluviatile—in origin, except for some marine strata near the base of the sequence in the Maryborough Basin on the Queensland coast. In the interior of the Australian continent there are a few small basins that contain Triassic fluvio-lacustrine sediments. Each of the major basins on the Western Australian coast, which had been initiated during the Palaeozoic, contains marine to brackish water Triassic sequences of limited lateral extent. In addition, fluvio-lacustrine deposits occur in the Canning and Perth Basins.

STRATIGRAPHY
Eastern and Central Australia (Lower Triassic)

The Early Triassic saw the continuation of sedimentation in several of the eastern Australian Permian depositional areas—the Tasmania Basin, at Bacchus Marsh, the Sydney Basin, the Bowen Basin, and the Springsure–Corfield Shelf (Fig. 8.1). In general, the Triassic is conformable upon the Permian, but disconformities occur on the eastern margin of the Tasmania Basin, at Bacchus Marsh in Victoria, and on the western margin of the Bowen Basin and the eastern Springsure–Corfield Shelf. Angular unconformity between Permian and Triassic deposits is known on the western margin of the Bowen Basin near Arcadia (Jensen *et al.*, 1964/61) and in the Lochinvar district west of Newcastle in the Sydney Basin, but is probably only of local significance in each case.

To the east of these Permo-Triassic basins four new basins were initiated, all lying within the region that was affected by the Hunter–Bowen Orogeny during the Late Permian. In two, the Lorne and Clarence–Moreton Basins, the earliest Triassic rocks lie unconformably on deformed Palaeozoic rocks. In the remainder, the Mulgildie and Maryborough Basins, the Triassic lies with apparent angular unconformity on sediments as young as Permian (Fig. 8.1).

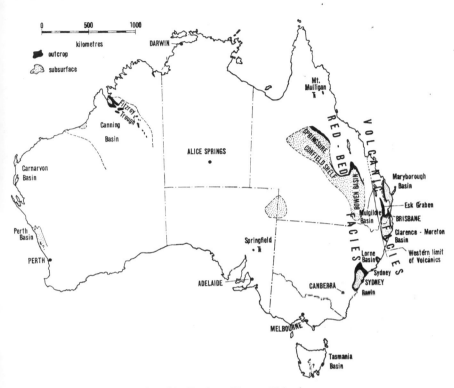

FIG. 8.1. Distribution of Lower Triassic strata.

During the Early Triassic, marine deposition was restricted to part of the Maryborough Basin. Most of the terrestrial deposits accumulated on the western side of the Hunter–Bowen mountain chain as a red-bed facies (Fig. 8.1). This facies is also developed in one intramontane area, the Lorne Basin. In the other intramontane basins thick volcanic and pyroclastic sequences accumulated, forming a volcanic facies. Fluviatile sediments are intercalated with the volcanics.

The Early Triassic stream patterns (Fig. 8.2) are largely conjectural, although there is some control from palaeocurrent measurements in New South Wales (Crook, 1957) and Tasmania (Spry and Banks, eds., 1962).

VOLCANIC FACIES

The volcanic facies is developed in the **Clarence–Moreton Basin**, the southern part of the **Maryborough Basin**, and the **Mulgildie Basin**. Flows, tuffs, and fluviatile sandstones and conglomerates containing volcanic detritus, are characteristic of this facies. In the north of the Clarence–Moreton Basin the Neara Volcanics are predominantly andesitic, with some

FIG. 8.2. Early Triassic palaeogeography.

basalt and rhyolite. The North Arm Volcanics of the Maryborough Basin, and unnamed equivalent strata in the Mulgildie Basin are similar. In contrast the Chillingham Volcanics in the southern part of the Clarence–Moreton Basin are predominantly rhyolitic. The volcanic facies is thickest (3000 m) in the **Esk Graben**, a northern offshoot of the Clarence–Moreton Basin.

Volcanics are poorly developed in the Maryborough Basin, where the Lower Triassic typically consists of shale with some sandstone (Brooweena

Formation). This, in part, reflects a change to marine conditions, for a Lower Triassic fauna including the bivalves *Myalina* sp. cf. *M. putiatensis*, *Bakevellia*, and a myophorid, and the cephalopod *?Protophiceras*, has been reported from the Brooweena Formation (Denmead, 1964). This is the only marine Lower Triassic known in eastern Australia.

RED-BED FACIES

The red-bed facies is developed in the **Sydney, Lorne,** and **Bowen Basins,** and the **Springsure–Corfield Shelf***, and comprises a variegated, green and red sequence of mudstones, shales, lithic sandstones, and conglomerates, all of fluviatile origin. In the Bowen Basin the name Rewan Formation is applied to this sequence, whereas in the Sydney Basin it forms the Clifton Sub-Group and equivalents, these being parts of the Narrabeen Group (see Table 8.1 (p. 243)).

Malone (1964) has discussed some aspects of the distribution of the red-bed facies in Queensland, and presented an isopach map. Other data are available from petroleum search wells and seismic surveys. The red-bed facies outcrops along the northeastern margin of the Springsure–Corfield Shelf, but it thins rapidly towards the southwest, where its limits are poorly known. Outliers, in part subsurface, occur on the Queensland–South Australian border, and perhaps also near Hawker in South Australia (see below) and Mount Mulligan in north Queensland (Pepperpot Sandstone) (Amos and De Keyser, 1964) (Fig. 8.1).

The Rewan Formation exceeds 3000 m in thickness along the eastern side of the Bowen Basin, and thins to the north, west, and south (Malone, 1964). The Clifton Sub-Group is thickest (500 m) near Sydney and also thins to the north, west, and south.

Three petrographic provinces have been recognized within the Clifton Sub-Group and its equivalents, corresponding to different source areas (Crook, 1957). That in the western part of the basin was derived from the west, and comprises quartz-rich detritus with an appreciable percentage of low grade metamorphic rock fragments. That in the north was derived from the northeast. The detritus in it is less quartz-rich, and jasper and sedimentary rock fragments are common. The third province is marked by a quartz-poor detritus and a great variety of rock fragments, including volcanic and plutonic rock types. It is well represented in the east of the basin, and is thought to have been derived from a fold-mountain belt, probably of Hunter–Bowen age, dying off the present coast line to the east.

In the eastern province in particular, but to some extent in the others, red-brown claystones are developed. These are kaolinite- or illite-rich, and are believed to be piedmont deposits (Loughnan *et al.*, 1964).

* Now generally referred to as the Galilee Basin.

?Lower Triassic strata occur in South Australia in the **Springfield Basin**, a small structural basin preserved within the folded Adelaidean strata of the Flinders Ranges near Hawker (Johnson, 1960). The lower part of the sequence in this basin comprises 350 m of coarse, mauve to purple, oligomictic conglomerate, muddy quartz sandstone, and red, chocolate, and grey shales, some of which are gypseous.

Near **Bacchus Marsh** in Victoria thin sequences of mudstone and quartz-rich sandstone occur in fault zones and overlie marine Permian strata. The plant *Dicroidium* has been collected from these Triassic strata.

In the **Tasmania Basin**, Lower Triassic sediments are not well known. Neither red beds nor volcanics occur, the Lower Triassic being composed of quartzose and volcanic lithic sandstones.

Eastern and Central Australia (Middle and Upper Triassic)

The Middle and Late Triassic saw sedimentation in each of the basins already mentioned (Fig. 8.3). In the Clarence–Moreton, Lorne, Sydney, and Tasmania Basins the succession from Lower to Middle Triassic is conformable. The relations between the Lower and Middle Triassic in the Maryborough and Mulgildie Basins are not known, but the successions are probably conformable.

Over much of the Bowen Basin a disconformity separates the Rewan Formation from overlying strata. This relationship also obtains on the Springsure–Corfield Shelf. However, along the eastern margin of the Bowen Basin there is little evidence of a disconformity.

The slight earth movements, towards the end of Early Triassic time, which produced the disconformities, caused a withdrawal of the sea from the eastern margin of the continent and a change in river patterns (Fig. 8.4). There is good control for much of the pattern shown (Olgers *et al.*, 1964/26; Jensen *et al.*, 1964/61; Standard 1961*b*; Spry and Banks, eds., 1962). The climate was sufficiently warm and moist to allow intense weathering in source areas, for the quartzose sandstones that were extensively developed at this time are thought to have been derived from a complex igneous–sedimentary–metamorphic source terrain. In certain of the intramontane areas peat swamps developed.

In the basins west of the Hunter–Bowen Mountains the quartzose sandstones were in due course followed by shales and lithic sandstones, which contain sporadic acritarch hystrichospheres suggestive of some marine influence. This change in sediment type was possibly coeval with tectonic movements in the mountain region to the east, for discordances occur at the base of the Bundamba Group and its equivalents in the Mulgildie and Clarence–Moreton Basins. Subsequent quiescence allowed the deposition of further fluviatile sediments in the intramontane areas.

Towards the end of the Triassic, sedimentation in the Bowen Basin was terminated by gentle folding. A predominantly planar erosion surface was

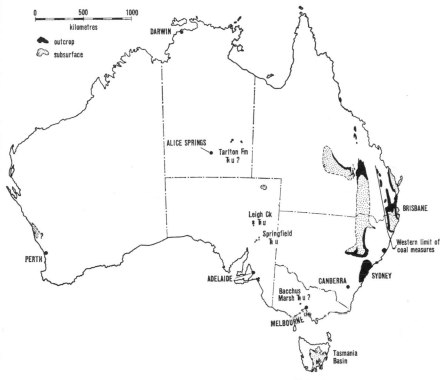

FIG. 8.3. Distribution of Middle and Upper Triassic strata.

cut into the upturned Permo-Triassic formations, and a strongly leached, silicified, and locally ferruginous, regolith developed (A. R. Jensen, pers. comm.). Across this surface, in the Early Jurassic, there spread the basal sands of the Great Artesian Basin Jurassic sequence.

TERRIGENOUS FACIES

The Middle and Upper Triassic sediments of the **Sydney, Lorne,** and **Bowen Basins** and **Springsure–Corfield Shelf** have much in common. The basal unit in each is dominantly quartz-rich sandstone with minor grey shale—the Gosford Formation and Hawkesbury Sandstone of the Sydney Basin, and the Clematis Sandstone of the Bowen Basin and Springsure–Corfield Shelf. The Wianamatta Group of the Sydney Basin and the Moolayember Formation of the Bowen Basin and Springsure–Corfield Shelf overlie the quartz sandstones. These units also are similar, both consisting of argillaceous rocks with some lithic sandstone, especially in the upper part of the sequence. Dark grey shale is typical of the Wianamatta Group,

FIG. 8.4. Middle and Late Triassic palaeogeography.

whereas olive-green to brown mudstones predominate in the Moolayember Formation. Coal seams are rare.

The distribution of the Clematis–Moolayember sequence is more limited than that of the Rewan, save for an extension southward from the Bowen Basin into New South Wales. The sequence is absent from southwestern Queensland, but a buried outlier occurs in the northeast of South Australia (Fig. 8.3). Thicknesses of less than 300 m are general except in the central part of the Bowen Basin where the sequence thickens rapidly to about 2400 m (Malone, 1964), the thickening occurring in the Moolayember Formation.

The Middle and Upper Triassic of the Sydney Basin is more limited in extent than the Lower, probably because of Cainozoic erosion. It reaches a maximum thickness of about 450 m near Camden, southwest of Sydney.

The **Maryborough Basin** and **Esk Graben** each contain more than 450 m of quartzose sandstone (the Myrtle Creek and Wivenhoe Sandstones respectively) similar to those of the Bowen and Sydney Basins. Some inter-bedded grey shales are present also.

COAL-BEARING FACIES

In the **Tasmania** and **Mulgildie Basins**, and the main part of the **Clarence–Moreton Basin**, the Middle and Upper Triassic contains coal measures, a feature that it shares with sequences of similar age in South Australia. In the Clarence–Moreton Basin, quartz sandstone, kaolinite shale, and bituminous to sub-bituminous coals (Ipswich Coal Measures and equivalents) predominate. These reach 1000 m in thickness and are overlain disconformably in the north and unconformably in the south by an extensive unit predominantly of quartz sandstone with conglomerate at the base and some siltstone at the top (Bundamba Group), which is up to 1500 m thick.

A similar break in the sequence may be present in the Mulgildie Basin where a disconformity is believed to occur within the Triassic sequence (Hoyling and Stewart, 1964) which, in addition to coal, contains much lithic sandstone and some volcanics. Precise correlations remain to be established.

Up to 600 m of quartzose and lithic sandstone, shale, and bituminous coal occurs in the Tasmania Basin.

The Middle and Upper Triassic in South Australia, like the Lower Triassic, occurs in isolated structural basins, of which those forming the **Leigh Creek Coalfield** are best known. Other occurrences are in the **Springfield** and **East Boolcunda Basins** near Hawker. In all basins the sequences consist dominantly of grey shale, with quartz sandstone and impure sub-bituminous coal seams. At Leigh Creek these coal measures are productive and reach 600 m in thickness. From them Playford and Dettman (1965) have described a very Late Triassic or possibly Early Jurassic micro-flora. In the Springfield Basin, the sequence is about 500 m thick, and is generally conformable on the ?Lower Triassic, although the non-conglo-meratic portions of these older beds are overlapped by the basal sandstone of the coal-bearing sequence.

In the **Tarlton district** of the southeastern Northern Territory, up to 60 m of quartz sandstone and conglomerate (Tarlton Formation), containing fossil wood and leaves of possible Late Triassic age, lie unconformably on Cambrian or Ordovician strata (Smith, 1964). The Tarlton Formation forms small mesas, and its relationship to the extensive Mesozoic deposits to the east and south is unknown.

Western Australia

Triassic rocks are well developed in the northern part of the **Perth Basin**, where they are known principally in the subsurface (Fig. 8.1). The oldest unit, the Kockatea Shale, is marine, and contains basal Lower Triassic ammonites and bivalves, together with microplankton, spores, and pollen and a labyrinthodont skull roof (Dickins and McTavish, 1963; Balme, 1963). The Kockatea lies on Precambrian gneiss near Geraldton but elsewhere is unconformable on Permian strata (Pudovskis, 1963). Along the coast subsurface thicknesses vary from 240 to 300 m, but the unit thickens markedly to the east, reaching a maximum of 1044 m in the Woolmulla No. 1 well (Pudovskis, 1963).

The Kockatea Shale is overlain by up to 220 m of Lower Triassic quartz-sandstone which is separated from the overlying "Lesueur Sandstone" by a disconformity. The "Lesueur" and the conformably overlying "Multi-coloured Member" of the Cockleshell Gully Formation reach 960 m in thickness and are principally quartz-sandstones with some shale. The "Lesueur" is probably Middle Triassic at its base, and the Triassic–Jurassic boundary is somewhere near the top of the "Multi-coloured Member".

Triassic rocks are unknown in outcrop in the **Carnarvon Basin** to the north of the Perth Basin, but occur in the subsurface beneath the Jurassic in the northwestern part of the basin (Fig. 8.2). Triassic strata are known to occur in the subsurface in the southwestern corner of the **Canning Basin** (Fig. 8.1) where 25 m of siltstone and shale yielded spores, including *Taeniaesporites* sp. cf. *T. kraeuseli*, and microplankton similar to those from the Kockatea Shale (Balme, *in* Bastian, 1962/168).

The Blina Shale, a grey shale containing a similar microflora, together with *Isaura*, *Lingula*, and vertebrate remains, outcrops in the Fitzroy Trough, on the northeastern margin of the Canning Basin, where it may be conformable on the Permian Liveringa Formation (Veevers and Wells, 1961). It reaches its maximum thickness (300 m) in the Derby Town Bore. To the southeast the Blina Shale lies unconformably on Upper Permian units, and in the Minnie Range possible Blina is underlain conformably by up to 60 m of cross-stratified quartz-sandstone (Culdiva) with *Dicroidium*. A similar sandstone (Erskine) conformably overlies the Blina Shale in the Fitzroy Trough. To the southwest of the Fitzroy Trough Triassic strata are absent in both outcrop and subsurface.

Veevers and Wells (1961) envisage the Blina Shale as accumulating during the Early Triassic in an arm of the sea, with the Culdiva Sandstone being derived from Permian units and accumulating on land to the southeast. Transgression subsequently extended the Blina Shale over the Culdiva. Towards the end of the Early Triassic the sea withdrew and the Erskine Sandstone, a fluviatile deposit, spread over the Blina Shale.

Isaura-bearing shales that are similar to the Blina Shale occur in the Northern Territory in the northeast of the **Bonaparte Gulf Basin** (Fig. 8.1) where they form the upper part of the Port Keats Group (Thomas, 1957). They are poorly known, and overlie Permian strata.

New Zealand

In the Late Permian and Early Triassic, the New Zealand Geosyncline was bordered on the west by a landmass or geanticline, and land areas also occupied the southeastern margins of the trough. The geanticline had developed from the elevated axis of the Permian volcanic arc from which the volcanics were stripped by erosion, and then the underlying metamorphic and granitic core was exposed. The materials thus provided form the sediments of the lower Lower Triassic sequence. As in the Permian System, the rocks of Triassic age may be classified as *axial* and *marginal* facies respectively, with some intermingling in places (Fig. 8.5).

Although we may clearly detect the presence of these geotectonic units, there is no direct evidence at present of the position of the shorelines of the land masses, except perhaps in Southland. That they were not far distant at times, however, is evidenced by the presence of plant remains in the Rhaetian rocks of mid-Canterbury and North Otago, which are probably of deltaic origin, spreading over the shelves and even towards the axis of the trough (Fleming, 1962). Volcanoes were active and were probably for the most part of submarine type. They contributed substantial amounts of ash and tuff to the sinking trough and extensive limestones are absent from the Triassic sequences. The tuffaceous rocks frequently have interbedded flows of fine-grained spilitic and variolitic basalt, often with thin lenses of chert and limestone, the whole mass characteristically red and green in colour. Throughout the period there is an overall decrease in volcanism, with a concomitant change from basic to acidic tuffs.

The relations between the oldest known Triassic formations and those of the Permian System are obscure. In the **Kawhia Syncline**, Permian formations are not known, whereas in the Nelson region the Permian and Triassic are in contact only along faults. An angular unconformity exists at this level in the Takitimu area of the Southland Syncline, but it has been pointed out (Waterhouse, 1963*d*, p. 174) that there is probably a passage sequence in the Livingstone Range within the beds of the Countess Formation, which span the Permian and Triassic. This requires further investigation.

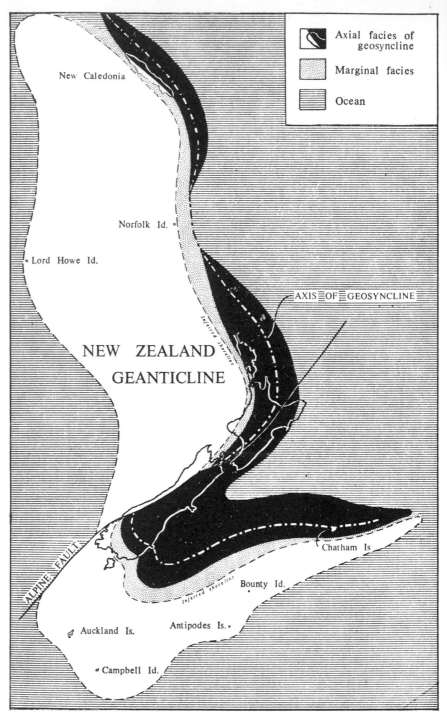

FIG. 8.5. Triassic palaeogeography of New Zealand. (After Fleming, 1962, by permission of *Tuatara*.)

The Triassic System in New Zealand has two divisions, the Lower and Middle Triassic Gore Series, and the Upper Triassic Balfour Series.

AXIAL FACIES

The axial rocks are mainly greywacke-type accumulations, almost unfossiliferous, with thin interbedded layers of spilitic basalt, altered and strongly deformed. They occupy areas in Northland, the central portion and the main mountain ranges of the North Island and the Southern Alps, and the eastern piedmont of the South Island.

It is impossible at present to estimate the proportion of Triassic components in the greywacke sequences of the New Zealand area. The occurrences of Triassic fossils in the rocks of this facies (Torlesse Group) are extremely scattered, but in almost every case they belong to species (e.g. *Monotis richmondiana* Zittel) commonly found in the rocks of the marginal facies, and were probably transported from the shelf areas to the pelagic zone. The greywackes also frequently contain remains of tube-worms (*Terebellina, Titahia*) and plant fragments. Recent finds in the South Island have also included polyzoans ("*Monotrypella*") and an ammonite aptychus (see Campbell and Warren, 1965).

MARGINAL FACIES

On the shelf margins of the New Zealand Geosyncline sands, muds, and often very coarse conglomerates were deposited. These are now exposed in the southwest Auckland, Nelson, and Southland regions. With the exception of the Nelson area, the Triassic rocks underlie Jurassic formations and are involved with them in folding of a relatively simple nature. The southwest Auckland and Nelson Triassic strata form part of a large synclinal structure extending southwards along the west coast of the North Island from about the latitude of Huntly into the Nelson area. They are partly obscured by the Tasman Sea and by the younger sediments and volcanics of the Taranaki region. It is reasonable to suppose that, prior to movement along the Alpine Fault in Middle Mesozoic times, this synclinal structure also joined with the Southland Syncline. Limestones are rare in the Triassic marginal facies as compared with their abundance in that of the Permian System.

SOUTH AUCKLAND REGION

The Mesozoic rocks occupy the north-trending **Kawhia Syncline** which, in fact, includes two major synclines, a major anticline and minor parallel folds, broken by a number of meridional strike faults. Triassic rocks appear on both flanks of the structure and are characterized by steep dips (70–90°). The sequence is quite incomplete and no rocks of the Gore Series are known to be present (Fig. 8.6).

The lowest part of the exposed Triassic sequence, which is here apparently restricted to the Balfour Series, comprises the Moeatoa Conglomerates (1200 m), outcropping on the southwest flank of the structure south of the Marakopa River. Boulders in the conglomerate range up to 2·5 m in diameter, and they are angular to rounded, badly sorted, and poorly bedded. Many of them consist of markedly stressed, acid holocrystalline igneous types, presumably derived from a landmass immediately to the west. The unit is placed in the Oretian Stage since it is overlain disconformably by about 300 m of indurated sandstones and siltstones with some tuffaceous material which, further to the northeast, contain the bivalve *Halobia*.

The sequence then continues through about 2000 m of beds typical of Triassic areas elsewhere in New Zealand, namely indurated sandstones and siltstones with frequent admixture of tuffaceous material, containing the characteristic fossils of the Otamitan, Warepan, and Otapirian Stages. The beds of the last-named stage are markedly coarser in texture than those of the older formations, and contain fossils only in the southwest part of the region.

NELSON REGION

The Triassic sequence forms a northeasterly-trending strip about 30 km long with a maximum width of about 3 km, just to the southwest of Nelson City. Along its eastern margin it is everywhere in thrust-fault contact with Upper Permian formations, so that its base is not seen, and the oldest Triassic rocks exposed belong to the Kaihikuan Stage. These are unfossiliferous, indurated sandstones of unknown thickness. This is in contrast to the very coarse, bouldery conglomerates at the base of the exposed Triassic sequence in the South Auckland region. In the vicinity of Wairoa Gorge, however, there are excellent sections in the Oretian, Otamitan, Warepan, and Otapirian Stages which are closely similar to those in the South Auckland area (Fig. 7.11).

It was in the Richmond area, near Nelson, that Hochstetter (1865, p. xxxiii) recorded the oldest rocks found by him during his visit to New Zealand in 1859. He recognized in these rocks ". . . species of *Monotis* and *Halobia* that are not distinguishable from the European forms . . . from the Trias of the Alps" (Fleming, 1959*b*, p. 15). Although the similarities at the specific level cannot now be entirely justified, he did draw attention to the remarkable resemblances between the marine Triassic faunas of Europe and those of equivalent age in New Zealand.

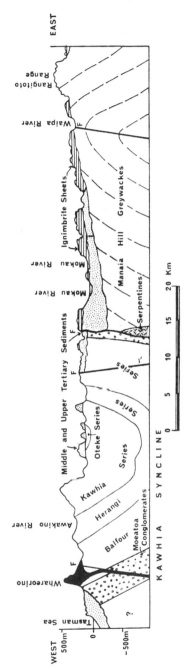

Fig. 8.6. Section across southern end of Kawhia Syncline, North Island, New Zealand. (After Kear, 1960, Section C–D.)

SOUTHLAND REGION

The Triassic rocks occupy a broad linear belt along the northern flank of the **Southland Syncline** and outcrop over a considerable area of its western culmination in the North Range, Taringatura Hills, and Wairaki Downs region. In these areas, the strata are from 3000 to 9000 m thick, in contrast to a much thinner development on the southern part of the syncline east of Mataura Island. It is in the former area that the most complete sequence of the New Zealand Triassic rocks occurs and this is taken as the standard section for correlations in the Dominion. In general, the coarseness of the sediments, the occurrence of plant remains and the abundance of fossils, indicate the deposition of these rocks in shallow water (Fig. 6.5).

Before proceeding further with the stratigraphy, it should be noted that the very thick Triassic sequence of the North Range contains a number of almost complete and uncomplicated sections which show clearly the general trend of a low-grade metamorphism bridging the wide gap between the sedimentary processes and the higher metamorphic facies (zeolite facies—prehnite-pumpellyite zone—greenschists) (Coombs, 1954; Coombs *et al.*, 1959).

The oldest-known Triassic rocks of the Gore Series (pre-Etalian) outcrop in the Wairaki Downs area on the western margin of the syncline. Their relationship to the uppermost beds of the Upper Permian Productus Creek Group is not known but is probably angularly unconformable. Their lithology is dominantly tuffaceous sandstone with some pebbly layers.

The Etalian Stage is represented in the same area by dark, blue–grey, banded, fossiliferous mudstones, but on the northern limb of the syncline it contains much more tuffaceous material.

The succeeding Kaihikuan Stage has a very much wider distribution. It consists of fine-grained, indurated, blue–grey sandstones and shales with an admixture of volcanic breccia, extending westnorthwestwards from the coast at Nugget Point along the northern flank of the syncline to the Wairaki Hills. It is also known at isolated points in other parts of the South Island in North Otago and mid-Canterbury. Like the preceding stages it has not been recorded in the North Island.

The Gore Series in the Southland Syncline, as a whole, varies in thickness from zero to more than 600 m. The shoreline extended roughly from south of Nugget Point through Ohai to north of Milford Sound. The thickest sections were developed towards the axial margin of the Early Triassic shelf, in the North Range, north of Gore, and at Clinton.

The transition from the Gore Series to the Balfour Series is marked chiefly by a faunal change, with the pteriid bivalve *Halobia* making its first appearance in the Oretian Stage. Thick beds of vitric and mottled tuffs indicate a renewal of volcanism, and in the basal conglomerates of this stage there are noted, for the first time, pebbles derived from the igneous and metamorphic rocks of the Fiordland area.

In the Otamitan Stage which follows, the rocks are dark blue–grey siltstones and mudstones and less common tuffaceous sandstones. There are also thick shell-beds consisting of the bivalve *Manticula* which make useful marker horizons.

The strata of the Warepan Stage at the western culmination of the Southland Syncline probably exceed 500 m in thickness, but elsewhere in the structure they are thin and impersistent because of unconformities both above and below. According to Mutch (1957) they lack primary tuffs and consist mainly of blue–grey coarse sandstones and pebble conglomerates. The occurrence of the characteristic fossil *Monotis richmondiana* (Zittel) is somewhat spasmodic, but readily serves to distinguish rocks of this age. For this reason also, Warepan rocks have frequently been recorded in areas where strongly deformed rocks of the axial facies are developed.

The youngest unit of the Balfour Series, the Otapirian Stage, is represented in the western part of the syncline by sandstones, siltstones, and fine conglomerates up to 1500 m thick in the North Range. Its boundaries with the Warepan Stage below and with the Jurassic System above are recognized on the basis of faunal changes.

PALAEONTOLOGY

Direct correlation between the Triassic sequences in Australia and those in New Zealand is not at present possible owing to the paucity of marine fossils in Australia and the lack of information on the New Zealand Triassic microflora. In view of the arbitrary nature of the Permo-Triassic boundary in Australia, and floral differences between the Triassic of Europe and Australia, indirect correlation has not been attempted, and separate correlation charts (Tables 8.1 and 8.2) are presented for each country.

Australia

All the conformable sequences in Australia that can be expected to contain the Permo-Triassic boundary are of fluviatile origin. The boundary is therefore defined on a change which is evident in both macro- and microflora. This boundary has not been satisfactorily related to the Permo-Triassic boundary of other continents. Correlation within the Triassic System in Australia is principally palynological (Evans, 1963; De Jersey, 1964). The scheme of Evans (1963) has been followed herein.

In place of the *Glossopteris* flora of the Permian, the Triassic flora is one dominated by *Dicroidium* [*Thinnfeldia*]. *Sphenopteris, Cladophlebis, Ginkgoites,*

Baiera, Taeniopteris, and *Phyllotheca* are characteristic associated forms. This change is reflected in the microflora by the replacement of the Late Permian *Striatites amplus–Dulhuntyspora parvolitha* assemblage by an assemblage containing *Quadrisporites horridus, Nuskoisporites radiatus,* and *Trizonaesporites* sp., and distinctive forms of *Alisporites.* In Western Australia a different microflora containing *Lundbladispora* and distinctive forms of *Taeniaesporites* and *Kraeuselisporites* occurs with a very early Triassic marine fauna (Balme, 1963). The relationship of this microflora to those in eastern Australia is in doubt. *Taeniaesporites* occurs in the earliest Triassic assemblages in the east, but does not become abundant until higher in the sequence, where it is joined by *Aratrisporites.*

Taeniaesporites does not extend into the Middle and Upper Triassic. There *Alisporites* is dominant, together with *Aratrisporites* and new forms, *Polypodiisporites ipsviciensis* and *Saturnisporites* sp. The last is absent from the youngest Triassic strata.

Marine fossils are known only from the Lower Triassic in the Carnarvon, Perth, and Maryborough Basins and include such genera as the ammonites *Ophiceras* and *Subinyoites,* and the bivalves *Trigonucula* and *Bakevellia.* Labyrinthodont amphibians are known from both east and west Australia. The remains of freshwater fish are locally common in the Sydney Basin and include dipnoans (*Ceratodus*) and chondrosteans (*Cleithrolepis* and *Brookvalia*) (Wade, 1935). Insect remains, including the giant *Clathrotitan,* are not uncommon associates of the fossil fish.

New Zealand

One of the striking characteristics of the Triassic System in New Zealand, first noted by Hochstetter (1865), is the similarity in faunal content to that of the coeval rocks in the European Alps, a feature now considered to have been the result of faunal migration along the Sea of Tethys.

The very sparse fauna of the axial facies of the Triassic System has already been noted (see p. 233). In contrast, however, the rocks of the marginal facies contain an abundance of fossils which have been extensively used for stratigraphical subdivision.

Some of the most reliable fossils for correlation are, of course, the ammonoids. It should be noted, however, that Kummel (1960, p. 489) believes that virtually all the ammonoid genera in the Triassic of New Zealand are common forms widely distributed in Tethys and in the geosynclines around the north Pacific region. He suggests that this indicates ". . . that the seaways in and around New Zealand during the Triassic were openly joined with and a part of the Circum-Pacific margin and with Tethys".

No terrestrial animals are known from the New Zealand Triassic deposits, but it is likely that ancestors of some of the present archaic forms like the tuatara (*Sphenodon*) and the native frog (*Leiopelma*) had already established themselves at this time.

In the oldest known (pre-Etalian) Triassic rocks from the Wairaki Downs area of the Southland Syncline (western culmination), Kummel (1959) has identified the middle Scythian ammonoids *Owenites*, *Flemingites*, *Subvishnuites*, and *Wyomingites*. A late Scythian ammonoid, *Prosphingites*, has recently been reported from South Otago (Kummel, 1965).

In the Etalian Stage, which is also recognized only in the Southland Syncline, another ammonoid fauna has been found, including the genera *Ptychites*, *Leiophyllites*, *Parapopanoceras*, *Monophyllites*, *Tropigastrites* and *Discophyllites* of Anisian age. The gastropods *Mellarium* and *Worthenia* have also been reported from this stage.

A reliable correlation of these two stratigraphical units has been made on the basis of the ammonites, but later Triassic faunas are rather more indigenous. Links with the Alpine Triassic of Europe are, however, frequently obtained through the similar geosynclinal sequences known in the Spiti region of India.

For instance, in the Kaihikuan Stage, there are numerous fossils, the more abundant including species of the bivalve *Daonella* similar to those in Spiti and the European Alps, indicating a correlation with the Ladinian Stage. Very early trigoniid genera, *Agonisca* and *Praegonia*, are also characteristic, along with several species of dielasmatid and spiriferinid brachiopods. Fleming (1964) has postulated that the trigoniids, so characteristic of the Mesozoic Era, originated from myophoriid ancestors in the Middle Triassic in the South Pacific area and from there spread to other parts of the globe. It is also of interest to note that, on the northern spurs of Mount Potts, mid-Canterbury, Kaihikuan beds have yielded the remains of a large marine reptile, *Ichthyosaurus hectori*. Plant remains are also well represented in this stage and include the earliest known araucarians and podocarps.

The incoming of the Balfour Series is, as noted earlier, marked by the first appearance of the pteriid bivalve *Halobia* in the Oretian Stage. Spiriferinid brachiopods are common and an indeterminate species of the ammonoid *Epigymnites* has been recorded, but correlation with the Lower Carnian of Europe is based mainly on the presence of *Halobia*. The early trigoniids of the Kaihikuan Stage are replaced by *Maoritrigonia*, a member of the subfamily Minetrigoniinae which spread widely over the Pacific area during the Late Triassic (Fleming, 1964).

There is a particularly abundant fossil fauna in the blue–grey siltstones and mudstones of the Otamitan Stage. Especially prominent is the bivalve *Manticula problematica* (Zittel) which, in places, forms solidly packed shell beds exceeding 8 m in thickness. *Halobia* still persists along with *Triaphorus* and

Palaeocardites, and the cephalopods *Grypoceras, Proclydonautilus, Rhacophyllites, Cladiscites, Arcestes, Epigymnites,* and *Pinacoceras,* to mention the chief constituents. A species of ichthyosaur has recently been reported in upper Otamitan strata in the Hokonui Hills (Campbell, 1965a). A late Carnian age is indicated by this fauna.

As mentioned above, the Warepan Stage is recognized chiefly by the widespread distribution of *Monotis richmondiana* (Zittel), a member of a species group that established itself in great abundance along the Sea of Tethys and around the Pacific region. This provides a most reliable correlation with the Norian Stage in Europe.

The Otapirian Stage is ushered in at the type locality, Otapiri Valley, by the appearance of the spiriferinid brachiopod *Rastelligera diomedea* Trechmann and closes with the incoming of the first psiloceratid ammonites of Early Jurassic age. Other characteristic fossils are the brachiopod *Clavigera* and the bivalve *Otapiria dissimilis* (Cox). All of these, however, are quite indigenous, so that correlation with the Rhaetian Stage of Europe is achieved through the presence in Otapirian strata of the ammonoids *Arcestes* and *Aulacoceras* and the pteriid bivalve *Rhaetavicula.* Beds of this age at Mount Potts, Clent Hills, and Mount St. Mary, contain Rhaetian plant remains.

CLIMATE

Despite the high palaeolatitude of Australia during the Triassic, when eastern Australia ranged between 60°S′ in Queensland and 75°S′ in Tasmania, and western Australia ranged from 48°S′ to 58°S′ (Irving, 1964) (Fig. 8.7) neither the fauna and flora nor the sediments show evidence of cold conditions.

The accumulation of red beds in the fluviatile exogeosynclinal basins of eastern Australia that were associated with the Hunter–Bowen mountain chain, suggests warm conditions with strongly seasonal rainfall.

The Triassic climate in the New Zealand area is assumed to have been warm temperate, though this is largely based on negative evidence. For instance, there is no record of reef corals and the small amount of Triassic vegetation known from the area gives no clue in regard to temperature zonation.

TECTONISM AND IGNEOUS ACTIVITY

One striking feature of the Australia–New Zealand region is the localization on its eastern margin of Triassic tectonism and acid to basic calc-alkaline volcanic activity. Epi-Permian folding is limited to northeastern

New South Wales, eastern Queensland, and New Zealand, and the Early Triassic volcanicity follows a similar pattern. Folding later in the Triassic affected an even smaller area: certain of the intramontane basins in eastern Australia and the southern part of the New Zealand Geosyncline. Triassic granites are confined to New Zealand, as are virtually all Middle and Upper Triassic volcanics.

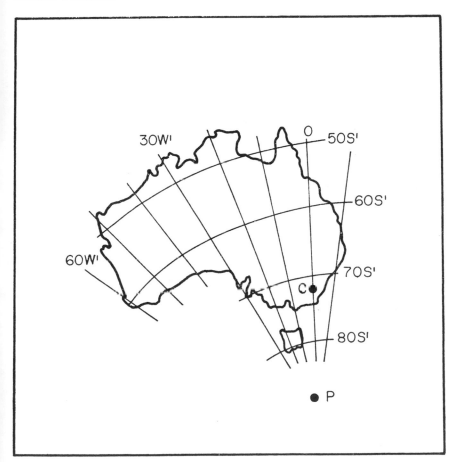

Fig. 8.7. Triassic palaeolatitudes, and palaeomeridians based on Canberra. Reliability A. (After Irving, 1964, by permission of John Wiley & Sons Inc.)

Australia

The sources of the calc-alkaline andesites, rhyolites, and basalts in the Lower Triassic of the Clarence–Moreton, Maryborough, and Mulgildie Basins are not known. No dated igneous intrusives of Triassic age are known in Australia, but several intrusive masses in the Esk Graben, of trachyte, dacite, and gabbro are regarded as probably Triassic. This would accord with the maximal development of volcanics in this part of the Clarence–Moreton Basin. Undoubtedly, local sources in other areas remain undiscovered.

Folding during the Triassic was weak, angular discordances being confined to the southern part of the Clarence–Moreton Basin, within the Middle and Upper Triassic succession. Elsewhere in the intramontane basins the movement is expressed either by disconformities, or by an absence of uppermost Triassic strata, as, for example, in the Lorne and probably the Maryborough Basins.

The exogeosynclinal basins, west of the Hunter–Bowen Mountain chain, seem not to have been deformed by this Middle or Late Triassic movement. They had, however, been affected by weak movements at the end of the Early Triassic, which produced disconformities in many places. No signs of this ep-Early Triassic movement are visible in the Triassic sequences of the intramontane basins. However, it seems to have caused withdrawal of the sea from the entire present land area of the Australian continent.

New Zealand

The axial facies of the New Zealand Geosyncline includes numerous interstratified flows of spilitic and variolitic basalts, commonly associated with tuffaceous greywacke, and lenses of chert and limestone. They are believed to have been erupted from fissures in the trough or in the flanks of the geanticline to the west. Because of the general disruption of these strata during the later eversion of the trough, it is difficult to give an age to the majority of these conspicuous, though not very extensive, marker beds. However, in some places, for instance, Harper Pass, Canterbury, a good correlation is available in the close association between such flows and Warepan limestones containing *Monotis richmondiana* (Zittel).

On the New Zealand Geanticline to the west and south of the geosyncline, sporadic volcanism supplied considerable quantities of andesitic and dacitic tuffs to the sediments accumulating on the shelf margins of the trough. In Southland also, there are some small porphyrite intrusions in the Triassic sediments.

In Southland, where the New Zealand Triassic is most typically developed, and probably also in the Nelson area, Wellman (1956, p. 25) considers that each stage thickens towards the schist basement. On the west side of the Southland Syncline, the dips of the Triassic strata are gentle and may represent the initial dips associated with the thickening. However, the characteristically steep dips on the east side of the Southland and Nelson synclines

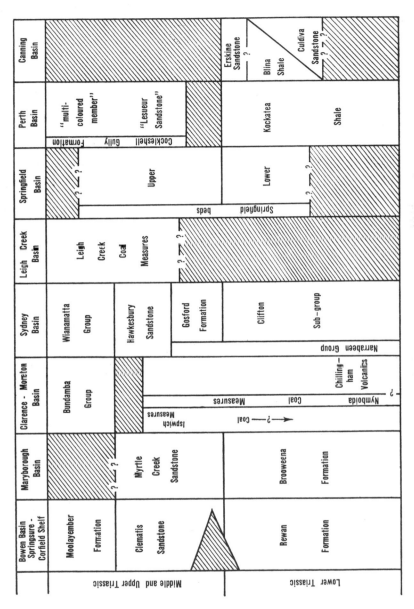

TABLE 8.1. CORRELATION TABLE FOR THE TRIASSIC SYSTEM IN AUSTRALIA

were formed during the deformation and eversion of the New Zealand Geosyncline as the thicker sediments were pressed against the stable geanti-clinal shelf. It should be noted, however, that Coombs (*in* Coombs *et al.*, 1959) contests the validity of the hypothesis that there is thickening towards the schist basement, and considers that in the Early Mesozoic there were, in southern New Zealand, more or less separate depositional troughs for the two sedimentary facies.

Emplacement of granites may also have occurred at this time in the west Nelson region, as well as in the vicinity of the Bounty Islands, about 850 km east of Stewart Island. Wasserburg *et al.* (1963) have recently dated a granite from the Bounty Islands at 188 ± 5 m.y. (K/A); 139 ± 5 m.y. (Rb/Sr), which is close to the Triassic–Jurassic boundary.

CHAPTER 9

The Jurassic System

JURASSIC strata in Australia are confined to the Canning, Carnarvon, and Perth Basins in Western Australia, and to the Carpentaria, Laura, Maryborough, Great Artesian, Polda, Mulgildie, and Clarence–Moreton Basins in eastern Australia (Fig. 9.1). They reached their greatest areal extent in Late Jurassic times. The deposits in eastern Australia are almost exclusively non-marine. Much of the Western Australian Jurassic is marine, but only that in the western part of the Carnarvon Basin is regarded as a deep-water deposit. Volcanism was greatly restricted both in time and space in the Jurassic of Australia.

In New Zealand the Jurassic rocks are geographically associated and, on the whole, conformable with those of the Triassic System. They are also lithologically similar to the Triassic but, especially in their upper portions, they are less indurated, finer bedded, and contain more mudstone and less visible feldspar. In general, they also have gentler dips and enter less into the structure of the mountain regions. In contrast to the Australian Jurassic, the products of volcanism still contributed a great deal to the marine sedimentary accumulations though they tended to diminish in amount as emergence of much of the area took place in the Middle and Late Jurassic.

STRATIGRAPHY

Australia

During the Early Jurassic the principal area of deposition lay in the north-eastern part of the continent (Fig. 9.2) where the Triassic drainage had been modified so as to form a new sedimentary basin, the Great Artesian Basin. This basin had precursors in the Permo-Triassic Bowen Basin and Springsure–Corfield Shelf, but it occupied a larger and somewhat different area. The Great Artesian Basin has a history extending into the Cretaceous during which period it reached its greatest areal extent. In the Early Jurassic, as later, the smaller Clarence–Moreton and Mulgildie Basins to the east seem to have been connected to the Great Artesian Basin, the whole forming a single drainage system. In North Queensland the Laura Basin was initiated

245

by fluviatile deposits lying athwart Precambrian and Palaeozoic structures.
Both this and the Great Artesian Basin were subjected to minor marine
incursions during the Early Jurassic.

   In Western Australia the Perth Basin was a site of fluviatile deposition from
the Late Triassic to the end of the Early Jurassic, whereas further north in

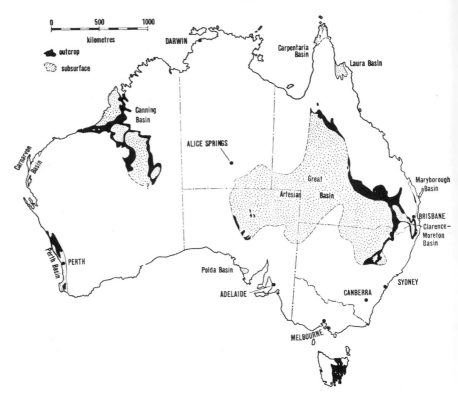

FIG. 9.1. Distribution of Jurassic strata.

the Carnarvon Basin the little known Lower Jurassic is marine, and its
relationship to the Triassic is not clear.

   This basic pattern for the continent was modified during the Middle
Jurassic by extension and ponding of the Great Artesian Basin which
permitted coal accumulation (Fig. 9.3). The Maryborough Basin on the
northeast coast and the Canning on the northwest, which had been non-
depositional areas since the Triassic, once again became sites of fluviatile
deposition. With the accumulation of fluviatile deposits in north Queensland
and southwest Papua, a new basin, the Carpentaria, was initiated. A marine
transgression occurred in the Perth Basin early in the epoch but was

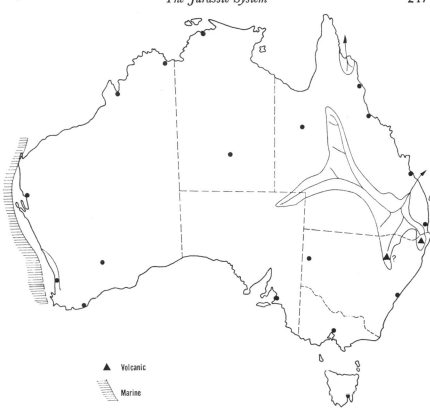

Volcanic

Marine

FIG. 9.2. Early Jurassic palaeogeography.

shortlived. Another affected the Carnarvon Basin towards the end of the epoch.

Further extension of fluviatile deposition in the Great Artesian Basin took place during the Late Jurassic and deposition commenced in the Polda Basin. The Maryborough and possibly the Carpentaria Basins were not sites of deposition (Fig. 9.4). The Canning Basin developed remarkably with marine incursions covering a wide area and fluviatile deposition extending some hundreds of kilometres inland. In the Carnarvon Basin marine deposition continued and was slightly more widespread than during the Middle Jurassic. In other basins deposition continued much as before.

EASTERN AND SOUTHERN AUSTRALIA

The Early Jurassic saw the initiation of sedimentation in the **Great Artesian Basin** of Queensland on an erosion surface cut into Upper Triassic and older units. In the adjoining **Clarence-Moreton** and **Mulgildie**

Basins deposition may have been continuous from the Late Triassic into the Jurassic. These basins seem to have been appendages of the Great Artesian Basin during the Jurassic. Cross-stratification measurements in the Clarence–Moreton Basin (Hill and Denmead, eds., 1960) suggest that streams flowed through it into the Great Artesian Basin, depositing quartz-rich sands (Marburg Sandstone). In the Great Artesian Basin coeval quartz-rich

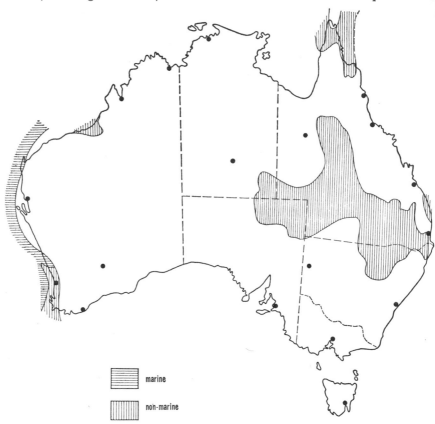

marine

non-marine

FIG. 9.3. Middle Jurassic palaeogeography.

sands (Precipice Sandstone) were spread over the old land surface by an extensive river system. The sediments on the northeastern margin of the basin were derived from the west, northwest, and east (Jensen *et al.*, 1964/61). Rivers appear to have gained access to the sea by way of the Mulgildie Basin (Fig. 9.2). The Precipice Sandstone is an important producer of oil at Moonie and natural gas near Roma.

Although sands continued to accumulate in the Clarence–Moreton Basin throughout the Early Jurassic (McElroy, 1963), finer material (Evergreen

Shale) with some lithic sandstone succeeded the Precipice Sandstone in the Great Artesian and Mulgildie Basins. The Evergreen may be marine in part, for swarms of acritarch hystrichospheres occur at several localities (Evans, 1962/115).

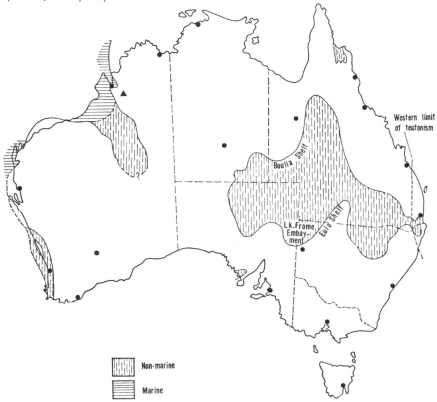

FIG. 9.4. Late Jurassic palaeogeography.

A return to fluviatile conditions probably occurred with the deposition of the quartz-rich Hutton Sandstone which is the most widespread of the Lower Jurassic units, extending from Queensland into New South Wales and South Australia (Fig. 9.2).

Minor extrusions of basalt took place at this time in the Clarence–Moreton Basin (Towallum Basalt). Probably contemporaneous volcanism also occurred in the southernmost part of the Great Artesian Basin (Garrawilla Volcanics) (Dulhunty, 1965). The latter reach 180 m in thickness. The maximum thickness of the Lower Jurassic sequence in each basin is about 600 m. This thickness is reached in the Great Artesian Basin only in the eastern part.

The Middle Jurassic saw a marked increase in the area of sedimentation in the Great Artesian Basin (Fig. 9.3). Throughout this basin, and the Mulgildie and Clarence–Moreton Basins, a sequence of lithic sandstone, shale, sideritic mudstone and sub-bituminous coal (Walloon and Mulgildie Coal Measures) accumulated, apparently under fluviatile to swamp conditions. The Walloon reaches a maximum thickness of 600 m in the Clarence–Moreton Basin where it extends into the Upper Jurassic at least. Elsewhere it is confined to the Middle Jurassic, and rarely exceeds 300 m, being much thinner towards the margins of the Great Artesian Basin.

By Late Jurassic times the area of sedimentation in the Great Artesian Basin had extended over the shelving borderlands of the basin, where thin sandstone–shale sequences were deposited. On the "Boulia Shelf", which borders the Precambrian inlier of western Queensland, the Longsight Sandstone accumulated. Equivalent strata west of Lake Eyre form the Algebuckina Sandstone. Deposition also occurred in the Lake Frome Embayment in South Australia, and on the margins of the Eulo Shelf in New South Wales and Queensland. Probably much of this marginal deposition took place near the close of the Jurassic.

The Upper Jurassic sequence in the Great Artesian Basin is best known in Queensland, and comprises three units, the basal Gubberamunda Sandstone, the Orallo Formation (formerly known as the "Fossil Wood Beds"), and the Mooga Sandstone Member of the Blythesdale Formation (Day, 1964). Previously these have been regarded as Cretaceous, but palynological studies (Evans, 1963) suggest that their age is Late Jurassic. These units are recognized throughout the basin, although near its margins all but the Mooga may be missing. Over much of the basin where all three units are present, they have an aggregate thickness of about 450 m. Their maximum thickness of about 1500 m occurs in the eastern part of the basin near Cabawin. They are entirely terrestrial, probably largely fluviatile. The sandstones in the Orallo Formation are lithic whereas those in the Gubberamunda Sandstone and Mooga Sandstone Member are quartzose. Shale and thin coal seams occur in the two upper units, particularly in the Orallo.

The Algebuckina Sandstone of South Australia, which is probably an equivalent of the Mooga, contains well-rounded quartz grains and dreikanter and locally exhibits very large-scale cross-stratification (Wopfner, pers. comm.). These features indicate aeolian deposition and its location in the interior of the continent suggests local desert conditions.

Part of the Walloon Coal Measures in the Clarence–Moreton Basin is known, on microfloral evidence, to be coeval with the lower part of the Blythesdale Group in the Great Artesian Basin, but the precise age limits of the Walloon as a whole are in doubt. It may be wholly Jurassic, or the upper part may be Lower Cretaceous, as young as Aptian or even Albian (Rade, 1964).

The possible equivalents of the Orallo and Mooga in the Clarence–Moreton Basin are the Kangaroo Creek Sandstone and the overlying Grafton Formation, which have a combined thickness of 400 m. The Kangaroo Creek Sandstone is quartz-rich. It lies, probably unconformably, on the Walloon Coal Measures. The movement that produced this unconformity may be expressed further north by the absence of Upper Jurassic strata from the Maryborough Basin. The Grafton Formation resembles the Orallo Formation, consisting of lithic sandstone, siltstone, claystone, and minor sub-bituminous coal seams.

The Jurassic System in the southern part of South Australia is confined to the small **Polda Basin** on the west side of Eyre Peninsula (Fig. 9.1), which contains 75 m of terrestrial lignitic and micaceous silts and clays with an Upper Jurassic microfloral assemblage (Harris, 1964).

Sedimentation commenced in the **Laura Basin** of north Queensland after the start of Jurassic time. The lower parts of the Dalrymple Sandstone, predominantly a quartz sandstone with some conglomerate and shale, which reaches about 450 m in thickness, are non-marine—probably fluviatile and lacustrine—and were derived largely from the eastern side of the basin (Lucas, 1962/149, 1964/93). The presence of some microplankton high in the Lower Jurassic sequence suggests some marine influence in the depositional environment at this time. During the remainder of the Jurassic the Dalrymple Sandstone continued to accumulate under non-marine conditions. It is overlain, disconformably near the margins of the basin, by Lower Cretaceous strata.

Although widely separated geographically, the **Maryborough and Carpentaria Basins** have in common the absence of recognized Lower and Upper Jurassic strata. Subsurface studies in the Carpentaria Basin may yet reveal Upper Jurassic strata, however.

The Middle Jurassic of both basins is a coal-bearing sequence. That of the Carpentaria contains much sandstone and is similar to the sequence in the Morehead Basin of southwestern Papua (A.P.C., 1961). The Tiaro Coal Measures of the Maryborough Basin lie disconformably on the Triassic Myrtle Creek Sandstone. They comprise an unknown thickness of coals, carbonaceous shales and lithic sandstones, much disturbed by faulting, folding and igneous intrusions.

WESTERN AUSTRALIA

Sedimentation was continuous from Late Triassic into Jurassic in the **Perth Basin** (McWhae *et al.*, 1958). There, in Early Jurassic times, a fluviatile sequence accumulated, reaching 500 m in thickness. This is dominantly quartz sandstone (Chapman Group and upper Cockleshell Gully Formation), with some shale and one extensive coal seam. The sea entered the northern part of the Perth Basin at the start of the Middle Jurassic, and a thin (*c.* 30 m) but richly fossiliferous sequence of limestone, shale, and sandstone (Champion Bay Group) was deposited. Fluviatile equivalents of this unit are present further south lying in a meridional trough between the shield on the east and a "high" of Triassic sediments, Beagle Ridge, on the west (Dickins and McTavish, 1963).

By the end of the Bajocian the sea had withdrawn from the basin, following some minor earth movements. Over 1000 m of fluviatile quartz-rich sandstone with some shale and conglomerate (Yarragadee Formation) succeeds the Champion Bay Group, locally disconformably, and extends into the Lower Cretaceous, reaching a maximum thickness of 1650 m. During the Late Jurassic the area of fluviatile sedimentation extended southwards to Perth, where some 180 m of quartz sandstone is known in subsurface, and beyond to the southern coast where the Capel River Group, some 600 m of sandstone and shale, outcrops. The upper parts of this group are Cretaceous.

In the **Carnarvon Basin** the lower part of the Dingo Claystone—a monotonous, grey to black, silty claystone and siltstone with minor greywacke, which exceeds 3500 m in thickness—is probably Lower Jurassic, and it may extend into the Triassic. It is the only open-sea Lower Jurassic unit known in Australia, and probably accumulated in fairly deep water.

Deposition of the Dingo Claystone continued throughout the Middle and Late Jurassic without interruption. However, towards the end of the Middle Jurassic a marine transgression covered the region to the east of the main trough with more than 600 m of muddy sandstone, conglomerate, and carbonaceous shale containing marine fossils (Learmonth Formation). This unit lies unconformably on Permian strata and is considered to be a paralic deposit. It extends into the Upper Jurassic. Marine conditions persisted in this area until the end of the Jurassic, and towards the end of the period a further transgression eastwards appears to have occurred. A sandy unit up to 100 m thick, with bivalves in some places (Wogatti Sandstone), was deposited. This overlies the Learmonth Formation, possibly disconformably. Further east and south possible equivalents of the Wogatti (Curdamurda Sandstone, Wittecarra Formation respectively) lie unconformably on Palaeozoic strata.

Deposition of Jurassic strata in the **Canning Basin** commenced late in the Middle Jurassic (Bathonian or Callovian). In the southwestern corner of the basin (Fig. 9.3), sandstones and claystones (lower part of Callawa Formation) were deposited, probably under fluviatile conditions. Sedimentation continued unbroken into the Late Jurassic, and covered wider areas (Fig. 9.4). The sediments initially became coarser—conglomerates and sandstones—

and some of these (upper Callawa, Jurgurra and Wallal Sandstones) may be of Middle Jurassic age.

Sedimentation in the Canning Basin was widespread in the Late Jurassic, but a lack of fossils from the interior of the basin prevents accurate reconstruction of its former extent. Veevers and Wells (1961) consider that many of the lithological units deposited at this time are strongly diachronous, but more recent macrofaunal data (Brunnschweiler, 1960) and unpublished palynological data suggest that this is not the case.

With the exception of a small area of marine Tithonian siltstone (Langey Beds) near Derby, deposition was confined to the Oxfordian and Kimmeridgian. A regional unconformity surface separates the youngest Kimmeridgian strata from the overlying Lower Cretaceous. The lowermost unit, of sandstone and conglomerate with some shale, comprises the Jurgurra Sandstone and much of the Wallal Sandstone and Callawa Formation. It reaches a maximum thickness of about 300 m in the southeast of the basin and thins to the northeast and east. A fine-grained unit, dominantly of siltstone and shale (Jarlemai Siltstone and Alexander Formation) overlies the coarse unit locally disconformably. This fine-grained unit thins east and south from Broome where it is about 300 m thick.

New Zealand (Table 8.2)

More or less continuous deposition in the New Zealand Geosyncline took place from the Late Triassic to the end of the Jurassic Period (Fig. 9.5). The distribution of Jurassic rocks is similar to that of the Triassic System but there are no remnants preserved in the Nelson region. There were signs, however, of change heralding the collapse of the trough, later culminating in the Rangitata or post-Hokonui Orogeny. As in the Triassic System, the sediments were dominantly sands, muds, and conglomerates, but in the upper part of the Jurassic System, non-marine or estuarine formations became very prominent. Again, both marginal and axial facies are recognizable in the Jurassic marine sediments. Active volcanism continued on the western landmass (geanticline) and supplied ashy debris to the geosyncline. It is possible that some of the younger granites of the west Nelson area were emplaced at this time.

A long narrow trough covered the present Northland, Auckland, and Taranaki areas of the North Island and extended towards the Nelson region in the South Island (Grindley, 1961b). The western margin of the trough, which lay very close to, but beyond, the present western coast line of New Zealand, marked the eastern margin of the geanticline. The trough itself was bounded on the east by a narrow arc of land, broken in the Taupo–Bay of Plenty region by a shallow strait connecting it to another sub-parallel

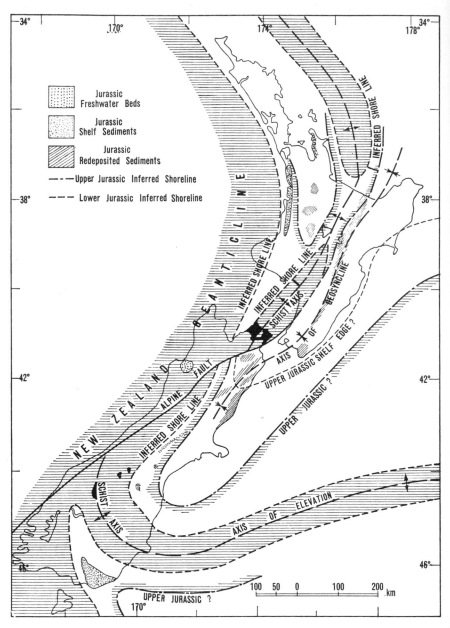

Fig. 9.5. Jurassic palaeogeography of New Zealand. (After Grindley, 1961*b*.)

geosyncline extending from the East Cape area along the eastern coastal regions of both islands as far south as North Otago. Yet another trough was located in the eastern Southland region (Fig. 9.5).

In Middle Jurassic times, the New Zealand Geosyncline began to collapse and, in the tectonic depressions formed in the rising sectors of a new geanticline, freshwater beds accumulated, as in inland Canterbury where they are overlain by andesites and rhyolites. Coeval volcanism is probably also expressed at Gebbies Pass on Banks Peninsula, whereas in the North Island geosynclinal keratophyric volcanics of probable Middle Jurassic age are found in Northland. In eastern Southland, forests of large trees became established on the newly elevated land during this epoch. The oldest coal mined in New Zealand is from deposits of Middle Jurassic age in Southland.

The Upper Jurassic rocks consist of marine and non-marine types. Mudstones, sandstones, and conglomerates abound, often with considerable accumulations of coal. At this time, tectonic movements begun in the Middle Jurassic, reached their climax in the Rangitata Orogeny. Suggate (1963) considers this orogenic disturbance to have been associated with a major transcurrent movement along the Alpine Fault of the order of 480 km (see also Reed, 1964; Kupfer, 1964; Wellman and Wilson, 1964). These tectonic movements were accompanied in the Northland and East Cape regions by basalt–dolerite and ultramafic–gabbroic eruptives. In Westland, there are coarse conglomerates and breccias (Ohika Beds) of this age, probably originating as fanglomerate rubble shed from scarps along the growing Alpine Fault and subsidiary fractures.

SOUTH AUCKLAND REGION

A reasonably complete sequence of Jurassic rocks occupies the axis of the **Kawhia Syncline**, partly obscured by Cainozoic sediments and volcanics, and extends from the south shore of Port Waikato almost to the Mokau River (see Fig. 8.6, p. 235). The well-exposed sequence about Kawhia Harbour is the standard section for correlation of all New Zealand Jurassic rocks, representing six stages.

The lowest Jurassic beds of the Herangi Series are clearly exposed on the sea coast south of the entrance to Kawhia Harbour. No recent biostratigraphical work has been carried out on these rocks and there is some uncertainty about their boundaries and the actual nature of the contact with the Triassic Otapirian beds. They consist, however, of siltstones and sandstones, with horizons of roundstone conglomerates. The shallow-water nature of the sediments and the nearness of the shoreline is shown by the occurrence of carbonaceous layers and tree stumps in the uppermost parts of the Ururoan sequence.

The remainder of the Jurassic sequence, the Kawhia and Oteke Series, is well-developed in the Kawhia Syncline (Fleming and Kear, 1960; Kear, 1960). The lowest part of the Kawhia Series (as defined by Marwick, 1953) here comprises the Rengarenga Group (810 m), consisting mainly of terrestrial, coarse-grained, carbonaceous sediments, with some conglomerates, and interbedded marine sediments from which the type fossils of the Temaikan Stage have been obtained.

The overlying Kirikiri Group (1400 m) is entirely marine, consisting of siltstone, with some sandstone beds particularly towards the top. Bivalves and ammonites are abundant throughout.

The Ahuahu Group (830 m), at the top of the series, has conglomerates at the base passing upwards into sandstone and finally siltstone, with abundant cephalopods. This probably represents a change from paralic to fully marine deposition, and the paucity of benthonic bivalves in the siltstone may reflect the stagnant condition of the depositional basin (Fleming and Kear, 1960).

Throughout the Kawhia Series a few tuffaceous bands are present, but volcanism was evidently on a minor scale as compared with that in the Triassic Period.

The Kawhia Series is considerably thicker towards the axial region of the geosyncline to the east of the Kawhia Syncline and passing northwards into the Coromandel Peninsula. There, the Manaia Hill Group, predominantly poorly bedded sandstones and roundstone conglomerates, is at least 10,500 m thick, with few fossils (Kear, 1960).

The Oteke Series, at the top of the Jurassic, is represented in the Kawhia Harbour region by the Owhiro Group which exceeds 1000 m in thickness, and, according to Kear (1960), the series may exceed 3000 m in other parts of the Kawhia Syncline. This sequence exhibits a lithological pattern similar to that of the Ahuahu Group below, but the non-indurated siltstones contain both bivalves and cephalopods. The upper part of the sequence which is best displayed in the north at Port Waikato, comprises the Huriwai Formation (700 m). This is a terrestrial unit of coarse sandstones, conglomerates, and breccias with thin coal lenses and abundant plant remains (Purser, 1961). It is either very late Jurassic or Early Cretaceous in age, and is overlain by Eocene non-marine strata.

SOUTHLAND REGION

In the **Southland Syncline**, where Jurassic beds occupy the axial region, the sequence is far less complete than in the South Auckland region. At this time, the present Southland area was a shelf environment, and breaks in the sequence are the result of oscillations of sealevel during which parts of the shelf were exposed to erosion. Tuffaceous components are rather more prominent in these beds than in the North Island, and crystal and lithic tuffs, tuffaceous greywackes and tuffaceous arkoses are common (Fig. 6.5).

The sequence begins with marine strata, conformably overlying the Otapirian (Triassic) sandstones, and in most places markedly finer-grained than the latter.

On the northwestern flank of the syncline, the Diamond Peak Group, some 1250 m thick, consists chiefly of marine strata with numerous tuffaceous greywackes, ranging from earliest Liassic to Callovian in age. In the Hokonui Hills the equivalent beds are the Bastion and Flag Hill "Series", about 1000 m thick, of similar lithology. The highest beds are coarse tuffaceous sandstones with *Pleuromya milleformis* (Marwick), coeval with the Temaikan Stage of the Kawhia Syncline.

The Ferndale Group (1320 m) which follows is marked by the appearance of shallow-water features. The feldspathic and tuffaceous muddy and well-sorted sandstones and mudstones contain abundant fragmentary plant remains and many intraformational conglomerates. They are cross-bedded and ripple-marked and marine fossils are very rare. In these ways they indicate the transition to the estuarine sequence that follows.

The youngest Jurassic rocks in the axis of the syncline comprise the Mataura Group, some 720 m thick at Mataura River and 1050 m thick in the eastern Hokonui Hills. The rocks are tuffaceous sandstones and arkoses with round-stone conglomerates and they include the well-known Mataura and Mokoia plant beds. Like the underlying Ferndale Group, they appear to be correlatives of the Temaikan marine stage of the Kawhia sequence.

In the southeastern part of the Southland Syncline, about 4400 m of tuffaceous sediments of Aratauran to Temaikan age which were deposited in estuarine and shallow marine environments are now exposed. They are overlain by the New Haven Group of late Temaikan age. This, the youngest unit in the Southland syncline consists of 180 m of unfossiliferous conglomerates, rudaceous grits, and sandstones with much carbonaceous material (Speden, 1961).

OTHER JURASSIC AREAS

The greywacke ranges of the southeastern part of Auckland Province, and the younger greywackes of Coromandel Peninsula, include Jurassic components of the axial facies (Torlesse Group). They also form basement inliers east of the North Island main ranges and in Marlborough Province in the South Island. The basement rocks of the Inland Kaikoura Range are mapped as Jurassic and consist of graded-bedded greywacke and argillite, overlain by massive greywacke with "cannon-ball" concretions and conglomerates. In the Seaward Kaikouras they are similar, with the grade reaching the Chlorite subzone 1 near the major faults.

Freshwater deposits of probable Jurassic age have been recorded in the Malvern Hills and at Mount Somers in Canterbury, and also at Preservation Inlet in southwest Fiordland, in addition to those already recorded in the Kawhia and Southland synclines. Special mention must be made of the Porarari Group of southwest Nelson and north Westland. The lowest strata, the Ohika Beds, rest unconformably on the Berlins Porphyry (?Lower Jurassic) and Greenland Group (?Precambrian). They consist of sandstones, conglomerates, shales, and thin coals, and are unconformably overlain by the Hawks Crag Breccia, a formation composed of two facies, one uranium-bearing and derived from a granite source, and the other derived from the ?Precambrian greywackes of the Greenland Group. These facies interdigitate to form a mixed facies in the Buller Gorge area (Bowen, 1964). There are abundant plant microfossils present in both these formations, but the absence of angiospermous pollen is considered an indication of an age prior to Late Jurassic, and probably Middle Jurassic. The next unit above, the Topfer Formation, may also in part be Jurassic in age, but is probably mainly Early Cretaceous.

PALAEONTOLOGY

FAUNAS

Lower Jurassic. In Australia, no marine macrofossils of Early Jurassic age are known.

On the other hand, in New Zealand the Lower Jurassic, like the Triassic, has a relatively rich fauna. Overseas correlations, however, are somewhat insecure owing to the marked provincialism in the molluscan and brachiopod benthos. This isolation of the so-called Maorian Province is illustrated by the absence, until after Liassic times, of any Lower Jurassic belemnites and trigoniids, so widespread elsewhere in the Pacific region. As in the Triassic sequence, no terrestrial fauna is known from any of the Jurassic rocks.

The principal correlations for the Herangi Series (Lower Jurassic) are based mainly on an isolated occurrence of the ammonite *Psiloceras* (Hettangian–Sinemurian) in the Aratauran Stage of Southland and the ammonite *Dactylioceras* (Toarcian) in the Ururoan Stage of the Kawhia coast. The characteristic pteriid bivalves, *Otapiria marshalli* for the Aratauran Stage and *Pseudaucella marshalli* for the Ururoan Stage, are indigenous, although valuable for local correlations.

Middle Jurassic. In Australia, Middle Jurassic faunas are well known in the Perth Basin and include ammonites (*Fontannesia, Pseudotoites*), bivalves

(*Isognomon, Trigonia*) and belemnites (*Belemnopsis*). Similar forms occur in the Carnarvon Basin.

The Middle Jurassic (Temaikan Stage) saw the immigration into the New Zealand area of the pteriid bivalve *Meleagrinella* cf. *echinata*, and the breaking down of the isolation of other benthos as links were established with the Tethyan area and even with Europe. For instance, the trigoniids, which have not been recorded from the New Zealand Liassic rocks, reappear in the Temaikan Stage. They are represented by *Trigonia* and various subgenera of *Vaugonia* (Fleming, 1964). Belemnites (*Hibolithes*) are also present for the first time since the Otapirian (Rhaetian) Stage.

The Temaikan strata are poor in fossils that provide reliable overseas correlations. The occurrence of *Meleagrinella* indicates the presence of Bajocian and Bathonian correlatives, but the only indication of the Callovian Stage is an isolated macrocephalitid ammonite from the Southland Syncline.

Upper Jurassic. There are similarities between the Upper Jurassic faunas from the Canning and Carnarvon Basins in Western Australia and those of the Kawhia Syncline in New Zealand. These areas contain formations with the ammonites *Perisphinctes* and *Kossmatia*, the bivalves *Meleagrinella, Malayomaorica, Buchia subspitiensis*, and *B. subpallasi*, and the belemnite *Belemnopsis* sp. cf. *B. aucklandica* (Brunnschweiler, 1960, 1963).

Microplankton is particularly abundant in the Upper Jurassic, a large number of forms having been described by Cookson and co-workers (see Cookson and Eisenack, 1960). They include *Scriniodinium, Gonyaulax, Cannosphaeropsis*, and *Nannoceratopsis*. Tintinnids (*Calpionella*) are known from the Canning Basin (Brunnschweiler, 1960).

In the Late Jurassic there was again some restriction on the entry of new forms of organisms into the New Zealand area. For instance, the previously cosmopolitan faunas were replaced by more provincial types of Pacific, Boreal, and Tethyan origin.

No marine fossils of definite Oxfordian age have been identified anywhere in the Dominion, and the base of the Upper Jurassic Heterian Stage is marked by the appearance of *Inoceramus galoi*, together with the lower Kimmeridgian ammonites *Subneumayria, Epicephalites*, and *Holcophylloceras*.

The Heterian, Ohauan, and Puaroan Stages, which span the time interval from early Kimmeridgian to early Tithonian, contain an abundance of fossils, ammonites being the most valuable. For local correlations the much more numerous pteriids and inoceramids have also proved of considerable value.

The lower part of the Heterian Stage contains, in addition to the index forms mentioned above, the ammonites *Lytoceras* and *Idoceras*, and numerous bivalves, for example *Malayomaorica malayomaorica, Pleuromya*, and *Haastina*.

Upper Heterian strata have also yielded some rich collections of ammonites including *Partschiceras, Aspidoceras, Paraboliceras,* and *Kossmatia.*

The appearance of *Inoceramus haasti* marks the base of the Ohauan Stage. Phylloceratid ammonites and *Kossmatia* are characteristic of the lower parts of the stage, but the richest cephalopod faunas come from the top of the stage and include *Calliphylloceras, Partschiceras, Uhligites, Kossmatia,* and several species of *Paraboliceras* (Fleming and Kear, 1960), together with an interesting species of the crinoid *Phyllocrinus* (Speden, 1959).

In the absence of any recorded upper Kimmeridgian faunas, the position of the lower boundary of the Tithonian cannot be precisely identified within the New Zealand stages. However, the faunas of the Puaroan Stage, overlying the Ohauan, are clearly lower Tithonian. They contain abundant ammonites, including *Aulacosphinctoides, Calliphylloceras,* and *Uhligites,* as well as numerous pteriids, inoceramids, and other bivalves. The brachiopods *Burmirhynchia* and *Holcothyris* (?) have recently been described from ?Puaroan rocks of the Torlesse Group in north Canterbury (Campbell, 1965*b*).

FLORAS

The Jurassic flora of Australia, which contains a large number of species, includes forms such as *Cladophlebis australis, Taeniopteris spatulata, Brachyphyllum crassum,* and *Sagenopteris rhoifolia.* Plant microfossils are abundant, and are valuable for zonation (Evans, 1963; De Jersey and Paten, 1964). The Lower Jurassic is characterized by *Classopolis torosus, Callialasporites segmentatus, C. dampieri,* and *Cadargasporites,* the first three of which continue into higher beds. The Middle Jurassic includes *Cingulatisporites granulatus, C. saevus,* and *Annulispora folliculosa,* whereas the Upper Jurassic has *Muraspora florida* and *Contignisporites cooksonae.* The last continues into the Cretaceous.

In New Zealand, the Lower Jurassic flora includes the earliest known podocarps in the Dominion, together with representatives of the equisetalians, cycadophytes and ginkgos, now extinct (except for human re-introduction).

In the west of the South Island, the Ohika Beds and the Hawks Crag Breccia have yielded much spore material believed, because of the absence of angiospermous pollens, to be Middle to Late Jurassic in age. The commonest forms are *Osmundacidites, Cyathidites, Lycopodacidites, Podocarpidites,* and ?*Pilularia.*

Other plant localities include the Middle Jurassic fossil forest at Curio Bay, Southland; the Mataura and Mokoia plant beds of the same age in the Southland Syncline; the Wakaepa Beds in Canterbury of Late Jurassic age; and the above-mentioned Huriwai plant beds at Port Waikato which contain a varied flora dominated by *Cladophlebis* and *Taeniopteris* (Purser, 1961).

CLIMATE

Too few data have been obtained from sediments or organisms to justify any definitive statement on climates during the Jurassic. Irving (1964) has suggested relatively high (45°–70°S') palaeolatitudes for the Jurassic depositional areas of Australia (Fig. 9.6). The variety of marine organisms, including cephalopods, does not suggest very cold conditions. However, these organisms are confined to palaeolatitudes lower than 50°S' on Irving's estimate. The occurrence of possible desert conditions at the end of the Jurassic in South Australia suggested by features of the Algebuckina Sandstone at a palaeolatitude of about 70°S' would require a climatic zonation relative to the Jurassic palaeoequator rather different from that now occurring.

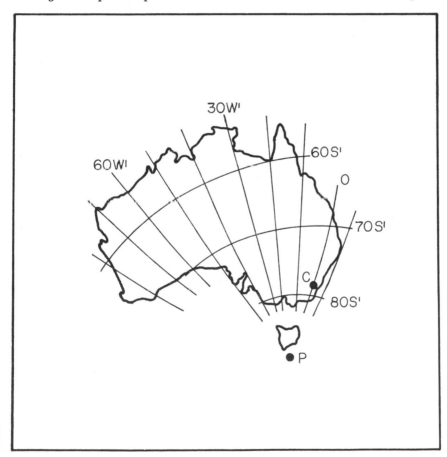

FIG. 9.6. Jurassic palaeolatitudes and palaeomeridians based on Canberra. Reliability A. (After Irving, 1964, by permission of John Wiley & Sons Inc.)

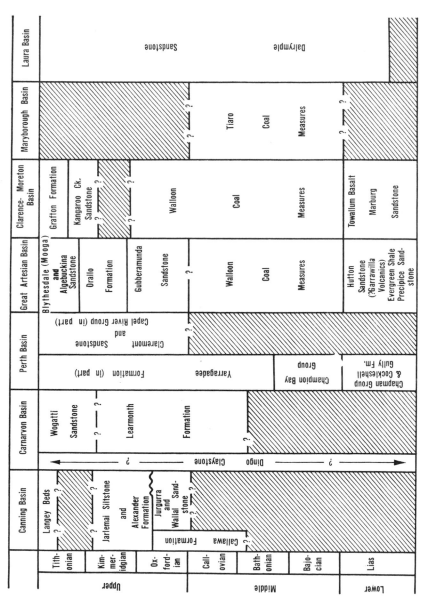

TABLE 9.1. CORRELATION TABLE FOR THE JURASSIC SYSTEM IN AUSTRALIA

The Early Jurassic of New Zealand was presumably climatically like the Triassic, with which it is closely allied, and was probably warm temperate. In the Middle Jurassic, although such organisms as reef-corals have not been recorded, there is a strong suggestion of very warm, possibly subtropical, conditions with lush forests such as that represented by the accumulations of tree trunks at Curio Bay, Southland.

TECTONISM AND IGNEOUS ACTIVITY

In Australia the Jurassic was a period of limited volcanicity. Lower Jurassic basalts occur in the Clarence–Moreton Basin and the southeastern arm of the Great Artesian Basin. Plugs of leucite lamproite intrude Permian strata in the northern Canning Basin (Prider, 1960) and these have been dated radiometrically as Late Jurassic. Large areas of the Permo-Triassic Tasmania Basin were intruded during the Jurassic by tholeiitic dolerite sills, aggregating up to 450 m in thickness. These have been described petrologically by Edwards (1942) and McDougall (1962), and dated at 160–165 m.y. (McDougall, 1961). The Mount Gibraltar Microsyenite at Bowral, southwest of Sydney and the Prospect Teschenite on the western outskirts of Sydney are of similar age (Evernden and Richards, 1962).

Although disconformities may occur locally within the Jurassic sequence, Jurassic folding is known only in the Maryborough and Clarence–Moreton Basins. This occurred in Late Jurassic times and was most intense in the Maryborough Basin, where the Lower Cretaceous Grahams Creek Volcanics lie on upturned Triassic to Middle Jurassic strata. After the folding, granites and associated porphyrites and andesites were intruded into these, and older strata. These igneous rocks are also Jurassic.

In New Zealand, basalt–dolerite and ultramafic–gabbroic eruptives of Middle Jurassic to Early Cretaceous age in Northland and at East Cape accompanied the tectonic movements in conjunction with the collapse of the New Zealand Geosyncline. In the extreme north of New Zealand, a small ultramafic intrusion comprises serpentinized dunites, lherzolites, and wehrlites, with varieties of gabbros, including a strongly gneissic type, occurring as sheet-like bodies within the intrusion. The whole intrusive body is associated with, and in places intersects, basaltic and pillow lavas and agglomeratic volcanics (Tangihua Volcanics) containing Jurassic–Lower Cretaceous fossils.

At Three Kings Islands and at points on the northernmost mainland, there are geosynclinal keratophyric and spilitic volcanics of probable Middle Jurassic age (Mount Camel Volcanics).

In the East Cape region there are extensive areas of basic intrusives penetrating and surrounded by masses of basaltic pillow lavas, agglomerates, and tuffs (Matakaoa Volcanics). Occasional interbedded sedimentaries of the

Table 9.2. Correlation Table for the Jurassic System in New Zealand

AGE	NEW ZEALAND SERIES	STAGE	KAWHIA SYNCLINE	SOUTHLAND SYNCLINE WEST	SOUTHLAND SYNCLINE EAST	SOUTH ISLAND WEST COAST	BIOZONES (after Fleming & Kear, 1960, p. 44) Ammonites	Pterids	Inoceramids
Upper Tithonian	OTEKE SERIES	PUAROAN	Huriwai plant-beds; OWHIRO GROUP 1100 m+ (Puti Siltstone, Waiharakeke Conglomerate)			? TOPFER FORMATION	Aulacosphinctoides brownei	Buchia plicata, B. hochstetteri, B. aff. misolica, B. cf. plicata	Inoceramus aff. everesti, I. aff. everesti, I. sp nov.
Lower Tithonian	OTEKE SERIES	PUAROAN							
Upper Kimmeridgian (not recorded)									
Middle Kimmeridgian	KAWHIA SERIES	OHAUAN	AHUAHU GROUP 930m (Kinohaku Siltstone, Takatahi Conglomerate, Kowhai Point Siltstone)			HAWKS CRAG BRECCIA	Paraboliceras sp. nov. A.	Malayomaorica malayomaorica	Inoceramus haasti / I. cf. subhaasti
Lower Kimmeridgian	KAWHIA SERIES	HETERIAN	KIRIKIRI GROUP (Waikiekie Tuffaceous Sandstone, Waikutakuta Siltstone, Kiwi Sandstone); GROUP 1400m (Ohineruru Sst. and Siltstone, Capt. King's Shellbed, Oraka Sandstone)		NEW HAVEN GROUP 180m	OHIKA BEDS 350 - 1500m	Kossmatia sp. nov. A.; Idoceras sp. nov. aff. humboldti; ? Epicephalites cf. epigonus	M.malayomaorica — M.malayomaorica	I. galoi, I. galoi
Oxfordian (not recorded)									
Callovian	HERANGI SERIES	TEMAIKAN	Wharetanu Measures; RENGA-RENGA GROUP 830m; Opapaka Sandstone; Urawitiki Measures	MATAURA GROUP 1000m; FERNDALE GROUP 1320m	CATLINS GROUP 1650 - 2000m		Macrocephalites	Meleagrinella	I. incondtus
Bathonian	HERANGI SERIES	TEMAIKAN							
Bajocian	HERANGI SERIES	TEMAIKAN							
Toarcian	HERANGI SERIES	URUROAN	Ururoan Sandstone; c. 1000m	FLAG HILL "SERIES" DIAMOND PEAK GROUP (in part)	BERESFORD GROUP 950 - 1400m	BERLINS PORPHYRY	Dactylioceras	Pseudaucella marshalli	—
Pliensbachian	HERANGI SERIES	URUROAN							
Sinemurian	HERANGI SERIES	ARATAURAN	Aratauran Sandstone; c. 1000m	BASTION "SERIES" DIAMOND PEAK GROUP (in part)	GLENOMARU GROUP 1100m	(Age uncertain)	Psiloceras	Otapiria marshalli	—
Hettangian	HERANGI SERIES	ARATAURAN							

(The Southland Syncline and South Island West Coast columns include diagonally-hatched "EMERGENCE" zones and the vertical label "PORARARI GROUP".)

axial facies have yielded specimens of the bivalve *Malayomaorica*, indicating an approximately Late Jurassic age, and suggesting that the volcanics originated as thick flows on the ocean floor of the geosyncline.

In the South Island, the freshwater beds of the Mount Somers district of inland Canterbury are overlain by tuffs and flow rocks of hypersthene–andesite, dacite and biotite–garnet rhyolite (Mount Somers Volcanics). The age of these volcanics is considered to lie within the range Late Jurassic–Maestrichtian, but some Cainozoic units may also be present. Similar volcanics occupy large areas of the high country in mid-Canterbury and have been mapped near Gebbies Pass on Banks Peninsula.

The Upper Jurassic Ohika conglomerates of southwest Nelson are traversed by small acidic intrusions, probably almost contemporaneous with the deposition of the sediments.

CHAPTER 10

The Cretaceous System

Deposits of Cretaceous age are present in outcrop or subsurface over approximately one-third of the present landmass of Australia. Their great extent is due principally to widespread deposition in Lower Cretaceous (Aptian–Albian) epeiric seas which divided the continent into three distinct landmasses (Fig. 10.2). The earliest Cretaceous deposits are somewhat more limited in extent than those of Aptian age, and are predominantly terrestrial. Upper Cretaceous deposits are even more limited in extent, and reasonably complete sequences are known only in certain of the coastal basins of Victoria and Western Australia. Part of the east coastal region of Queensland was strongly deformed during the Late Cretaceous Maryburian Orogeny. This marked the close of orogenic activity within the Tasman Orthogeosyncline.

Although Cretaceous rocks have a widespread distribution in both islands of New Zealand and have been known for many years, their stratigraphy, especially in the Lower Cretaceous portion, has been greatly confused, largely because of complex structural relationships and paucity of fossils. However, Wellman (1959), after a detailed study of the fossil *Inocerami*, has been able to resolve many of the difficulties and to clarify the Cretaceous succession as a whole. The account of the New Zealand Cretaceous that follows is extracted largely from his masterly survey, with modifications by Hall (1963).

STRATIGRAPHY

Australia (Lower Cretaceous)

Each of the basins that had been a site of sedimentation during the Jurassic received some sediment in the Early Cretaceous (Fig. 10.2), with the possible exception of the Clarence–Moreton Basin in which the age of the uppermost units is either Late Jurassic or Early Cretaceous. Sedimentation was widespread in the Carpentaria Basin, and the sea gradually spread over the Northern Territory Shelf. In the southern part of the continent three new basins were initiated—the Gippsland and Otway Basins in Victoria and the Eucla Basin in South and Western Australia. On the east coast of Queensland a small area was covered by sea during the Neocomian, to form the Styx Basin.

Marine transgression, commencing in the Late Neocomian and continuing through into the Albian gradually inundated each of these basins except the Gippsland. The boundaries of the main intracontinental basins—the Canning and Great Artesian—extended until the basins met in the interior of Western Australia. Deposition in the Murray Basin was initiated at this time, when the sea entered from the north.

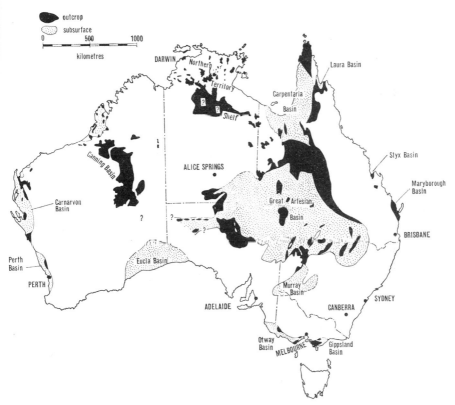

FIG. 10.1. Distribution of Cretaceous strata.

The Early Cretaceous palaeogeography of Australia (Fig. 10.2) is known with some certainty from both outcrop and subsurface data. Postulated marine connexions between the main basins in the south central part of the continent are based on faunal similarities (Skwarko, 1962/11), and on the deposition of strata around the margins of the presumed area of inter-connexion, which is at present unmapped.

Crespin (1963), using Early Cretaceous arenaceous Foraminifera, has interpreted the environment in the Artesian Basin during the Aptian as varying from inner sublittoral with high turbidity and low salinity to outer sublittoral with moderate turbidity and salinity, the latter occurring in the north, south, and southwestern parts of the basin. In the Albian a striking change occurred, with open sea conditions of low turbidity and normal salinity throughout much of the basin.

EASTERN SEABOARD

The oldest marine faunas (Neocomian) occur in sandstones near **Stanwell** west of Rockhampton (Hill and Denmead, eds., 1960). Nearby, and again a little further north in the **Styx Basin**, lithic sandstones and shales with coal seams (Styx Coal Measures) occur. One marine interbed containing Albian microplankton is known in this sequence.

To the south in the **Maryborough Basin** the Cretaceous commences with 1350 m of andesitic volcanics (Grahams Creek) including lavas, tuffs, and their re-worked derivatives, together with some trachyte and rhyolite. The Grahams Creek Volcanics probably extend to sea northeastwards for at least 80 km, and occur in the base of the Wreck Island No. 1 Well (Derrington *et al.*, 1960).

The volcanics lie unconformably on the Jurassic Tiaro Coal Measures and are overlain conformably by 1800 m of marine shales and cherts of Aptian age (Maryborough Formation). A reversion to terrestrial conditions took place in the Albian, and the resultant Burrum Coal Measures (1650 m) consist of lithic sandstone and siltstone with shales and bituminous coals.

Of these seaboard occurrences, those in the Styx Basin and near Stanwell are preserved by down faulting whereas those in the Maryborough Basin form part of the strongly folded belt of Mesozoic rocks which was formed during the Late Cretaceous Maryburian Orogeny.

GREAT ARTESIAN BASIN AND ENVIRONS

Deposition was continuous from Jurassic to Cretaceous in the **Great Artesian Basin** (Hill and Denmead, eds., 1960) where the upper members of the Blythesdale Formation, up to 180 m thick, are of Neocomian to Early Aptian age. Although the top member (Minmi) of the Blythesdale Formation contains marine fossils, chiefly bivalves, most of the sequence appears to be of fluviatile origin (Day, 1964). The Blythesdale Formation consists of quartzose and feldspathic sublabile sandstone, silty shales, and thin coal seams in the lower part.

With the onset of the Aptian transgression the areas of non-marine Neocomian sedimentation were gradually inundated. The Roma Formation, a fossiliferous blue, grey, and brown calcareous claystone with minor sandstone and impure limestone, was deposited over much of the Great Artesian Basin, lying conformably on the Blythesdale. The Roma extends westwards into South Australia and its equivalents may extend across the Shield into

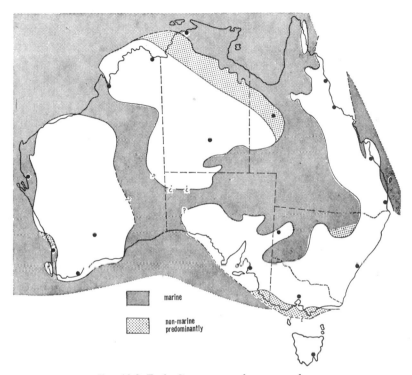

marine

non-marine
predominantly

FIG. 10.2. Early Cretaceous palaeogeography.

the Eucla and Canning Basins (Fig. 10.1). The Roma is overlain by the lithologically similar Tambo Formation, which is poorly defined, but contains Albian macrofossils. These two units together reach a maximum thickness of 960 m at Springleigh.

In the northern part of the basin the equivalent of the Roma and lower Tambo is the Wilgunya Formation (Vine and Day, 1965), comprising up to 420 m of mudstone and calcareous siltstone, with minor lithic sandstone and one limestone member (Toolebuc) of possible Middle Albian age. The Wilgunya Formation is succeeded by up to 240 m of interbedded lithic sandstone and mudstone (Mackunda Formation) which contain Late Albian marine fossils (Vine *et al.*, 1964/39). The Albian part of the Great Artesian Basin sequence does not extend east of the Eulo Shelf, and is thickest (300 m) in the Queensland–South Australian border district.

During the Early Cretaceous up to 420 m of largely marine sandstones and shales accumulated in the **Murray Basin** which at this time appears to have been connected to the southern part of the Artesian Basin (Fig. 10.2). These strata are known only in the subsurface in the Loxton, Company's, Wentworth No. 1, and Tolarno Bores (Haites, 1962), and in Ivanhoe No. 1 and North Renmark No. 1 Bores (Grasso, 1963). In all except the last well they are less than 105 m thick. The strata range in age from probable Neocomian to Albian. In view of the non-marine character of the strata of this age in the Otway Basin to the south, a southward connexion to the open ocean seems unlikely. The Padthaway Horst between the Murray and Otway Basins was apparently land at this time.

Northern Seaboard

Lower Cretaceous deposits accumulated over much of the northern seaboard of the continent and extended southward to coalesce with those of the Great Artesian Basin. The centre of Cretaceous deposition lay in the Carpentaria Basin. A subsidiary centre to the east lay in the Laura Basin, but connexion between the basins was maintained for at least part of the Early Cretaceous. Westwards and southwestwards from the Carpentaria Basin a thin sequence accumulated on the Northern Territory Shelf.

In the **Carpentaria Basin** the Cretaceous for the most part lies directly on a Palaeozoic or Precambrian basement. The basal conglomerates and quartz-rich sandstones (Gilbert River Formation, Wrotham Park Sandstone), about 30 m thick, extend over much of the basin. Like the Blythesdale Formation, the Gilbert River Formation contains marine macrofossils of early Aptian age in its upper parts.

The Gilbert River Formation and its equivalents are overlain by a succession which is very similar to that in the north of the Artesian Basin. It reaches 750 m in thickness and comprises the Blackdown Formation, the Kamileroi Limestone which is equivalent to the Toolebuc, and the Normanton Formation. The last bears more similarity to the Mackunda Formation than to the upper part of Wilgunya Formation.

The earliest Cretaceous strata in the **Laura Basin** (Battle Camp Formation) are both marine and non-marine, and overlie the Upper Jurassic disconformably at least near the margins of the basin (Lucas, 1962/149, 1964/93). They consist principally of quartzose sandstones and shaley sandstones, locally glauconitic, with conglomerates at the base. In some places Neocomian marine fossils appear at or not far above the base of the succession, but in the Flinders Islands the Neocomian appears non-marine throughout. Thin lacustrine sediments underlie the transgressive marine Neocomian locally in the southeast.

The upper part of the Battle Camp Formation is predominantly shale, and contains Aptian marine fossils, principally bivalves. The formation exceeds 300 m in thickness. It is overlain, with unknown stratigraphic relation, by about 120 m of Albian calcareous claystones (Wolena Claystone). These are equivalents of the Blackdown Formation of the Carpentaria Basin, and are of restricted extent.

In the Mullaman Beds of the **Northern Territory Shelf** Skwarko (1964) has recognized thin but widespread non-marine quartz sandstones which lie unconformably on a Precambrian or Cambrian basement. In the coastal regions (Fig. 10.2) the sandstones pass upwards into marine Neocomian strata. Further inland, non-marine deposition may have also commenced in the Neocomian but the bulk of the deposition there took place in the Aptian, and the upper parts of the Mullaman Beds over much of the Shelf are of Aptian and Albian age. The maximum preserved thickness of the whole unit is only 40 m, although stripping of overlying strata has undoubtedly occurred.

In the Aptian–Albian portion of the sequence Skwarko (1964) has recognized a Coastal Belt of quartz sandstone and silty sandstone which is marine, and an Inland Belt with a sandstone, silty sandstone, and claystone sequence of which only the upper part is marine.

WESTERN AUSTRALIA

The Cretaceous in Western Australia is extensively developed in the **Canning Basin** where an embayment of the sea extended far inland during the Early Cretaceous (Veevers and Wells, 1961) (Fig. 10.2). Neocomian marine strata, chiefly quartz sandstone and conglomerate (Broome Sandstone and equivalents), lie disconformably on the Jurassic over the northwestern part of the Basin. They are thickest (165 m) in the vicinity of Broome, and thin rapidly eastwards. Marine Aptian sandstones, the Frezier and Melligo, overlie these strata conformably in a belt of country running from south of Broome northeastwards across the Dampier Peninsula. No Albian strata are known.

Inland in the southwest and south of the basin, and locally in the east, Cretaceous strata are widespread. They extend southwards into the interior of Western Australia (Wells, 1963/59) (Fig. 10.1), whence Skwarko (1963/2) has described an Aptian fauna similar to that of the Roma Formation in the Great Artesian Basin. Skwarko (1962/11) considers that marine connexions with both the Great Artesian and Eucla Basins may have been present at this time (Fig. 10.2). Neocomian strata may also be present in the south of the Canning Basin.

During much of the Neocomian the Jurassic units in the **Carnarvon Basin** were being eroded following the mild Late Jurassic folding. Late in the Neocomian the sea again entered the basin, initiating deposition of a marine sequence which was to continue to accumulate through into the Late Cretaceous. The Lower Cretaceous part of this sequence is about 300 m thick in outcrop, where it overlies Palaeozoic strata. It thickens westwards in the subsurface to about 600 m. The sequence, in ascending order, comprises the Birdrong Formation, Muderong Shale, Windalia Radiolarite, and the lower part of the Gearle Siltstone. The lower three are shallow-water deposits. All four contain abundant microplankton and forams, and the Windalia and Gearle also contain radiolarians, bivalves, and ammonites. The Birdrong, which is dominantly quartz sandstone, glauconitic in part, yielded oil in non-commercial quantities at the Rough Range No. 1 Well in 1953. Outliers of sandstone and siltstone (Nanutarra Formation), with a marine fauna (Cox, 1961), occur in the northeast of the basin. These may be Upper Neocomian (Skwarko, 1964) in which case they are equivalents of the Birdrong. The Muderong consists of shale, siltstone, and greensand, and the Windalia, which is predominantly non-terrigenous, contains some claystone, greensand, and chert in addition to the predominant radiolarite. The Gearle comprises bentonitic siltstone, claystone, and shale.

In the **Perth Basin** non-marine deposition was continuous from Jurassic to Cretaceous in the northern and southern parts of the basin (Edgell, 1964*b*). The Yarragadee Formation in the north, consisting of quartz sandstone and siltstone, extends to the top of the Neocomian, and the Capel River Group in the south, comprising shale and quartz sandstone with an interbedded tholeiitic basalt flow (Bunbury Basalt), extends up to the top of the Aptian. The group is partly marine in its upper parts.

In the vicinity of Perth the South Perth Formation, some 300 m of interbedded marine quartz sandstones, siltstones, and claystones, containing some pyrite and carbonaceous beds, was deposited disconformably on the Jurassic Claremont Sandstone during the late Neocomian to early Albian. It is succeeded conformably by the Osborne Formation which is also marine, comprising up to 115 m of glauconitic sandstone and shale with abundant microfossils.

Marine conditions persisted in this part of the Perth Basin until the end of the Early Cretaceous, and perhaps into the Cenomanian, after which the sea withdrew.

To the north of Perth there is no record of Aptian sedimentation, but a marine incursion in the Albian led to the deposition of the quartz-rich Dandaragan Sandstone unconformably on the Yarragadee Formation.

This unit may extend into the Upper Cretaceous. By the end of the Ceno-manian this area was probably again land.

SOUTHERN SEABOARD

On the southern coasts of the continent three new basins were initiated in Early Cretaceous times. The **Eucla Basin** of South and Western Australia is predominantly Tertiary, but contains up to 20 m of quartz sandstone and conglomerate (Loongana Conglomerate) overlain by 200 m of shale, sand-stone, and greensand (Madura Shale). The Madura Shale is at least partly marine, having yielded Aptian bivalves which are very similar to those in the Roma Formation in Queensland.

The other two southern basins lie across the eroded surface of the folded Palaeozoic strata of the Tasman Geosyncline. The westernmost, the **Otway Basin**, extends from South Australia into Victoria, whereas the **Gippsland Basin** to the east lies entirely within Victoria. The two basins were con-nected during the Early Cretaceous when a sequence of lithic sandstones, mudstones, and conglomerates was deposited under fluviatile conditions in both basins, forming the Korumburra Group. This was derived from the north (Philip, 1958) and thickens rapidly seawards off the Palaeozoic basement, where subsurface thicknesses are known to exceed 2100 m in the Otway Basin and 2450 m in the Gippsland Basin.

The occurrence of hystrichospheres and rare dinoflagellates in the top-most beds of the Korumburra Group in some wells in the Otway Basin suggests that a marine influence began to be effective late in the Albian. This was to develop strongly in the Late Cretaceous.

Australia (Upper Cretaceous)

By the end of the Early Cretaceous the sea had withdrawn from much of the continent (Fig. 10.3), and deposition had ceased in the Maryborough, Styx, and Laura Basins, the Canning and Eucla Basins, and the Gippsland Basin. Only the western end of the Northern Territory Shelf continued to receive sediment, and deposition in the Carpentaria Basin was restricted in extent. The Perth and Carnarvon Basins show little change, although much of the lower Upper Cretaceous sequence is missing in each. The Otway Basin, in which deposition may have been continuous throughout the Cretaceous, was of more limited extent than formerly.

The withdrawal of the sea from the Great Artesian Basin at the close of the Early Cretaceous permitted an extensive river system to develop (Fig. 10.3), which deposited the Winton Formation and its equivalents. The pat-tern of this system is largely conjectural although Vine (pers. comm.)

has noted evidence of north-flowing currents in the Winton Formation in the north of the basin.

GREAT ARTESIAN BASIN AND NORTHERN SEABOARD

In the **Great Artesian Basin** deposition was somewhat more restricted than during the Early Cretaceous, but nonetheless covered a wide area. The transition was gradual, the most notable feature being a change from marine to non-marine conditions. The Winton Formation, the product of Cenomanian fluvio-lacustrine deposition, occupies much of the basin west of the Eulo Shelf, and reaches a maximum thickness of 630 m near the Queensland–South Australian border. It consists of thick beds of mudstone and sandstone and a few coal seams. The Winton appears to overlap the Tambo Formation along the western side of the Eulo Shelf, whence it extends southeastwards into New South Wales (Fig. 10.3). In this eastern area the Winton lies directly on the Roma Formation (Rade, 1954). Either the Winton there is Albian in part, and contains freshwater equivalents of the Tambo, or the Roma–Winton contact is a disconformity, with Cenomanian overlying Aptian.

The Winton is the youngest Cretaceous unit preserved except in the northeast of South Australia where, at Mount Howie, 45 m of cross-stratified quartz sandstones with some shale (Mount Howie Sandstone) lie disconformably on the Winton (Wopfner, 1963). Plant fossils suggest a Late Cretaceous age.

Cenomanian marine shales occur locally in the **Carpentaria Basin**, in the Mornington Island Well. They contain Foraminifera and microplankton. Strata of similar age, which may not be marine, are known in the subsurface along the western side of Cape York Peninsula. Probably the rivers of the Great Artesian Basin flowed northwards to the sea during the Cenomanian (Fig. 10.3).

In the Darwin–Bathurst Island area of the **Northern Territory Shelf,** sedimentation continued from Early Cretaceous (Aptian) through the Turonian, whereas elsewhere in the Territory sedimentation seems to have ceased in the Albian (Skwarko, 1964). The sequence consists of more than 300 m of quartz sandstone and shale, and is richly fossiliferous.

WESTERN AUSTRALIA

The Upper Cretaceous of the **Carnarvon Basin** is divided into two parts by a mild unconformity. The older comprises the upper parts of the Gearle Siltstone, which is conformable with the Albian lower part of the Gearle Siltstone. It is of Cenomanian to early Turonian age (Belford, 1958). Calcareous green claystones with microplankton and marine macrofossils are prominent in the upper part of the Gearle.

The younger strata, which reach 270 m in thickness, are calcareous and richly fossiliferous. They comprise the Toolonga Calcilutite, Korojon Calcarenite, and the Miria Marl, and range in age from Santonian to Maestrichtian.

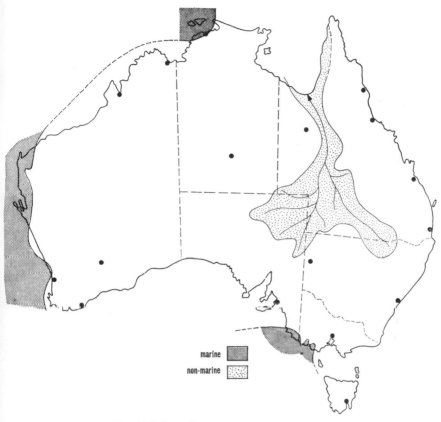

FIG. 10.3. Late Cretaceous palaeogeography.

The history of the **Perth Basin** during the Late Cretaceous is in some doubt owing to the lack of diagnostic fossils from most units. Deposition was continuous from Early Cretaceous into Cenomanian times in the Perth area and an area to the north, but the sea withdrew from both areas by the end of the Turonian if not earlier. Later in the Cretaceous the area north of Perth was again inundated (Fig. 10.4). According to Belford (1958) the 90 m of Upper Cretaceous strata that accumulated in the area north of Perth do not form a continuous sequence. The Molecap Greensand which forms the lower part of this sequence is thought to be of Cenomanian to early Turonian age, whereas the richly fossiliferous Gingin Chalk and the overlying Poison Hill Greensand which form the upper part are Santonian to possibly Maestrichtian in age. Alternatively one may follow Edgell (1964b) and regard this sequence as continuous, ranging in age from Coniacian to Campanian.

Belford (1958) has presented a series of palaeogeographic maps of the Carnarvon and Perth Basins covering most of Late Cretaceous time (Fig. 10.4). Both basins are depicted as non-depositional during the late Turonian and Coniacian.

SOUTHERN SEABOARD

Deposition, which continued throughout the Late Cretaceous, was confined to the **Otway Basin** which had, however, been somewhat reduced in size by Cenomanian times (Fig. 10.5). The sequence (lower Wangerrip Group) thickens rapidly southwards off the Palaeozoic basement, and in the marginal areas of the basin the youngest units lie disconformably on the Korumburra Group. The known thickness exceeds 1950 m in the subsurface, three units having been recognized. The Waarre Sandstones and Flaxman Formation at the base consist of quartzose and glauconitic sandstones with Cenomanian microplankton. They pass up into a thick and monotonous mudstone sequence, locally glauconitic (Belfast Mudstone), with Turonian to possibly Campanian forams and microplankton. This is overlain by the Paaratte Formation, consisting of dolomitic quartz sandstones and siltstones and containing a Santonian to Maestrichtian fauna. The succession passes up conformably into the Palaeocene Pebble Point Formation.

Facies relationships within the Otway Basin are complex, the whole sequence being paralic and cyclic in character (Taylor, 1964; Bock and Glenie, 1965). The lower part of the sequence is thought on the basis of lithology and forams to have been deposited in a shallow turbid marine environment. This was succeeded by deposits of a neritic clear-water environment as transgression continued. Subsequently, with the commencement of the Late Cretaceous regression, facies differentiation developed, with landward "marginal marine deposits" of deltaic, lagoonal, and bay origin and a seaward facies of deep-water origin, but anaerobic benthonic conditions.

New Zealand (Fig. 10.6)

By the close of the Jurassic Period, the **New Zealand Geosyncline** had become much restricted in size, and in earliest Cretaceous times, its contents were folded and uplifted by the deforming movements of the Rangitata Orogeny. It appears likely that the eversion of the geosyncline resulted in the retreat of the sea from most of the present New Zealand area, for marine

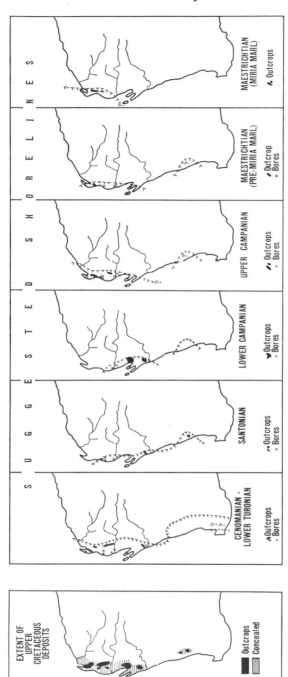

FIG. 10.4. Late Cretaceous palaeogeography of the Carnarvon and Perth Basins. (After Belford, 1958.)

strata of undoubted Neocomian age have not yet been positively identified. Freshwater beds of probable Early Cretaceous age (Topfer Formation) with conglomerates and thin coal-seams are present in north Westland. Considerable volcanism accompanied the orogenic movements as a continuation of the Late Jurassic activity.

Partial resubmergence of the region took place in Aptian times when the so-called **East Coast Geosyncline** was established along the East Cape–Hawkes Bay–East Wellington–Marlborough axis. Along the margins of this trough the land was mountainous and faulting was marked, yielding a supply of detritus in the form of rapidly deposited mudstones and conglomerates (Taitai Series) to the trough. Contemporaneous igneous rocks are known in the East Cape region, and there is evidence that a considerable amount of this material was derived from the east, as well as from the west, where a geanticline was emergent in the Rotorua–Coromandel area (Kingma, 1959).

The East Coast Geosyncline persisted into Late Cretaceous times, towards the end of which a marginal sea extended southwards along the present eastern coastal margins of the South Island beyond Dunedin. In the closing stages of the period, the sea extended even almost to Campbell Island and Late Cretaceous marginal transgressions are recorded also in the vicinity of the Chatham Islands.

Across the geanticline to the west of the East Coast Geosyncline, an erosion surface developed in Late Cretaceous times, extending from Marlborough to east Otago. A littoral strip of swampy lowlands and gravel-covered plains bordered a land of low relief, on which long-continued chemical weathering resulted in the formation of quartzose gravels and sands. Fleming (1962) suggests that this erosional phase, with its quartzose sedimentation, which continued locally into Cainozoic times, may be the only really stable phase in the history of the New Zealand Geosyncline since the Devonian Period. Across this erosion surface, during the Late Cretaceous and Early Cainozoic, there was a steady marine transgression westwards, so that marine sediments are found resting there on slightly older terrestrial beds.

While marine deposition was taking place during the Late Cretaceous on the margins of the East Coast Geosyncline, terrestrial deposits with valuable coal-seams were being formed in the fault-angle depressions on the hinterland in northwest Nelson, Westland, and Otago. These Upper Cretaceous freshwater deposits with coals on the west coast (Paparoa Beds) clearly show the rapid rise to prominence of the angiosperms, which made their appearance in New Zealand in the Raukumara Serieson on the West Coast of the South Island.

Lower Cretaceous marine sediments are restricted in their distribution. They comprise the coarse-grained Taitai Series of the axial facies of the North

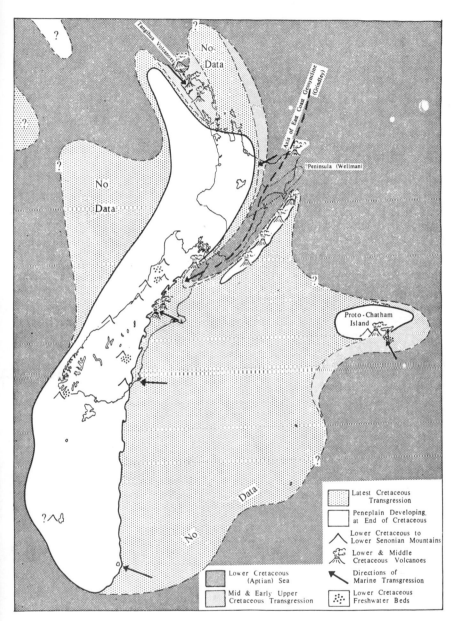

FIG. 10.6. Cretaceous palaeogeography of New Zealand.
(After Fleming, 1962, by permission of *Tuatara*).

GJ

Island and small areas of sandstones, mudstones, and conglomerates of Albian–Aptian age in the East Cape region and Marlborough. The Upper Cretaceous marine rocks, on the other hand, are much more widespread in both islands. They are divided into three series. The two older, the Clarence and the Raukumara, consist of siltstones, mudstones, and redeposited sandstones. The youngest, the Mata Series, is by far the most widespread. In its lower part it comprises well-sorted, medium-grained, fossiliferous sandstones, but towards the top it shows considerable facies variation from shallow- to deep-water sediments, often with a yellowish coating due to the presence of iron sulphides.

NORTHLAND REGION

The succession of Cretaceous rocks here is not well-known, largely because of deep weathering, poor exposure, and complex structural relations. Their widespread occurrence and the presence of most of the stages between the Motuan and Haumurian inclusive, is indicated by scattered fossils such as the various species of *Inoceramus*. The beds belong for the most part to the sand–shale facies of shallow-water marine origin.

Perhaps one of the most interesting units here is the lower portion of the Mangakahia Group of Haumurian age. It consists of micaceous sandstones with cone-in-cone limestone concretions containing, at Batley, an abundance of ammonites, some of very large size.

EAST CAPE REGION

Whether the Cretaceous deposits here were laid down within the East Coast Geosyncline proper or in a separate subsidiary trough as depicted by Wellman (1959, Fig. 1) must remain in doubt until further data are obtained.

At the base of the Taitai Series there is a unit (Mokoiwi Mudstone) of crushed dark argillite with lenses of volcanic material and small calcareous concretions. These rocks are distinguished from the considerably younger Tapuwaeroa Mudstone (Mata Series), with which they were for long confused, by the presence in them of the bivalve *Inoceramus warakius*. In the Tapuwaeroa Valley where the Mokoiwian strata typically occur, they are several thousand metres thick, but their precise base is not known and the lowest parts may include Upper Jurassic horizons. The unit appears to thin rapidly southwards and is only recognized by the presence of the index fossil in the east coast ranges. It is not known in the South Island.

The next overlying sequence is the Taitai Sandstone, comprising the bulk of the Korangan Stage. It is a green massive sandstone and pebbly conglomerate, derived from a volcanic source, forming a number of the high points on the Raukumara Range known as "taipos" (for example, Taitai, Hikurangi, and Aorangi) which are clearly, in places, large lensoid masses forming anticlinal (piercement) massifs surrounded by Upper Cretaceous and Lower Cainozoic sediments (Grindley *et al.*, 1959, p. 26). The Taitai Sandstone is unfossiliferous, except probably at Koranga.

The Clarence Series which follows consists of three stages, the Urutawan, Motuan, and Ngaterian, in ascending order. Shallowing of the East Coast Geosyncline towards the south is indicated by a distinct change in facies from the redeposited sandstone (axial) type in the north to the transitional shale and mudstone facies with very thin redeposited sandstones at Koranga. At Motu, where the Clarence sequence is virtually complete, the siltstones and redeposited sandstones are 1100 m thick, while at Koranga, the transitional sediments are about 1000 m thick.

The overlying Raukumara Series, comprising the Arowhanan, Mangaotanean, and Teratan Stages, most clearly indicates the filling of the geosyncline (see Table 10.2) (p. 292). At Raukokere in the extreme north of the Cretaceous sequence, the redeposited facies, representing the three stages, measures some 1500 m in thickness. In the Tapuwaeroa Valley this is reduced to 1200 m and transitional mudstones appear at the top, while in the Mangaotane Valley the sediments are entirely transitional in type and total 1000 m in thickness. This thickness rapidly diminishes southward until at Koranga the Raukumara Series is represented by about 150 m of transitional and shelf (marginal) sediments, a condition maintained throughout the marine sections in the South Island.

Erosion has removed much of the record of the rocks of the Mata Series in the northern sections in the East Cape region. However, geosynclinal conditions, with redeposited sediments, still persisted in the extreme northeastern parts, but elsewhere transitional and shelf sediments were deposited. Rocks of the Haumurian Stage, of a monotonous, creamy-grey argillite facies, are widespread over the southern areas. In all cases, there is a marked coarsening of the sediments towards the east, indicating a source of supply in that direction as shown by Fleming's reconstruction of Cretaceous geography (Fig. 10.6). No freshwater deposits are recorded in this area.

North Island East Coast and East Marlborough Region

The distinction of this region from the East Cape region is based on Wellman's concept (1959) of a northeasterly-trending peninsula in Cretaceous times located in the Gisborne district, which lay between these two regions. The palaeogeographical reconstruction accepted by Fleming (Fig. 10.6) suggests that the East Coast Geosyncline extended without such interruption along the line of the present east coast of both islands as far south as Marlborough.

In the east coast region of the North Island, Cretaceous rocks are scattered over a wide and structurally complicated area between the southern shore of Hawke Bay and the eastern shore of Palliser Bay. Most of the New Zealand Cretaceous stages are partially represented, one of the most interesting being a sequence of beds in the Motuan Stage at Tinui which has yielded ammonite and saurian remains. As in the East Cape region, the uppermost Cretaceous is marked by the widespread occurrence of creamy-grey rhyolitic tuffs, formerly referred to as argillites (J. T. Kingma, pers. comm.).

The East Marlborough and North Canterbury occurrences of Cretaceous rocks were the earliest discovered in the Dominion and for long were regarded as typical of the New Zealand sequence. Wellman has recently shown that considerable gaps in the sequence exist in this area and that the best representation of the system is given by the East Cape sections.

The East Marlborough region is the original locality for the Clarence Series. These oldest rocks of the series are graded-bedded greywackes and concretionary argillites with conglomerate bands, referred to the uppermost part of the Torlesse Group (Lensen, 1963), that grade upwards into massive mudstones or sandstones. Freshwater beds also make their appearance near the top of the sequence. The series is 1300 m thick at Coverham decreasing rapidly to 170 m in the Seymour River area where marine sediments of Urutawan age are overlain by freshwater grits and conglomerates with coal measures at the base, and by thick marine and terrestrial basalt flows and tuffs. In this area also, the Clarence sediments rest directly on the Jurassic basement (Fig. 10.7).

Farther south at Amuri Bluff, for long a classical locality for the New Zealand Upper Cretaceous sequence, the Clarence Series is also missing and the Pinipauan Stage, represented by a thin freshwater unit, rests directly on the Jurassic greywackes. Even in the more northern areas of Marlborough the marine sediments of the Raukumara Series—massive quartz sandstones, glauconitic sandstones with conglomerates—rarely exceed 200 m in thickness, although there is evidence in the Seaward Kaikoura Range of a progressive northeastward transgression at this time, the sea also entering the area of the present Awatere Valley.

This temporary interval of slow emergence was succeeded by a further general marine transgression along the east coast region, with the deposition of the Mata Series. These rocks cover a greater area than the other series in all the Cretaceous regions in New Zealand, and the same remarks apply, in respect of stages, to the Haumurian Stage.

At Amuri Bluff, virtually the type area for the series, the beds are about 200 m thick and consist chiefly of shallow-water sandstones and sulphur-coloured siltstones with a considerable fauna of molluscs and saurian bones. This section is incomplete at the top.

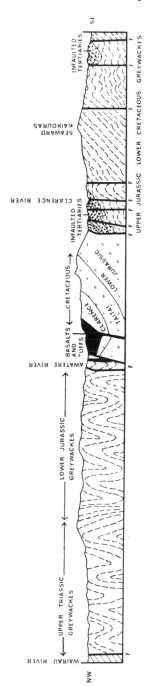

Fig. 10.7. Section from the Wairau River to the vicinity of Kaikoura, South Island, New Zealand. (After Lensen, 1963, part of Section A–A'.)

SOUTH ISLAND—EAST COAST

Along the remaining coastal section of the South Island as far south as Kaitangata and extending inland as far as Trelissick Basin, there is evidence of a similar marine transgression. Very shallow-water marine sediments in this coastal area spread over swamp and freshwater deposits which had been laid down along a fringe of a low hilly land to the west. These terrestrial deposits consist mainly of quartz gravels and sands derived by long-continued chemical weathering. In the southern districts, these sediments in turn rest directly on the schistose basement.

The uppermost Cretaceous marine sediments of the Mata Series are everywhere along the South Island east coast similar to those at Amuri Bluff. Greensands are frequently developed, and bands of large siliceous and/or calcareous septarian concretions, sometimes up to 4 m in diameter, occur near the top of the sequence. These are commonly associated with saurian and molluscan remains.

WEST COAST REGION (Fig. 10.8)

The Cretaceous sequence here is entirely non-marine and very incomplete. In the south Nelson area, the Upper Jurassic (?) Ohika Beds grade upwards into the Hawks Crag Breccia, which in turn is overlain with gradational passage by the Topfer Formation—conglomerates, sandstones, siltstones, and thin coal-seams. This formation also contains plant microfossils, similar to those of the Hawks Crag Breccia in having no angiospermous elements. The formation is tentatively dated as Neocomian–Albian in age.

In north Westland, an important unit of Late Cretaceous age is the Paparoa Coal Measures which rests with a basal breccia–conglomerate directly on Greenland (?Precambrian) greywackes and argillites. The coal measures vary in thickness from about 600 to 960 m and contain a microflora suggesting correlation with the Senonian Stage of Europe. They are referred by Suggate and Couper (1952), in their threefold classification of New Zealand coals, to the Lower Coal Measures. During the considerable period of tectonic quiet that prevailed in the Late Cretaceous, much of the New Zealand area was peneplained and a deeply leached erosion surface was cut across these Lower Coal Measures and all older rocks, prior to the deposition of the Middle Coal Measures of youngest Cretaceous and Early Cainozoic age.

PALAEONTOLOGY

Fossils are abundant in Cretaceous strata in many parts of Australia. Recent work by Cox (1961), Dickins (1960/69), Skwarko (1963), Woods (1961) and C. W. Wright (1963) on Mollusca; Crespin (1963), Taylor

(1964), and Belford (1960) on Foraminifera; and Cookson and Eisenack on microplankton, has added considerably to our knowledge of Cretaceous faunas. Balme, Cookson, Dettman, and Evans have each made important contributions to our knowledge of Australian plant microfossils, as Couper (1960) has done for New Zealand forms.

Faunas. In Australia, typical Neocomian molluscs include the bivalves *Iotrigonia* (*Zaletrigonia*), *Nototrigonia*, *Pterotrigonia* (*Rinetrigonia*), *Austretrigonia*, and *Maccoyella*, and the ammonite *Hatchericeras lakefieldense.*

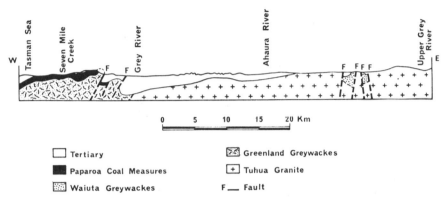

FIG. 10.8. West–east section from Point Elizabeth to Upper Grey River, Westland, New Zealand. (After Bowen, 1964, Section X–Y.)

The oldest known Cretaceous rocks in New Zealand, the Karanga Sandstone in the East Cape region, contains fragmentary remains of the large *Inoceramus warakius*, which is so far the only known macrofossil except probably for the bivalve *Maccoyella incurvata*, described by Waterhouse (1959) from a compacted mudstone below typical Mokoiwi beds. On this basis, the compacted mudstones are regarded as probably Aptian or possibly Albian in age and the Mokoiwian Stage as early Aptian.

The Aptian rocks in Australia contain new species of *Nototrigonia*, accompanied by *Laevitrigonia lineata*, *Maccoyella barklyi*, *M. reflecta*, *Pseudavicula anomala*, *Fissilunula clarkei*, and *Cyrenopsis meeki*. Other important fossils include the ammonites *Australiceras* and *Tropaeum*, the belemnite *Peratobelus oxys*, the brachiopod *Rhynchonella croydonensis*, and the sponge *Purisiphonia clarkei*.

The presence of *Maccoyella magnata*, *Aucellina* spp., and *Dicranodonta* in the rocks of the New Zealand Korangan Stage indicate an Aptian age also. Inoceramids are present, but only as indeterminate fragments.

Ammonites are common in the Albian rocks of both countries. In Australia, they include *Myloceras*, *Labeceras*, *Beudanticeras*, and *Appurdiceras*. *Dimitobelus* is typical of the belemnites. Three trigoniid species occur that range up from the Aptian. Other bivalves are *Aucellina hughendenensis, Cyrenopsis huddlestoni, Maccoyella rockwoodensis, Pseudavicula papyracea,* and *Inoceramus* spp.

In New Zealand, two stages of the Clarence Series appear to correspond to the Albian of Europe. The lower, Urutawan Stage, is characterized by *Inoceramus kapuus,* and many other fossils including two species of ammonites and the correlation with the lower Albian is based on the conformable relations between the Urutawan Stage and the overlying Motuan Stage (with *Inoceramus ipuanus*). In the East Wellington region, Motuan strata have yielded *Puzosia, Phyllopachyceras, Anagaudryceras,* and *Wellmanites,* together with saurian remains and *Pachydesmoceras* has been found in correlative beds in Marlborough. Brachiopods, bivalves (including the last *Aucellinae*), gastropods and echinoids are also present in rocks of this age. The correlation of the Motuan Stage seems, on the basis of the ammonites, to be fairly clearly with the middle and upper Albian.

The Late Cretaceous faunas of Australia are less well known than those of the Early Cretaceous. Molluscs are abundant, ammonites dominating among the described forms. Typical Cenomanian ammonites include *Turrilites costatus, Stomohamites simplex, Hypoturrilites, Euomphaloceras,* and *Acanthoceras. Collignoniceras* has been described from the Turonian.

In New Zealand, on the contrary, the youngest Cretaceous faunas are quite prolific and well known. In so far as the boundary between the Lower and Upper Cretaceous in Europe is placed between the Albian and Cenomanian Stages, this appears to lie in New Zealand within the Clarence Series, and the upper unit of this series, the Ngaterian Stage, is correlated with the Cenomanian. Rocks of Ngaterian age, characterized by *Inoceramus fyfei* and *I. hakarius,* contain a number of ammonites, for example *Sciponoceras, Scaphites, Hypoturrilites, Desmoceras,* and *?Ptychoceras,* which have distinct Cenomanian affinities. *Otoscaphites,* a genus with upper Turonian affinities, is also present. The weight of evidence, however, supported by the occurrence of the ammonite *Mariella* in company with *Inoceramus concentricus* (a European species) near the base of the stage, supports correlation with the Cenomanian. Other important fossils are the bivalves *Eselaevitrigonia, Iotrigonia,* and *Exogyra,* the hexacoral *Haimesiastraea,* and useful species of globigerinids.

The Raukumara Series in New Zealand also comprises three stages. Apart from the index inoceramids, which are of value for local correlations, there are few fossils that provide a direct link with overseas sequences. On stratigraphical grounds the Raukumara Series must closely approximate to the Coniacian and Santonian Stages of Europe, with some extension downwards perhaps into the Turonian Stage.

The Santonian to Maestrichtian sequence in Western Australia has yielded an abundant fauna including the bivalves *Inoceramus*, *Gryphaea*, and *Ostrea*, the ammonites *Paraphylloceras*, *Pseudophyllites*, *Hauericeras*, *Kossmaticeras*, *Eubaculites*, and *Pachydiscus*, and the crinoids *Uintacrinus* and *Marsupites*. Vertebrate remains, including the marine reptiles *Ichthyosaurus*, *Kronosaurus*, and *Plesiosaurus*, are known from Queensland and elsewhere.

The youngest and most widespread Cretaceous rocks in New Zealand comprise the Mata Series. The lower, Piripauan Stage, is characterized by the abundance and wide distribution of its index inoceramids, *Inoceramus pacificus* and *I. australis*. Other macrofossils occur at only a few places and appear to be confined to a restricted facies within the marginal sediments (Wellman, 1959). Although there is a considerable number and variety of fossils known from this stage, including ammonites such as *Kossmaticeras*, *Gaudryceras*, and *Baculites*, many of these require revision. Correlation with the middle and upper Campanian is therefore based largely on stratigraphical grounds, though partially on the resemblance of *Inoceramus australis* to *I. balticus* from the Campanian of Germany.

The upper, Haumurian Stage, is currently regarded as the uppermost Cretaceous unit in New Zealand. Its upper limit is marked by the last ammonites and belemnites, with the inoceramids disappearing from the record slightly earlier. This boundary is believed to correspond to the top of the Maestrichtian Stage in Europe, a correlation confirmed by the presence of some key Maestrichtian forams in the Haumurian rocks.

Important fossils in the Haumurian Stage include bivalves (*Inoceramus matatorus*, *Ostrea lapillicola*, *Lahillia*, *Callistina*, and *Pacitrigonia*), gastropods (*Struthioptera*, *Perissoptera*, and *Conchothyra parasitica*), ammonites (*Phyllopachyceras*, *Pseudophyllites*, *Ptychoceras*, *Gaudryceras*, *Diplomoceras*, *Gunnarites*, *Vertebrites*, *Jacobites*, and *Maorites*), belemnites (small forms of *Cheirobelus*), elasmobranch fishes (*Synechodus*, *Lamna*, and *Callorhynchus*), and marine reptiles (*Elasmosaurus*, *Mauisaurus*, *Cimoliosaurus*, *Tylosaurus*, and *Taniwhasaurus*).

It is now generally accepted practice in New Zealand to regard the Teurian Stage (together with the Wangaloan "Stage" of south Otago), for long reckoned as the uppermost portion of the Mata Series, as Palaeocene in age and correlated with the Danian Stage of Europe. Belemnites, earlier reported in Teurian strata, have been shown to come from Haumurian rocks. Fleming (pers. comm.) has also indicated that the supposed occurrence of saurian remains in the Waipara Greensands of North Canterbury, identified as Teurian in age on the basis of Foraminifera, has not been confirmed by collections made since McKay's original report in 1877.

Floras. Plant macrofossils of Cretaceous age are abundant at many localities in Australia, but are of limited stratigraphical value. Typical forms include

Taeniopteris spatulata, Cladophlebis australis, Elatophyllum, Pterophyllum, Ptilophyllum, Nathorstia, and *Elatocladus.*

A varied microplankton assemblage occurs in the Lower Cretaceous of Western Australia (Cookson and Eisenack, 1958), being dominated by *Deflandrea, Gonyaulax* and *Hystrichosphaeridium. Dingodinium cerviculum* and *Muderongia* are characteristic forms. Upper Cretaceous microplankton are known both from Western Australia (Cookson and Eisenack, 1962) and Victoria where they have been used for zonation (Douglas, 1962). The most important genera are *Deflandrea, Nelsoniella, Odontochitina,* and *Amphidiadema.*

Lower Cretaceous plant microfossils have proved valuable for correlation in Australia (Dettman, 1963; Evans, 1963). Dettman (1963) has recognized three assemblages spanning the Lower Cretaceous. The oldest is characterized by *Crybelosporites stylosus* and is regarded as probably Late Jurassic in age by Evans (pers. comm.). The next assemblage is named for *Dictotosporites speciosus,* and for the youngest *Coptospora paradoxa* is diagnostic.

The plant microfossils from the Australian Upper Cretaceous have been less adequately studied, but the advent of angiospermous pollen is first recorded in the Belfast Mudstone (Turonian) of the Otway Basin (Evans 1962/57).

In New Zealand, plant macrofossils are found in Upper Cretaceous strata and include the first record of the southern beeches of the *Nothofagus brassi* group and a species of *"Dryandra".* Plant microfossils are somewhat spasmodic in occurrence in the Cretaceous rocks, but they have proved of considerable value for correlation in many places. In the freshwater beds of the Topfer Formation, which overlies the probably Middle and Upper Jurassic Hawks Crag Breccia and Ohika Beds in north Westland, there are pollens (*Microcachryidites, Podocarpidites, Gleichenia,* and *Blechnum*) which are not known from New Zealand Jurassic strata. Moreover, the absence of angiospermous pollens from the Topfer Formation places an upper limit on its age and supports a tentative correlation with the Neocomian Stage of Europe.

No plant remains are known from the rocks of the Taitai Series, nor from the lower part of the Clarence Series. In the Ngaterian Stage (as revised by Hall (1963)), however, numerous spores and pollens occur including the earliest dicotyledonous form (?*Tricolpites*) known from New Zealand. Other genera present include *Osmundacidites, Podocarpidites, Cyathidites,* and *Trilites.* Rich floras from the Gridiron Formation of the Clarence Valley include abundant *Trisaccites* and other coniferous pollens.

In the Raukumara Series, spores and pollens are known from the Paparoa Group of the west coast of the South Island. These include characteristic Upper Cretaceous species of *Dacrydiumites, Nothofagus,* and *Tricolpites,* with *Triorites* and *Proteacidites* appearing near the top of the sequence. On this evidence, this entirely non-marine sequence is assigned a post-Ngaterian and pre-Haumurian age.

The Mata Series, which was deposited under paralic conditions, contains many formations with abundant microfloras (Couper, 1960) that can be accurately dated by comparison with the faunas of the interfingering marine strata.

CLIMATE

Irving (1964) has suggested that Australia lay between 45°S′ and 75°S′ during the Cretaceous. Ammonites are known over much of this palaeolatitude range and large reptiles occur in the Great Artesian Basin. These imply a temperate or warm equable climate throughout.

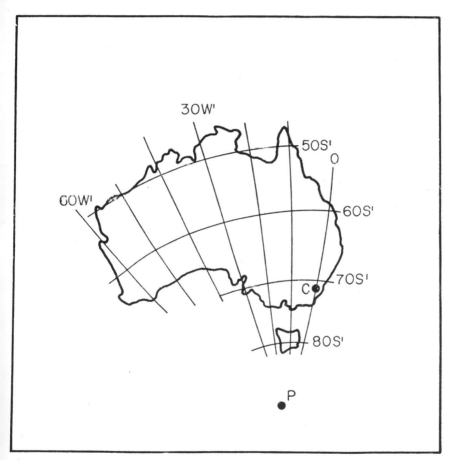

FIG. 10.9. Cretaceous palaeolatitudes and palaeomeridians based on Canberra. (After Irving, 1964, by permission of John Wiley & Sons Inc.)

There are numerous records in the literature of striated and faceted blocks up to 1·5 m in diameter in all units of the Lower Cretaceous in the south-western Artesian Basin. This led David and Browne (1950) to conclude that this area had been glaciated during Cretaceous times. Parkin (1956) has reviewed the evidence and concluded that all occurrences can be explained by the reworking of blocks from Permian tills, which are widespread in this area. These blocks either are incorporated in the Lower Cretaceous sediments, or have been derived directly from the Permian and scattered over the present land surface by Cainozoic erosive processes, so that they now rest on areas underlain by Cretaceous strata.

The climatic conditions of the New Zealand Cretaceous are somewhat obscure and may be deduced on rather negative evidence. For instance, the absence of rudistids, reef corals and large forams suggests that in the Late Cretaceous, at least, the temperatures were not tropical. The presence in deposits of this age in the South Island, however, of marine reptiles and the pollen *Anacolosidites*, representing the tropical family Olacaceae, suggests a climate warmer than at present, probably moist warm-temperate (Fleming, 1962, p. 66). It is doubtful whether the virtual absence of limestones from the New Zealand Cretaceous has any climatic significance. No glacial deposits have been confirmed.

TECTONISM AND IGNEOUS ACTIVITY

Australia

The Cretaceous was a period during which igneous activity was absent from much of the continent. The only volcanics occur in the Lower Cretaceous of the Maryborough and Perth Basins. The Grahams Creek Volcanics of the Maryborough Basin are predominantly andesitic, with some trachytes and rhyolites, whereas the Bunbury Basalt of the Perth Basin is a tholeiite.

Certain intrusive masses have been shown by radiometric dating (Evernden and Richards, 1962; Webb and McDougall, 1964) to be of Cretaceous age. These are the Mount Dromedary shoshonitic complex on the south coast of New South Wales, the Cygnet intrusions of syenite and alkaline intermediate porphyry at Point Cygnet in Tasmania, and certain granites in the Eungella district, Queensland. The last are Early Cretaceous in age.

As in the Jurassic, folding of any intensity is confined to the Maryborough Basin. The youngest strata involved are Albian in age and the orogeny is referred to the Late Cretaceous. In the Wreck Island No. 1 Bore on the Barrier Reef, probably Grahams Creek Volcanics are overlain unconformably by Lower Miocene limestone, which sets an upper limit to the age of this Maryburian Orogeny.

Elsewhere in the continent, regional tectonic influences have resulted

Table of stratigraphic correlation (rotated chart). Stages listed down the left (Upper: Maestrichtian, Campanian, Santonian, Coniacian, Turonian, Cenomanian; Lower: Albian, Aptian, Neocomian), basins across the top.

Series	Stage	Gippsland Basin	Otway Basin	Eucla Basin	Perth Basin	Carnarvon Basin	Canning Basin	N.T. Shelf – Coastal & Inland Belts	N.T. Shelf – Darwin-Bathurst Is.	Maryborough Basin	Styx Basin – Stanwell	Laura Basin	Carpentaria Basin	Great Artesian Basin
Upper	Maestrichtian		Paaratte Formation		Poison Hill Greensand	Miria Marl								
Upper	Campanian		Belfast Mudstone		Gingin Chalk	Korojon Calcarenite								Mt. Howie Sst.
Upper	Santonian		Flaxman Fm. / Waarre Sandstone		Molecap Greensand	Toolonga Calcilutite								
Upper	Coniacian													Winton Formation
Upper	Turonian				Osborne Formation & Dandaragon Sandstone	Gearle Siltstone		Mullaman Beds	Mullaman Beds	Burrum Coal Measures	Styx Coal Measures		Unnamed	
Upper	Cenomanian												Normanton Formation	
Lower	Albian	Korumburra Group	Korumburra Group		South Perth Formation	Windalia Radiolarite	Frezier and Melligo Sandstone			Maryborough Formation	Unnamed strata near Stanwell	Wolena Claystone	Kamileroi Limestone / Blackdown Formation	Mackunda Fm. / Wilgunya Fm. (upper) / Toolebuc Member / Wilgunya Fm. (lower)
Lower	Aptian			Madura Shale		Muderong Shale				Grahams Ck. Volcanics		Battle Camp Formation	Gilbert River Fm. / Wrotham Park Sandstone	Tambo Fm. / Roma F. / Miami Mem.
Lower	Neocomian			Loongana Congl.		Birdrong Fm. / Nanutarra Fm.	Broome Sandstone & equivalents							Blythesdale Formation

TABLE 10.1. CORRELATION TABLE FOR THE CRETACEOUS SYSTEM IN AUSTRALIA

only in broad warping. Several such large structures occur in the Artesian Basin, particularly near the Queensland–South Australian border (Wopfner, 1960; Freeman, 1963). They are of either Late Cretaceous or Early Cainozoic age.

In the Carnarvon Basin the Cretaceous rocks have been involved in Late Tertiary folding, although there is some evidence of Turonian–Coniacian deformation in addition (McWhae *et al.*, 1958).

New Zealand

Volcanism on a considerable scale took place in Early Cretaceous times along the Northland Trough, and probably along a line of islands to the east of the East Coast Geosyncline. These were an accompaniment to the deforming movements of the Rangitata Orogeny which culminated at this time, and which resulted in large-scale emergence of the New Zealand area. For instance, the North Cape Ultramafics, the Tangihua and Matakaoa volcanics, the North Canterbury Syenites and associated igneous rocks, and the alkaline intrusions of the Haast Pass and north Westland, probably include rocks of Early Cretaceous age. Kingma (1959) believes that the Lower Cretaceous sediments of the East Cape region (Mokoiwi–Taitai rocks) were derived from a geanticlinal structure to the west, namely, in the present Rotorua–Coromandel area.

The partial resubmergence of the New Zealand region in Aptian times, in which fracturing and faulting played a major role, was accompanied by further volcanism with eruptions of basalts, pillow lavas, and conspicuous tuffs that outcrop in the Raukumara Range. Probably coeval non-marine tuffs and agglomerates, largely of acid composition, with dolerite dykes (Kirwan Intrusives), are known in the Topfer Formation near Reefton.

With the onset of the Clarence Epoch, tectonic activity decreased markedly. This is reflected in the formation of extensive erosion surfaces on which Upper Cretaceous marine sediments frequently rest, and also in the diminution of volcanic activity, at least in so far as spatial distribution of these rocks is concerned. Volcanics of Clarence age are known only from the Awatere and Clarence Valleys in Marlborough. It is estimated that thick flows of olivine basalt with interbedded tuffs, partly marine and partly non-marine, formerly covered an area of at least 750 sq km. A large accumulation in the Upper Awatere Valley extends over 25 sq km and is at least 900 m thick. The neighbouring Taitai and older rocks are traversed by numerous dyke-swarms, mostly vertical in attitude and trending dominantly northnorth-eastwards or eastsoutheastwards.

Raukumara volcanics are limited to two places on the West Coast of the South Island. On the east side of the Greymouth coalfield there are thick flows, tuffs and agglomerates thinning to the west within the lower Paparoa Coal Measures. Basalt interbedded with coal measures is also known at Kowhitirangi Hill, Westland.

A rather temporary and perhaps local revival of tectonism may have occurred in the Late Cretaceous in the East Cape region when the Tapuwaeroa grits and conglomerates of the lower Tapuwaeroa Valley were deposited. Apart from this, however, there is little to suggest that the end of the Cretaceous was anything other than a time of peneplanation and extremely low relief on the hinterland.

There is even less evidence of Mata igneous rocks. They are known with certainty only in the Wairarapa region of the North Island. Erosion near Ngahape has exposed teschenitic and doleritic intrusions with flows of variolitic pillow basalts interbedded with Mata sediments. An ash flow in the Shag Valley, north Otago, is believed to be interbedded with sediments of Senonian age (Steiner *et al.*, 1959).

CHAPTER 11

The Tertiary System

THE Tertiary histories of Australia and New Zealand have been treated separately, chiefly because of their markedly differing degree of relative importance in the geological picture of each country, and to a lesser extent, because of the difficulties of making precise correlations across the Tasman at this time. In Australia, the Tertiary marine deposits are in large measure marginal to the continent, their sequences are discontinuous and rather fragmentary, and there is still room for improvement in the correlation schemes proposed for individual areas. The relative importance of Tertiary terrestrial deposits in Australia is very considerable in contrast to New Zealand where such deposits are insignificant. In the latter country, however, marine deposits are widely distributed in both islands, many continuous sequences are available, and they have probably been investigated more thoroughly than any deposits of other ages.

The tectonic setting for Tertiary sedimentation is also quite different in the two countries. In Australia, although there was large scale volcanism in the east and southeast of the continent, tectonic movements were restricted to those of the epeirogenic type. The New Zealand regime, on the other hand, was one of increasing diastrophism and orogenesis reaching a climax with the Kaikoura movements in the Late Tertiary and Early Quaternary.

AUSTRALIA

STRATIGRAPHY

MARINE DEPOSITS

Marine Tertiary rocks are known only from the southern and western parts of the continent, and from the Great Barrier Reef Platform off the Queensland coast. The sediments which are at present observable were laid down along the margins of basins that encroached onto what is now the edge of the landmass. This encroachment was of very limited extent in Tasmania and along the southern coast of Victoria, but was much more extensive in the Murray, Eucla, and Carnarvon Basins. In all the epicontinental basins the sequence tends to be similar, the broad outline being as follows. At the base there are paralic or littoral sandstones and shales, often carbonaceous and sometimes glauconitic. These are usually Palaeocene or lower Eocene but continue on into the upper Eocene in some places. There was a widespread extension of marine conditions in the late Eocene, followed by withdrawal in the Oligocene and a yet more widespread transgression in the late Oligocene or early Miocene. Pliocene sediments are not common and are mainly estuarine or lagoonal sands.

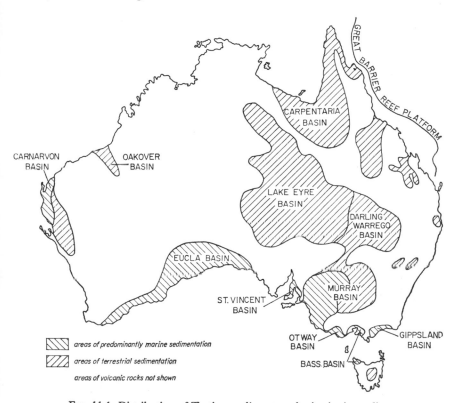

Fɪɢ. 11.1. Distribution of Tertiary sedimentary basins in Australia.

Great Barrier Reef Platform. Tertiary marine rocks are probably widespread along the Great Barrier Reef, but proof of this awaits a drilling programme. At Wreck Island, approximately 360 m of limestones, calcarenites and glauconitic quartzose sandstones representing continuous deposition over the early Miocene–late Pliocene interval, have been found in a well (Derrington *et al.*, 1960). These rocks are unconformable on basement, and are overlain by 170 m of Pleistocene and Holocene carbonates.

Gippsland Basin. In the Tertiary this was a small depositional basin with its long axis more or less parallel to the trend of the present coast line, and separated from the Bass Basin to the west by a rising area of Lower Cretaceous sediments and older rocks against which the Tertiary sediments thin out. Lignites are both widespread and thick in the early sediments (the Latrobe Valley Coal Measures); and in the northern part of the basin at Yallourn and Morwell, where coal-measure conditions were more continuous and

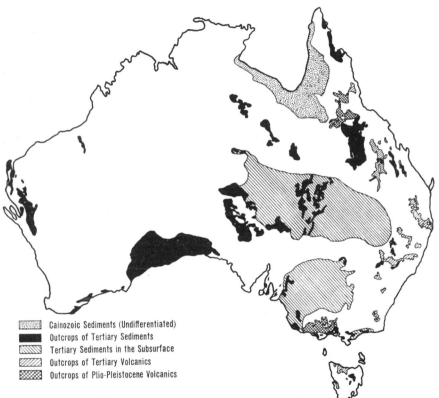

Cainozoic Sediments (Undifferentiated)
Outcrops of Tertiary Sediments
Tertiary Sediments in the Subsurface
Outcrops of Tertiary Volcanics
Outcrops of Plio-Pleistocene Volcanics

Fig. 11.2. Distribution of Tertiary strata.

subsidence more rapid than further south, economically important seams reach a total thickness of over 300 m, and one seam is up to 160 m thick. Locally there are interbedded basalts.

Following a marine transgression in the eastern part of the basin in the late Oligocene, greensands, marls, and limestones (the Lakes Entrance Formation) were deposited (Carter, 1964; Hocking and Taylor, 1964). During the Miocene there was a gradual shallowing of the basin due to sedimentation, and the Gippsland Limestone formed under quiet water conditions. Towards the top of the formation erosional gaps occur. Organic limestones and marls are the dominant rocks. Lepidocyclines occur in the middle part and the echinoid *Clypeaster gippslandicus* is common near the top. This phase terminated with the deposition of limonitic or glauconitic marls (the Tambo River Formation). Uplift with tilting followed in the Pliocene and the landward part of the basin rose above sealevel. In the seaward parts there is continuity of sedimentation, and the Jemmys Point Formation of carbonaceous and glauconitic marls is conformable on the Tambo River Formation. The sequence is completed by widespread terrestrial gravels and sands, the Haunted Hill Gravels, which extend up into the Pleistocene.

Bass Basin. This basin occupies the greater part of Bass Strait, and sediments deposited around its margins outcrop in the Port Phillip area to the north, northern Tasmania to the south, and the Furneaux Islands in the east. In the first area the whole Tertiary sequence is less than 350 m thick, and it rests with angular unconformity on Cretaceous or older rocks. The rocks of the paralic Palaeocene–Eocene phase occur in the present coastal areas and are divided into three formations—the Eastern View Coal Measures, Boonah Sandstone, and Demons Bluff Formation (Raggatt and Crespin, 1955). There was regression in the early Oligocene and then in the late Oligocene an extensive marine transgression occurred which reached the present limits of the basin and beyond, and in which were laid down the clays, sands, and fossiliferous glauconitic calcarenites of the Jan Juc Formation (=Lower Maude Formation; Bowler, 1963). During the Miocene the sea deepened slightly, but there is evidence that there were only slight migrations of the shoreline. As would be expected, the lithological units are diachronous. Contemporary movement along north–south faults or monoclines in the basement have also complicated the depositional pattern. Some of the benthonic organisms can be shown to be strictly limited in distribution by bottom conditions. There are two formations in this interval, the lower to middle Miocene Batesford Limestone (equivalent to the Maude Basalt and upper Maude Formation), and the upper Miocene Fyansford Clay. The former consists of poorly bedded limestone and calcarenite in the upper parts of which there is an abundance of *Lepidocyclina* and *Cycloclypeus*. The latter is made up of clays, marls, and argillaceous limestones with well preserved molluscs and forams. Following a shallowing of the sea again at the end of the Miocene there was a short period of emergence before the Pliocene shallow-water marine to terrestrial sediments of the Moorabool Viaduct Sands were deposited. Upper Pliocene to Quaternary basalts (the Newer Basalts) cap this sequence. The sediments remain almost horizontal except in the vicinity of the basement faults or monoclines.

On the islands of Bass Strait and in northern Tasmania, outcrops are isolated and of limited extent. No Palaeocene or Eocene rocks are known, but by late Oligocene times, thin coquinites, calcarenites, and sandstones were forming (Table Cape Group and equivalents). These contain the oldest known Australian marsupial *Wynyardia bassiana* and a microfauna similar to that of the Jan Juc Formation. Further limestones developed during the Miocene and late Pliocene.

Otway Basin. This basin still existed in both South Australia and Victoria. The Kanawinka Hinge was active along the western half of its northern edge, and the Tertiary sediments wedge out rapidly towards it (Sprigg and Woolley, 1963). In the north they rest with angular unconformity on the Lower Cretaceous or earlier rocks, but beneath the present coast line drilling has indicated a Tertiary section up to 1500 m thick, conformable on the Upper Cretaceous. In fact, the Cretaceous–Palaeocene boundary probably lies within the Paaratte Formation. In the east the Tertiary rocks thin out against a ridge of Lower Cretaceous sediments which forms a discontinuous divide between the Otway and Bass Basins.

Stratigraphic nomenclature within the basin is in urgent need of standardization, each area examined in detail at present having its own system (Baker, 1950; Carter, 1958a; Ludbrook, 1961b; Boutakoff, 1963; Bock and Glenie, 1965). The part of the basin preserved on the mainland appears to have been a continental terrace which rapidly subsided in the early Tertiary, but became progressively more stable. Towards the south, there is an increase in the marine component in the sediments, and the sequence is apparently unbroken. Northwards lagoonal, tidal flat, and some lacustrine deposits are found, and minor breaks in the sequence are common.

At the southeastern end of the basin, at least, the stratigraphy can be interpreted in terms of three transgressive–regressive cycles (see Fig. 10.5; p. 278) corresponding with the units Upper Wangerrip Group, Nirranda Group, and Heytesbury Group (Bock and Glenie, 1965). In places the breaks between the cycles are considerable—for example that between cycles 3 and 4 involves the loss of Faunal Unit 4 in most sections. In general, during the transgressive phases marls and muds were widespread, and during the regressions carbonaceous and quartzose sandstones, thin coals, and minor gravels spread seawards.

Murray Basin. Stability and slow subsidence characterize this large, roughly circular basin. The maximum thickness of Tertiary sediments is in the west central part where it reaches about 500 m, a figure considerably less than that recorded in the Otway Basin to the south. A thin veneer of terrestrial Quaternary deposits obscures the early rocks over most of the basin, but there are good outcrops along the lower reaches of the Murray River, and several deep wells have yielded much information. As elsewhere, Tertiary deposition began with paralic gravels, sands, clays, and carbonaceous silts. These cover a large part of the basin, indicating the presence of a more or less planate depositional surface. Since the marine influence is restricted to the southwestern quadrant, the sea must have entered from this direction. Shallow-water marine deposition began during the Oligocene and continued on into the early Miocene with conglomerates, marls, and bioclastic limestones of the Glenelg Group (Ludbrook, 1961*b*, 1963; Johns and Lawrence, 1964). These spread at least as far east as longitude 143° 30′E and as far north as latitude 33°S. After a depositional break during most of the late Miocene, marine conditions returned in the latest Miocene and Pliocene (the Murray Group). A complicated facies picture was produced by partial withdrawal and re-entry of the sea during this interval, as is well illustrated by Fig. 11.3. It is probable that many of the northerly to northwesterly trending ridges with red sandstone cores in the Mallee district of western Victoria are barrier dunes formed during the late Pliocene retreat of the sea (Blackburn, 1962).

St. Vincent Basin. There may have been Cretaceous sedimentation on the site of the present St. Vincent Gulf as the result of Cretaceous graben formation, but certainly by Early Tertiary times the sea had invaded this area and was spilling onto the present landmass both east and west. The land surfaces were being rejuvenated by normal faulting which continued throughout the Tertiary, and the encroaching seas formed sediments of varying facies and thicknesses in the consequent topographical irregularities. The Mount Lofty Range area was never covered by the sea and this basin therefore was never connected directly to the Murray Basin.

The lower Eocene sediments were carbonaceous sands and lignites of deltaic origin (the North Maslin Sand) and these have a patchy distribution. They are covered by glauconitic sands and richly fossiliferous marls and limestones (the South Maslin Sand, Tortachilla Limestone, and Blanche Point Marl) laid down in a transgressing late Eocene sea. After a distinct hiatus, deposition of polyzoan limestones and marls resumed in the late Oligocene and early Miocene (the Port Willunga Beds), when the Tertiary seas attained their widest extent in this basin. During the middle and late Miocene there was uplift, normal faulting, and monoclinal folding causing a re-shaping of the shorelines, and when the sea entered again in the Pliocene sediments were laid down with disconformity and angular unconformity on the lower Miocene, as well as directly on Precambrian and Palaeozoic rocks. These Pliocene sediments (the Hallett Cove and Dry Creek Sands) are mainly white and yellow sands and sandy limestones.

Eucla Basin. A thin veneer of Tertiary limestones covers a shelf area of some 110,000 sq km at the head of the Great Australian Bight. The maximum thickness of Tertiary sediment is probably nowhere much in excess of 300 m. The only terrigenous sediments are thin, irregularly distributed carbonaceous silts, quartz sands, and conglomerates (the Pidinga Formation) laid down in the original Eocene transgression. Subsequent rocks are largely organic limestones with abundant well-preserved macro- and microfaunas. The lower or Wilson Bluff Limestone is soft and chalky and is conformable or slightly disconformable on the Pidinga Formation. It is of late Eocene age and contains numerous polyzoans and the distinctive echinoid *Australanthus longianus*. There is a major disconformity at the base of the overlying Nullarbor Limestone which in most places is hard, white, and crystalline. In places small patch reefs of coralline and algal material were developed. It is of early Miocene age and is much less extensive than the Wilson Bluff Limestone. No subsequent deposition has taken place in the basin, and everywhere the sediments remain almost horizontal.

To the west of the present limits of the Eucla Basin are several isolated outcrops of marine Tertiary rocks, the largest of which are in the vicinity of Albany where they are known as the Plantagenet Beds. All of these sediments are less than 100 m thick and they lie unconformably on the Precambrian. They consist of siltstones, spongolites, limestones, and occasional lignites, and represent relics of a once extensive sheet of sediments laid down during the Eocene transgression.

Perth Basin. There was only minor deposition in this basin. The only Tertiary unit recognized is the Kings Park Shale which is known in the subsurface at Perth. It is of late Palaeocene age (McGowran, 1964) and is up to 300 m thick.

Carnarvon Basin. In the vicinity of the Giralia and Rough Ranges there was only a slight break in sedimentation at the end of the Cretaceous. Greensands and calcarenites were deposited during the Palaeocene and early to middle Eocene, and though they total less than 100 m in thickness they have been divided into five formations. Fossils, particularly forams, echinoids (*Cardiaster*, *Holaster*), bivalves, and nautiloids (*Aturoidea*, *Teichertia*), have

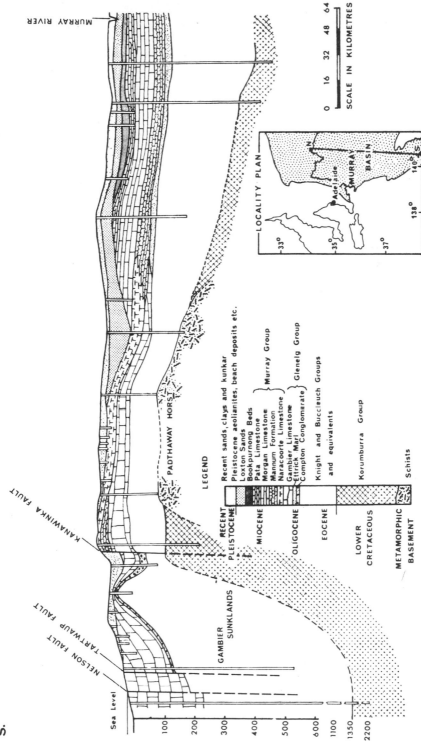

FIG. 11.3. Section through the Murray Basin along the South Australia–Victoria border. (Modified after Ludbrook, 1961.)

provided a firm basis for correlation. The late Eocene was a period of wide transgression when about 90,000 sq km of the present continent were covered in a meridional belt up to 270 km wide. Away from the shoreline the sediments consist of fossiliferous calcarenites and hard limestones with glauconite, whereas shorewards they are predominantly quartz sandstones and siltstones (the Merlinleigh Sandstone) which lie with marked angular unconformity on Upper Palaeozoic sediments. Significant fossils at this level are the forams *Nummulites* and *Discocyclina* and the nautiloids *Aturia* and *Aturoidea*.

During the Oligocene slight uplift of the Eocene sediments took place accompanied by the formation of low, meridionally elongated domes. Subsidence was renewed along the western half of the basin in the early Miocene, and the widespread Cape Range Group was deposited. Terrigenous material is present only as clean white sands representing the beach deposits of the early part of this transgression, and all the other sediments are limestones. They rest disconformably on the Eocene in most places, but on the crests of the above-mentioned domes there is slight angular unconformity. Once again, forams are the dominant fossils, and include *Lepidocyclina*, *Cycloclypeus*, and *Miogypsina*.

The remainder of the Tertiary was a period of uplift over the whole basin except for a narrow strip near the present coast where a thin calcareous sandstone (the Vlaming Sandstone) was deposited during the Pliocene, possibly under brackish conditions.

TERRESTRIAL DEPOSITS

Terrestrial deposits are of two main types—those of relatively small lakes and river systems of the eastern highlands and coastal plain, and those of the great internal drainage systems covering parts of the old Drummond, Georgina, Amadeus, and Great Artesian Basins. These last deposits may properly be regarded as continuing the history of the Great Artesian Basin. In addition, there are small areas of sediment associated with the rivers of the Pilbara region and Carnarvon Basin of Western Australia.

Small patches of shale, quartzose sandstone and conglomerate, which were laid down in standing bodies of fresh water and along water courses draining into them, are a feature of the geology from Cape York in the north to Tasmania in the south. The most extensive of these deposits, covers well over 10,000 sq km, and in places the sediments are up to 300 m thick, though the average figure is about 100 m. Most of the sediments are either Eocene or Oligocene in age, the structures which they fill having been initiated by Eocene epeirogenic movements, and they are unconformable on a variety of earlier rocks. The commonest sediments are quartzose gravels and sands which often have ferruginous cement, but clays and mudstones are far from rare. Occasional lignites, oil shales and cherty limestones are also present. Plant fossils and freshwater fish are found at several localities. In many places the rocks are covered by volcanics and the old stream channels form deep leads which have been of economic importance for the gold and tin they contain. Diatomaceous earths and kaolinites developed in shallow basins on the volcanics in several areas. Late Tertiary lake deposits are present on a restricted scale in north Queensland.

During the Tertiary great internal drainage systems occupied an area comparable with that which the Lake Eyre drainage system occupies today. This, however, was apparently not focused on a single centre but on several more or less ephemeral centres. Only the Lake Eyre Basin has retained a degree of permanence (Johns and Ludbrook, 1963). During the Eocene–Miocene interval a sequence of grey clays, silts, and dolomitic mudstones (the Etadunna Formation), reaching a maximum known thickness of about 70 m, was deposited. This lies with only slight erosional disconformity on the Cretaceous Winton Formation. The Etadunna Formation contains a fauna of marsupials which is possibly as old as Oligocene (Stirton *et al.*, 1961). There seem to be few deposits of Early and Middle Tertiary age outside the Lake Eyre Basin proper, but 160 km northeast of Alice Springs there are probable Miocene lake deposits which have a rich avian fauna and a eucalypt flora (Newsome and Rochow, 1964).

During the Late Tertiary deposition was much more widespread. Over much of the northern and northeastern edges of the Great Artesian Basin and the Carpentaria Basin there are dissected sheet-like fluviatile deposits generally 30–60 m thick (the Glendower and Lynd Formations). They have gravels at the base and pale-coloured silts and muds toward the top, the gravels containing, *inter alia*, the products of the erosion of laterites. They are therefore considered to be Late Tertiary or early Pleistocene in age. Further west, across much of the Georgina Basin and the western side of the Great Artesian Basin, there are dissected sheets of silicified limestones interbedded with minor clayey sandstones, for example the Springvale and Horse Creek Formations and the Marion and Austral Downs Limestones (Vine, 1964). These limestones are well bedded and contain freshwater gastropods, algae, and faecal pellets in many places; forams and ostracods are also known in the Austral Downs Limestone. Some limestones are at least partly the result of spring action, but most of them are the result of chemical and biological deposition under fresh or brackish water conditions (Paten, 1964). In the Lake Eyre Basin there was little deposition during the Late Tertiary and there is evidence of active erosion in places. Stream channel deposits, the Mampuwordu Sands and the Tirari Formation, occur locally and contain rich mammalian faunas.

In the Canning Basin area of Western Australia there are Early Tertiary fluviatile and lacustrine deposits a few tens of metres thick formed by the ponding of rivers (Oakover Formation). Late Tertiary sands and limestones formed in the coastal regions (Veevers and Wells, 1961).

LAND SURFACES AND SOILS

Much of the Australian landscape consists of land surfaces that were formed during the Tertiary and are now in varying states of dissection. Older surfaces are being exhumed in some sedimentary basins by the stripping of sediments varying in age from younger Precambrian to Cretaceous, but the only known contemporary land surface that has persisted unburied since pre-Tertiary times occurs in the Macdonnell Ranges, Central Australia, and is thought to have developed prior to the Cretaceous (Mabbutt, pers. comm.)

The numbers and relationships of Tertiary land surfaces are known only for parts of the continent, and a synthesis cannot yet be made. Commonly two, and sometimes more, highly planate surfaces are observed (Twidale, 1956). In semi-arid regions the older land surface is present as outlying mesas that rise above the plains of the younger land surface and pass laterally into extensive plateaux. The degree of planation of both surfaces, particularly of the older, has led many workers to call them peneplains.

In the more humid eastern highlands the Tertiary surfaces were uplifted to varying extents during the Late Tertiary (?) Kosciusko epeirogenic movement. Dissection is variable, and scarps are much more subdued, but the planate surfaces are easily discernible and account for the widespread tableland landscapes throughout the highlands (Voisey, 1957). Indeed, the straight skyline so typical of panoramic views throughout the Australian continent reflects these Tertiary land surfaces.

The Tertiary land surfaces carry weathering profiles that not uncommonly exceed 50 m in depth (Langford-Smith and Dury, 1965). The profiles are typically lateritic, usually with a thick pisolitic ferruginous indurated zone, and in some cases with silcrete in the mottled and pallid zones (Whitehouse, 1940). Locally, as at Weipa, Queensland, highly aluminous indurated zones are mined as bauxite (Evans, 1965). Laterite occurs in all States on a wide range of lithologies, and although it is developed on Tertiary land surfaces of all ages, in general the profile is best developed on the oldest of these (R. L. Wright, 1963).

In the interior of the continent, silcrete ("billy") is widespread forming a surficial cap or duricrust. It occurs on more than one land surface. Some workers (Jessup, 1961) believe that the silcretes are younger than the oldest laterites, and the widespread silicification of the Austral Downs Limestone and its equivalents, which overlie laterites (Paten, 1964), accords with this view. Others believe the silcrete and laterite to be contemporaneous (Stephens, 1964). The silcrete may be related to the younger extensive land surface, occurrences with laterite on the oldest land surface being the result of double pedogenesis.

The age of the land surfaces and the palaeosols is a matter of debate. Eocene laterite dated by marine fossils is known from North West Cape, Western Australia. The older land surface bevels Cretaceous (Turonian) strata and the laterites it bears are older than the Austral Downs Limestone, which is probably Miocene or Pliocene. The silcrete would then be late Miocene or Pliocene. However, the lack of precision in dating the Tertiary terrestrial sediments, and the likelihood of several periods of laterite formation leave the question unresolved.

PALAEONTOLOGY AND CLIMATE

Little integrated work has been done on the biostratigraphy of the terrestrial deposits, though there is much scattered palynological literature on isolated occurrences (Cookson and Pike, 1954; Cookson, 1958). An attempt has been made to correlate certain sections in the Murray Basin by the distribution of *Nothofagus* and *Triorites* pollens (Evans and Hodgson, 1963/95). By contrast, the biostratigraphy of the marine deposits, especially those of southern Australia, has a long and involved history. Singleton's scheme of stages (Singleton, 1941) based on field mapping and all the then available palaeontology, has been modified by recent workers among whom there is now a large measure of agreement (Carter 1958b, 1959, 1964; Ludbrook, 1963; Reed, 1965; Wade, 1964; Wilkins, 1963). Redefinition of the stages has been based largely on foraminiferal studies which have taken into account both planktonic and benthonic forms (Table 11.1). While little doubt remains about the succession of stages, there is still disagreement about overseas correlation; in particular the position of the Janjukian in the Oligocene and that of the Balcombian and Bairnsdalian in the Miocene, remain matters of dispute (Table 11.2). The southern Australian stages have not been recognized in the marine basins of Western Australia.

The Carnarvon Basin was characterized by warm-water faunas during the Tertiary. This is perhaps best brought out by the forams which are represented by *Nummulites, Discocyclina,* and *Asterocyclina* in the Eocene, *Nummulites* and *Eulepidina* in the Oligocene, lepidocyclines and *Cycloclypeus* in the Miocene, and large numbers of such warm-water species as *Marginopora vertebralis* and *Sorites marginalis* in the Pliocene. These forms indicate Indo-Pacific affinities of the province throughout the entire Tertiary. On the other hand, larger forams are absent from the Bass Strait Province except for a

Species / Faunal units	EOCENE 1	2	? 3	OLIGOCENE 4	5	6	MIOCENE 7	8	9	10	
Hantkenina alabamensis compressa	▬	▬									
Asterigerina adelaidensis	▬	▬									
Lamarckina airensis	▬	▬									
Globigerinella micra	▬										
Globigerinoides index	▬	▬	▬	▬	▬						
Crespinina kingscotensis			▬	▬							
Planorbulinella johannae			▬								
Globigerina linaperta	▬	▬	▬	▬							
Vaginulinopsis acanthonucleus	▬	▬	▬	▬							
Alabamina westraliensis	▬	▬	▬	▬							
Anomalina perthensis	▬	▬	▬	▬	▬						
Cibicides pseudoconvexus	▬	▬	▬	▬	▬						
Guembelina rugosa	▬	▬	▬	▬	▬	▬					
Victoriella plecte				▬	▬	▬					
Sherbornina atkinsoni				▬	▬	▬					
Globigerina ouachitaensis - G. bulloides group				▬	▬	▬	▬				
Amphistegina sp.						▬	▬				
Calcarina mackayi						▬	▬				
Lamarckina glencoensis						▬	▬				
Astrononion centroplax							▬	▬	▬	▬	
Globigerina ciperoensis							▬	▬	▬		
Globoquadrina dehiscens							▬	▬	▬		
Operculina victoriensis							▬	▬			
Sherbornina cuneimarginata							▬	▬			
Hofkerina semiornata							▬	▬			
Globigerina apertura								▬	▬	▬	
Globigerinoides triloba								▬	▬	▬	
Planorbulinella plana								▬	▬		
Planorbulinella inaequilateralis								▬	▬		
Gypsina howchini								▬	▬		
Globigerinoides bispherica								▬	▬		
Globigerinoides rubra									▬	▬	
Cycloclypeus victoriensis									▬		
Lepidocyclina (Trybliolepidina) howchini									▬		
Globigerinoides transitoria									▬	▬	
Orbulina suturalis										▬	▬
Orbulina universa										▬	▬
Biorbulina bilobata										▬	▬
Cibicides victoriensis										▬	▬

TABLE 11.1. DISTRIBUTION OF FORAMINIFERA IN THE FAUNAL UNITS OF CARTER, ESTABLISHED FOR SOUTHEASTERN AUSTRALIA. (After Carter, 1959.)

short interval during the early Miocene when *Trybliolepidina* and *Cycloclypeus* were locally abundant. Presumably larger forams were excluded at other times because of lower temperatures. The Eucla Basin lacks *Nummulites*, *Discocyclina* and lepidocyclines, but it is considered that the faunas have Indo-Pacific affinities (Crespin, 1950). Certainly the climate was warm enough to support reefs in early Miocene times, but the affinities of the faunas as a whole seem to be with the Bass Strait Province rather than the Carnarvon Basin. Lepidocyclines are known from the lower Miocene at Wreck Island on the Great Barrier Reef, but there is no evidence yet of the provincial relationships of the later Tertiary faunas.

The echinoid fauna is rich and diversified and is almost entirely of Indo-Pacific origin in all basins. The extinction of a large number of genera in the late Miocene in southern Australia is probably indicative of cooling and can be related to the recession of the larger forams. Genera of interest are *Phyllacanthus*, which is widespread and known from the Oligocene to the Holocene; *Australanthus*, of which one species *A. longianus* is a valuable upper Eocene index; *Lovenia*, which is particularly abundant at certain levels between the Oligocene and upper Miocene; and *Clypeaster*, which is important in the upper Miocene (Philip, 1963, 1964b; Carter, 1964).

Polyzoans are abundant at several horizons, particularly in the lower Miocene, and numerous species have been described (Brown, 1957). Most of the polyzoan genera are long-ranging, but *Plagiosmittia* (Eocene–Oligocene), *Cucullipora* (Miocene), and species of *Aspidostoma* and *Crateropora* (Early Tertiary) are useful indexes.

Brachiopods are common locally, but of far greater importance are the molluscs. Species of *Glycimeris*, *Cucullaea*, *Limopsis*, *Chlamys*, *Pecten*, *Neotrigonia*, *Eotrigonia*, *Zenatiopsis*, *Eucrassatella*, and *Venericardia* among the bivalves, and *Turritella*, *Cypraea*, *Volutospira*, *Tylospira*, *Polinices*, and *Murex* among the gastropods have been valuable in establishing intrabasinal correlations (Gill and Darragh, 1963). Species of the nautiloids *Aturia*, *Aturoidea*, and *Teichertia* have been used mainly in the correlation of Eocene deposits, though some species are of value as late as the Miocene (Glenister *et al.*, 1956).

Vertebrate fossils are sparse in the marine and paralic sediments (Woods, 1962). The oldest of these are the marsupial *Wynyardia bassiana* and the whale *Prosqualodon davidi* from the Oligocene of northern Tasmania. Recently two very rich vertebrate faunas of probable Miocene (?Oligocene) and Pliocene ages, have been found in the Lake Eyre region. The older fauna (Etadunna Formation) includes dipnoans, teleosts, chelonians, crocodiles, and birds, as well as dasyurid, phascolarctid, macropodid, and diprotodontid marsupials. The Pliocene fauna of the Mampuwordu Sands includes members of several of the above groups but is less diverse (Stirton *et al.*, 1961). Ride (1964) has recently given a review account of Australian fossil marsupials.

Most of our present knowledge of the Tertiary floras is almost confined to those of the southern half of the continent. In the Eocene and early Miocene a mesophytic flora, which included species of *Cinnamomum*, *Nothofagus*, *Podocarpus*, *Casuarina*, *Banksia*, and probably *Eucalyptus*, was widespread and, in fact, flourished in the Lake Eyre region which is now desert. These data suggest humid, warm conditions over wide areas, and this is in accord with the evidence of the spread of laterites (Crocker, 1959). During the late Miocene and Pliocene it is thought that the flora became much more differentiated than it had been previously, owing to the development of new habitats and barriers to migration on the epeirogenically deforming land surface. Members of the *Compositeae* and *Acacia* became abundant, and *Eucalyptus* spread and diversified. In general, however, the terrestrial climate was probably still humid and warm, and it is possible that sub-tropical conditions were widespread; the cool conditions as evidenced in the marine Pliocene in southern Australia were probably the result of ocean currents (Fig. 11.4).

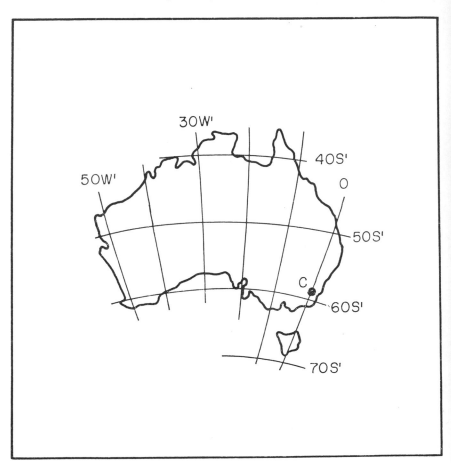

Fig. 11.4. Palaeogene palaeolatitudes and palaeomeridians based on Canberra. (After Irving, 1964, by permission of John Wiley & Sons Inc.)

TECTONICS

The Australian continent was relatively stable throughout the Tertiary, and vertical movements, both positive and negative, predominate. Compressional folding is present only in the Carnarvon Basin, and even there it is very mild and related to faulting in underlying rocks. Four Tertiary tectonic elements may be recognized—the Eastern Highlands, the Murray–Artesian Depression, the Uplifted Shield, and the Marginal Basins (see map).

In the **Eastern Highlands** normal faults are predominant. As much as 800 m of uplift has taken place since Early Tertiary times, mainly along eastern boundary faults most of which remain unmapped. Further west the movement was accommodated by warping. Horsts and gräben, as well as meridional normal faults, occur in the highland area (Spry and Banks, eds., 1962). The dating of these movements is a matter of difficulty owing to the general absence of marine sediments and the lack of work on the microfloras. A denudation chronology has been proposed by various workers (Voisey, 1957; Davies, 1959), and this is being gradually checked by radiometric and palynological studies. Uplift probably began on a small scale in the Eocene and was episodic throughout the Cainozoic. The major period of elevation appears to have been in the late Miocene—an event which was apparently part of a movement of much wider significance, since there was widespread withdrawal of the seas from the marginal basins at this time.

Subsidence in the **Murray–Artesian Depression** continued from the Cretaceous through the Tertiary, but during this whole interval it did not amount to more than 500 m in any one place. Most of the Tertiary sediments remain horizontal, but in places they form elongated, *en échelon* domes with local dips of up to 20° on the flanks. These have been interpreted as drape structures formed over persistently moving basement shears (Sprigg, 1961).

Most of the **Uplifted Shield** was subjected to upwarping during the Tertiary (McWhae *et al.*, 1958; Hills, 1961). In Western Australia flat-lying Eocene marine limestones are as much as 300 m above sealevel, and it is thought that most of this movement took place in the Late Tertiary, though some of it was probably Pleistocene.

In the **Marginal Basins** the marine sediments have been only slightly disturbed. Monoclines and gentle anticlines resulting from basement fracture are known in the Gippsland, Bass, and Otway Basins; block faulting has dominated the St. Vincent Basin; and in the Carnarvon Basin there are simple meridionally trending anticlines up to 80 km in length and with closures of up to 450 m, formed over reversed faults in the basement.

IGNEOUS ACTIVITY

A feature of the geology of Australia is the spread of Tertiary volcanics forming a broad but discontinuous belt down the eastern highlands, around into western Victoria and South Australia and across to Tasmania. Study of these rocks is proceeding and much remains to be learned. Although it is not intended to be all-inclusive, a preliminary subdivision into three main associations provides a useful way of dealing with them: (1) a strongly undersaturated basalt association which forms flows of great lateral and vertical extent, as well as numerous extensive sills; (2) an alkali basalt–peralkaline trachyte association which is somewhat more limited in geographical extent; (3) a tholeiitic association which is much less common as flows, but which also occurs in several small intrusive complexes.

(1) Rocks of the strongly undersaturated basalt association form much of the tablelands of North Queensland, the New England district, the southern tablelands of New South Wales, Lord Howe Island, the highlands of Tasmania, and possibly the Older Basalts of Victoria. In all these areas they form very fertile soils. They are not all of the same age. Those of northern Queensland and at least some from Tasmania are of Late Tertiary to Pleistocene age, while the bulk of those from New South Wales and some from Tasmania and Lord Howe Island are probably Oligocene to early Miocene and the Older Basalts of Victoria are Palaeocene and Eocene. The oldest volcanics at Lord Howe Island are Early Tertiary or older (Standard 1963). Over thirty centres of eruption are known in Tasmania (Spry and Banks, eds., 1962), and another large number from northern Queensland. In New South Wales, however, they have proved difficult to locate, and eruption is thought to have been of the fissure type. The most abundant rock type is olivine basalt, but smaller quantities of analcime basalts, basanites, and limburgites are widespread (McDougall, 1959; Wilkinson, 1962).

Differentiated sills of teschenite, generally thought to be of Tertiary age, have been found intruding Mesozoic and Permian sandstones in New South Wales (Wilkinson, 1958; Wilshire, 1959) and in places invade the olivine basalt piles. Some of the sills of this type have been radiogenically dated as Jurassic and others as Cretaceous (Evernden and Richards, 1962), and thus there may have been a long-continued series of them.

(2) Areally important occurrences of the peralkaline trachyte association are to be found in the Springsure–Clermont area of central Queensland, the Canoblas, Warrumbungle, and Nandewar Mountains of New South Wales, and the Newer Basalts of Victoria. In all these areas basic types are the predominant rocks, and they form sheets covering areas of thousands of square kilometres. They include olivine basalts, oligoclase basalts (mugearites), and trachy-basalts. Associated with them in various places are aegirine and riebeckite trachytes and phonolites. The centres of extrusion in some places were apparently shield volcanoes, for example the Nandewar Mountains, but elsewhere, as in the Glasshouse Mountains to the north of Brisbane, there are isolated plugs arranged in a more or less linear fashion.

(3) Flows of tholeiitic basalt are more restricted in extent, but members of the tholeiitic suite form remarkable intrusive complexes in southeast Queensland. Ring dykes, cone sheets, sills, and bosses of granophyre, rhyolite, and

Table arranged with geological epochs as rows (left) and sedimentary basins as columns.

Epoch	Carnarvon Basin	Eucla Basin	St. Vincent	Murray Basin	Otway Basin (Portland Sunklands / Gambier Sunklands)	Cape Otway	Australian Stages	Anglesea	Bass Basin — Geelong	Gippsland Basin	Lake Eyre Basin
PLIOCENE	Vlaming Sandstone (?)		Hallet Cove Sandstone	Norwest Bend Formation / Loxton Sands / Bookpurnong Beds	Whaler's Bluff Formation; Grange Burn Formation (Normanby Group)		Werrikooian (?) / Kalimnan (?)		Moorabool Viaduct Sands	Haunted Hill Gravels (lower part) / Jemmy's Point Formation	Tirari Formation (?) / Mampuwordu Sands (?)
MIOCENE	Trealla Limestone / Tulki Limestone / Mandu Calcarenite	Nullarbor Limestone	Myponga Limestone / Port Willunga Beds	Pata Limestone / Morgan Limestone / Mannum Formation / Ettrick Formation	Gambier Limestone (Gambier Sunklands); Muddy Creek Formation; Nirranda Formation (Glenelg Group)	Fishing Point Marls / Upper Glen Aire Clays / Calder River Limestone / Lower Glen Aire Clays / Castle Cove Limestone	Cheltenhamian / Mitchellian / Bairnsdalian / Balcombian / Batesfordian / Longfordian	Puebla Formation / Point Addis Limestone / Jan Juc Formation	Fyansford Clay / Batesford Limestone / Upper Maude Fm / Maude Basalt / Lower Maude Fm	Tambo River Formation / Bairnsdale Limestone / Glencoe Limestone / Wuk Wuk Marl / Longford Limestone (Gippsland Limestone)	
OLIGOCENE	Giralia Calcarenite / Jubilee Calcarenite			Buccleuch Group		Browns Creek Clays	Janjukian	Demons Bluff Formation		Lakes Entrance Formation	Etadunna Formation
EOCENE	Cashin Calcarenite / Pirie Calcarenite / Wadera Calcarenite	Wilson Bluff Limestone / Hampton Conglomerate (?)	Blanche Point Marls / Tortachilla Limestone / Sth Maslin Sands / North Maslin Sands	Moorlands Coal Measures (Knight Group) (?)	Greensands / Dartmoor Formation / Bahgallah Formation / Parraate Formation (Knight Group)	Johanna River Sands	Johannian	Boonah Sandstone / Eastern View Coal Measures		Latrobe Valley Coal Measures	Non-marine silts and sands
PALAEOCENE	Boonerooda Greensand					Rotten Point Sands					

TABLE 11.2. CORRELATION TABLE FOR THE AUSTRALIAN TERTIARY SEQUENCE

GK

dolerite are known from several areas (Stephenson, 1959; Stevens, 1959). They intrude Jurassic sandstones, but an upper limit to their age has not been fixed.

The position in this scheme of the thick volcanics (up to 1000 m) in the Macpherson Ranges of the Queensland border is problematical and awaits further study (Joplin, 1964). Here there is a sequence of rhyolites lying between two series of basalts in both of which there are flows with and without olivine.

NEW ZEALAND

The Tertiary rocks of New Zealand have received considerable attention from geological investigators. Unlike their Australian counterparts, which lie almost undisturbed along the continental margins and in the inland areas, the New Zealand Tertiary strata have been subjected to orogenic movements of varying intensity, culminating in Pliocene–Pleistocene times in the Kaikoura Orogeny. For this reason, unconformities in them are common.

Throughout the Mesozoic Era, the structural pattern of the New Zealand region was dominated by a small number of large downwarps and intervening land areas. By the end of the Cretaceous Period, the major part of the present South Island was emergent and had been reduced to a surface of low relief. This surface extended northeastwards to include the central and western parts of the North Island area.

In contrast to this pattern of rather broad folds and geosynclinal troughs of earlier times, the depositional areas of the Tertiary were on a much finer scale, with relatively small folds, welts and troughs, interfingering and branching, so as to resemble an archipelago (Fleming, 1962). There were rapid changes in the development of the troughs and their complementary upfolds or fault-blocks, so that even in neighbouring regions the stratigraphical and lithological sequences may be quite dissimilar (Fig. 11.5).

A period of relative tectonic quiet in the Early Tertiary resulted in a slow spreading of the seas on to the peneplained land surface, and the usual sequence encountered is one of coal measures resting on a leached basement followed by marine sandstones, siltstones, and, finally, by argillaceous and pure shelly limestones. In several eastern areas, this type of development had begun in Late Cretaceous times so that in such places there is an essentially continuous sequence from the Senonian into the Eocene. In these places also, the sediments supplied by the source area of low relief were generally fine-grained and light-coloured, often bentonitic. Greensand horizons are frequent. Macrofossils are almost completely unknown (with one unusual exception) from the Palaeocene deposits, but there is a rich foraminiferal fauna in many places. Here and elsewhere throughout the rest of the Tertiary

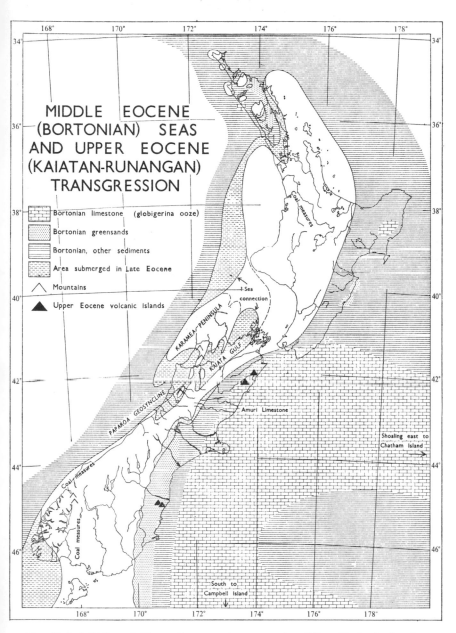

MIDDLE EOCENE
(BORTONIAN) SEAS
AND UPPER EOCENE
(KAIATAN-RUNANGAN)
TRANSGRESSION

Bortonian limestone (globigerina ooze)

Bortonian greensands

Bortonian, other sediments

Area submerged in Late Eocene

Mountains

Upper Eocene volcanic islands

Fig. 11.5. Middle and Upper Eocene palaeogeography of New Zealand, showing main types of sediment of Bortonian Stage and transgression in Kaiatan and Runangan times. (After Fleming, 1962, by permission of *Tuatara*.)

sequence, forams and molluscs have formed the basis for recognizing twenty-three stages, mainly as the result of the painstaking work of Finlay and Marwick (1940, 1947).

Above the definitely Cretaceous strata of the Haumurian Stage comes a sequence of sediments grouped in the Teurian Stage. These sediments, which are markedly calcareous in contrast to the Haumurian rocks, have many distinctively Cretaceous elements in the faunas present, but they lack any traces of ammonites, belemnites, or inoceramids which occur, often in abundance, in the Haumurian formations. For this reason, and because of strong Danian affinities in the microfaunas, the Teurian Stage is now grouped with the lower part, at least, of the Waipawan Stage in the lower Dannevirke Series of Palaeocene age. These two stages are irregularly distributed along the east coast of both islands from Gisborne southwards and they also occur in Northland.

On the basis of recent work (N. Hornibrook, pers. comm.) it appears that the upper part of the Waipawan Stage along with the Mangaorapan and most of the Heretaungan Stages belong to the lower Eocene, the Porangan and Bortonian Stages are middle Eocene, and the Kaiatan and Runangan Stages are upper Eocene.

It should be particularly stressed at this point that the use of European stages, especially as applied to the Cainozoic, does not imply precise correlation between the New Zealand sequence and that in Europe. It is well known that the so-called typical areas of Lyell's divisions in Europe are quite often incomplete and that their boundaries can seldom be defined in terms that would permit correlation on a worldwide basis. For this reason, it is customary to employ local stage names almost exclusively.

Progressive inundation of the Late Cretaceous land surface continued through the Eocene and culminated in middle Oligocene times with a transgression that submerged most of the present land area, with the exception of the Tauranga–Rotorua–Taupo region in the north and the eastern Southland–south central Alpine region in the south, and left its mark in the widespread, thick-bedded, often argillaceous limestones mentioned above. Before the end of the Oligocene, however, some retreat of the sea had taken place, especially in eastern districts of the North Island, and tectonic movements were initiated that were eventually to rise in intensity to the Kaikoura Orogeny. During the Late Tertiary, this increasing diastrophic activity was reflected in the formation of many rather small, rapidly sinking basins which were filled with sediment often thousands of metres thick, eroded from bordering rising welts or geanticlines.

The present outline of the Dominion began to take shape in Pliocene times, though large portions of the south and east of the North Island remained in a shallow submerged condition until the beginning of Pleistocene times.

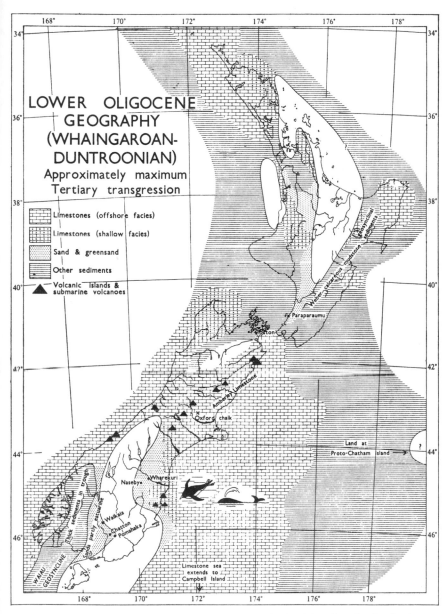

FIG. 11.6. Lower Oligocene palaeogeography of New Zealand, based on the distribution of sediments of the Whaingaroan and Duntroonian Stages. (After Fleming, 1962, by permission of *Tuatara*.)

Lower Tertiary

STRATIGRAPHY

NORTH ISLAND

Northland Region

In Northland, where for most of the time, a shallow marine trough flanked by land areas existed, the sequence is essentially continuous from the Upper Cretaceous, with varicoloured calcareous shales and sandstones and argillaceous limestones of Palaeocene age forming the upper part of the Mangakahia Group. These are followed by lower Eocene shales and greensands of the Waiomio Group, though they also rest directly in places on Mesozoic greywackes or on strata of Late Cretaceous age. Middle Eocene greensands are well displayed in the eastern parts of Northland, and are overlain by upper Eocene glauconitic siltstones or, as in the Whangarei area, by coal measures. The Oligocene witnessed an inundation of the sea right across the Northland Peninsula and the extensive deposition of both pure and argillaceous limestones, and much greensand. The extent of the Duntroonian submergence exceeded that of the Whaingaroan, but by Waitakian times there were local signs of emergence and instability. For instance, in the Auckland area, limestones were replaced by mudstones and graded-bedded sandstones, suggesting an increase in the supply of sediment from rising land areas.

South Auckland and Taranaki Region

In the western part of the North Island, south of Auckland, the earliest Tertiary deposits are of middle Eocene age and consist of coal measures resting directly on leached Mesozoic greywackes. They extend into the upper Eocene and are then superseded by Oligocene marine limestones, siltstones, and calcareous sandstones of the Te Kuiti Group. By late Oligocene times, thick geosynclinal mudstones with redeposited sandstone bands were being deposited in central Taranaki and the King Country. At Kapuni, in southwestern Taranaki, a deep bore passed through about 3900 m of an almost complete Tertiary sequence to reach Eocene coal measures which have yielded large quantities of gas.

East Coast Region

Throughout the Early Tertiary, the eastern parts of the North Island appear to have been separated for much of the time from the western regions by a meridional ridge or island of low relief. The depositional pattern is, however, very similar to that in other parts of the Dominion.

In the East Cape region, sedimentation seems to have been remarkably uniform throughout the whole of the period from the Late Cretaceous to the Oligocene, with the deposition of light-coloured siliceous shales and mudstones, often with large calcareous concretions. Towards the top of this sequence (Mangatu Group), these sediments become much more calcareous and glauconitic sandy limestones appear.

There are some quite noteworthy differences to be observed in the sequences in the Hawkes Bay and east Wellington districts. Here again, the succession is continuous from the Upper Cretaceous, and the standard area for the New Zealand Palaeocene and lower Eocene (Dannevirke Series) is located in the Waipawa district where these rocks conformably overlie Maestrichtian sediments (Whangai Shale). The basal Palaeocene sediments consist of calcareous siltstones, greensands and bentonitic clays of the Wanstead Group. These sediments (Upper Cretaceous and Palaeocene) are thought to have been derived from the east (see Fig. 11.5), since there is a distinct increase in grainsize in that direction (Kingma, 1962). In the Palaeocene succession elsewhere, there may be detected the beginnings of tectonic movements which resulted in the formation of small basins 15–30 km long and 10–15 km wide, in which banded sediments up to 4500 m thick accumulated. At the top of the Teurian Stage, and widely distributed through Hawkes Bay, is a very characteristic dark brown shale member some 6–15 m thick known as the Waipawa Chocolate Shale. This grades eastwards into a glauconitic sandstone of similar colour.

A distinct change is seen at the incoming of the lower Eocene (Waipawan Stage) sediments. In these, and later sediments of the Dannevirke Series, the grainsize increases towards the west. Uplift of land in that direction has been postulated, but it was probably not of great magnitude since the derived sediments continue to be fine-grained with mudstones predominating (Kingma, 1962). They are markedly calcareous and rich in forams.

In the middle and late Eocene, silty mudstones continued to accumulate with gradual increase in lime content and the appearance of thin limestone lenses with time. Bentonitic clays are common in the eastern sections.

The early part of the Oligocene is represented by the Weber Mudstone, a continuation of the calcareous, fine-grained deposition of the Eocene Period, but a major change occurred in the middle Oligocene (Duntroonian Stage) when unsorted, silty sandstones began to appear, presumably deposited over a broad shelf area. Tectonic movements are reflected also in the contemporaneous occurrence in small basinal areas of sorted sediments with well-developed rhythmic banding.

SOUTH ISLAND

Nelson and Westland Region

Elevation above sealevel of this region appears to have been maintained from the onset of the deforming movements of the Rangitata Orogeny until early Eocene times. In Westland, the resulting erosion surface which had been cut across the Paparoa Coal Measures (Upper Cretaceous), formed the site for the deposition of further paralic sediments, the Brunner Coal Measures, in the middle Eocene. These coal measures are conformably overlain by a massive, moderately fine-grained, grey, calcareous, marine sandstone (Island Sandstone), also containing middle Eocene fossils. This marine incursion represents the early stages of a newly forming or extending trough, the **Paparoa Geosyncline,** the axis of which lay parallel to the present alpine trend. It gradually spread widely over the northern areas of the South Island, except for the extreme northwest which, as seen in Fig. 11.5, remained as a large projection named by Fleming (1962) the Karamea Peninsula. In the resulting "Kaiata Gulf", thick, massive, calcareous, brownish-grey siltstones, frequently carbonaceous, were laid down and overlapped widely onto coal measures and pre-Cretaceous rocks. On the eastern flank of the Paparoa Geosyncline, as seen on the east side of the Greymouth Coalfield, the carbonaceous siltstones are represented by coarse breccia conglomerates with large blocks of greywacke in contorted slump-bedded mudstones (Omotumotu Beds).

Much the same sequence in the middle and upper Eocene is observed in the southwest Nelson area where coal measures rest on leached Mesozoic basement and are themselves covered by marine siltstones, algal limestones and glauconitic sandstones (Maruia and Matiri Formations).

By early Oligocene times, almost three-quarters of the South Island had become submerged in the limy seas. The former Karamea Peninsula had disappeared, and in northwest Nelson shallow-water limestones were deposited. In Westland at this time, the sediments were at first muddy, but they were rapidly replaced by pure calcareous deposits giving rise to crystalline limestones. Distinct traces of this calcareous sedimentation may be seen along the western coastal strip. To the southwest of Bruce Bay, the Oligocene limestones forming the coastal cliffs are interbedded with thick basalt flows.

Northeast Coastal Region

Here are considered the districts of southeast Marlborough and north Canterbury, where predominantly calcareous sedimentation took place throughout Lower Tertiary times.

In the shallow coastal waters, which gradually encroached westwards on the Cretaceous landmass, muddy deposits with much glauconite and bentonitic material accumulated, whilst in the deeper offshore areas, muddy foraminiferal oozes built up considerable thicknesses of material now represented by the Amuri Limestone, a strongly diachronous unit ranging in age from early Eocene to Oligocene. This same type of deposition took place in the seas covering the sites of the present Chatham Islands to the east and Campbell Island to the south.

Calcareous sedimentation continued on into Oligocene times as the sea spread extensively and inundated almost the whole of the northern half of the South Island (Amberley Limestone, Oxford Chalk, and Weka Pass Stone). Volcanism, probably mainly of submarine or volcanic island (calc-alkaline) type, occurred along the site of the eastern flanks of the Southern Alps.

Southeast Coastal Region

The Early Tertiary history of this region is somewhat different from that of the northern areas in that its sediments are uniformly of shallow-water origin, frequently estuarine in places, and volcanism of the island arc type broke out on a considerable scale in the north Otago area.

The earliest Tertiary deposits in this region, which rest on Upper Cretaceous coal measures, are usually dark grey to black, muddy sandstones, weathering to light grey or pale yellowish brown, frequently containing large elliptical and spheroidal septarian concretions (for example the Katiki Formation at Shag Point). Thick greensands also commonly occur, but there are very few fossils present.

A notable exception to this generalized account of the earliest Cainozoic deposits of the South Island is that of the Wangaloa Formation which has an extremely restricted distribution in south Otago, and in a boulder from the East Wellington area. At Wangaloa itself, Upper Cretaceous coal measures pass upwards into a ferruginous, quartz-pebble conglomerate and glauconitic, concretionary sandstone of littoral marine origin containing large numbers of macrofossils, mostly molluscs, of a peculiar and interesting type (see section on Palaeontology and Climate; also Hornibrook and Harrington, 1960).

In the coastal areas of north Otago, the Palaeocene strata are overlain by a conformable sequence of mudstones, often with thick greensand horizons, which show transition to deeper-water environments as the sea gradually extended westwards. This marine incursion had not reached the present inland areas, such as Naseby, until late Eocene or early Oligocene times, for there the earliest Tertiary deposits comprise quartz conglomerates with

	Approximate European Stage	Series	New Zealand Stage	NORTHLAND	SOUTH AUCKLAND AND TARANAKI	EAST CAPE	HAWKES BAY AND EAST WELLINGTON
OLIGOCENE	Rupelian	LANDON	Waitakian (Lw)	Limestones (Pokapu - W; 1350m) (Whangarei - E; 75m)	TE KUITI GROUP limestones, siltstones and sandstones	MANGATU GROUP calcareous shales	WEBER GROUP Brown sandstones and dark-grey mudstones
			Duntroonian (Ld)				
	Lattorfian		Whaingaroan (Lwh)				Mudstones (60-3000m)
EOCENE	Priabonian	ARNOLD	Runangan (Ar)	Ruatangata glauconitic sandstones and siltstones (0-60m)	Waikato coal measures (60-300m)	Siliceous shales and mudstones	WANSTEAD GROUP Light grey calcareous mudstones and pure limestones (15-600m)
			Kaiatan (Ak)	Kamo coal measures (15m)			
	Lutetian		Bortonian (Ab)	Opahi greensands and shales (375m)			
		DANNEVIRKE	Porangan (Dp)	Waiomio shales and greensands (100-500m)			Light grey mudstones and bentonitic clays
	Ypresian		Heretaungan (Dh)				
			Mangaorapan (Dm)				Blue-grey mudstones
PALAEOCENE			Waipawan (Dw)				
	Danian		Teurian (Dt)	Mangakahia shales and sandstones (450-1350m)			Siltstones, greensands and bentonitic clays

▌ TYPE LOCALITY FOR N.Z. STAGE

TABLE 11.3. CORRELATION TABLE FOR NEW ZEALAND LOWER TERTIARY SEQUENCE

NELSON	WESTLAND	MARLBOROUGH	NORTH CANTERBURY	SOUTH CANTERBURY AND NORTH OTAGO	DUNEDIN AND SOUTH OTAGO	WESTERN SOUTHLAND AND WESTERN OTAGO
Crystalline limestone (15-300m)	Basalts	Basalts, pillow lavas	Grey Marls	Waitaki limestone		Limestones
	Cobden	Marly limestones, chalk, glauconitic sandstones (1500m)	Calcareous siltstone and glauconitic limestone			
Matiri glauconitic sandstones, quartz sandstones, mudstones, conglomerates	limestone (200-300m)		Weka Pass limestone (9-30m)	Kokoamu greensands (10-50m)		Sandstones and mudstones
	Port Elizabeth mudstone (50-300m)		Amberley limestone	McDonald limestone Deborah volcanics		Concretionary micaceous sandstones and grits
Maruia siltstones, algal limestones, glauconitic sandstones (60m)	Dark shales, conglomerates	AMURI GROUP ↑ Greensands and calcareous mudstones	Glauconitic calcareous	Totara limestone	Burnside marl	Feldspathic sandstones, grits and conglomerates
	Kaiata mudstone (1800m)			Waiareka volcanics		
				Raki siltstone (30m)		Coal measures, basal conglomerates
Coal measures (300m)	Island sandstone (180m) Brunner coal measures (30-120m)	Pillow lavas and tuffs	sandstones,	Hampden mudstone (75m)	Green Island loose sand	
		Argillaceous limestones, bentonitic clays, and some lavas	siltstones, mudstones and bentonitic clays (50⁺m)	Kurinui mudstone	Abbotsford ↑ glauconitic mudstone	
				Moeraki siltstones and glauconitic concretionary mudstones (90-100m)		
		Bedded │ flints	Waipara greensands Sulphur mudstones	Otepopo greensands (30-75m) Katiki mudstone (100m)	Wangaloa shell-bed	

coals (Hogburn Beds) of middle Eocene age resting directly on a leached schist basement.

In the late Eocene, volcanism broke out on a grand scale in the Oamaru district where the thick deposits of tuffaceous breccias and sandstones, together with massive sills, dykes, and pillow lavas, indicate probable derivation from offshore island centres to the east of the present coast line. This volcanism, which continued on into the early Oligocene, was accompanied by the deposition of thick limestones and greensands containing large numbers of well-preserved fossils, especially brachiopods, molluscs, and echinoids.

The Eocene sequence of the south Otago area is very similar to that already described for north Otago, except for the absence of volcanism. But in Oligocene times, however, the area was apparently uplifted epeirogenically and remained emergent throughout the period, so that near Dunedin, for instance, the upper Eocene offshore deposits of the Burnside Marl are disconformably overlain by Miocene sandstones.

Western Southland and Western Otago Region

In the southwest of the South Island, a new geosynclinal downwarp began to develop in late Eocene times. Following the Late Cretaceous planation the land surface lay close to sealevel, and by the middle Eocene, coal measures with thick conglomerates were being deposited on the exposed Palaeozoic and Mesozoic basement. In early Oligocene times, a meridional trough, the **Waiau Geosyncline**, had become established along the site of the present Waiau–Te Anau–Hollyford depression, and thick, rather shallow-water sediments accumulated in it. By late Oligocene times, this inundation had extended eastwards and northwards beyond the Lake Wakatipu area where a belt of limestones and coarser clastics (120 m) is involved as a narrow, deeply infaulted strip along the steeply dipping Moonlight Fault which may be traced from Bobs Cove on Lake Wakatipu northnortheastwards for a distance of about 35 km.

To the west, across the present Fiordland area, typical calcareous deposits of the Oligocene sea were formed, while on the eastern flank of the new geosyncline against the greatly reduced land area, estuarine sands were the principal sediments.

PALAEONTOLOGY AND CLIMATE

Forams are by far the most useful and widespread fossils in the fine-grained Lower Tertiary rocks, occurring almost to the exclusion of all others in the Palaeocene and lower Eocene deposits. Many Cretaceous forams persist into strata of the Teurian Stage, but are there accompanied by typical Tertiary lineages of pelagic globigerinids, and by such Tertiary genera as *Zeauvigerina* and *Aragonia*. Correlation of the lower part of the Teurian Stage with the European Danian Stage is now reasonably confirmed on the basis of small planktonic globigerinids of the *Globigerina triloculinoides* type (Hornibrook, 1958, and pers. comm.; Jenkins, 1964*b*).

Hornibrook (pers. comm.) has recently suggested that the Palaeocene–Eocene boundary comes somewhere within the Waipawan Stage. This is based on the occurrence in that stage of *Globigerina pseudoiota*, a species that appears to be of early Eocene age in other parts of the world (Jenkins, 1964*b*). The palaeontology of the Waipawan Stage is almost entirely restricted to a microfauna including the forams *Truncorotalia* aff. *crassata aequa* and *Tappanina glaessneri*, and there is good reason to believe that the lower part of the stage correlates with the upper Velasco shale of Mexico, regarded as late Palaeocene in age (Jenkins, 1964*b*).

The earliest Tertiary faunas in New Zealand are fairly clearly of moderately warm-water type for, although there are no nummulitids present (with the exception of a *Nummulitella* in the uppermost Eocene), the orbitoid *Asterocyclina* appeared in the lower Eocene deposits of south Canterbury and the Chatham Islands (Cole, 1962) and, after an apparent absence, reappeared in the late Eocene along with shallow-water tropical genera such as *Carpenteria*, *Asterigerina*, *Amphistegina*, *Halkyardia*, and *Peneroplis*. The most significant invasion from the point of view of correlation was the appearance of *Hantkenina*, a genus that achieved worldwide distribution in the middle Eocene, together with many ubiquitous and long-ranging lineages including those of *Notorotalia*, *Rotaliatina*, *Heronallenia*, and *Astrononion*. The last appearance of discocyclines occurred in the uppermost Eocene deposits.

The Oligocene microfaunas, though of warm-water type, also have a very poor representation of the larger forams, which indicates sub-tropical rather than fully tropical conditions at this time. The re-invasion by *Operculina*, *Carpenteria*, and *Asterigerina*, along with an abundance of *Calcarina mackayi* in the Duntroonian Stage, suggests a temperature maximum at this time.

Corals are little known from the Palaeocene and lower Eocene deposits, but are quite well represented in the middle Eocene and later. *Balanophyllia* is abundant in the middle Eocene and is associated with other corals having distinct affinities with Australia (*Odontocyathus*) and the American Gulf Coast and the West Indies (*Discotrochus*). The Oligocene is especially characterized by an almost explosive development of alcyonarian corals, especially in north Otago and south Canterbury (*Isis*, *Moltkia*, and *Graphularia*), a feature which supports the hypothesis of a sub-tropical climate at this time (Squires, 1958). Solitary scleractinian corals (*Notocyathus*, *Stephanocyathus*, and *Conocyathus*) emphasize the Indo-Pacific relationships of the fauna.

New Zealand is famed for the richness of its Tertiary brachiopod faunas, especially in the South Canterbury and North Otago coastal areas. The tuffaceous bands commonly associated with the upper Eocene and Oligocene limestones contain abundant and beautifully preserved remains of these fossils.

Probably the most interesting molluscan fauna is that from the glauconitic, concretionary sandstone immediately above the coal measures at Wangaloa and other places in South Otago. This rich fauna includes a strange mixture of Cretaceous (for example, the bivalves *Conchothyra*, *Perissodonta*, *Struthioptera*, and *Lahillia*) and Tertiary elements (for example the bivalves *Limopsis* and *Venericardia* and the gastropods *Polinella*, *Sigaretotrema*, *Globisinum*, and *Proficus*). Unfortunately, no foraminiferal microfaunas are known from the Wangaloan Beds, but associated microplankton and microflora (see below) support the assessment of a Danian age for this horizon.

With the possible exception of another puzzling fauna from Otaio Gorge, South Canterbury, few lower Eocene Mollusca have been recorded. Genera included here are the bivalves *Costacallista* and *Monalaria*, and the gastropods *Perissodonta*, *Priscoficus*, and *Notoplejona* (Marwick, 1960).

Middle Eocene molluscan faunas (Bortonian) are rich, distinctive, and quite widely distributed. Bivalves and gastropods are the commonest forms, and cephalopods are represented by *Hercoglossa* and *Brazaturia* (Fleming, 1945). The marked warming of the climate in the late Eocene is indicated by the appearance of the bivalve *Hinnites* and by mitrid and conid gastropods.

The Oligocene saw several marked changes in the molluscan faunas, especially noteworthy being the introduction of bivalve genera of Australian affinity (*Bassina*, *Eucrassatella*, and *Zenatia*) and the appearance of the characteristic New Zealand gastropod *Struthiolaria*, a descendant of the Cretaceous aporrhaids through the lower Eocene *Monalaria*.

Three genera of decapod crustaceans have been described from middle Eocene and Oligocene strata in the South Island (Glaessner, 1960). In north Canterbury, the Waipara Greensands and about 30 m of the underlying sulphur-coloured mudstones, which contain a Teurian microfauna, have, in addition, fish teeth and peduncles of the cirripede *Euscalpellum* (Wilson, 1963, p. 28).

Cidarid echinoids are especially plentiful in the Oligocene deposits, with one Eocene record. The Oligocene genera include *Histocidaris*, *Stereocidaris*, *Eucidaris*, *Phyllacanthus*, and *Goniocidaris*, and are regarded by Fell (1954) as indicating sub-tropical or tropical climates in the early and middle Oligocene. Also notable is the occurrence of the regular echinoid *Brochopleurus australiae* in the upper Oligocene sequence, as compared with its presence in the Janjukian beds in Australia.

The vertebrate fauna of the Lower Tertiary in New Zealand is practically limited to the Oligocene, though the lower Eocene in Canterbury has provided the earliest record of the penguins. The Oligocene fauna includes abundant penguins and whales (zeuglodonts and squalodonts).

Floras. Couper (1960) has given a valuable account of Cainozoic plant microfossils in New Zealand and Fleming (1963) has made considerable use of information from plant fossils in his reconstruction of southern biogeography.

On the land, the early part of the Cainozoic Era was dominated by Cretaceous-type podocarp forests. Pollen-analysis shows the persistence of most Late Cretaceous coniferous pollens with the addition of *Dacrydiumites mawsonii*. *Podocarpidites otagoensis* appears for the last time, the characteristic Tertiary dicotyledon *Triorites harrisii* for the first time, and the southern beech *Nothofagus waipawaensis* (*N. fusca* group) is restricted to the Teurian Stage. *Metrosideros* is also present for the first time. Microplankton from this stage includes *Cannosphaeropsis* sp. cf. *C. fenestrata*, *Deflandrea*, and *Eisenackia* (last appearance).

The lower Eocene flora, as a whole, is separable from that of the Palaeocene by the first appearance of a few characteristic Tertiary species and the relative abundance of *Triorites harrisii*. The occurrence of *Cupanieidites*, a genus of tropical and subtropical affinities, is significant. Microplankton includes *Hystrichosphaera* sp. aff. *H. ramosa*.

The middle and upper Eocene (Arnold Series) is often separable into two zones, the lower with southern beeches of the *Nothofagus fusca* group and the upper characterized by the *N. brassi* group. The latter at this time replaced the conifers of Cretaceous origin as the forest dominants. Of living plant genera, *Dysoxylum*, *Rhopalostylis*, *Elytranthe*, *Phormium*, and *Phyllocladus*, make their first appearance in the record.

The Oligocene flora is essentially dominated by the *Nothofagus brassi* group. Representatives of present-day tropical and sub-tropical families such as the Bombacaceae and Ephedraceae are also prominent. *Microcachryidites brevisaccatus* is a characteristic pollen of late Oligocene and early Miocene age.

In summary, the evidence for climatic changes, deduced from the foraminiferal, coral, echinoid, and plant biotas of the Lower Tertiary, is reasonably consistent. This indicates a gradual warming-up of the New Zealand area until late Eocene times when, as estimated on the basis of the corals (Squires, 1958), the sea temperature was about $10°–15°C$. These conditions were almost certainly maintained throughout most of the Oligocene, though the general absence of larger forams and the occurrence of abundant remains of penguins and cetaceans in deposits of this age suggest that true tropical conditions were not attained. On the land, the climatic changes appear to be reflected in the forest dominants, *Nothofagus* of the *N. fusca* group along with abundant podocarps indicating somewhat cooler conditions than those prevailing when the *N. brassi* group was in the ascendant.

IGNEOUS ACTIVITY

In Northland, eruptions of basaltic pillow lavas, breccias, and tuffs, and intrusions of dolerite and teschenite, appear to have continued spasmodically from Cretaceous times, since the sequence known as the Tangihua Volcanics is interbedded in places with sediments ranging in age from Middle Cretaceous to middle Eocene. Elsewhere in the North Island, there is little evidence of igneous activity except in the East Cape–northern Hawkes Bay region where the upper parts of the Mangatu Group appear to be composed in some measure of rhyolitic tuffs, and widespread bentonitic clays of Lower Tertiary age suggest possible derivation from acid volcanics.

In the South Island, activity was restricted to two narrow linear belts parallel to and on either side of the present alpine chain. In Westland, extensive basalt flows occurred in the Oligocene, while on the eastern side, volcanism in linear island belts took place in south Marlborough, north Canterbury, and north Otago, accompanied by the intrusion of sills and dykes, frequently gravitationally differentiated as at Moeraki Peninsula, north Otago.

Upper Tertiary

During the Late Tertiary, sediments of both shelf and geosynclinal type were deposited. Miocene sediments in many places are unconformable on Early Tertiary and older rocks, owing to a marked alteration in the pattern of the geosynclines and the associated geanticlines as the main axial arches began to rise.

With the present concept of the Miocene, embracing a rather larger interval of geological time than formerly, mainly at the expense of the Oligocene, the Miocene of New Zealand is now regarded as including the Pareora Series (formerly correlated with the upper Oligocene), the Southland Series, and the Taranaki Series. Recently, the Oligocene–Miocene boundary has been even further lowered to lie below the Waitakian Stage, the upper stage of the Landon Series (Jenkins, 1964a) (see also Eames et al., 1964; Jenkins, 1964c).

The beginning of the Miocene marks a considerable change in the palaeogeography of the New Zealand area. The phase of dominant submergence begun in the Late Cretaceous, which reached its maximum in middle Oligocene times, now rapidly changed to a phase of emergence. In some places, especially in the central North Island, increased topographical relief had shown itself in the late Oligocene. The emergence of rising axes led to a marked change in the nature of the sediments, and many small-scale basins were formed which became filled with thousands of metres of detritus derived from the adjacent rising geanticlines. Where the sea remained, the extensive calcareous deposits of the Oligocene now gave place to dominant sandstones and mudstones, though in the southern areas of Southland, and in the Takaka district of northwest Nelson, limestones and greensands persisted for a short time in the early Miocene (Fig. 11.7).

The Pliocene was a time of greatly increased tectonic unrest as the climax of the Kaikoura Orogeny approached. Along a zone stretching southwestwards from the East Cape region through the main mountain axes of both islands to Fiordland, there was a highly mobile belt in which the greatest movements occurred. To the northwest and southeast of this belt lay the more stable areas of Northland and east Otago respectively, and the movements here were much less powerful (Fig. 11.9).

STRATIGRAPHY

NORTH ISLAND

Northland Region

In the early Miocene, the Northland Peninsula was the site of a narrow, shallow marine trough, apparently flanked on both sides by land ridges, on each of which lines of volcanoes were in active eruption. The western ridge, now totally submerged, supplied much of the material for the rapidly accumulating Otaua and Waitemata Groups, composed of graded-bedded sandstones, tuffs, conglomerates, and some greensands. The volcanoes of the eastern ridge are now represented by the rugged peaks of Whangaroa, Great Barrier, and Coromandel.

By middle Miocene times, the sea had retreated from most of the Auckland area, and since then only very minor marginal incursions have taken place. Tectonically, the area is now one of distinct stability as compared with the mobile volcanic belt to the south.

In the Pliocene, the region approximated its present shape with some minor inundations. Shallow-water polyzoal limestones were deposited in the Three Kings Islands area.

Southwest Auckland and Taranaki Region

It is probable that, in the early Miocene, the marine trough along the Northland Peninsula area extended southwards through the Waikato Basin to link with the deeper marine gulf occupying the southwest Auckland and

Taranaki region. In this geosynclinal trough, massive calcareous siltstones with thin sandy limestones (Mahoenui Group) were deposited at first, and were followed by increasingly sandy formations with much tuffaceous material derived from a group of middle and upper Miocene volcanics located to the west of the Awakino District.

Extensive emergence occurred towards the end of the Miocene, but in Pliocene times shallow shelf seas continued to inundate the Taranaki area, and silts, sands, and shelly limestones were deposited.

East Coast Region

In the early part of the Miocene, marine sedimentation was confined to the Raukumara Peninsula area and a small embayment in northeast Wellington. In both areas, shallow shelf sediments predominated but some graded beds deposited in narrow troughs may be discerned.

With the advent of the late Miocene, the Eastern Geosyncline took on its earlier form so that practically the whole of the East Coast region was submerged and deposition even extended across the present Ruahine–Raukumara axis. Shelf sands and thin conglomerates were dominant, but in subsiding areas, as near Lake Waikaremoana, graded sediments were deposited. These, according to Kingma, were the result of active transcurrent faulting movements, producing fresh supplies of detritus.

Through Pliocene times, shallow seas continued in the Gisborne area and in Hawkes Bay. Silts, sands, and shelly limestones were deposited, some of the last-named being rich in polyzoans and, on occasions, cirripede plates (Te Aute Limestone). Small emergent island highs appeared in the southern Hawkes Bay–east Wellington area; and an actively rising ridge joined the Wellington and Palmerston North districts, and probably extended across Cook Strait to the Marlborough Sounds and beyond.

South Island

East Coast Region

The area inundated by the great marine transgression of the Oligocene was now greatly reduced by the emergence and uplift of a large part of the present alpine chain during the early Miocene, though not to its present mountainous proportions. The resulting sediments to the east of the new divide were, in general, quite distinct from those of the Lower Tertiary. Limestones were now almost entirely absent, and greensands, marls, siltstones, and sandstones prevailed.

By late Miocene times, the rising mountain axis had caused the retreat of the sea from south Canterbury and Otago, whither it has never subsequently

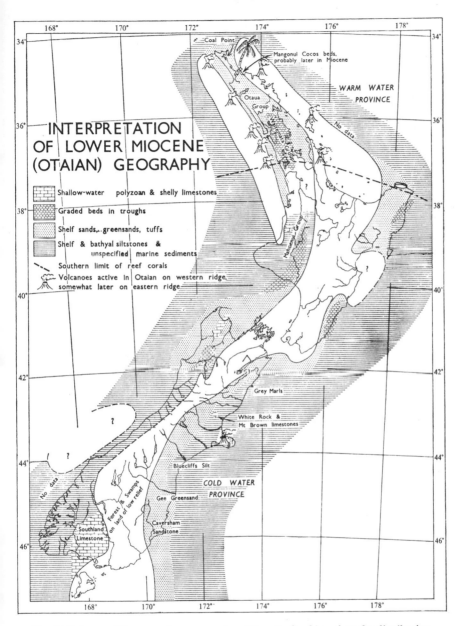

FIG. 11.7. Lower Miocene palaeogeography of New Zealand based on the distribution of sediments of the Otaian Stage. (After Fleming, 1962, by permission of *Tuatara*.)

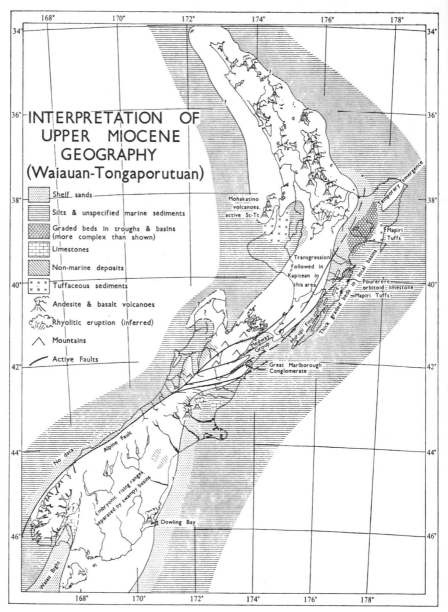

FIG. 11.8. Upper Miocene palaeogeography of New Zealand based on sediments of the Waiauan and Tongaporutuan Stages. (After Fleming, 1962, by permission of *Tuatara*.)

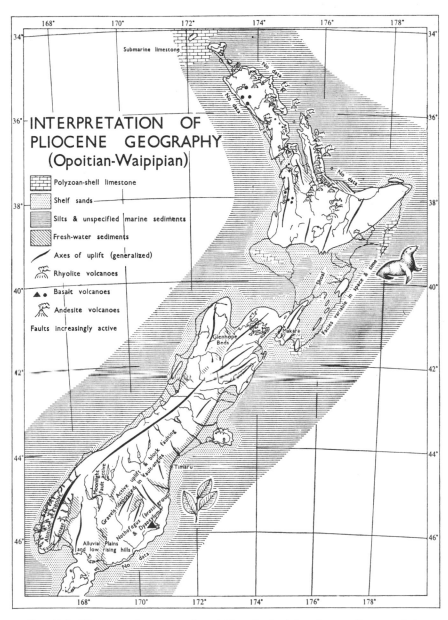

FIG. 11.9. Pliocene palaeogeography of New Zealand based on sediments of the Opoitian and Waipipian Stages. (After Fleming, 1962, by permission of *Tuatara*.)

returned. It remained, however, in central and north Canterbury where sands, silts and some offshore limestones were deposited.

In the northern parts of the South Island, considerable thicknesses of coarse, mainly freshwater, conglomerates are exposed over wide areas. In the east, the Great Marlborough Conglomerate, with huge subangular blocks of older Tertiary and pre-Tertiary rocks, some exceeding 30 m in length, probably reflects the rapid rise of the active fault blocks along the Alpine Fault Complex.

Marine Pliocene deposits are rather limited in distribution. They occur in the Awatere District of Marlborough in the form of massive concretionary mudstones and siltstones with sandstone bands, shell beds and breccias containing basic volcanics, and in coastal Canterbury as far south as Timaru.

The relief of the land was strong, but it had not yet reached its maximum which was to occur in the Pleistocene. Paludal deposits and lignitic coal seams are frequently found along the former coast lines and in many of the intermontane basins of the South Island where block-faulting accompanied the rapid uplifts of the orogenic prelude.

Nelson and West Coast Region

In general, Miocene marine deposits occupy the coastal strip west of the Alpine Fault and appear to have been deposited in a geosynclinal trough extending from the Murchison District to as far south as Milford Sound. Emergence of the mountain system clearly affected the nature of the sediments which are coarse sands and conglomerates, though shallow-water polyzoal and shelly limestones were deposited in the Takaka District of west Nelson. In the south, near Bruce Bay, the Tititira Formation of coarse breccias and sands appears to have been derived from the northwest. Elsewhere graded beds and siltstones were dominant. The middle and late Miocene was marked by the emergence of the northwest Nelson area, while in the Murchison area, the Longford Formation, some 1800 m of conglomerates, sandstones, and minor coal seams, represents material shed during the rapid rise of the Alpine Fault to the east.

This deposition of coarse fanglomerate material in freshwater environments continued on into Pliocene times (Glenhope Beds).

Southwestern Region

In the Oligocene, as noted, a rapidly sinking trough—the Waiau Geosyncline—developed in the western Southland area. In this trough in the early Miocene, shallow-water limestones were deposited, with muddier sediments to the west.

Region		
Southland and Western Otago	Greywacke gravels, brown pebbly sandstones	Blue-grey silts
	Sandstones and clays at Cliffden	Cliffden limestone
Naseby	Waipiata volcanics	Manuherikia beds / Quartz conglomerates and lignites — WEDDERBURN BEDS
South Otago	Dunedin volcanics	Dowling Bay limestone / Goodwood limestone / Caversham sandstone
North Otago	Conglomerates and sandstones — KUROW GROUP	Alliday siltstones / Rifle Butts siltstones / Gee greensand
Canterbury	Kowai gravels / Greta conglomerates and siltstones	Blue calcareous siltstone / Glenmark limestone / Hinnites shell-bed / Blue calcareous siltstones — "MOUNT BROWN LIMESTONES" / Calcareous siltstones and limestones / Waikari siltstones
Marlborough	Great Marlborough conglomerate	Dark-grey mudstones / Bedded calcareous mudstones and sandstones
Westland	Blue-grey siltstones and mudstones — "BLUE BOTTOM FORMATION"	
Buller	Glenhope non-marine sandstones, mudstones and lignites	Longford conglomerates and sandstones (estuarine) / Mangles mudstones with interbedded sandstones
Nelson	Grey sandstones, conglomerates, shales with lignites	Blue-grey massive sandstones and siltstones / Blue-grey massive sandstones / Tarakohe mudstones
	Mudstones, sandstones, shell-beds, limestones, conglomerates / Mudstones, siltstones, sand shell-beds / Mudstones and sandstones	Almost complete sequence in Bore at Kapuni
East Wellington	Te Aute coquina limestones / Blue calcareous siltstones	Siltstones / Calcareous siltstones / Tuffs *Amphistegina* / Massive calcareous sandy siltstones / Dark-grey muddy siltstones / Dark-grey siltstones alternating with thin sandstones
	Wharekahika sandstones, mudstones, and conglomerates	Tokomaru sandstones and shell-beds / Mapiri tuffs / Tutamoe / Ihungia mudstones and sandstones
	Volcanism / Kaawa pumiceous shell-beds and sandstones	Terrestrial / Volcanism / Mohakatino tuffaceous sandstones / Mokau sandstones / Mahoenui siltstones and sandstones
	Parahaki rhyolites and dacites	Wairakau andesites / ? Mangonui Cocos beds / Limestone at North Cape / Pakaurangi Point glauconitic sandstones / Waitemata sandstones and Manakau breccias

New Zealand	Stage	Series	Epoch
	Waitotaran (Ww)	WANGANUI	PLIOCENE
	Waipipian (Wp)		
	Opoitian (Wo)		
	Kapitean (Tk)	TARANAKI	UPPER MIOCENE
	Tongaporutuan (Tt)		
	Waiauan (Sw)	SOUTHLAND	MIDDLE MIOCENE
	Lillburnian (Sl)		
	Cliffdenian (Sc)		
	Altonian (Sa)		
	Awamoan (Pa)	PAREORA	LOWER MIOCENE
	Hutchinsonian (Ph)		
	Otaian (Po)		

The general emergence of large parts of the South Island towards the end of the Miocene led to a marked reduction in the extent of the Waiau Geosyncline. It became closed off from any northern connexion and remained as a narrow meridional gulf gradually retreating southwards. In it, sands and shallow-water limestones with rich brachiopod and foraminiferal faunas accumulated in the middle Miocene.

At this time also, the Moonlight Fault, trending almost due north from Lake Wakatipu for a distance of about 60 km and involving steeply-dipping Oligocene formations, was extremely active.

PALAEONTOLOGY AND CLIMATE

Only the most important members of the abundant Late Tertiary biota may be cited here, and the reader is referred to Fleming's (1962) masterly account of the changes, mostly at the generic level, that have been observed during this interval of time.

Amongst the Protozoa, probably the most important event was the appearance of the foram genus *Orbulina* at the base of the Lillburnian Stage (Jenkins, 1964c, p. 182), in the evolutionary sequence *Globigerinoides triloba–G. bispherica–Orbulina suturalis–O. universa*. This almost cosmopolitan genus indicates a middle Miocene age for these deposits, though a precise correlation in terms of European stages is still uncertain. Of more local and climatic significance was the appearance of orbitoids (*Nephrolepidina*) in the Otaian Stage and their marked abundance (*Trybliolepidina, Cycloclypeus, Eulepidina,* and *Miogypsina*) at intervals until the close of the Middle Miocene (Waiauan Stage). The sub-tropical maximum thus indicated was coincident with a striking invasion of Malayo-Pacific faunal and floral elements into the New Zealand area. The disappearance of the orbitoids at the close of the Waiauan Stage also marks a useful datum plane in the Indo-Pacific region.

In the Late Tertiary, when cooling of the globe had set in, there was an increasing trend towards biogeographical provincialism, and palaeontological criteria for world wide correlation are scarce. The arrival of *Bolivinita quadrilatera* from the Indo-Pacific region in the Taranaki Epoch is a useful datum but, by and large, the widespread and abundant Foraminifera are not particularly valuable for outside correlations. A most striking event in the Pliocene was the extinction of many Miocene warm-water groups, including the *Haeuslerella* and the *Globorotalia miozea* lineages.

The temperature maximum in the early Miocene was also marked by the only occurrence in the New Zealand Tertiary sequence of hermatypic corals (for example *Lobophyllia, Turbinaria,* and *Alveopora*). By middle and late Miocene times, many of the subtropical genera, established during the early Miocene, had been eliminated. However, in the Pliocene when the temperatures had cooled considerably, though probably not to present-day levels, newcomers included the scleractinian coral *Flabellum rubrum*, a common modern form.

Brachiopods flourished for a short time after their almost explosive development in the New Zealand Oligocene but as the climate cooled through the Tertiary, their significance as a faunal element waned considerably.

In so far as the molluscs are concerned, they probably form the most important introductions into the New Zealand fauna in the early Miocene. Fleming (1962, p. 76) distinguishes two strongly contrasting climatic provinces at this time (not confined to the molluscs), one that inhabited the area of the present eastern South Island area and little different from that of the preceding late Oligocene, and a subtropical fauna located in the Northland area in which many new genera of molluscs appear, including the Australian bivalve *Dimya*, gastropods of Australian origin such as *Ataxocerithium*, *Maoricolpus*, and *Murexsul*, the Malayo-Pacific bivalves *Cardita*, *Septifer*, *Ctenoides*, and *Chama*, and conid gastropods.

Although the climatic cooling in the latter half of the Miocene saw the extinction of many of the subtropical forms, Malayo-Pacific and Australian immigrants still entered, including the bivalves *Mactra*, *Atrina*, and *Striacallista*, and the gastropod *Zeacumantus*. *Cucullaea* persisted, as the temperatures remained higher than at present.

In the Pliocene, as with the forams, several Miocene warm-water genera were extinguished, including *Gemmula*, *Maoricardium*, and *Mauicassis*. An important event at the close of the Pliocene was the appearance of the pelagic mollusc *Hartungia postulata* which has close relatives in the Pliocene of the Azores, Morocco, and Australia (Fleming, 1953).

The vertebrate record is not large, but the late Miocene is marked by the first record of the moas and probably footprints of a kiwi. A Pliocene seal, *Arctocephalus* has been described from near Cape Kidnappers.

Lower Miocene vegetation differs from that of the Oligocene in the relatively greater abundance of podocarps, palms and ferns, and an increase in the beeches of the *Nothofagus fusca* group though the dominant trees are still of *N. brassi* group.

The tropical or subtropical climate of the early Southland Epoch, with rather drier conditions, saw a marked decrease in the podocarps and ferns. At this time also, the well-known *Cocos*-bearing beds of Coopers Beach, Northland, were deposited.

Beeches of the *N. brassi* group continued to dominate even in the cooler conditions of the Pliocene, but members of several tropical families died out at the end of the Tertiary. It is probable, however, that even in the uppermost Pliocene the temperature was warmer than at present as shown by the abundant *N. brassi* and rare pollen of tropical and subtropical species (*Ephedra* and *Cupanieidites*) not now living here.

IGNEOUS ACTIVITY

Since early Miocene times, igneous activity has occurred in two major volcanic regions separated by a central non-volcanic mobile belt. The northern volcanic region, mainly of basaltic and andesitic type, extends northwestwards from a northeast-trending line through the centre of the North Island. The southern volcanic region throughout the Late Tertiary was apparently entirely basaltic in type.

Andesitic volcanoes erupted in early Miocene times on both flanks of the marine trough occupying the site of the present Northland Peninsula. Their products are now largely preserved in the Manukau Breccias and the Waitemata tuffaceous sandstone. It is probable also that the Kapanga andesitic flows of the Coromandel Peninsula (also known as the "First Period Volcanics") were of this age, though they may be younger. Between these flanking andesitic belts, there was also some eruption of basalt lavas and pillow lavas in the area south of Hokianga Harbour. Elsewhere in New Zealand, there is little evidence of volcanic activity at this time.

In the late Miocene, activity in the Northland and Auckland areas remained andesitic and vigorous with a particular concentration along the Coromandel Peninsula and southwards of the Beesons Island Volcanics ("Second Period Volcanics"). According to Thompson (1961), the intrusions of serpentine, teschenite, and dunite in the Silverdale district are also late Miocene in age, many of them being distributed linearly along fault zones where sediments of the Mangakahia Group (Cretaceous–Palaeocene) are in contact with Waitemata tuffaceous sandstone (lower Miocene).

By Pliocene times, however, the picture had changed, with a resurgence of eruption in the eastern Northland area, this time of dacitic type, to be followed closely by eruptions of rhyolites ("Third Period"—Whitianga Group) along the Coromandel Peninsula–Great Barrier–Poor Knights arch. Finally, in the late Pliocene, a change to basaltic composition is seen in the remnants of volcanic cones and flows of the Waipoua District of Northland.

In the south Auckland region, the Orangiwhao and Kiwitahi andesite volcanic accumulations are classified as upper Miocene or lower Pliocene on their erosional form (Skeleton Stage) by Kear (1960).

Such andesitic sources in north Taranaki were also active and contributed large amounts of tuffaceous material to the Mohakatino Formation (middle Miocene). In the east coast districts of the North Island there are numerous occurrences of white rhyolitic tuffs which probably originated from eruptions in the Taupo region (Fleming, 1962, p. 50).

By late Pliocene or early Pleistocene times, basaltic and andesitic volcanism was in full swing in the south Auckland area. The large cones of Karioi and Pirongia and associated centres, with their alignment in a southeasterly direction belong to this sequence of eruptions.

In the South Island, basaltic volcanoes were active along the upper Miocene shoreline located about 60 km west of Christchurch (Harper Hills Volcanics). Further south in the Dunedin volcanic region, volcanism broke out in late Miocene times with trachytic explosive eruptions followed by alkaline (phonolitic) lava flows which continued through to the late Pliocene or early Pleistocene times. In the Waipiata area of north Otago, basaltic eruptions were also in full swing at this time. Towards the end of the Pliocene also, it is probable that basaltic eruptions of the Hawaiian shield volcano type were also in progress in the Banks Peninsula area.

CHAPTER 12

The Quaternary System

AUSTRALIA and New Zealand differ markedly in their Quaternary histories and deposits. Australia was the site of extensive fluviatile and aeolian deposition during this time, with only marginal marine incursions. Although there is some evidence of epeirogenic movements in the Eastern Highlands, and more particularly in the Torrens and St. Vincent Basins of South Australia, the continent as a whole was tectonically stable during the Pleistocene and is virtually aseismic at present. Glaciation was of very limited areal extent, only Tasmania and a small area in the Eastern Highlands being affected.

The New Zealand area, on the other hand, was partly submerged in the Early Quaternary and was affected by the paroxysmic convulsions of the Kaikoura Orogeny, the expiring phases of which are still expressed in the seismicity of much of the country and the igneous activity of the Central Volcanic Region of the North Island. Glaciation was widespread and severe, particularly in the South Island, and continues in the higher regions to the present day.

The Quaternary chronology in New Zealand is based on glaciations and marine faunas, and may be correlated reasonably well with the northern hemisphere standards. The criteria and bases used in New Zealand fail for much of the Australian Quaternary System, and no satisfactory chronology has been obtained for this country as yet. Few Quaternary correlations have been established between the two countries, and the history of each will therefore be described separately.

AUSTRALIA

Stratigraphy

The Australian Quaternary System contains a variety of deposits ranging from marine shelf sediments to till and aeolian desert sands. The continental margins and much of the interior areas have been and are sites of extensive deposition. Igneous activity has moulded the landscape in only two areas. Fluviatile and aeolian activity has been predominant over most of the continent, with glacial action restricted to small areas in the southeast. The disposition of the major deposits is shown in Fig. 12.1.

Most of the Quaternary System may be classed as "surficial", but the lithification of aeolian calcarenites in some coastal areas and at Lord Howe Island, and the interbedding of volcanic and sedimentary rocks coupled with tectonism and erosion in other places (e.g. Portland, Victoria), has produced Quaternary "solid" geology.

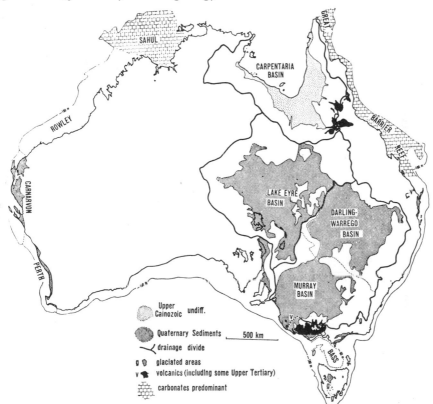

Fig. 12.1. Map showing distribution of principal Australian Quaternary deposits.

MARINE DEPOSITS

The Carpentaria, Gippsland, Otway, Murray, St. Vincent, Torrens, Perth, and Carnarvon Basins are ancient sedimentary basins that may be considered as having a depositional history extending into the Quaternary, and in which marine sediments are still accumulating. Extensive areas of continental shelf off the Eucla and Canning Basins may warrant the consideration of these basins in the same category. The Sahul Shelf, seawards of the Bonaparte Gulf Basin, probably constitutes a sedimentary basin in its own right, as does the major area of carbonate deposition that includes the Great Barrier Reef. In Bass Strait the entirely submerged Bass Basin (Jennings, 1959) contains several hundred metres of probable Cainozoic strata, but its Quaternary history is unknown.

Studies of Quaternary marine sediments in the Australian region are few. Carbonate sedimentation predominates over the Sahul Shelf and the Great Barrier Reef Platform and at Lord Howe Island. The Sahul Shelf has a submerged outer reef barrier, now dead, with adjacent calcarenite, a central mud-calcilutite zone, and a shoreward zone of calcarenite with some terrigenous detritus (van Andel *et al.*, 1961; von der Borch, 1965*b*). The low relief of the hinterland and drowning of river mouths has limited the influx of terrigenous material. The Barrier Reef Platform has been little studied, and is undoubtedly complex. It lies athwart the Palaeozoic and Mesozoic trends of the Tasman Orthogeosyncline and has a sedimentary history extending back to at least the Miocene (Derrington *et al.*, 1960). An outer actively growing barrier reef shelters numerous patch reefs, cays and intermittent fringing reefs (Fairbridge, 1950). Sediments vary widely in grainsize and composition, with terrigenous detritus increasing inshore. Major variations of carbonate sediments occur within small areas, as Maxwell *et al.*, (1961, 1964*a*, *b*) have shown at Heron Island.

From Warnbro Sound, in the southern part of the Perth Basin, Carrigy (1956) has described essentially non-terrigenous sands and muds, rich in carbon and nitrogen, in which mollusc fragments predominate. The sound is barred on the seaward side by drowned calcarenite dune barriers and receives no fluviatile inflow.

Preliminary studies of the eastern continental shelf (Phipps, 1963; Shirley, 1964) and of the shelf margining the western and southern coasts of Western Australia (Carrigy and Fairbridge, 1954) indicate that terrigenous sedimentation is widespread. In addition considerable areas of carbonate sediment, consisting of coral or shells, occur in the west. Coarse carbonate sediment composed of entire and fragmented molluscan shells margins the seaward edge of the continental shelf of New South Wales, in water depths exceeding 125 m, and is believed to be still forming.

COASTAL MORPHOLOGY AND SEDIMENTS

Evidence for both higher and lower stands of sealevel than the present is widespread along the Australian coast (Gill, 1964*a*), and there can be little doubt that some stands are eustatically controlled. However, there is scant agreement as yet on the dating of the various stands, or of their heights, for reasons outlined by Bauer (1961). It is unfortunate, but perhaps inevitable, that those regions which show most clearly the relative ages of events spanning much of the Quaternary, such as the Portland district, Victoria (Boutakoff, 1963), should be suspect as type areas, on the grounds of tectonic instability.

No recent review of Australian eustatic data is available, but Gentilli (1961) has provided a fairly comprehensive bibliography. Collation of data is rendered difficult not only by tectonic effects, which have been evaluated only rarely (Sprigg, 1952), but also by the variety of geomorphic features that occur and the problems of relating these to a precise datum. Erosional and constructional forms, both stranded and submerged, occur in varying states of preservation. They include erosional platforms, wave-cut notches, sea-caves and cliffs, beaches, beach ridge systems, barrier formations, cheniers, dune ridges with interdune flats, shell beds, submerged peat horizons, emerged coral reef forms, submarine canyons terminating at breaks in slope, rias, sediment-choked river valleys with bed-rock floors below sealevel, and thalassostatic river terraces (Bird, 1964).

The sealevels suggested range from $+240$ m to -180 m, but these limits seem excessive. Most values lie between $+75$ m and -135 m, with commonly occurring values of about $+30$ m, $+20$ m, $+15$ m, $+6$ m, $+3$ m, $+1\cdot5$ m, -1 m, -2 m to -4 m, -12 m, -55 m and -100 m. Ages of certain of these levels have been postulated by Boutakoff (1963), but Fairbridge (1961) has presented a somewhat different chronology for them. Fairbridge (1961) and others have reported widespread evidence of coastal emergence during the Holocene, arguing that the post-glacial marine transgression carried the sea temporarily up to 3 m above its present level before receding. The idea of Holocene higher sealevels has been criticized, however, by Shepard (1961) and others, and it may be that these apparently higher sealevels should be attributed to tectonic uplift of certain sections of the coast during the past few thousand years. However, Ward and Jessup (1965) claim that shorelines at altitudes in excess of 100 m on Yorke Peninsula in South Australia are younger than the latest tectonic movements in that area.

Shoreline deposits fringe much of the coastline, but occupy limited areas except along the coastal parts of Cainozoic sedimentary basins and in the vicinity of the mouths of certain east coast rivers. In these regions the Quaternary is represented by an extensive body of paralic clastic sediments up to a few hundred metres thick. In western Victoria and South and Western Australia (Fairbridge and Teichert, 1953; Bauer, 1961) the basic component of these deposits is lithified aeolian calcarenite, with subordinate quartz sand which together commonly occur as dunes or dune stumps. In some cases quartz-sand sheets are believed to have formed from the destruction of the dunes (Sprigg, 1959). Aeolian calcarenites also occur at Lord Howe Island (Standard, 1963).

The classic area for these paralic sediments is in the Murray and Otway

Basins (Sprigg, 1952), where more than fourteen sub-parallel dunes, some exceeding 130 km in length, occupy a 60–80 km wide coastal strip west of the Kanawinka Fault. Other dunes occur east of the fault. During the Pleistocene the shoreline retreated southwestwards and the dune system spans the whole of the Quaternary, with the easternmost dunes being of Tertiary age. At least one further dune lies submerged just off the present coast. The interdune corridors, some of which are several kilometres wide, contain both older marine deposits and contemporary peat with fresh- to brackish-water lake deposits. Remarkable among the lakes is the Coorong which extends behind the most recent dune barrier for 160 km southeast from the mouth of the Murray River. This is the site of contemporary evaporite sedimentation, dolomite, magnesite, calcite, and aragonite being the predominant minerals (von der Borch, 1965a).

On the coasts of eastern Victoria and New South Wales, dunes are present, but the characteristic deposits comprise quartz-sand barriers with lagoonal silt deposits landward (Bird, 1965). Multiple barriers are commonly developed (Thom, 1965), in which the Inner Barriers, believed to be of Pleistocene age, are well vegetated, and partly indurated to form sandrock. The lagoons landward of the Inner Barriers are commonly silted up, with the formation of peat, mud, and sandrock.

The coast of south Queensland is marked by striking accumulations of quartz sand in the form of parabolic dunes of Pleistocene age which are oriented northwest–southeast, obliquely to the present coast and rise locally to more than 200 m above sealevel (Coaldrake, 1961; Whitehouse, 1963). At Stradbroke Island these sands extend to depths of 60 m below sealevel, and the dunes are fixed, heavily vegetated, and include peat and sandrock layers. The sand is strongly iron-pigmented in many places.

Cheniers, which occur at several points on the Queensland coast, are particularly characteristic of the eastern shore of the Gulf of Carpentaria (Valentin, 1961) where they form a unit within the Quaternary paralic deposits of the Carpentaria Basin. Some ridge systems are contemporary, others are ancient. They overlie marine muds and give way landwards to salt mud-flats with older ridges and dunes. These pass into claysoil flats margining the huge gently sloping alluvial fans of the coastal rivers. Sand sheets, with abundant clay-pan depressions, cover much of these fans (Whitehouse, 1963).

INLAND TERRESTRIAL DEPOSITS

The river systems were the principal sites of terrestrial deposition—both fluviatile and aeolian—during the Quaternary, the volume of sediment being related to the size of the river system. The most notable deposits are associated with streams draining the interior, and the hinterland of the Gulf of Carpentaria, although deposits associated with shorter coastal streams are locally important and have received some study. Important Quaternary deposits occur in the Murray Basin, in the Lake Eyre and Darling–Warrego Basins (Fig. 12.1) which may be considered together as the Quaternary expression of the Great Artesian Basin, and in the Carpentaria Basin. Quaternary terrestrial deposits in other sedimentary basins are not well known.

The deposits of the Murray Basin may be taken as representative. They fall into three distinct regions, the downstream "Bungunnia" region with lacustrine clay and oolitic and algal limestone (Firman, 1965), the south bank "Mallee" region (Hills, 1939) in which aeolian activity, both Quaternary and Tertiary, has been dominant, and the upstream "Riverine Plain" region dominated by fluviatile deposition. The Quaternary deposits at Swan Hill (Churchward, 1963) lie on the junction between the second and last regions.

Butler (1966) has summarized our knowledge of the Riverine Plain deposits. The region is essentially a gigantic alluvial sheet spreading from the foothills of the Eastern Highlands. It represents the deposits of a system or systems of prior streams, some of which may have been as large as the Missouri River, U.S.A. (Langford-Smith, 1960). Intercalated with the fluviatile deposits, and mantling the whole landscape, there are sheets of clay-rich loess-like material ("parna") of aeolian origin (Butler, 1956). Butler (1959) recognizes three successive parna sheets each overlying fluviatile deposits. The youngest fluviatile deposits have associated parna dunes (lunettes) rather than sheets. Sand dunes are locally important being related to sand deposits of the prior streams.

Each body of fluviatile–aeolian sediment developed a soil mantle in its upper part during a subsequent non-depositional phase. This body of sediment with its soil mantle is, in Butler's terminology, a "ground surface". The sequence of partly or entirely buried ground surfaces is clearly cyclic, and is the basis for the K-cycle concept which has been widely applied to Australian surficial deposits. This concept (Butler, 1959) relates the development of ground surfaces to cyclic climatic change which causes an alternation of instability and stability of landscape. At the start of each K-cycle the landscape is unstable, and fluviatile and aeolian erosion and deposition build up the sedimentary portion of a ground surface. With the onset of more humid conditions this unstable phase of the K-cycle is succeeded by a stable phase during which the soil mantle is developed, and the ground surface development is completed. Six such K-cycles, from the contemporary K_0 to the K_5, which may be as old as middle Pleistocene, are evident in the deposits of the Riverine Plain and vicinity. The K_1 to K_4 ground surfaces contain parna components.

Similar ground surfaces occur elsewhere in the Eastern Highlands and in the coastal regions (Butler, 1966), but these lack recognizable aeolian components. The eastern part of the Darling–Warrego Basin also contains buried ground surfaces (Hill and Denmead, eds., 1960, p. 398) but these have been little studied.

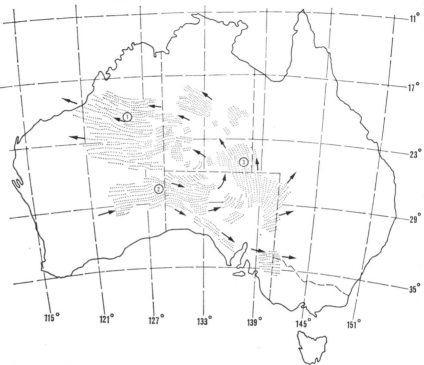

FIG. 12.2. Generalized arrangement of desert sand ridges. Arrows show deduced causal wind patterns. (After King, 1960.)

Surficial deposits comprising several ground surfaces occur in the Lake Eyre and western Darling–Warrego Basins, but the ground surfaces differ from those of the other basins in the predominance of the aeolian component (Jessup, 1961). The streams in the Lake Eyre Basin are braided and produce extensive sand and silt deposits and a characteristic "channel country" topography (Whitehouse, 1948). The topographically lower parts of the basin, some of which are below sealevel, have been the site of evaporite accumulation, principally halite, gypsum, and dolomite (Johns and Ludbrook, 1963; Bonython, 1956). Aeolian sand sheets and dunes represent an important part of the Quaternary sediments of this basin.

The sand-ridge deserts of the interior of the continent are striking examples of Quaternary sediment accumulation (King, 1960; Veevers and Wells,

1961), particularly in the Lake Eyre and Canning Basins. The ridges are dunes from 12 to 30 m high and are separated by corridors 270–450 m wide, and appear outwardly to consist of quartz sand, fixed, except at the crest, by vegetation. In plan the dunes vary somewhat in form (Veevers and Wells, 1961). Typically they are narrow, highly rectilinear, and tens of kilometres in length, with a few exceeding 320 km. Dune convergence is common, resulting in asymmetrical Y-shaped patterns which invariably point in the same direction in each locality. The convergences are directed down-wind and the regional pattern of the dunes (Fig. 12.2) reflects a wind regime but little different from the modern one (King, 1960). In South Australia at least, King (1960) believes that the dunes are of the windrift type, rather than the seif type, the sand having travelled only a short distance, and erosion having been predominant in the corridors. They probably resulted from deflation of drainage systems and weathered Mesozoic and older sandstones during the Quaternary arid cycles, and may have been initiated during the late Pleistocene. Dune systems are absent from those parts of the interior in which crystalline rocks or old laterite surfaces are predominant, the sand from these sources forming extensive sandplains.

Dunes of different types, the most notable of which are reticulate in plan, occur locally in Queensland, the Northern Territory and elsewhere. White-house (1963) ascribes their origin to two or more approximately equal wind systems of differing direction.

GLACIATION

Only a small portion of the Australian continent was glaciated during the Quaternary. Estimates of the area involved have been reduced in recent years from those given by Browne (1957), and recent workers recognize evidence for only one phase of glaciation, rather than three.

The principal region of Pleistocene glaciation in Australia was Tasmania, where an area of some 6000 sq km was covered by ice (Spry and Banks, eds., 1962). About 4000 sq km of the northwestern part of the Central Plateau lay under a single ice cap, and there were many smaller ice caps and cirque or valley glaciers (Fig. 12.1). The regional orographic snow line, which now lies between 1500 m and 1800 m, was probably from 900 to 1200 m, rising eastwards to 1450 m. Roches moutonnées, cirques and excavated lakes, fluted and hummocky moraine, terminal moraines, fluvioglacial outwash, and dammed lakes are common. Cirque-cut massifs with horn peaks, arêtes, and other erosion features occur locally. The glaciation is believed to be of Würm age.

Patterned ground, solifluxion mantles, block fields, and streams and residual stacks occur, and many are widespread although they have received scant study. Periglacial effects extend down to 450 m, and may still be active above 1200 m.

Glaciation on the Australian mainland was very limited in extent, covering only some 50 sq km of the highest country around Mount Kosciusko (2195 m) in southern New South Wales (Galloway, 1963). At its maximum the ice accumulated on the southeastern facing slopes of the high country, and forming confluent valley glaciers, descended eastwards some 8 km into the valley of the upper Snowy River, to an altitude of about 1650 m. Thirteen cirques, the lowest with a floor at 1845 m, head the valleys. A few contain roches moutonnées. Later retreat left erratics scattered along the Snowy Valley, and terminal, lateral and hummocky moraines in higher areas, several being associated with lakes. All these features are the result of a single glaciation probably during the Würm, although some of the larger cirques may have been initiated earlier.

Periglacial influences have been widespread, down to altitudes of 900 m, and are still active, but weak, above 1800 m. Solifluxion deposits such as stone-banked terraces and lobes, block fields, and block streams are not uncommon.

Soils and Land Surfaces

The widespread effects of K-cycles complicate greatly the distribution pattern of Australian soils. Stephens (1964) recognizes forty-seven Great Soil Groups in Australia. Many are strictly palaeosols, formed under environmental conditions far different from the present, and now at the surface as a result of protection from deposition or erosion, or due to stripping of surficial material. Thus the ages of the soils vary, some certainly being of Tertiary age.

The effects of stripping during the erosive stage of a K-cycle, and soil formation during the non-depositional stage, provide a mechanism for widespread renewal of soils on existing land surfaces (van Dijk, 1959). Thus the soils developed on the various geomorphic surfaces in Australia are in many cases much younger than the surfaces themselves. Since K-cycles are known to extend well back into the Pleistocene, probably to the middle Pleistocene at least, it is likely that most land surfaces of any extent were initiated in the Tertiary or earlier.

Tectonism and Igneous Activity

Australia lacks active volcanoes, but cessation of volcanicity took place subsequent to human settlement. Scarcely denuded cones with unweathered ejectamenta, flows intimately related to the present topography, and even craters with fumarolic deposits are known. Holocene volcanicity, yielding alkali-olivine basalts and other alkaline volcanics, occurred in north Queensland (White, 1961), central Queensland (Stevens, 1961) and western Victoria extending into the southeast of South Australia (Edwards, 1938; Sprigg, 1952; Boutakoff, 1963; Gill, 1964*b*). In the first and last regions earlier volcanicity of Pliocene to Pleistocene age was also important, and more than 100 vents of varying ages have been recognized in each region.

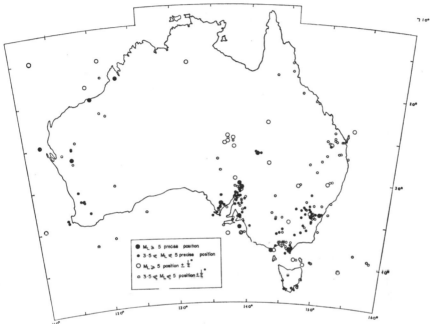

Fig. 12.3. Seismicity of Australia. (After Doyle, H. A., Everingham, I. B., and Sutton, D. J., pers. comm.)

Pliocene to Holocene basalt flows and tuffs cover about 13,600 sq km in north Queensland, in four separate areas, and occupy more than 26,000 sq km in Victoria–South Australia (Fig. 12.1). Scoria cones, composite cones, basalt domes, lava tunnels, and maars have been recognized, and disruption of drainage by both Holocene and older Quaternary flows is common. Post-eruption caldera subsidence has occurred at several places, for example in the region of Portland, Victoria, where it has combined with active marine erosion to present magnificent cross-sections through several of the volcanic piles.

The most recent eruptions in the southern province occurred at Mount Gambier in South Australia (4830 ± 70 yrs. B.P.) (Gill, 1955), and at Tower Hill in Victoria (4315 ± 195 yrs. B.P.) where dingo bones and an aboriginal grinding stone occur beneath the tuffs (Gill, 1964*b*).

Australia is regarded as a tectonically stable continent, few shocks of large magnitude having been recorded. However, intermediate to low magnitude shocks occur fairly frequently, particularly in the Pirie–Torrens Sunkland in South Australia and other tectonically active areas (Jaeger and Browne, 1958; H. A. Doyle, pers. comm.) (Fig. 12.3). Only within the last decade has a seismic network capable of locating low magnitude epicentres been available, and much of the continent is not covered by this network.

The relative stability of the continent probably does not extend far back into the Quaternary. Although the epeirogenic uplift of the eastern highlands is commonly placed in the Tertiary, some evidence suggests younger movements of considerable magnitude. Beavis (1960) describes the thrusting of Palaeozoic gneiss over presumably Quaternary river gravels in the Kiewa Valley, Victoria, on the margin of the Bogong High Plains. Jaeger and Browne (1958) have pointed out that the absence of marine Tertiary and Pleistocene deposits from low-lying parts of the Sydney and Newcastle districts implies depression of the central coastal region of New South Wales after the mid-Pleistocene high sealevels. The Lapstone Monocline, which forms the front of the Blue Mountains west of Sydney, would have attained its present form during this movement.

A succession of stranded and warped shore lines occurs in western Victoria and adjacent South Australia (Sprigg, 1952, 1959; Boutakoff, 1963) as a result of the interplay between slow warping and Quaternary eustatism.

Climate and Palaeontology

Evidences for variations in climate are widespread in the Australian Quaternary, and have been discussed by Gentilli (1961) and Galloway (1965). The proper dating of datum points presents a problem which has not yet been overcome. The preparation of a generally accepted pattern of Quaternary climatic change must await solution of this problem.

The K-cycle concept is of particular utility in interpreting Quaternary climatic data. Butler (1959) considers that the erosional–depositional (unstable) phase of each K-cycle is initiated by climatic change. This he ascribes to the onset of aridity, whereas Langford-Smith (1960) stresses pluvial conditions. Since parna layers follow fluviatile layers in the Riverina K-cycle deposits it is possible that a change to pluvial conditions initiates the cycle and later passes into drier conditions. Butler, however, considers that the stable phase of a K-cycle, during which soil formation occurs, is one of humid climate.

Further, the degree of stripping of the landscape, and extent of weathering and of the soil development, give indications of the magnitude of the climatic change and the duration of the stable phase that followed it (van Dijk, 1959).

In the Eastern Highlands the K_4 cycle, and probably also the K_5, seem to have involved changes of greater magnitude and occupied longer periods of time than the later cycles, even allowing for the cumulative effects of weathering during the interval since their initiation.

We thus see, in the six or seven cycles so far recognized, evidence of intervals of varying duration that were both more and less arid than at present. Presumably the soil-forming phases of K-cycles are related to interglacials or interstadials, but in the absence of glacial deposits older than Würm this must remain conjectural.

The base of the marine Quaternary in Australia is placed at the base of the Werrikoo Member in the Otway Basin, where both fauna and palaeo-temperature measurements indicate a cooling of the environment from that in the preceding Maretimo Member (Gill, 1957).

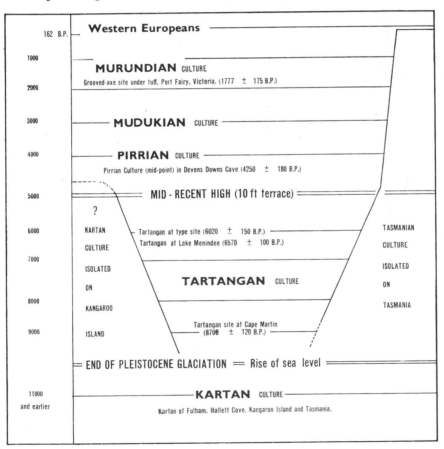

Fig. 12.4. Culture sequence and dates in southeastern Australia. (After Tindale, 1959.)

Quaternary marine faunas include certain distinctive forms. *Pecten meridionalis* is characteristic of the lower Pleistocene in the Otway Basin, and *Anadara trapezia*, a warm-water form, is dominant in mid-Holocene faunas in the Murray Basin. Other significant forms are mentioned by Sprigg (1952) and Valentine (1965).

The terrestrial vertebrate fauna includes several extinct marsupial genera and species (Woods, 1962), such as *Thylacoleo, Protemnodon, Procoptodon, Nototherium, Diprotodon*, and *Macropus titan*. The last two are giant forms. Some genera, notably *Diprotodon*, survived into the early Holocene. Others, such as *Thylacinus* and *Sarcophilus*, became extinct on the mainland but are still extant in Tasmania. Aboriginal man entered the continent sometime before 18,000 yrs. B.P., bringing with him the dingo (*Canis familiaris dingo*) which is believed to have been responsible for the extinction of certain mainland marsupials. The dingo did not reach Tasmania. A human culture sequence extending back to 11,000 yrs. B.P. (Fig. 12.4) has been worked out for southeastern Australia (Tindale, 1959).

Quaternary plant fossils remain largely unstudied, and very little can be said about the effects of climatic change on the Quaternary flora. Crocker (1959) has made some suggestions. Many genera first encountered in the Tertiary continue through to modern times. The present *Eucalyptus–Acacia*-dominated flora probably became established in something like its present form during the Quaternary; and the restriction of non-eucalypt forests, in which *Nothofagus* is prominent, to isolated humid areas, principally uplands of the eastern seaboard, probably occurred at this time.

Chronology

The insignificant development of glacial and periglacial deposits over the Australian continent poses special problems in establishing a Quaternary chronology, for the basis of the traditional northern hemisphere framework is absent (Butler, 1964). Stranded marine deposits are of limited extent, and fossils from them and from submarine units have been little studied. Terrestrial fossils are insufficiently common and do not yield a sufficiently fine time-subdivision. The principal sources of information which are likely to be significant in the establishment of a satisfactory chronology are: radiometric dates—^{14}C in the late Quaternary and K–Ar for the earlier parts, using volcanic rocks; K-cycles; eustatic changes; palaeotemperature determinations; and palynological studies. Only limited data are available from most of these sources.

Relatively few ^{14}C dates have been obtained from Australia (Dury, 1964), and almost all are from spot samples and are therefore uncontrolled.

K-cycles and eustatism have provided some useful data. On the New South

Wales coast, up to six ground surfaces, in the form of terraces, have been clearly equated with high sealevels (Butler, 1964). Three of these ground surfaces—K_1, K_2, and K_3 at Nowra—have been dated at 400, 3750, and 29,000 yrs. B.P. (Walker, 1962). The soils on the successive terraces in the coastal regions are very similar to those on successive ground surfaces elsewhere in southeastern Australia.

In the present state of our knowledge the presentation of even a tentative chronological chart for the Australian Quaternary does not seem warranted. Earlier chronologies (Browne, 1945; Boutakoff, 1963) have not found general acceptance. With the accumulation of more data a satisfactory Quaternary chronology using mapped ground surfaces as time-rock units may be developed. Relationships between ground surfaces and sealevels could be determined in coastal river valleys. Correlation with the northern hemisphere would require radiometric determination of the absolute age limits of the K-cycles to which the ground surfaces correspond.

NEW ZEALAND

Stratigraphy

Marked cooling of the New Zealand area became clearly defined in the deposits of the upper part of the Waitotaran Stage. The deterioration in climate, which resulted in a mean depression of the snow line, with reference to its present level, of about 1050 m and a reduction in the mean temperature of about 6°C (Willett, 1950) was accompanied by the paroxysmic phases of the Kaikoura Orogeny, during which almost all of the present land area of the Dominion was elevated above sealevel. This violent uplift and deformation has resulted in a very marked unconformity between the deposits of the Wanganui Series (Pliocene–early Pleistocene) and those of the Hawera Series (late Pleistocene and Holocene). The degree of disturbance at this time may be gauged from Suggate's recent estimate (1963) that vertical uplift to the east of the Alpine Fault in central Westland probably amounted to something of the order of 18,000 m with a horizontal movement of approximately the same magnitude. The amount of erosion since the end of the Middle Pleistocene has thus been sufficient to remove a thickness of some 15,000 m of rocks to leave such remnants as Mount Cook (3763 m).

Gage (1965) has recently reviewed the evidence for the climatic conditions prevailing in New Zealand during the cold phases of the Pleistocene. He concludes that running water played a more substantial part in the formation of the glacial deposits, as compared with conditions in the glaciated areas of the continental regions. He suggests that ". . . the winters were not seasons of continual frost, but were broken by spells of above-freezing weather".

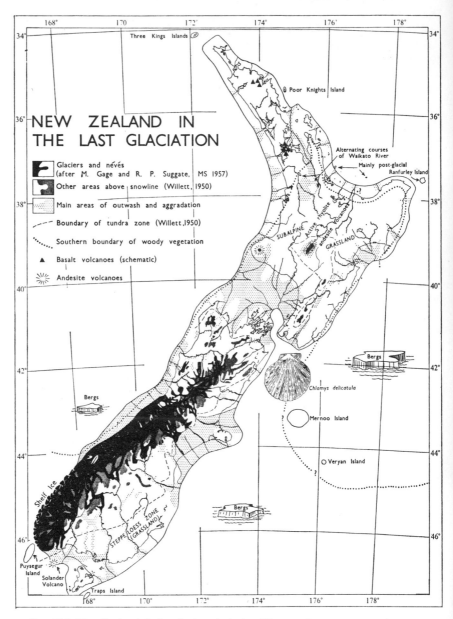

Fig. 12.5. New Zealand during the last glaciation. The map is an attempt to show conditions during the peak of the Otiran Glaciation. (After Fleming, 1962, by permission of *Tuatara*.)

NORTH ISLAND

Towards the end of the Pliocene, the present outlines of the island were established and extended as the climate deteriorated and sea level fluctuated. The shallow sea, which had spread over the southern half of the island, began to retreat as the axial ranges rose and separated an **eastern** (Hawkes Bay Province) **basin** from a **western** (Wanganui) **basin.** At times these remained interconnected by the narrow strait through the site of the present Manawatu Gorge. In the extreme north, the stack-like islands of the North Cape eruptives became welded on to the main Northland Peninsula by aggradation and the construction of a gigantic tombolo.

The first cooling maximum of the lower Pleistocene corresponds to the former Hautawan Stage, now considered by Boreham (1963) to be at least partly equivalent to the Mangapanian (upper Waitotaran) Sub-Stage. In some places, for example, the Wanganui Basin and Central Hawkes Bay, this is characterized by the appearance of a cold-water pectinid bivalve, *Chlamys delicatula*, in latitudes at least 480 km north of its present distribution. At this time, the rising Ruahine–Tararua ranges shed considerable quantities of gravels which caused the temporary closure of the Manawatu Strait.

An amelioration of the climate, known as the Marahauan Interglacial, led to a marked marine incursion into the earlier-named districts, with connexion re-established through the Manawatu Strait. At the same time, to the northwest of the rising mountain axis, highly acid volcanism, producing ignimbrite and pumice, broke out in the Taupo region.

Then came a further cooling—the Okehuan Stage—which, however, is not clearly marked as a truly glacial age, the main evidence for climatic deterioration being based on the elimination of many of the warm-water molluscs of the preceding stage at this time. Most of the Hawkes Bay–Wairarapa area was finally abandoned by the sea and there was also a temporary retreat from most of the Wanganui Basin. The latter was brought about largely by the vast amounts of erosion products from the rising mountain ranges and the ashy eruptiva from the volcanic belt. This material spread out in enormous fans and aprons across the shallow platform of the basin.

The warming-up of the Castlecliffian Stage was marked by the appearance of many new genera of molluscs of Australian affinities, while the sea encroached in many places along the coastal margins and as far inland as the western flank of the Ruahine Range, and on to the Heretaunga Plain on the east. The fauna indicates that the temperature was probably greater than at present.

The upper Pleistocene and Holocene (Hawera Series), as stated above, is clearly separated from the lower and middle Pleistocene, especially in the central areas of New Zealand. This series may, in fact, be considered as a post-orogenic unit that followed the Kaikoura Orogeny.

In the North Island, rocks of Hawera age are separated from older formations by a regional unconformity, and most of them, especially in the west, contain the products of the volcanoes of the Taranaki and Tongariro National Park areas. They comprise coastal terrace deposits, marking stands of high sealevel during interglacial stages, or fluvial deposits formed during intervals of low sealevel when rivers were aggrading and erosion was rapid. They also include formations laid down as a cover (alluvium, dune-sand, beach-sand, ash, lignite, etc.) on benches eroded by marine and fluviatile agencies subsequently to the gentle folding, faulting and planation of the upper Pliocene and lower Pleistocene Wanganui Series. In the south and west, these gentle deforming movements continued throughout the epoch accompanied by eustatic changes of sealevel. To the northwest of the main volcanic belt, however, conditions were much more stable and attempts have been made to correlate various late Pleistocene coastal surfaces (for example at South Kaipara and Waihi Beach) with similar levels of surfaces in Europe (Brothers, 1954; Kear and Waterhouse, 1961). Such correlations have, however, been strongly criticized by Cotton (1963).

Fleming (1953) has recognized two marine stages within the Hawera Series in the Wanganui area. These, the Terangian below and the Oturian above, are not faunally so well characterized as the stages of the underlying Wanganui Series, being representatives of much shorter periods of time. They are considered to be deposits of successive interglacial periods.

Only very minor areas of the North Island were glaciated during the Hawera Epoch, for instance, the highest parts of the Ruahine Range, Tongariro National Park, and Mount Egmont. Willett (1950) has suggested that these areas alone would have lain within a somewhat larger but not extensive zone of tundra type inside the midsummer 10°C isotherm, and that by and large the North Island would have been occupied by a forest zone.

SOUTH ISLAND

The effects of Pleistocene refrigeration were markedly more evident in the South Island. As shown in Fig. 12.5, glaciers and névés extended widely along the main alpine axis and covered most of the western littoral areas as well. Willett (1950) believes that the entire island, with the exception of small areas about Banks Peninsula, the north Canterbury coast, northern Marlborough and northwest Nelson, was subjected to a midsummer temperature of less than 10°C. This resulted in the lowering of the snow line by some 1050 m as compared with its present level, a depression of the average temperature by about 6°C, and the inclusion of most of the present lowland area and its extensions seawards caused by lowering of sealevel, within the periglacial zone.

The glacial sequences in the South Island have been closely studied by many workers in recent years, and a detailed stratigraphy for the moraines, outwash fans and erosion surfaces has been worked out, using field criteria such as differences in ice extent, erosion and weathering of deposits, and differences of altitude due to progressive lowering of river profiles (Gage, 1958, 1961; Gage and Suggate, 1958; Soons, 1963; Suggate, 1965). These investigations show that at least six or seven distinct glacial advances are recognizable in the Westland and Canterbury regions. By their very nature, it is difficult to correlate many of these features even within the South Island itself, let alone with the standard references for Europe and North America. The vast tectonic effects of the Kaikoura Orogeny culminating in the late Pleistocene must also have added considerable complications, so that some of the minor advances of outwash material that have been detected at particular localities may not necessarily be due to climatic cooling alone. Moreover, the preservation of the evidences of glaciation was affected in different ways by the diastrophic movements.

The earliest evidence of Pleistocene glaciation is to be seen at Ross, Westland, where morainic material and varved silts (Ross Glacials) conformably overlie marine Pliocene deposits, the whole having been strongly deformed by the Kaikoura orogenic movements. Unconformably overlying them are almost undeformed late Pleistocene moraines. The Ross Glaciation is believed to be coeval with the Hautawan marine stage of the Wanganui District in the North Island.

The record is somewhat obscured in the middle part of the Pleistocene when the orogenesis reached its maximum. The rapidly rising Southern Alps, however, shed on both sides enormous quantities of gravels which range in age from late Pliocene to middle Pleistocene (the Moutere Gravels of Nelson; the Old Man Gravels of the Grey–Inangahua Depression; the Kowai Gravels of the North Canterbury; and the Gore Piedmont Gravels of Southland).

The late Pleistocene and Holocene (Hawera Epoch) in the South Island was a time of alternate warming and cooling, so that stratigraphical records consist either of coastal terraces developed during interglacial periods of high sealevel or glacio-fluvial deposits formed during aggradation as sealevel fell, and erosion rapidly ensued following the deforestation of the mountain areas.

Four glaciations are recognized in the upper Pleistocene, the last (Otira) exhibiting two or three major advances, each with minor stadials when the ice advanced and interstadials when the temperature rose a little.

The earliest of these, the Porika Glaciation, is typically developed in the Upper Buller Valley where it is represented by weathered till, sub-glacial gravel and sand at high levels (up to 600 m) above the valley floor. Weathered but relatively undisturbed gravels in north Canterbury have also been correlated with this stage.

The Waimaunga Glaciation which follows, appears to represent a time when the glaciers were thicker and more extensive on both sides of the Southern Alps than at any later time. It was followed by a lengthy inter-glacial interval when rivers cut deeply into their beds (300 m in the Waimakariri Valley) and oxidation of the earlier deposits was deep. In the more stable parts of the Dominion, the rise of sealevel at this time is frequently marked by a 18–21 m beach.

The Waimea Glaciation has very recently been recognized (Suggate, 1965) as till and outwash gravel on the west coast of the South Island and is correlated with the Tophouse Formation of Nelson and the Woodlands Formation of Canterbury.

In the Otira (Last) Glaciation, glacial advances and recessions are well-marked in the South Island, although correlation of these is not unequivocal. The glacial maximum at this time corresponded with a fall in sealevel of at least 105 m, so that, as shown in Fig. 12.5 a large part of the continental shelf was exposed and the present North and South Islands were joined by land.

The effects of the glacial regime are widely displayed. In addition to the deep erosion of the rising mountain ranges and the deposition of moraines, huge fiords in the southwestern region of the South Island were carved by glaciers and many inland glacial valleys are now occupied by lakes. The outwash alluvium from the glacial fronts on the east side of the Southern Alps coalesced in great alluvial fans to form the Canterbury Plains. In addition, large parts of the eastern lowlands are covered by thick deposits of loess of aeolian origin (Raeside, 1964; Young, 1964).

Many data on radiocarbon dating of Late Quaternary events using peat, wood, calcareous shells, etc., are now available through the investigations of the Carbon Dating Laboratory of the New Zealand Institute of Nuclear Sciences (Grant-Taylor and Rafter, 1962).

Palaeontology

The marine faunas of the New Zealand Quaternary have some distinctive forms, though the chief faunal differences are concerned mainly with fluctuations in distribution.

With the onset of cold conditions in the early Pleistocene, many invertebrate groups, now characteristic of high, subantarctic latitudes, moved northwards and are found in deposits of Hautawan age in the south part of the North Island, for example the bivalves *Chlamys delicatula* and *Tawera subsulcata*, the gastropods *Zeacolpus (Stiracolpus) symmetricus* and *Maurea couperi*, the crab *Jacquinotia*, and possibly the echinoid *Notocidaris vellai* (see Fleming, 1962, p. 85). Vertebrate fossils include the seal *Ommatophoca*, now confined to the Antarctic regions.

The climatic deterioration is marked in the land floras by the presence of pollens of the mountain beech (*Nothofagus solanderi* var. *cliffortioides*) and the silver beech (*N. menziesii*) in deposits of Hautawan age in the south Auckland area. In South Island, subalpine grasses and scrub were widespread at low altitudes at this time also.

The interglacial intervals are of interest in that immigrants from the Australian area or further north appear. For instance, in the Nukumaruan Stage, the bivalves *Pterynotus angasi* and *Leucotina ambigua* are evident, while in the Castlecliffian, such genera and species as *Xenogalea*, *Pecten* (s. str.), *Anadara trapezia*, and *Bembicium melanostomum* are notable arrivals.

The late Pleistocene (Hawera Epoch) contains a poor shallow-water foraminiferal assemblage from which there is a marked absence of *Loxostomum karrerianum*, a widespread species in Holocene faunas. The presence of fossil remains of some molluscs in deposits south of their present distribution suggests somewhat warmer sea temperatures at that time. This is in accord with the evidence for a rather warm inter-glacial interval during the early part of the Hawera Epoch as shown by the deep weathering and "rubification" of old soils and land surfaces on the Wellington Peninsula.

In so far as terrestrial vertebrates are concerned, the Quaternary is virtually coincident with the racial history of the moa and other flightless birds (e.g. *Notornis*). Moreover, with the possible exception of an albatross bone, there are no pre-Pleistocene records of flying birds in New Zealand, and remains of the living subfamily of penguins are not known before the late Pleistocene.

Tectonism

It will be useful at this point to summarize the essential tectonic features of the Dominion and the surrounding oceanic region (Fig. 12.6).

The tectonic movements of the Quaternary in New Zealand are essentially those resulting from the maximal disturbances of the Kaikoura Orogeny in middle Pleistocene times and their decreasing intensity until the present day.

The emergent land area of New Zealand is part of an extensive series of crustal elevations, plateaux and ridges that alternate with basins and trenches. The present land area may be divided into two tectonic regions (Clark *et al.*, 1965), as follows:

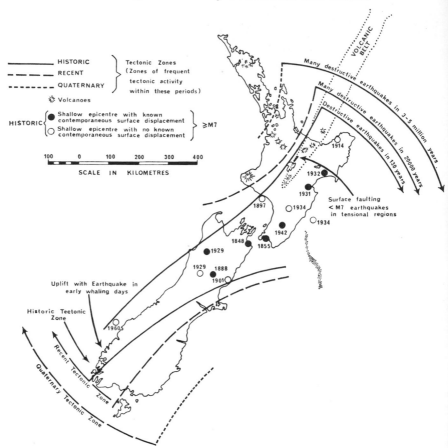

FIG. 12.6. Map of New Zealand showing deduced tectonic zones, historic earthquake epicentres, position of Late Cainozoic volcanoes, and the present active volcanic belt. (After Clark *et al.*, 1965.)

(1) The **Northland Peninsula**, a relatively "stable" region that appears to have escaped measurable deformation since at least Miocene times. There has been local volcanism which is no longer active.

(2) The **"Quaternary Tectonic Zone"**, comprising the remainder of the country, where seismic, thermal and some volcanic activity are still pronounced. Raised beaches, uplifted marine terraces and platforms on the coastal margins are expressions of this tectonic activity.

The sub-oceanic surroundings may in turn be divided into three provinces (Pantin, 1959):

(a) **The Northwestern Province.** Here are included the Lord Howe Rise (Standard, 1961*a*), the New Caledonia Basin, the Norfolk Island Ridge, and the Norfolk Basin. These have the northwesterly trend of the Northland Peninsula.

(b) **The Kermadec Province**. This includes the Colville Ridge and Havre Trough, the Kermadec Ridge with its steep eastern slope, and the narrow very deep Kermadec Trench extending southsouthwestwards into the Hikurangi Trench and northnortheastwards into the Tonga Trench, stretching in all some 2500 km.

(c) **The Chatham Province**. The Chatham Rise and Bounty Trough with an east-west trend, and the Campbell Plateau.

Since many of the sea-floor lineaments trend in a similar direction to that of the geological structures on the land, it is apparent that both the submarine and terrestrial features have been shaped by related tectonic movements. For this reason, it is thought that the structures of the Northwestern Province and Northland Peninsula, on the one hand, and those of the Chatham Province on the other were formed during the Rangitata Orogeny (Late Jurassic–Early Cretaceous), and those of the Kermadec Province and the "Quaternary Tectonic Zone" during the Kaikoura Orogeny (Late Cainozoic). The markedly greater relief of the latter areas strongly supports this hypothesis.

Geophysical investigations of the nature of dispersive waves have indicated that below much of the New Zealand land area the crust has a typical continental thickness of 30–40 km (Thomson and Evison, 1962). Gravity measurements (Bouguer anomalies) have also shown that major negative anomalies occur in both the main islands (see Figs 12.7 and 12.8). That in the North Island (the Rangitikel–Waiapu Anomaly) is believed to be an expression of the state of activity and inbalance of the nearby Tonga–Kermadec–Hikurangi Trenches. In the South Island, the Alpine Anomaly is believed to be the gravitational expression of the crustal roots of the Southern Alps and the mountains southwest of Blenheim. Approximate isostatic equilibrium appears to have been achieved in this region (Robertson and Reilly, 1958). According to Officer (1955) and Standard (1961a) the crustal thickness of the Tasman Basin which separates Australia and New Zealand is the same as that for the South Pacific Basin to the east of New Zealand, namely 5–10 km, whereas the thickness of the crust in the area of the Lord Howe Rise is 20–25 km.

Igneous Activity

The climax of the Kaikoura orogenic movements in New Zealand was naturally accompanied by considerable magmatic mobility expressed on the surface in volcanism, the effects of which may be seen in many parts of the Dominion, and which continues on a reduced scale at the present time.

FIG. 12.7. Bouguer anomaly map of New Zealand. Anomalies in milligals. (After Reilly, 1965.)

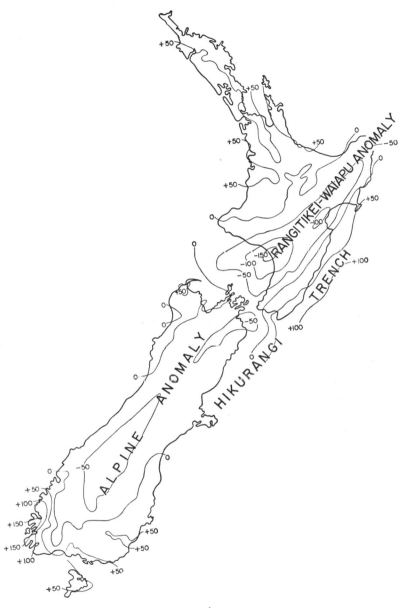

FIG. 12.8. Isostatic anomaly map of New Zealand, based on Airy–Heiskanen System ($T = 30$ km). Anomalies in milligals. (After Reilly, 1965.)

Many major structures and associated fractures that developed at this time are still active.

The Early Quaternary picture of igneous activity is essentially similar to that of the Late Tertiary. In the Northland Peninsula, eruptions of alkaline basaltic material (Horeke Basalts) continued on a reduced scale in the Bay of Islands and Whangarei (Kear and Thompson, 1964), as volcanicity migrated southwards towards the Central Volcanic Belt (Fig. 12.6) which was established at this time. These older Quaternary volcanics (referred by Kear (1959) to the Planeze Stage of erosional development, with some remnants of the original core form) are usually distinguished from a younger sequence (Taheke Basalts) which has well-preserved scoria cones and lava flows filling the valley floors (Kear's Volcano Stage).

Late Pleistocene and Holocene basaltic eruptions both explosive and effusive in type, took place in the Auckland City region, probably beginning about 50,000 yrs. B.P., and the latest, on radiocarbon dating, terminating about 1200 A.D.

In the south Auckland region, the prominent eroded basaltic and andesitic cones of Pirongia and Karioi are remnants of violent eruptions that probably continued from late Pliocene times into the early Pleistocene. The hypersthene andesites of Little Barrier Island and the rhyolites of Mayor Island are probably slightly younger (?middle Pleistocene).

The principal igneous activity of the Pleistocene was, however, concentrated in the Central Volcanic Region which comprises two broad ignimbrite plateaux sloping gently northnortheastwards from Tongariro National Park to the Bay of Plenty (Thompson, 1964). Between these plateaux is a graben which contains the Taupo Volcanic Zone and many andesitic, dacitic and rhyolitic accumulations.

The earliest eruptions in the region appear to have been andesitic in composition, though andesite is still being actively erupted at Mount Ngauruhoe in the Tongariro National Park. Mount Tongariro itself appears to be the oldest volcanic centre in this complex of five major volcanoes, its earliest effusives resting on sediments of early Pleistocene age. Shortly afterwards, there were intense eruptions of ignimbrites, dense welded vitric tuffs, often forming sheets up to 500 m thick, and distributed widely over the Central Volcanic Region. Small rhyolitic and dacitic domes were also formed and thick pumice–breccia deposits accumulated in the Taupo–Reporoa–Wairakei area. Grindley (1960) has correlated these various igneous events with climatic fluctuations recorded in the higher parts of the National Park area which were subjected to glaciation. Lahars (mud-flows) are also prominent components of the volcanic sequence.

The solfataric stages of this igneous episode are still active in the Rotorua–Taupo region, and they are potentially the most important economic resource

Table 12.1. Correlation Table for New Zealand Quaternary Sequence

	EUROPEAN ALTIMETRIC EQUIVALENT	NORTHERN HEMISPHERE GLACIAL EQUIVALENT	SERIES	STAGE	NORTH ISLAND (WANGANUI DISTRICT) (FLEMING, 1953)	NORTH CANTERBURY (GREGG, 1964)	WAIMAKARIRI VALLEY (GAGE, 1958, 1961)	RAKAIA VALLEY (SOONS, 1963)	UPPER CLUTHA VALLEY (McKELLAR, 1960)	NELSON-BULLER (BOWEN, 1964)	WESTLAND (SUGGATE, 1960)
HOLOCENE	FLANDRIAN			POST-GLACIAL	PAPAITI ALLUVIUM / ST JOHN'S TERRACE	SPRINGSTON	Recent	beach-sands, dune-sands	swamp deposits,	ash beds,	alluvium.
UPPER PLEISTOCENE	MONASTIRIAN (c. 20m TERRACE)	WÜRM = WISCONSIN	HAWERA	OTIRA GLACIAL / OTURIAN	RAPANUI FORMATION	ST BERNARD / BURNHAM / WINDWHISTLE / WINTERHOLME / PARIKAWA — WOODLANDS	POULTER (2 Advances) / BLACKW.TER (2 or 3 A.) / OTARAMA — WOODSTOCK	(?)ACHERON;3advances / BAYFIELD (2 Advances) / TUI CREEK — WOODLANDS	HAWEA / ALBERT TOWN / LUGGATE — LINDIS	SPEARGRASS — TOPHOUSE	MOANA LOOPLINE AWATUNA — WAIMEA KARORO
UPPER PLEISTOCENE	TYRRHENIAN (c. 33-35 m TERRACE)	RISS = ILLINOIS	HAWERA	WAIMEA GLACIAL / TERANGIAN	BRUNSWICK FORMATION					MANUKA ALBION	COCKEYE
UPPER PLEISTOCENE	MILAZZIAN (?)	MINDEL ? = KANSAS	HAWERA	WAIMAUNGA GLACIAL / WAIWHEROAN	KAIATEA FORMATION	HORORATA	AVOCA	?	CLYDE	PORIKA	?
UPPER PLEISTOCENE		? GÜNZ ? = NEBRASKAN		PORIKA GLACIAL							
MIDDLE PLEISTOCENE	SICILIAN (c. 100-120m TERRACE)	WAAL	UPPER WANGANUI	CASTLECLIFFIAN (= PUTIKIAN)	SHAKESPEARE GROUP / KAI-IWI GROUP / OKEHU GROUP	KOWAI GRAVELS	BANKS PENINSULA IGNEOUS PHASE	?	?	MOUTERE GRAVELS	OLD MAN GRAVELS
MIDDLE PLEISTOCENE		EBURON	UPPER WANGANUI	OKEHUAN							
EARLY PLEISTOCENE	CALABRIAN (c. 165m TERRACE)	TEGELEN	UPPER WANGANUI	MARAHAUAN	MAXWELL GROUP / NUKUMARU GROUP						
EARLY PLEISTOCENE		BRÖGGEN	UPPER WANGANUI	HAUTAWAN	OKIWA GROUP				MAORI BOTTOM GRAVELS	UPPER PART OF LONGFORD FORMATION	ROSS GLACIALS
UPPER PLIOCENE			LOWER WANGANUI	WAITOTARAN	PAPARANGI GROUP						

CULMINATION OF KAIKOURA OROGENY

of the district. Holes have been drilled for geothermal steam to depths of 1200 m at Wairakei and a 69 MW power station is in full operation, with planned development to 250 MW in the near future.

In western Taranaki, andesitic or dacitic volcanism has occurred since at least Miocene times in the Egmont region, apparently with a southward progression along a line ending in Mount Egmont itself about 1500 A.D.

Quaternary volcanism in the South Island is restricted to two small areas. At Banks Peninsula, the volcanic centres of the Hawaiian Shield type, from which basaltic and trachytic eruptions took place probably in Early and middle Pleistocene times, have been breached by the sea. Harrington and Wood (1958) also consider that the dacitic and andesitic lavas, tuffs, agglomerates and dykes on the Solander Islands are of late Pleistocene age.

References

Amos, A. J. (1958). Algunos Spiriferacea y Terebratulacea (Brach.) del carbonifero superior del "sistema de Tepuel" (provincia de Chubut). *Contrnes cient. Fac. Cienc. exact. fis. nat. Univ. B. Aires, (Geol.)*, **2**, 95–108.

Amos, A. J. (1961). Algunos Chonetacea y Productacea del Carbonifero inferior y superior del Sistema de Tepuel, Provincia de Chubut. *Revta Asoc. geol. argent.* **15**, 6–107.

Amos, B. J., and De Keyser, F. (1964). Mossman, Qd. 1:250,000 Geological Series Sheet E55/1. *Explan. Notes B.M.R.*

A.P.C. (The Australasian Petroleum Company Proprietary) (1961). Geological results of petroleum exploration in western Papua, 1937–1961. *J. geol. Soc. Aust.* **8** (1).

A.O.G. (1964). New names in Queensland stratigraphy. *Australas. Oil Gas J.* **10** (4), 26–27.

Australian Code of Stratigraphic Nomenclature, 4th edn., 1964. *J. geol. Soc. Aust.* **11**, 165–71.

Balme, B. E. (1960a). Notes on some Carboniferous microfloras from Western Australia. *Publs. Dep. Geol. Univ. West. Aust.* **220**, 25–31.

Balme, B. E. (1960b). Some palynological evidence bearing on the development of the *Glossopteris*-flora, in *The Evolution of Living Organisms*, Symp. R. Soc. Vict., pp. 269–80.

Balme, B. E. (1963). Plant microfossils from the Lower Triassic of Western Australia. *Palaeontology* **6**, 12–40.

Balme, B. E. (1964). The palynological record of Australian pre-Tertiary floras. *Ancient Pacific Floras*, Univ. Hawaii Press.

Balme, B. E., and Hassell, C. W. (1962). Upper Devonian spores from the Canning Basin. Western Australia. *Micropaleontology* **8**, 1–28.

Bauer, F. H. (1961). Chronic problems of terrace study in southern Australia. *Z. Geomorph.*, Suppl. **3**, 57–72.

Beavis, F. C. (1960). The Tawonga fault, north-east Victoria. *Proc. R. Soc. Vict.* **72**, 95–100.

Beck, A. C. (1964). Marlborough Sounds 1:250,000 geol. Map Ser. Sheet 14, geol. Surv. N.Z.

Belford, D. J. (1958). Stratigraphy and micropalaeontology of the Upper Cretaceous of Western Australia. *Geol. Rdsch.* **47**, 629–47.

Belford, D. J. (1960). Upper Cretaceous foraminifera from the Toolonga Calcilutite and Gingin Chalk, Western Australia. *Bull. B.M.R.* **57**.

Bennett, E. M. (1965). Lead–zinc–silver and copper deposits of Mount Isa. *8th Commonw. Min. Metall. Congr.* **1**, 233–46.

Benson, W. N. (1913). The geology and petrology of the Great Serpentine Belt of New South Wales. Part 1. *Proc. Linn. Soc. N.S.W.* **38**, 490–517.

Benson, W. N. (1956). Cambrian rocks and fossils in New Zealand (preliminary note). *Int. geol. Congr. 20* **2**(2), 285–88.

Benson, W. N., and Keble, R. A. (1935). The Geology of the regions adjacent to Preservation and Chalky Inlets, Fiordland, New Zealand. Part IV. Stratigraphy and palaeontology of the fossiliferous Ordovician rocks. *Trans. R. Soc. N.Z.* **65**, 244–94.

Berry, W. B. N. (1964). Siluro-Devonian graptolites from Eildon, Victoria. *Aust. J. Sci.* **26**, 223–4.

Berry, W. B. N. (1965). Description and age significance of *M. hercynicus* type monograptids from Eildon, Victoria. *Proc. R. Soc. Vict.* **78**, 1–14.

BINNS, R. A. (1963). Some observations on metamorphism at Broken Hill, N.S.W. *Proc. Australas. Inst. Min. Metall.* **207,** 239–61.

BINNS, R. A. (1964). Zones of progressive regional metamorphism in the Willyama Complex, Broken Hill district, New South Wales. *J. geol. Soc. Aust.* **11,** 283–330.

BIRD, E. C. F. (1964). *Coastal Landforms,* Aust. natn. Univ., Canberra.

BIRD, E. C. F. (1965). A geomorphological study of the Gippsland Lakes. *Publs. Dep. Geogr. Aust. natn. Univ. Canberra* G/1.

BLACKBURN, G. (1962). Stranded coastal dunes in north-western Victoria. *Aust. J. Sci.* **24,** 388–9.

BOCK, P. E. and GLENIE, R. C. (1965). Late Cretaceous and Tertiary depositional cycles in south-western Victoria. *Proc. R. Soc. Vict.* **79,** 153–63.

BONYTHON, C. W. (1956). The salt of Lake Eyre—its occurrence in Madigan Gulf and its possible origin. *Trans. R. Soc. S. Aust.* **79,** 66–92.

BOOKER, F. W. (1960). Studies in Permian sedimentation in the Sydney Basin. *Tech. Rep. Dep. Mines N.S.W.* **5,** 11–62.

BOREHAM, A. U. E. (1963). Some problems concerning the application of the Lower Nuku-maruan (Hautawan) Substage (Pleistocene, New Zealand). *N.Z. J. Geol. Geophys.* **6,** 3–27.

BOUCOT, A. J., CASTER, K. E., IVES, D., and TALENT, J. A. (1963). Relationships of a new Lower Devonian Terebratuloid (Brachiopoda) from Antarctica. *Bull. Am. Paleont.* **46** (207), 81–151.

BOUTAKOFF, N. (1963). The geology and geomorphology of the Portland area. *Mem. geol. Surv. Vict.* **22,** 1–172.

BOWEN, F. E. (1964). Buller 1:250,000 geol. Map Ser. Sheet 15, geol. Surv. N.Z.

BOWLER, J. M. (1963). Tertiary stratigraphy and sedimentation in the Geelong–Maude area, Victoria. *Proc. R. Soc. Vict.* **76,** 69–137.

BROTHERS, R. N. (1954). The relative Pleistocene chronology of the South Kaipara District, New Zealand. *Trans. R. Soc. N.Z.* **82,** 677–94.

BROWN, D. A. (1957). Fossil cheilostomatous Polyzoa from south-west Victoria. *Mem. geol. Surv. Vict.* **20.**

BROWN, D. A., CAMPBELL, K. S. W., and ROBERTS, J. (1965). A Viséan cephalopod fauna from New South Wales. *Palaeontology* **7,** 682–94.

BROWN, I. A. (1933). The Geology of the South Coast of New South Wales, with special reference to the origin and relationships of the igneous rocks. *Proc. Linn. Soc. N.S.W.* **53,** 334–62.

BROWNE, I. A. (1958). Stratigraphy and structure of the Devonian rocks of the Taemas and Cavan areas, Murrumbidgee River, south of Yass, N.S.W. *J. Proc. R. Soc. N.S.W.* **92,** 115–28.

BROWNE, W. R. (1945). An attempted post-Tertiary chronology for Australia. *Proc. Linn. Soc. N.S.W.* 70, 5–24.

BROWNE, W. R. (1957). Pleistocene glaciation in the Commonwealth of Australia. *J. Glaciol.* **3** (22), 111–15.

BRUNNSCHWEILER, R. O. (1960). Marine fossils from the Upper Jurassic and the Lower Cretaceous of Dampier Peninsula, Western Australia. *Bull. B.M.R.* **59.**

BRUNNSCHWEILER, R. O. (1963). A review of the sequence of *Buchia* species in the Jurassic of Australasia. *Proc. R. Soc. Vict.* **76,** 163–8.

BRYAN, W. H., and JONES, O. A. (1954). Contributions to the geology of Brisbane. No. 2. The structural history of the Brisbane Metamorphics. *Proc. R. Soc. Qd.* **65,** 25–50.

BUTLER, B. E. (1956). Parna, an aeolian clay. *Aust. J. Sci.,* **18,** 145–51.

BUTLER, B. E. (1959). Periodic phenomena in landscapes as a basis for soil studies. *Soil Publ. C.S.I.R.O. Aust.* **14.**

BUTLER, B. E. (1964). The place of soils in studies of Quaternary chronology in southern Australia. *Revue Géomorph. dyn.* **14,** 160–5.

BUTLER, B. E. (1966). Soil periodicity in relation to land-form development in south eastern Australia, *in* Jennings, J. N. and Mabbutt, J. A. (Eds.), *Landform Studies from Australia and New Guinea,* Aust. natn. Univ., Canberra.

CAMPANA, B., and HORWITZ, R. (1956). The Kanmantoo Group of South Australia considered as a transgression sequence. *Aust. J. Sci.* **18**, 128–9.

CAMPANA, B., HUGHES, F. E., BURNS, W. G., WHITCHER, I. G., and MUCENIEKAS, E., (1964). Discovery of the Hamersley iron deposits. *Proc. Australas. Inst. Min. Metall.* **210**, 1–30.

CAMPANA, B., and KING, D. (1963). Palaeozoic tectonism, sedimentation and mineralization in West Tasmania. *J. geol. Soc. Aust.* **10**, 1–53.

CAMPANA, B., and WILSON, R. B. (1955). Tillites and related glacial topography of South Australia. *Eclog. geol. Helv.* **48**, 1–30.

CAMPBELL, J. D. (1965a). New Zealand Triassic saurians. *N.Z. J. Geol. Geophys.* **8**, 505–09.

CAMPBELL, J. D. (1965b). New Species of Brachiopoda from the Torlesse Group of Kaiwara Valley, North Canterbury. *Trans. R. Soc. N.Z. (Geol.)* **3**, 95–97.

CAMPBELL, J. D., and WARREN, G. (1965). Fossil Localities of the Torlesse Group in the South Island. *Trans. R. Soc. N.Z. (Geol.)* **3**, 99–137.

CAMPBELL, K. S. W. (1957). A Lower Carboniferous brachiopod-coral fauna from New South Wales. *J. Paleont.* **31**, 34–98.

CAMPBELL, K. S. W., and ENGEL, B. A. (1963). The faunas of the Tournaisian Tulcumba Sandstone and its members in the Werrie and Belvue Synclines, New South Wales. *J. geol. Soc. Aust.* **10**, 55–122.

CAREY, S. W., and BROWNE, W. R. (1938). Review of the Carboniferous stratigraphy, tectonics and palaeogeography of New South Wales and Queensland. *J. Proc. R. Soc. N.S.W.* **71**, 591–614.

CARRIGY, M. A. (1956). Organic sedimentation in Warnbro Sound, Western Australia, *J. sedim. Petrol.* **26**, 228–39.

CARRIGY, M. A., and FAIRBRIDGE, R. W. (1954). Recent sedimentation, physiography and structure of the continental shelves of Western Australia. *J. Proc. R. Soc. West. Aust.* **38**, 65–95.

CARTER, A. N. (1958a). Tertiary foraminifera from the Aire district, Victoria. *Bull. geol. Surv. Vict.* **55**, 1–76.

CARTER, A. N. (1958b). Pelagic foraminifera in the Tertiary of Victoria. *Geol. Mag.* **95**, 297–304.

CARTER, A. N. (1959). Guide foraminifera of the Tertiary stages in Victoria. *Min. geol. J.* **6** (3), 2–7.

CARTER, A. N. (1964). Tertiary foraminifera from Gippsland, Victoria and their stratigraphical significance. *Mem. geol. Surv. Vict.* **23**.

CARTER, E. K., BROOKS, J. H., and WALKER, K. R. (1961). The Precambrian mineral belt of north-western Queensland. *Bull. B.M.R.* **51**.

CASEY, J. N. and TOMLINSON, J. G. (1956). Cambrian geology of the Huckitta–Marqua region, Northern Territory. *Int. geol. Congr. 20* **2** (2), 55–74.

CHALLIS, G. A. (1965). The Origin of New Zealand Ultramafic intrusions. *J. Petrology* **6**, 322–64.

CHAPPELL, B. W. (1961). The stratigraphy and structural geology of the Manilla–Moore Creek district, N.S.W. *J. Proc. R. Soc. N.S.W.* **95**, 63–75.

CHURCHWARD, H. M. (1963). Soil studies at Swan Hill, Victoria, Australia. IV. Ground-surface history and its expression in the array of soils. *Aust. J. Soil Res.* **1**, 242–55.

CLARK, R. H., DIBBLE, R. R., FYFE, H. E., LENSEN, G. J., and SUGGATE, R. P. (1965). Tectonic and earthquake risk zoning. *Trans. R. Soc. N.Z. (General)* **1** (10), 113–26.

CLARKE, E. DE C., PHILLIPS, H. T., and PRIDER, R. T. (1954). The Pre-Cambrian geology of part of the south coast of Western Australia. *J. Proc. R. Soc. West. Aust.* **38**, 1–64.

COALDRAKE, J. E. (1961). The Ecosystem of the coastal lowlands ("Wallum") of Southern Queensland. *Bull. Commonw. scient. ind. Res. Org.* **283**.

COATS, R. P. (1965). Tent Hill Formation correlations—Port Augusta and Lake Torrens areas. *Q. Notes geol. Surv. S. Aust.* **16**, 9–11.

COCHRANE, G. W., and SAMSON, H. R. (1947). The Geology of the Nowa Nowa, South Buchan area, Victoria. *Proc. R. Soc. Vict.* **60**, 93–122.

COCKBAIN, A. E. (1965). Note on Devonian stromatoporoids from Reefton. *N.Z. J. Geol. Geophys.* **8**, 745–51.

COLE, W. S. (1962). *Asterocyclina* from New Zealand and the Chatham Islands. *Bull. Am. Paleont.* **44** (203), 339–57.

COLEMAN, P. J. (1957). Permian Productacea of Western Australia. *Bull. B.M.R.* **40**.

COMPSTON, W., CRAWFORD, A. R., and BOFINGER, V. M. (1966). A radiometric estimate of the duration of sedimentation in the Adelaide geosyncline, South Australia. *J. geol. Soc. Aust.* **13**, 229–76.

COMPSTON, W., and PIDGEON, R. T. (1962). Rubidium–strontium dating of shales by the total-rock method. *J. geophys. Res.* **67**, 3493–3502.

CONOLLY, J. R. (1963). Upper Devonian stratigraphy and sedimentation in the Wellington–Molong district. N.S.W. *J. Proc. R. Soc. N.S.W.* **96**, 73–106.

CONOLLY, J. R. (1965). The stratigraphy of the Hervey Group in central New South Wales. *J. Proc. R. Soc. N.S.W.* **98**, 37–83.

COOKSON, I. C. (1958). Fossil pollen grains of *Nothofagus* from Australia. *Proc. R. Soc. Vict.* **71**, 25–30.

COOKSON, I. C., and EISENACK, A. (1958). Microplankton from Australia and New Guinea Upper Mesozoic sediments. *Proc. R. Soc. Vict.* **70**, 19–79.

COOKSON, I. C., and EISENACK, A. (1960). Upper Mesozoic microplankton from Australia and New Guinea. *Palaeontology* **2**, 243–61.

COOKSON, I. C., and EISENACK, A. (1962). Additional microplankton from Australian Cretaceous sediments. *Micropaleontology* **8**, 485–507.

COOKSON, I. C., and PIKE, K. M. (1954). Some dicotyledonous pollen types from Cainozoic deposits in the Australian region. *Aust. J. Bot.* **2**, 197–219.

COOMBS, D. S. (1954). The nature and alteration of some triassic sediments from Southland, New Zealand. *Trans. R. Soc. N.Z.* **82**, 65–109.

COOMBS, D. S., ELLIS, A. J., FYFE, W. S., and TAYLOR, A. M. (1959). The Zeolite Facies, with comments on the interpretation of Hydrothermal Syntheses. *Geochim. cosmochim. Acta* **17**, 53–107.

COOPER, J. A., RICHARDS, J. R., and WEBB, A. W. (1963). Some potassium–argon ages in New England, New South Wales. *J. geol. Soc. Aust.* **10**, 313–16.

COOPER, R. A. (1965). Lower Paleozoic Rocks between Upper Takaka and Riwaka, north-west Nelson. *N.Z. Jl. Geol. Geophys.* **8**, 49–61.

COTTON, C. A. (1963). The question of high Pleistocene shorelines. *Trans. R. Soc. N.Z. (Geol.)* **2**, 51–62.

COUPER, R. A. (1960). New Zealand Mesozoic and Cainozoic plant microfossils. *Palaeont. Bull. Wellington* **32**.

COX, L. R. (1961). The Molluscan fauna and probable Lower Cretaceous age of the Nanutarra Formation of Western Australia. *Bull. B.M.R.* **61**.

CRAWFORD, A. R. (1963). The Wooltana Volcanic Belt, South Australia. *Trans. R. Soc. S. Aust.* **87**, 123–54.

CRESPIN, IRENE (1943). Conodonts from Waterhouse Range, Central Australia. *Trans. R. Soc. S. Aust.* **67**, 231–2.

CRESPIN, IRENE (1950). Australian Tertiary microfaunas and their relationships to assemblages elsewhere in the Pacific region. *J. Paleont.* **24**, 421–29.

CRESPIN, IRENE (1958). Permian foraminifera of Australia. *Bull. B.M.R.* **48**.

CRESPIN, IRENE (1963). Lower Cretaceous arenaceous foraminifera of Australia. *Bull. B.M.R.* **66**.

CROCKER, R. L. (1959). Past climatic fluctuations and their influence upon Australian vegetation, in *Biogeography and Ecology in Australia*, The Hague, pp. 283–90.

CROCKFORD, JOAN (1957). Permian Bryozoa from the Fitzroy Basin, Western Australia. *Bull. B.M.R.* **34**.

CROOK, K. A. W. (1957). Cross-stratification and other sedimentary features of the Narrabeen Group. *Proc. Linn. Soc. N.S.W.* **82**, 157–66.

CROOK, K. A. W. (1959). Lithotopic relationships in deep-water troughs. *J. sedim. Petrol.* **29**, 336–42.

CROOK, K. A. W. (1960). Classification of arenites. *Am. J. Sci.* **258**, 419–28.

CROOK, K. A. W. (1961a). Stratigraphy of the Tamworth Group (Lower and Middle Devonian), Tamworth–Nundle district, N.S.W. *J. Proc. R. Soc. N.S.W.* **94**, 173–88.

CROOK, K. A. W. (1961b). Stratigraphy of the Parry Group (Upper Devonian–Lower Carboniferous), Tamworth–Nundle district, N.S.W. *J. Proc. R. Soc. N.S.W.* **94**, 189–207.

CROOK, K. A. W. (1964). Depositional environments and provenance of Devonian and Carboniferous sediments in the Tamworth Trough, N.S.W. *J. Proc. R. Soc. N.S.W.* **97**, 41–53.

DAILY, B. (1956). The Cambrian in South Australia. *Int. geol. Congr.* **20 2** (2), 91–147.

DAILY, B. (1963). The fossiliferous Cambrian succession on Fleurieu Peninsula, South Australia. *Rec. S. Aust. Mus.* **14**, 579–601.

DALGARNO, C. R. (1964). Report on the Lower Cambrian stratigraphy of the Flinders Ranges, South Australia. *Trans. R. Soc. S. Aust.* **88**, 129–44.

DANIELS, J. L. (1966). The Proterozoic geology of the north-west division of Western Australia. *Proc. Australas. Inst. Min. Metall.* **219**, 17–26.

DAVID, T. W. E. (1922). Occurrence of remains of small crustacea in the Proterozoic (?) or Lower Cambrian (?) rocks of Reynella, near Adelaide. *Trans. R. Soc. S. Aust.* **46**, 6–8.

DAVID, T. W. E. (1950). *The Geology of the Commonwealth of Australia*, Vol. I (Ed. W. R. Browne), Arnold, London.

DAVIES, J. L. (1959). High level erosion surfaces and landscape development in Tasmania. *Aust. Geogr.* **7**, 193–203.

DAY, R. W. (1964). Stratigraphy of the Roma–Wallumbilla area. *Publs. geol. Surv. Qd.* **318**.

DE JERSEY, N. J. (1964). Triassic spores and pollen grains from the Bundamba Group. *Publs. geol. Surv. Qd.* **321**.

DE JERSEY, N. J., and PATEN, R. J. (1964). Jurassic spores and pollen grains from the Surat Basin. *Publs. geol. Surv. Qd.* **322**.

DE KEYSER, F. (1963). The Palmerville Fault—a "fundamental" structure in North Queensland. *J. geol. Soc. Aust.* **10**, 273–8.

DE KEYSER, F. (1964). Innisfail, Qd. 1:250,000 Geological Series Sheet 3E/55–6. *Explan. Notes B.M.R.*

DE KEYSER, F. (1965). The Barnard Metamorphics and their relation to the Barron River Metamorphics and the Hodgkinson Formation, North Queensland. *J. geol. Soc. Aust.* **12**, 91–103.

DE LA HUNTY, E. (1963). Balfour Downs, West Aust. 1:250,000 Geological Series Sheet SF/51–9. *Explan. Notes geol. Surv. West. Aust.*

DENMEAD, A. K. (1964). Note on marine macrofossils with Triassic affinities from the Maryborough Basin, Queensland. *Aust. J. Sci.* **27**, 117.

DERRINGTON, S. S., CRESPIN, I., MORGAN, W. R., BOCK, P. E. and HOUSTON, B. R. (1960). H.B.R. No. 1 Bore Wreck Island, Queensland, of Humber Barrier Reef Oils Pty. Ltd. *Publs. Petrol. Search Subsidy Acts Aust.* **4**.

DETTMAN, MARY E. (1963). Upper Mesozoic microfloras from south-eastern Australia. *Proc. R. Soc. Vict.* **77**, 1–131.

DICKINS, J. M. (1963). Permian pelecypods and gastropods from Western Australia. *Bull. B.M.R.* **63**, 1–203.

DICKINS, J. M., and McTAVISH, B. A. (1963). Lower Triassic marine fossils from the Beagle Ridge (BMR 10) Bore, Perth Basin, Western Australia. *J. geol. Soc. Aust.* **10**, 123–40.

DICKINS, J. M., and THOMAS, G. A. (1959). The marine fauna of the Lyons Group and the Carrandibby Formation of the Carnarvon Basin, Western Australia. *Rep. B.M.R.* **38**, 65–96.

DICKINS, J. M., MALONE, E. J., and JENSEN, A. R. (1964). Subdivision and correlation of the Permian Middle Bowen Beds, Bowen Basin, Queensland. *Rep. B.M.R.* **70**.

DICKINSON, S. B. (1942). The structural control of ore deposition in some South Australian copper fields. *Bull. geol. Surv. S. Aust.* **20.**

DOUGLAS, J. G. (1962). Microplankton of the Deflandreidae group in western district sediments. *Min. geol. J.* **6,** (4), 17–33.

DOW, D. B. (1965). Evidence of a Late Precambrian Glaciation in the Kimberley Region of Western Australia. *Geol. Mag.* **102,** 407–14.

DRISCOLL, E. G. (1960). Geology of the Mundubbera District. *Pap. Dep. Geol. Univ. Qd.* **5** (5), 1–27.

DULHUNTY, J. A. (1964). Our Permian heritage in central eastern New South Wales. *J. Proc. R. Soc. N.S.W.* **97,** 145–55.

DULHUNTY, J. A. (1965). The Mesozoic age of the Garrawilla Lavas in the Coonabarabran–Gunnedah District. *J. Proc. R. Soc. N.S.W.* **98,** 105–9.

DULHUNTY, J. A., and PACKHAM, G. H. (1962). Notes on Permian sediments in the Mudgee district, N.S.W. *J. Proc. R. Soc. N.S.W.* **95,** 161–6.

DUNN, P. R. (1963). Hodgson Downs 1:250,000 Geological Series Sheet SD53–14. *Explan. Notes B.M.R.*

DUNN, P. R. (1964). Triact Spicules in Proterozoic rocks of the Northern Territory of Australia. *J. geol. Soc. Aust.* **11,** 195–7.

DUNN, P. R., PLUMB, K. A., and ROBERTS, H. G. (1966). A proposal for time-stratigraphic sub-division of the Australian Precambrian. *J. geol. Soc. Aust.* **13,** 593–608.

DUNN, P. R., SMITH, J. W. and ROBERTS, H. G. (in prep.). Geology of the Carpentaria Proterozoic Province, Northern Territory. Part 1. Roper River to the Queensland border. *Bull. B.M.R.*

DURY, G. H. (1964). Australian Geochronology: Checklist 1. *Aust. J. Sci.* **27,** 103–9.

EAMES, F. E., BANNER, F. T., BLOW, W. H., and CLARKE, W. J. (1964). New Zealand mid-Tertiary stratigraphical correlation. *Nature, Lond.* **203** (4941), 180–2.

EDGELL, H. S. (1964*a*). Precambrian fossils from the Hamersley Range, Western Australia, and their use in stratigraphic correlation. *J. geol. Soc. Aust.* **11,** 235–61.

EDGELL, H. S. (1964*b*). The correlative value of microplankton in the Cretaceous of the Perth Basin, W. A. *Annu. Rep. geol. Surv. West. Aust.* (1963), 50–55.

EDWARDS, A. B. (1938). The Tertiary volcanic rocks of central Victoria. *Q. J. geol. Soc. London.* **94,** 243–320.

EDWARDS, A. B. (1942). Differentiation of the dolerites of Tasmania. I and II. *J. Geol.* **50,** 451–610.

EDWARDS, A. B. (1956). The Rhyolite–Dacite–Granodiorite association of the Dandenong Ranges. *Proc. R. Soc. Vict.* **68,** 111–49.

EDWARDS, A. B., and CLARKE, E. DE C. (1940). Some Cambrian basalts from the East Kimberley, Western Australia. *J. Proc. R. Soc. West. Aust.* **26,** 77–94.

ENGEL, B. A. (1962). Geology of the Bulahdelah–Port Stephens district. N.S.W. *J. Proc. R. Soc. N.S.W.* **95,** 197–215.

EVANS, H. J. (1965). Bauxite deposits of Weipa. *8th Commonw. Min. Metall. Congr.* **1,** 396–401.

EVANS, P. R. (1963). The application of palynology to stratigraphy in Australia. *ECAFE Min. Resour. Dev. Ser.* **18** (1), 285–90.

EVERNDEN, J. F., and RICHARDS, J. R. (1962). Potassium–Argon ages in eastern Australia. *J. geol. Soc. Aust.* **9,** 1–49.

FAIRBRIDGE, R. W. (1950). Recent and Pleistocene coral reefs of Australia. *J. Geol.* **58,** 330–401.

FAIRBRIDGE, R. W. (1961). Eustatic changes in sea level. *Physics Chem. Earth* **4,** 99–185.

FAIRBRIDGE, R. W., and TEICHERT, C. (1953). Soil horizons and marine bands in the coastal limestones of Western Australia. *J. Proc. R. Soc. N.S.W.* **86,** 68–87.

FELL, H. B. (1954). Tertiary and Recent Echinoidea of New Zealand: Cidaridae. *Palaeont. Bull. Wellington* **23**.

FINLAY, H. J., and MARWICK, J. (1940). The divisions of the Upper Cretaceous and Tertiary in New Zealand. *Trans. R. Soc. N.Z.* **70**, 77–135.

FINLAY, H. J., and MARWICK, J. (1947). New divisions of the New Zealand Upper Cretaceous and Tertiary. *N.Z. J. Sci. Technol.* **28B**, 228–36.

FINUCANE, K. J. (1964). The blue asbestos deposits of the Hamersley Ranges. *Proc. Australas. Inst. Min. Metall.* **211**, 75–84.

FIRMAN, J. B. (1965). Late Cainozoic lacustrine deposits in the Murray Basin, South Australia. *Q. Notes geol. Surv. S. Aust.* **16**, 1–4.

FLEMING, C. A. (1945). Some New Zealand Tertiary cephalopods. *Trans. R. Soc. N.Z.* **74**, 411–18.

FLEMING, C. A. (1953). The Geology of Wanganui Subdivision. *Bull. geol. Surv. N.Z.* **52**.

FLEMING, C. A. (1959a). Wanganui 1:250,000 geol. Map Ser. Sheet 10, geol. Surv. N.Z.

FLEMING, C. A. (1959b). *Geology of New Zealand* (translated from F. C. von Hochstetter), Gov. Printer, Wellington.

FLEMING, C. A. (Editor) (1959c). *Lexique stratigraphique international*, Vol. VI, Océanie, Fasc. 4, New Zealand, C.N.R.S., Paris.

FLEMING, C. A. (1962). New Zealand biogeography: a paleontologist's approach. *Tuatara* **10**, 53–108.

FLEMING, C. A. (1963). Paleontology and southern biogeography. *Proc. Pacif. Sci. Congr.* **10**, 369–85.

FLEMING, C. A. (1964). History of the bivalve family Trigoniidae in the south-west Pacific. The geological background to an Australian "living fossil". *Aust. J. Sci.* **26**, 196–204.

FLEMING, C. A., and KEAR, D. (1960). The Jurassic sequence at Kawhia Harbour, New Zealand. *Bull. geol. Surv. N.Z.* **67**.

FLETCHER, H. O. (1964). New Linguloid shells from Lower Ordovician and Middle Palaeozoic rocks of New South Wales. *Rec. Aust. Mus.* **26**, 283–94.

FORBES, B. G. (1960). Magnesite of the Adelaide system: petrography and descriptive stratigraphy. *Trans. R. Soc. S. Aust.* **83**, 1–10.

FORBES, B. G. (1961). Magnesite of the Adelaide system: a discussion of its origin. *Trans. R. Soc. S. Aust.* **85**, 217–22.

FORMAN, D. J. (1965). Regional geology of the south-west margin, Amadeus Basin, Central Australia. *Rep. B.M.R.* **87**.

FORMAN, D. J., MILLIGAN, E. N., and McCARTHY, W. R. (1965). Regional geology and structure of the north-east margin, Amadeus Basin, Northern Territory. Part I. *Rep. B.M.R.* **103**.

FREEMAN, R. N. (1963). Highlights of recent developments in the central and western areas of the Great Artesian Basin. *J. Aust. Petrol. Explor. Ass.* (1963) 29–34.

FREEMAN, R. N. (1964). Oil exploration in the western Great Artesian Basin. *Proc. Australas. Inst. Min. Metall.* **211**, 85–114.

FYFE, W. S., TURNER, F. J., and VERHOOGEN, J. (1958). Metamorphic reactions and metamorphic facies. *Mem. geol. Soc. Am.* **73**.

GAGE, M. (1958). Late Pleistocene glaciations of the Waimakariri Valley, Canterbury, New Zealand. *N.Z. J. Geol. Geophys.* **1**, 123–55.

GAGE, M. (1961). New Zealand glaciations and the duration of the Pleistocene. *J. Glaciol.* **3**, 940–3.

GAGE, M. (1965). Some characteristics of Pleistocene cold climates in New Zealand. *Trans. R. Soc. N.Z.* (*Geol.*) **3** (2), 11–21.

GAGE, M., and SUGGATE, R. P. (1958). Glacial chronology of the New Zealand Pleistocene. *Bull. geol. Soc. Am.* **69**, 589–98.

GALLOWAY, R. W. (1963). Glaciation in the Snowy Mountains; a re-appraisal. *Proc. Linn· Soc. N.S.W.* **88**, 180–98.

GALLOWAY, R. W. (1965). Late Quaternary climates in Australia. *J. Geol.* **73**, 603–18.

GEMUTS, I. (1965). Regional metamorphism in the Lamboo Complex, East Kimberley area. *Annu. Rep. geol. Surv. West. Aust.* (1964), 36–41.

GENTILLI, J. (1961). Quaternary climates of the Australian region. *Ann. N.Y. Acad. Sci.* **95**, 465–501.

GILL, E. D. (1949). Devonian fossils from Sandys Creek, Gippsland, Victoria. *Mem. natn. Mus. Vict.* **16**, 91–115.

GILL, E. D. (1950). Preliminary account of the palaeontology and palaeoecology of the Eldon Group formations of the Zeehan area, Tasmania. *Pap. Proc. R. Soc. Tasm.* (1949), 231–58.

GILL, E. D. (1951). Two new brachiopod genera from Devonian rocks in Victoria. *Mem. natn. Mus. Vict.* **17**, 187–205.

GILL, E. D. (1952). Palaeogeography of the Australian–New Zealand region in Lower Devonian time. *Trans. R. Soc. N.Z.* **80**, 171–85.

GILL, E. D. (1955). Radiocarbon dates for Australian archaeological and geological samples. *Aust. J. Sci.* **18**, 49–52.

GILL, E. D. (1957). The Pliocene–Pleistocene boundary in Australia. *Aust. J. Sci.* **20**, 86.

GILL, E. D. (1964a). Quaternary shorelines in Australia. *Aust. J. Sci.* **26**, 388–91.

GILL, E. D. (1964b). Rocks contiguous with the Basaltic cuirass of western Victoria. *Proc. R. Soc. Vict.* **77**, 331–55.

GILL, E. D., and CASTER, K. E. (1960). Carpoid echinoderms from the Silurian and Devonian of Australia. *Bull. Am. Paleont.* **41**, (185), 1–71.

GILL, E. D., and DARRAGH, T. A. (1963). Evolution of the Zenathiinae (Mactridae : Lamellibranchiata). *Proc. R. Soc. Vict.* **77**, 177–90.

GLAESSNER, M. F. (1960). The fossil decapod Crustacea of New Zealand and the evolution of the order Decapoda. *Paleont. Bull. Wellington* **31**.

GLAESSNER, M. F. (1962). Pre-Cambrian fossils. *Biol. Rev.* **37**, 467–94.

GLAESSNER, M. F., and DAILY, B. (1959). The geology and late Precambrian fauna of the Ediacara Fossil Reserve. *Rec. S. Aust. Mus.* **13**, 369–401.

GLAESSNER, M. F., and PARKIN, L. W. (Editors) (1958). The geology of South Australia. *J. geol. Soc. Aust.* **5** (2), 1–153.

GLENISTER, B. F. (1958). Upper Devonian ammonoids from the *Manticoceras* Zone, Fitzroy Basin, Western Australia. *J. Paleont.* **32**, 58–96.

GLENISTER, B. F. (1960). Carboniferous conodonts and ammonoids from northwestern Australia. *C. r. Congr. Int. Strat. Géol. Carb.* (1958) **1**, 213–17.

GLENISTER, B. F., and FURNISH, W. M. (1961). The Permian ammonoids of Australia. *J. Paleont.* **35**, 673–736.

GLENISTER B. F., and GLENISTER, A. T. (1958). Discovery of subsurface Ordovician strata, Broome Area, Western Australia. *Aust. J. Sci.* **20**, 183.

GLENISTER, B. F., MILLER, A. K., and FURNISH, W. M. (1956). Upper Cretaceous and Early Tertiary nautiloids from Western Australia. *J. Paleont.* **30**, 492–503.

GLOVER, J. E. (1960). A contribution to the petrology of the Yandanooka Group. *J. Proc. R. Soc. West. Aust.* **43**, 97–103.

GRANT-TAYLOR, T. L., and RAFTER, T. A. (1962). New Zealand radiocarbon age measurements. 5. *N.Z. J. Geol. Geophys.* **5**, 331–59.

GREEN, D. H. (1959). Geology of the Beaconsfield District, including the Anderson's Creek ultrabasic complex. *Rec. Queen Vict. Mus.* **10**, 1–25.

GREGG, D. R. (1964). Hurunui 1:250,000 geol. Map Ser. Sheet 18, geol. Surv. N.Z.

GRINDLEY, G. W. (1960). Taupo 1:250,000 geol. Map Ser. Sheet 8, geol. Surv. N.Z.

GRINDLEY, G. W. (1961a). Golden Bay 1:250,000 geol. Map Ser. Sheet 13, geol. Surv. N.Z.

GRINDLEY, G. W. (1961b). Mesozoic orogenies in New Zealand. *Proc. Pacif. Sci. Congr. 9, Geol. Geophys.* **12**, 71–75.

GRINDLEY, G. W., HARRINGTON, H. J., and WOOD, B. L. (1959). The geological map of New Zealand 1:2,000,000. *Bull. geol. Surv. N.Z.* **66**.

GRINDLEY, G. W., and WODZICKI, A. (1960). Base metal and gold–silver mineralisation on the south-east side of the Aqrere Valley, north-west Nelson. *N.Z. J. Geol. Geophys.* **3**, 585–92.

GUPPY, D. J., LINDNER, A. W., RATTIGAN, J. H., and CASEY, J. N. (1958). The geology of the Fitzroy Basin, Western Australia. *Bull. B.M.R.* **36**.

GUSTAFSON, J. K., BURRELL, H. C., and GARRETTY, M. D. (1950). Geology of the Broken Hill ore deposit, Broken Hill, N.S.W., Australia. *Bull. geol. Soc. Am.* **61**, 1369–1438.

HALL, W. D. M. (1963). The Clarence Series at Coverham, Clarence Valley. *N.Z. J. Geol. Geophys.* **6**, 28–37.

HARRINGTON, H. J., and WOOD, B. L. (1958). Quaternary andesitic volcanism at the Solander Islands. *N.Z. J. Geol. Geophys.* **1**, 419–31.

HARRIS, W. J., and THOMAS, D. E. (1954). Notes on the geology of the Wellington–Macalister area. *Min. geol. J.* **5** (3), 34–49.

HARRIS, W. K. (1964). Mesozoic sediments of the Polda Basin, Eyre Peninsula. *Q. Notes geol. Surv. S. Aust.* **12**, 6–7.

HEALY, J., *et al.* (1964). Rotorua 1:250,000 geol. Map Ser. Sheet 5, geol. Surv. N.Z.

HILL, D. (1954). Coral faunas from the Silurian of New South Wales and the Devonian of Western Australia. *Bull. B.M.R.* **23**.

HILL, D. (1955). Ordovician corals from Ida Bay, Queenstown and Zeehan, Tasmania. *Pap. Proc. R. Soc. Tasm.* **89**, 237–54.

HILL, D. (1956). Palaeozoic corals from New Zealand. Part I. The Devonian corals of Reefton, New Zealand. *Paleont. Bull. Wellington* **25**, 5–14.

HILL, D. (1957a). Ordovician corals from New South Wales. *J. Proc. R. Soc. N.S.W.* **91**, 97–107.

HILL, D. (1957b). Explanatory notes on the Springsure 4-mile geological sheet. *Explan. Notes B.M.R.* Sheet G/55-3.

HILL, D. (1958). Distribution and sequence of Silurian coral faunas. *J. Proc. R. Soc. N.S.W.* **92**, 151–73.

HILL, D., and DENMEAD, A. K. (Editors) (1960). The geology of Queensland. *J. geol. Soc. Aust.* **7**, 1–474.

HILLS, E. S. (1939). The physiography of north-western Victoria. *Proc. R. Soc. Vict.* **51**, 297–323.

HILLS, E. S. (1958a). A brief review of Australian fossil vertebrates, in *Studies on Fossil Vertebrates*, pp. 86–107, London.

HILLS, E. S. (1958b). Record of *Bothriolepis* and *Phyllolepis* (upper Devonian) from the Northern Territory of Australia. *J. Proc. R. Soc. N.S.W.* **92**, 174–5.

HILLS, E. S. (1959). Cauldron subsidences, granitic rocks, and crustal fracturing in S.E. Australia. *Geol. Rdsch.* **47**, 543–61.

HILLS, E. S. (1961). Morphotectonics and the geomorphological sciences with special reference to Australia. *Q. J. geol. Soc. Lond.* **117**, 77–89.

HILLS, E. S., and THOMAS, D. E. (1954). Turbidity currents and the graptolitic facies in Victoria. *J. geol. Soc. Aust.* **1**, 119–33.

HOCKING, J. B., and TAYLOR, D. J. (1964). The initial marine transgression in the Gippsland Basin, Victoria. *J. Aust. Petrol. Explor. Ass.* (1964), 125–32.

HORNIBROOK, N. DE B. (1958). New Zealand Upper Cretaceous and Tertiary foraminiferal zones and some overseas correlations. *Micropaleontology* **4**, 25–38.

HORNIBROOK, N. DE B., and HARRINGTON, H. J. (1960). The status of the Wangaloan Stage. *N.Z. J. Sci. Technol.* **38B**, 655–70.

HORWITZ, R. C. (1962). Some features of the lower part of the Marinoan Series of the Adelaide System. *Aust. J. Sci.* **24**, 355–6.

HORWITZ, R. C., and SOFOULIS, J. (1963). The stratigraphic sequence in the Warburton Range, Eastern Division. *Annu. Rep. geol. Surv. West. Aust.* (1962), 37.

HORWITZ, R. C., THOMSON, B. P., and WEBB, B. P. (1959). The Cambrian–Precambrian boundary in the eastern Mt. Lofty Ranges region: South Australia. *Trans. R. Soc. S. Aust.* **82**, 205–18.

HOWCHIN, W. (1929). *The Geology of South Australia*, 2nd edn. Gov. Printer, Adelaide.

HOWCHIN, W. (1935). Notes on the geological sections obtained by several borings situated on the plain between Adelaide and Gulf St. Vincent. *Trans. R. Soc. S. Aust.* **59**, 68–102.

HOYLING, N. H. V., and STEWART, H. W. J. (1964). Well Completion Report. A. P. Abercorn No. 1, Queensland. Amalgamated Petroleum Exploration Pty. Ltd. Rep. Petrol. Search Subsidy Acts Aust. (unpublished).

HUGHES, F. E., and MUNRO, D. L. (1965). Uranium ore deposit at Mary Kathleen. *8th Commonw. Min. Metall. Congr.* **1**, 256–63.

HURLEY, P. M., FISHER, N. H., PINSON, W. H., Jr., and FAIRBAIRN, H. W. (1961). Geochronology of Proterozoic granites in Northern Territory, Australia. Part 1. K–Ar and Rb–Sr age determinations. *Bull. geol. Soc. Am.* **72**, 653–62.

HUTTON, C. O. (1940). Metamorphism in the Lake Wakatipu region, western Otago, New Zealand. *Geol. Mem. N.Z.* **5**.

IRVING, E. (1964). *Paleomagnetism*, Wiley, New York.

IRVING, E., and PARRY, L. G. (1963). The magnetism of some Permian rocks from New South Wales. *Geophys. J.* **7**, 395–411.

IVANAC, J. F. (1954). The geology and mineral deposits of the Tennant Creek gold-field Northern Territory. *Bull. B.M.R.* **22**.

JAEGER, H. (1962). Das Alter der ältesten bekannten Landpflanzen (*Baragwanathia*-Flora) in Australien auf Grund der begleitender Graptolithen. *Paläont. Z.* **36**, 7.

JAEGER, J. C., and BROWNE, W. R. (1958). Earth tremors in Australia and their geological importance. *Aust. J. Sci.* **20**, 225–7.

JENKINS, D. G. (1964a). Foraminiferal evidence for the Oligocene–Miocene boundary in New Zealand. *N.Z. J. Geol. Geophys.* **7**, 888–90.

JENKINS, D. G. (1964b). Location of the Danian–Upper Paleocene–Eocene boundaries in North Canterbury. *N.Z. J. Geol. Geophys.* **7**, 890–1.

JENKINS, D. G. (1964c). Reply to "New Zealand Mid-Tertiary stratigraphical correlation" (by Eames *et al.*) *Nature, Lond.* **203** (4941), 180–2.

JENNINGS, J. N. (1959). The submarine topography of Bass Strait. *Proc. R. Soc. Vict.* **71**, 49–72.

JESSUP, R. W. (1961). A Tertiary–Quaternary pedological chronology for the south-eastern portion of the Australian arid zone. *J. Soil Sci.* **12**, 199–213.

JOHNS, M. W., and LAWRENCE, C. R. (1964). Aspects of the geological structure of the Murray Basin in north-western Victoria. *Rep. Undergr. Wat. Invest. geol. Surv. Vict.* **10**.

JOHNS, R. K., and LUDBROOK, N. H. (1963). Investigation of Lake Eyre. Parts I and II. *Rep. Invest. Dep. Mines S. Aust.* **24**, 1–104.

JOHNSON, J. E. (1963). Basal sediments of the north side of the Officer Basin. *Q. Notes geol. Surv. S. Aust.* **7**, 7.

JOHNSON, W. (1960). Exploration for coal, Springfield Basin in the Hundred of Cudla-Mudla, Gordon Cradock District. *Rep. Invest. Dep. Mines. S. Aust.* **16**.

JOHNSTON, M. R., LAIRD, M. G., and SKWARKO, S. K. (1965). Age of Wangepeka Formation and Mt. Arthur Marble, Mount Owen, north-west Nelson. *N.Z. J. Geol. Geophys.* **8**, 854–8.

JOKLIK, G. F. (1955). The geology and mica-fields of the Harts Range, Central Australia. *Bull. B.M.R.* **26**.

JOPLIN, GERMAINE A. (1947). Petrological studies in the Ordovician of New South Wales. IV. The northern extension of the north-east Victorian metamorphic complex. *Proc. Linn. Soc. N.S.W.* **72**, 87–124.

JOPLIN, GERMAINE A. (1962). An apparent magmatic cycle in the Tasman Geosyncline. *J. geol. Soc. Aust.* **9**, 51–69.

JOPLIN, GERMAINE A. (1964). *A Petrography of Australian Igneous Rocks*, Angus & Robertson, Sydney.

KEAR, D. (1959). Stratigraphy of New Zealand's Cenozoic volcanism north-west of the volcanic belt. *N.Z. J. Geol. Geophys.* **2**, 578–89.

KEAR, D. (1960). Hamilton 1:250,000 geol. Map Ser. Sheet 4, geol. Surv. N.Z.

KEAR, D., and HAY, R. F. (1961). North Cape 1:250,000 geol. Map Ser. Sheet 1, geol. Surv. N.Z.

KEAR, D., and THOMPSON, B. N. (1964). Volcanic risk in Northland. *N.Z. J. Geol. Geophys.* **7**, 87–93.

KEAR, D., and WATERHOUSE, B. C. (1961). Quaternary surfaces and sediments at Waihi Beach. *N.Z. J. Geol. Geophys.* **4**, 434–45.

KING, D. (1960). The sand ridge deserts of South Australia and related aeolian landforms of the Quaternary arid cycles. *Trans. R. Soc. S. Aust.* **83**, 99–108.

KINGMA, J. T. (1959). The tectonic history of New Zealand. *N.Z. J. Geol. Geophys.* **2**, 1–55.

KINGMA, J. T. (1962). Dannevirke 1:250,000 geol. Map Ser. Sheet 11, geol. Surv. N.Z.

KLEEMAN, A. W. and WHITE, A. J. R. (1956). The structural petrology of portion of the eastern Mt. Lofty Ranges. *J. geol. Soc. Aust.* **3**, 17–31.

KONECKI, M. C., DICKINS, J. M., and QUINLAN, T. (1958). The geology of the coastal area between the Lower Gascoyne and Murchison Rivers, Western Australia. *Rep. B.M.R.* **37**.

KRÄUSEL, R. (1961). *Lycopodiopsis derbyi* Renault und einige andere Lycopodiales aus den Gondwana-Schichten. *Palaeontographica* **109B**, 62–90.

KRÖMMELBEIN, K. (1954). Devonische Ostracoden aus der Gegend von Buchan und von der Kuste der Waratah Bay. *Senckenberg. leth.* **35**, 193–229.

KUMMEL, B. (1959). Lower Triassic ammonoids from western Southland, New Zealand. *N.Z. J. Geol. Geophys.* **2**, 429–47.

KUMMEL, B. (1960). New Zealand Triassic ammonoids. *N.Z. J. Geol. Geophys.* **3**, 486–503.

KUMMEL, B. (1965). New Lower Triassic ammonoids from New Zealand. *N.Z. J. Geol. Geophys.* **8**, 537–47.

KUPFER, D. H. (1964). Width of the Alpine fault zone, New Zealand. *N.Z. J. Geol. Geophys.* **7**, 685–701.

LAMBERT, I. B., and WHITE, A. J. R. (1965). The Berridale wrench-fault. *J. geol. Soc. Aust.* **12**, 25–34.

LANGFORD-SMITH, T. (1960). The dead river systems of the Murrumbidgee. *Geogr. Rev.* **50**, 368–89.

LANGFORD-SMITH, T., and DURY, G. H. (1965). Distribution, character, and attitude of the duricrust in the northwest of New South Wales and the adjacent areas of Queensland. *Am. J. Sci.* **263**, 170–90.

LAUDER, W. R. (1964). The geology of Pepin Island and part of the adjacent mainland. *N.Z. J. Geol. Geophys.* **7**, 205–41.

LAUDER, W. R. (1965a). The geology of Dun Mountain, Nelson, New Zealand. Part 1. The petrology and structure of the sedimentary and volcanic rocks of the Te Anau and Maitai Groups. *N.Z. J. Geol. Geophys.* **8**, 3-34.

LAUDER, W. R. (1965b). The Geology of Dun Mountain, Nelson, New Zealand. Part 2. The petrology, structure, and origin of the ultrabasic rocks. *N.Z. J. Geol. Geophys.* **8**, 475–504.

LEGGO, P. J., COMPSTON, W., and TRENDALL, A. F. (1965). Radiometric ages of some Precambrian rocks from the north-west division of Western Australia. *J. geol. Soc. Aust.* **12**, 53–65.

LENSEN, G. J. (1963). Kaikoura 1:250,000 geol. Map Ser. Sheet 16, geol. Surv. N.Z.

LEWIS, B. R., FORWARD, P. S., and ROBERTS, J. B. (1965). Geology of the Broken Hill lode reinterpreted. *8th Commonw. Min. Metall. Congr.* **1**, 319–32.

LINDNER, A. W. (1953). The geology of the coastline of Waratah Bay between Walkerville and Cape Liptrap. *Proc. R. Soc. Vict.* **67**, 77–92.

LOGAN, B. W., and CHASE, R. L. (1961). The stratigraphy of the Moora Group, Western Australia. *J. Proc. R. Soc. West. Aust.* **44**, 14–32.

LOUGHNAN, F. C., KO KO, M., and BAYLISS, P. (1964). The red-beds of the Triassic Narrabeen Group. *J. geol. Soc. Aust.* **11**, 65–77.

LUDBROOK, N. H. (1961a). Subsurface stratigraphy of the Maralinga area, South Australia. *Trans. R. Soc. S. Aust.* **84**, 51–59.

LUDBROOK, N. H. (1961b). Stratigraphy of the Murray Basin in South Australia. *Bull. geol. Surv. S. Aust.* **36**, 1–96.

LUDBROOK, N. H. (1961c). Permian to Cretaceous subsurface stratigraphy between Lake Phillipson and The Peake and Denison Ranges, South Australia. *Trans. R. Soc. S. Aust.* **85**, 67–80.

LUDBROOK, N. H. (1963). Correlation of the Tertiary rocks of South Australia. *Trans. R. Soc. S. Aust.* **87**, 5–15.

McDOUGALL, I. (1959). The Brighton Basalts. *Pap. Proc. R. Soc. Tasm.* **93**, 17–28.

McDOUGALL, I. (1961). Determination of the age of a basic igneous intrusion by the potassium–argon method. *Nature, Lond.* **190** (4782), 1184–6.

McDOUGALL, I. (1962). Differentiation of the Tasmanian dolerites: Red Hill dolerite–granophyre association. *Bull. geol. Soc. Am.* **73**, 279–316.

McDOUGALL, I., DUNN, P. R., COMPSTON, W., WEBB, A. W., RICHARDS, J. R., and BOFINGER, V.M. (1965). Isotopic Age determinations on Precambrian Rocks of the Carpentaria region, Northern Territory, Australia. *J. geol. Soc. Aust.* **12**, 67–90.

McDOUGALL, I., and LEGGO, P. J. (1965). Isotopic age determinations on granitic rocks from Tasmania. *J. geol. Soc. Aust.* **12**, 295–332.

McELROY, C. T. (1963). The Geology of the Clarence–Moreton Basin. *Mem. geol. Surv. N.S.W.* **9**.

McELROY, C. T., and ROSE, G. (1962). Reconnaissance geological survey: Ulladulla 1-mile Military Sheet, and southern part of Tianjara 1-mile Military Sheet. *Bull. geol. Surv. N.S.W.* **17**, 1–65.

McGOWRAN, B. (1964). Foraminiferal evidence for the Paleocene age of the King's Park Shale (Perth Basin, Western Australia). *J. Proc. R. Soc. West. Aust.* **47**, 81–86.

MACKAY, R. M. (1961). The Lambie Group at Mount Lambie. Part 1. Stratigraphy and structure. *J. Proc. R. Soc. N.S.W.* **95**, 17–21.

McKELLAR, I. C. (1960). Pleistocene deposits of the upper Clutha Valley, Otago, New Zealand. *N.Z. J. Geol. Geophys.* **3**, 432–60.

MACLEOD, W. N., DE LA HUNTY, L. E., JONES, W. R., and HALLIGAN, R. (1963). A preliminary report on the Hamersley iron province, north-west division. *Annu. Rep. geol. Surv. West. Aust.* **4**, 44–54.

McWHAE, J. R. H., PLAYFORD, P. E., LINDNER, A. W., GLENISTER, B. F., and BALME, B. E. (1958). The stratigraphy of Western Australia. *J. geol. Soc. Aust.* **4**, 1–155.

MALONE, E. J. (1962). Pine Creek, N.T. 1:250,000 Geological Series Sheet D/52-8. *Explan. Notes B.M.R.*

MALONE, E. J. (1964). Depositional evolution of the Bowen Basin. *J. geol. Soc. Aust.* **11**, 263–82.

MALONE, E. J., CORBETT, D. W. P., and JENSEN, A. R. (1964). The Geology of the Mount Coolon 1:250,000 Sheet Area, Queensland. *Rep. B.M.R.* **64**.

MARWICK, J. (1953). Divisions and faunas of the Hokonui System (Triassic and Jurassic). *Paleont. Bull. Wellington* **21**.

MARWICK, J. (1960). Early Tertiary Mollusca from Otaio Gorge, South Canterbury. *Paleont. Bull. Wellington* **33**.

MASON, B. H. (1962). Metamorphism in the Southern Alps of New Zealand. *Bull. Am. Mus. nat. Hist.* **123**, 211–48.

MATHEWS, R. T. (1954). The greenstones of the Petrie–Mount Mee Area, Queensland. *Pap. Dep. Geol. Univ. Qd.* **4**(6), 1–28.

MAXWELL, W. G. H. (1953). Upper Palaeozoic formations in the Mt. Morgan district—stratigraphy and structure. *Pap. Dep. Geol. Univ. Qd.* **4** (4), 1–14.

MAXWELL, W. G. H. (1961*a*). Lower Carboniferous brachiopod faunas from Old Cannindah, Queensland. *J. Paleont.* **35**, 82–103.

MAXWELL, W. G. H. (1961*b*). Lower Carboniferous gastropod faunas from Old Cannindah, Queensland. *Palaeontology* **4**, 59–70.

MAXWELL, W. G. H. (1964). The Geology of the Yarrol region. Part 1. Biostratigraphy. *Pap. Dep. Geol. Univ. Qd.* **5** (9), 1–79.

MAXWELL, W. G. H., DAY, R. W., and FLEMING, P. J. G. (1961). Carbonate sedimentation on the Heron Island Reef, Great Barrier Reef. *J. sedim. Petrol.* **31**, 215–30.

MAXWELL, W. G. H., JELL, J. S., and McKELLAR, R. G. (1964*a*). Differentiation of carbonate sediments in the Heron Island reef. *J. sedim. Petrol.* **34**, 294–308.

MAXWELL, W. G. H., and MAIKLEM, W. R. (1964*b*). Lithofacies analysis, southern part of the Great Barrier Reef. *Pap. Dep. Geol. Univ. Qd.* **5** (11), 1–21.

MIRAMS, R. C. (1961). Field relationships of the Anabama granite. *Trans. R. Soc. S. Aust.* **85**, 121–31.

MIRAMS, R. C. (1964). A Sturtian glacial pavement at Merinjina Well. *Q. Notes geol. Surv. S. Aust.* **11**, 4–5.

MOLLAN, R. G., KIRKEGAARD, A. G., EXON, N. F., and DICKINS, J. M. (1964). Note of the Permian rocks of the Springsure area and proposal of a new name, Peawaddy Formation. *Qd. Govt. Min. J.* **65**, 577–81.

MOORE, B. R. (1965). The geology of the Upper Yarra region, Central Victoria. *Proc. R. Soc. Vict.* **78**, 221–39.

MUTCH, A. R. (1957). Facies and thickness of the Upper Paleozoic and Triassic sediments of Southland. *Trans. R. Soc. N.Z.* **84**, 499–511.

MUTCH, A. R. (1963). Oamaru 1:250,000 geol. Map Ser. Sheet 23, geol. Surv. N.Z.

NEWSOME, A. E., and ROCHOW, K. A. (1964). Vertebrate fossils from Tertiary sediments in Central Australia. *Aust. J. Sci.* **26**, 352.

NOAKES, L. C. (1956). Upper Proterozoic and sub-Cambrian rocks in Australia, *in* Symposium, *Int. geol. Congr.* **20 2** (2), 239–84.

NOAKES, L. C., CARTER, E. K., and ÖPIK, A. A. (1959). Urandangi 4-mile Geological Series Sheet F/54-5. *Explan. Notes B.M.R.*

NOAKES, L. C., and ÖPIK, A. A. (1954). Geology and geomorphology, in *Canberra a nation's capital.* Part II. The Australian Capital Territory as a region, 115–52 (ed. H. L. White).

NOAKES, L. C., and TRAVES, D. M. (1954). Part III. Outline of the geology of the Barkly region, in Survey of Barkly region 1947–8, *Land Res. Ser. C.S.I.R.O. Aust.* **3**, 34–41.

NOLDART, A. J., and WYATT, J. D. (1962). The geology of portion of the Pilbara goldfield. *Bull. geol. Surv. West. Aust.* **115**.

OFFICER, C. B. (1955). Southwest Pacific crustal structure. *Trans. Am. geophys. Un.* **36**, 449–59.

ÖPIK, A. A. (1953). Lower Silurian fossils from the "*Illaenus* Band" Heathcote, Victoria. *Mem. geol. Surv. Vict.* **19**.

ÖPIK, A. A. (1956*a*). Cambrian geology of Queensland. *Int. geol. Congr.* **20 2** (2), 1–24.

ÖPIK, A. A. (1956*b*). Cambrian geology of the Northern Territory. *Int. geol. Congr.* **20 2** (2), 25–54.

ÖPIK, A. A. (1956*c*). Cambrian palaeogeography of Australia. *Int. geol. Congr.* **20 2** (2), 239–84.

ÖPIK, A. A. (1958*a*). The geology of the Canberra City district. *Bull. B.M.R.* **32**.

ÖPIK, A. A. (1958*b*). The Cambrian trilobite *Redlichia*: organization and generic concept. *Bull. B.M.R.* **42**, 1–50.

ÖPIK, A. A. (1959). Tumblagooda sandstone trails and their age. *Rep. B.M.R.* **38**, 3–20.

ÖPIK, A. A. (1961*a*). Alimentary caeca of agnostids and other trilobites. *Palaeontology* **3**, 410–38.

ÖPIK, A. A. (1961*b*). The geology and palaeontology of the headwaters of the Burke River, Queensland. *Bull. B.M.R.* **53**.

ÖPIK, A. A. (1963). Early Upper Cambrian fossils from Queensland. *Bull. B.M.R.* **64**, 1–107.

ÖPIK, A. A. (1967). The Mindyallan fauna of north-west Queensland. *Bull. B.M.R.* **74.**

PACKHAM, G. H. (1960). Sedimentary history of part of the Tasman geosyncline in south eastern Australia. *Int. geol. Congr.* **21** (12), 74–83.

PACKHAM, G. H. (1962). An outline of the geology of New South Wales, in *A Goodly Heritage*, ed. A. P. Elkin, pp. 24–35.

PACKHAM, G. H., and STEVENS, N. C. (1955). The Palaeozoic stratigraphy of Spring and Quarry Creeks, west of Orange, N.S.W. *J. Proc. R. Soc. N.S.W.* **88**, 55–60.

PANTIN, H. M. (1959). The sea floor round New Zealand, in *A Descriptive Atlas of New Zealand*, p. 12, Gov. Printer, Wellington.

PARKIN, L. W. (1956). Notes on the younger glacial remnants of northern South Australia. *Trans. R. Soc. S. Aust.* **79**, 148–51.

PATEN, R. J. (1964). Tertiary geology of the Boulia region, western Queensland. *Rep. B.M.R.* **77**.

PEDDER, A. E. H. (1963). Two new genera of Devonian tetracorals from Australia. *Proc. Linn. Soc. N.S.W.* **88**, 364–7.

PERRY, W. J., and DICKINS, J. M. (1960). The geology of the Badgeradda area, Western Australia. *Rep. B.M.R.* **46**, 1–38.

PHILIP, G. M. (1958). The Jurassic sediments of the Tyers Group, Gippsland, Victoria. *Proc. R. Soc. Vict.* **70**, 181–199.

PHILIP, G. M. (1960). Victorian Siluro-Devonian faunas and correlations. *Int. geol. Congr.* **21**, 143–57.

PHILIP, G. M. (1962). The palaeontology and stratigraphy of the Siluro–Devonian sediments of the Tyers area, Gippsland, Victoria. *Proc. R. Soc. Vict.* **75**, 123–246.

PHILIP, G. M. (1963). The Tertiary echinoids of southeastern Australia. I. Introduction and Cidaridae (1). *Proc. R. Soc. Vict.* **76**, 118–226.

PHILIP, G. M. (1964*a*). The age of the strata at Eildon. *Aust. J. Sci.* **27**, 23.

PHILIP, G. M. (1964*b*). The Tertiary echinoids of south-eastern Australia. *Proc. R. Soc. Vict.* **77**, 433–77.

PHILIP, G. M. (1965). Lower Devonian conodonts from the Tyers Area, Gippsland, Victoria. *Proc. R. Soc. Vict.* **79**, 95–117.

PHILIP, G. M., and PEDDER, A. E. H. (1964). A re-assessment of the age of the Middle Devonian of south-eastern Australia. *Nature, Lond.* **202** (4939), 1323–4.

PHILLIPS, JUNE R. P. (1956). Geology of the Queanbeyan district. *J. Proc. R. Soc. N.S.W.* **89**, 117–26.

PHILLIPS-ROSS, JUNE R. P. (1961). Ordovician, Silurian, and Devonian Bryozoa of Australia. *Bull. B.M.R.* **50**.

PHIPPS, C. V. G. (1963). Topography and sedimentation of the continental shelf and slope between Sydney and Montague Island—N.S.W. *Australas. Oil Gas J.* **10** (3), 40–46.

PIDGEON, R. T., and COMPSTON, W. (1965). The age and origin of the Cooma granite and its associated metamorphic zones, New South Wales. *J. Petrology* **6**, 193–222.

PLAYFORD, G., and DETTMANN, MARY E. (1965). Rhaeto-Liassic plant microfossils from the Leigh Creek Coal Measures, South Australia. *Senckenberg. leth.* **46**, 127–81.

POCOCK, K. J. (1964). *Estaingia*, a new trilobite genus from the Lower Cambrian of South Australia. *Palaeontology* **7**, 458–71.

PRICHARD, C. E., and QUINLAN, T. (1962). The geology of the southern half of the Hermannsburg 1:250,000 sheet. *Rep. B.M.R.* **61**.

PRIDER, R. T. (1954). The Pre-Cambrian succession in Western Australia. *Proc. pan-Indian Ocean Sci. Congr.*, Section C (Geol.), pp. 69–78.

PRIDER, R. T. (1960). The Leucite Lamproites of the Fitzroy Basin, Western Australia. *J. geol. Soc. Aust.* **6**, 71–118.

PRIDER, R. T. (1961). The "greenstones" of south western Australia. *J. Proc. R. Soc. West. Aust.* **44**, 1–9.

PRIDER, R. T. (1965). Geology and mineralization of the Western Australian shield. *8th Commonw. Min. Metall. Congr.* **1**, 56–65.

PUDOVSKIS, V. (1963). Well completion report. Woolmulla No. 1, Western Australia. Western Australian Petroleum Pty. Ltd., Rep. Petrol. Search Subsidy Acts Aust. (unpublished).

PURSER, B. H. (1961). Geology of the Port Waikato region (Onewhero Sheet N.51). *Bull. geol. Surv. N.Z.* **69**.

RADE, J. (1954). Geology and sub-surface waters of the area north of the Darling River between longitudes 145° and 149°E., N.S.W. *J. Proc. R. Soc. N.S.W.* **88**, 24–32.

RADE, J. (1964). Lower Cretaceous sporomorphs from the northern part of the Clarence Basin, New South Wales. *J. Proc. R. Soc. N.S.W.* **97**, 175–6.

RAESIDE, J. D. (1964). Loess deposits of the South Island, New Zealand, and soils formed on them. *N.Z. J. Geol. Geophys.* **7**, 811–38.

RAGGATT, H. G. (1936). Probable Late Silurian age of serpentine, Condoblin–Trundle district, New South Wales. *J. Proc. R. Soc. N.S.W.* **70**, 402–5.

RAGGATT, H. G., and CRESPIN, IRENE (1955). Stratigraphy of Tertiary rocks between Torquay and Eastern View, Victoria. *Proc. R. Soc. Vict.* **67**, 75–142.

RANDAL, M. A. (1962). Fergusson River, N.T. 1:250,000 Geological Series Sheet D/52-12. *Explan. Notes B.M.R.*

RANFORD, L. C., COOK, P. J., and WELLS, A. T. (1965). The geology of the central part of Amadeus Basin, Northern Territory. *Rep. B.M.R.* **86**.

RATTIGAN, J. H. (1964). Occurrence and stratigraphic position of Carboniferous coals in the Hunter Valley, N.S.W. *Aust. J. Sci.* **27**, 82.

REED, J. J. (1958). Granites and mineralization in New Zealand. *N.Z. J. Geol. Geophys.* **1**, 47–64.

REED, J. J. (1964). Mylonites, cataclasites, and associated rocks along the Alpine fault, South Island, New Zealand. *N.Z. J. Geol. Geophys.* **7**, 645–84.

REED, K. J. (1965). Mid-tertiary smaller Foraminifera from a bore at Heywood, Victoria, Australia. *Bull. Am. Paleont.* **49** (220), 43–104.

REID, I. W. (1965). Iron ore deposits of Yampi Sound. *8th Commonw. Min. Metall. Congr.* **1** 126–31.

REILLY, W. I. (1965). Gravity Map of New Zealand 1:4,000,000. Isostatic and Bouguer Anomalies (1st edn.). *N.Z. Dep. scient. ind. Res.*

RHODES, J. M. (1965), The Geological Relationships of the Rum Jungle Complex, Northern Territory. *Rep. B.M.R.* **89.**

RICHARDS, J. R., COOPER, J. A., and WEBB, A. W. (1963). Potassium–argon ages on micas from the Precambrian region of north-western Queensland. *J. geol. Soc. Aust.* **10**, 299–316.

RICHARDS, J. R., and PIDGEON, R. T. (1963). Some age measurements on micas from Broken Hill, Australia. *J. geol. Soc. Aust.* **10**, 243–59.

RICHARDS, J. R., WHITE, D. A., WEBB, A. W., and BRANCH, C. T. (1967). Isotopic ages of acid igneous rocks in the Cairns hinterland, North Queensland. *Bull. B.M.R.* **88**.

RIDE, W. D. L. (1964). A review of Australian fossil marsupials. *J. Proc. R. Soc. West. Aust.* **47**, 97–131.

RINGWOOD, A. E. (1955). The geology of the Deddick–Wulgulmerang area, East Gippsland. *Proc. R. Soc. Vict.* **67**, 19–66.

RIPPER, ELIZABETH A. (1938). Notes on the middle Palaeozoic stromatoporoid faunas of Victoria. *Proc. R. Soc. Vict.* **50**, 221–43.

ROBERTS, J. (1965). Lower Carboniferous zones and correlations based on faunas from the Gresford–Dungog district, New South Wales. *J. geol. Soc. Aust.* **12**, 105–22.

ROBERTSON, E. I., and REILLY, W. I. (1958). Bouguer anomaly map of New Zealand. *N.Z. J. Geol. Geophys.* **1**, 560–4.

Ross, R. J., Jr., and Berry, W. B. N. (1963). Ordovician graptolites of the Basin Ranges in California, Nevada, Utah, and Idaho. *Bull. U.S. geol. Surv.* **1134**, 1–177.

Runnegar, B. (1965). The bivalves *Megadesmus* Sowerby and *Astartila* Dana from the Permian of eastern Australia. *J. geol. Soc. Aust.* **12**, 227–52.

Russell, R. T., and Lewis, B. R. (1965). Gold and copper deposits of the Cobar district. *8th Commonw. Min. Metall. Congr.* **1**, 411–19.

Ryan, G. R. (1961). The geology and mineral resources of the Hatches Creek wolfram field, Northern Territory. *Bull. B.M.R.* **6**.

Ryan, G. R. (1964). A reappraisal of the Archaean of the Pilbara Block. *Annu. Rep. geol. Surv. West. Aust.* (1963), 25–28.

Ryan, G. R. (1965). The geology of the Pilbara Block, Western Australia. *Proc. Australas. Inst. Min. Metall.* **214**, 61–94.

Ryan, G. R., and Kriewaldt, M. (1964). Facies changes in the Archaean of the West Pilbara Goldfield. *Annu. Rep. geol. Surv. West Aust.* (1963), 28–30.

Schleiger, N. W. (1964a). Primary scalar bedding features of the Siluro–Devonian sediments of the Seymour district, Victoria. *J. geol. Soc. Aust.* **11**, 1–31.

Schleiger, N. W. (1964b). Some quantitative studies of coarse-bedded conglomerates of Late Silurian–Early Devonian age in the Tallarook and Seymour East synclines, Victoria. *J. geol. Soc. Aust.* **11**, 217–33.

Shepard, F. P. (1961). Sea level rise during the past 20,000 years. *Z. Geomorph.*, Suppl. 3, 30–35.

Sherrard, Kathleen M. (1953). The assemblages of graptolites in New South Wales. *J. Proc. R. Soc. N.S.W.* **87**, 73–101.

Sherrard, Kathleen M. (1959). Some Silurian lamellibranches from N.S.W. *Proc. Linn. Soc. N.S.W.* **84**, 356–72.

Shirley, J. (1938). The fauna of the Baton River Beds (Devonian), New Zealand. *Q. J. geol. Soc. Lond.* **94**, 459–506.

Shirley, J. (1964). An investigation of the sediments on the continental shelf of New South Wales, Australia. *J. geol. Soc. Aust.* **11**, 331–41.

Singleton, F. A. (1941). The Tertiary geology of Australia. *Proc. R. Soc. Vict.* **53**, 1–125.

Singleton, O. P. (1965). Geology and mineralization of Victoria. *8th Commonw. Min. Metall. Congr.* **1**, 440–9.

Skevington, D. (1963). A correlation of Ordovician graptolite-bearing sequences. *Geol. För. Stockh. Förh.* **85**, 298–319.

Skwarko, S. K. (1958). The Lower Ordovician of Cape Providence: a new graptolite zone and a new species of *Schizograptus*. *N.Z. J. Geol. Geophys.* **1**, 256–62.

Skwarko, S. K. (1962). Graptolites of Cobb River–Mount Arthur area north-west Nelson, New Zealand. *Trans. R. Soc. N.Z. (Geol.)* **1**, 215–47.

Skwarko, S. K. (1963). Australian Mesozoic trigoniids. *Bull. B.M.R.* **67**.

Skwarko, S. K. (1964). Cretaceous stratigraphy and palaeontology of the Northern Territory. *Bull. B.M.R.* **73**.

Smith, G. J. (1966). New graptolite localities in the Aorangi mine area, north-west Nelson. *Trans. R. Soc. N.Z. (Geol.)*. **4**, 171–175.

Smith, J. W., and Roberts, H. G. (1963). Mount Drummond, N.T. 1:250,000 Geological Series. *Explan. Notes B.M.R.*

Smith, K. G. (1963). Hay River, N.T. 1:250,000 Geological Series. *Explan. Notes B.M.R.*

Smith, K. G. (1964). Progress report on the geology of the Huckitta 1:250,000 Sheet, N.T. *Rep. B.M.R.* **67**.

Smith, K. G., Stewart, J. R., and Smith, J. W. (1961). The regional geology of the Davenport and Murchison Ranges, Northern Territory. *Rep. B.M.R.* **58**.

Snelling, N. J. (1960). The geology and petrology of the Murrumbidgee batholith. *Q. J. geol. Soc. Lond.* **116**, 187–215.

Sofoulis, J. (1963). Boorabbin, 1:250,000 Geol. Series, Sheet SH/51-13. *Explan. Notes geol. Surv.West. Aust.*

SOONS, JANE M. (1963). The glacial sequence in part of the Rakaia Valley, Canterbury, New Zealand. *N.Z. J. Geol. Geophys.* **6**, 735–56.

SPEDEN, I. G. (1959). *Phyllocrinus furcillatus* sp. nov., a cyrtocrinoid from the Upper Jurassic of Kawhia, New Zealand. *Palaeontology* **2**, 150–5.

SPEDEN, I. G. (1961). Papatowai 1:63,360 geol. Map Ser. Sheet S184, geol. Surv. N.Z.

SPENCER-JONES, D. (1965). The geology and structure of the Grampians area, Western Victoria. *Mem. geol. Surv. Vict.* **25**.

SPRIGG, R. C. (1952). The geology of the south-east province, South Australia, with special reference to Quaternary coastline migrations and modern beach developments. *Bull. geol. Surv. S. Aust.* **29**.

SPRIGG, R. C. (1959). Stranded sea beaches and associated sand accumulations of the upper south-east. *Trans. R. Soc. S. Aust.* **82**, 183–93.

SPRIGG, R. C. (1961). On the structural evolution of the Great Artesian Basin. *Conf. Pap. Aust. Petrol. Explor. Ass.*, pp. 37–56.

SPRIGG, R. C., and WOOLLEY, J. B. (1963). Oil and gas prospects of the Geltwood Beach anticline, Millicent, South Australia. *J. Aust. Petrol. Explor. Ass.*, pp. 69–79.

SPRY, A., and BANKS, M. R. (Editors) (1962). The geology of Tasmania. *J. geol. Soc. Aust.* **9**, 107–362.

SQUIRES, D. F. (1958). The Cretaceous and Tertiary corals of New Zealand. *Palaeont. Bull. Wellington* **29**.

STANDARD, J. C. (1961*a*). Submarine geology of the Tasman Sea. *Bull. geol. Soc. Am.* **72**, 1777–1788.

STANDARD, J. C. (1961*b*). A new study of the Hawkesbury Sandstone: preliminary findings. *J. Proc. R. Soc. N.S.W.* **95**, 145–6.

STANDARD, J. C. (1963). Geology of Lord Howe Island. *J. Proc. R. Soc. N.S.W.* **96**, 107–21.

STANTON, R. L. (1956). The Palaeozoic rocks of the Wiseman's Creek–Burraga area, N.S.W. *J. Proc. R. Soc. N.S.W.* **89**, 131–56.

STEINER, J., BROWN, D. A., and WHITE, A. J. R. (1959). Occurrence of ignimbrite in the Shag Valley, north-east Otago. *N.Z. J. Geol. Geophys.* **2**, 380–4.

STELCK, C. R., and HOPKINS, R. M. (1962). Early sequence of interesting shelf deposits, Central Australia. *J. Alberta Soc. Petrol. Geol.* **10**, 1–12.

STEPHENS, C. G. (1961). The soil landscapes of Australia. *Soil Publ. C.S.I.R.O. Aust.* **18**, 1–43.

STEPHENS, C. G. (1964). Silcretes of Central Australia. *Nature, Lond.* **203** (4952), 1407.

STEPHENSON, P. J. (1959). The Mt. Barney central complex, south-east Queensland. *Geol. Mag.* **96**, 125–36.

STEVENS, N. C. (1952). Ordovician stratigraphy at Cliefden Caves, near Mandurama, N.S.W. *Proc. Linn. Soc. N.S.W.* **77**, 114–20.

STEVENS, N. C. (1954). A note on the geology of Panuara and Angullong, south of Orange, N.S.W. *Proc. Linn. Soc. N.S.W.* **78**, 262–68.

STEVENS, N. C. (1957). Further notes on Ordovician formations of central New South Wales. *J. Proc. R. Soc. N.S.W.* **90**, 44–50.

STEVENS, N. C. (1958). Palaeozoic geology of the Cooleman Caves district, New South Wales. *Proc. Linn. Soc. N.S.W.* **83**, 251–8.

STEVENS, N. C. (1959). Ring-structures of the Mt. Alford district south-east Queensland. *J. geol. Soc. Aust.* **6**, 37–49.

STEVENS, N. C. (1964). Upper Cainozoic volcanism near Gayndah, Queensland. *Proc. R. Soc. Qd.* **72**, 75–82.

STEVENS, N. C., and PACKHAM, G. H. (1953). Graptolite zones and associated stratigraphy at Four Mile Creek, south-west of Orange, N.S.W. *J. Proc. R. Soc. N.S.W.* **86**. 94–99.

STIRTON, R. A., TEDFORD, R. H., and MILLER, A. H. (1961). Cenozoic stratigraphy and vertebrate paleontology of the Tirari Desert, South Australia. *Rec. S. Aust. Mus.* **14**, 19–61.

STRUSZ, D. L. (1960). The geology of the Parish of Mumbil, near Wellington, N.S.W. *J. Proc. R. Soc. N.S.W.* **93**, 127–36.

STRUSZ, D. L. (1961). Lower Palaeozoic corals from New South Wales. *Palaeontology* **4**, 334–61.

STRUSZ, D. L. (1964). Devonian trilobites from the Wellington–Molong district of New South Wales. *J. Proc. R. Soc. N.S.W.* **97**, 91–97.

STRUSZ, D. L. (1965). A note on the stratigraphy of the Devonian Garra Beds of New South Wales. *J. Proc. R. Soc. N.S.W.* **98**, 85–90.

SUGGATE, R. P. (1957). The geology of Reefton Subdivision. *Bull geol. Surv. N.Z.* **56**.

SUGGATE, R. P. (1959). Christchurch 1:250,000 geol. Map Ser. Sheet 21, geol. Surv. N.Z.

SUGGATE, R. P. (1961). Rock-stratigraphic names for the sediments of the New Zealand geosyncline. *N.Z. J. Geol. Geophys.* **4**, 392–9.

SUGGATE, R. P. (1963). The Alpine Fault. *Trans. R. Soc. N.Z.* (*Geol.*) 2, 105–29.

SUGGATE, R. P. (1965). Late Pleistocene geology of the northern part of the South Island, New Zealand. *Bull. geol. Surv. N.Z.* **77**.

SUGGATE, R. P., and COUPER, R. A. (1952). The stratigraphic relations and plant micro-fossils of the New Zealand coal measures. *N.Z. J. Sci. Technol.* **34B**, 106–17.

TALENT, J. A. (1956). Devonian brachiopods and pelecypods of the Buchan Caves Limestone, Victoria. *Proc. R. Soc. Vict.* **68**, 1–56.

TALENT, J. A. (1959a). Notes on Middle Palaeozoic stratigraphy and diastrophism in eastern Victoria. *Min. geol. J.* **6** (3), 57–58.

TALENT, J. A. (1963). The Devonian of the Mitchell and Wentworth Rivers. *Mem. geol. Surv. Vict.* **24**, 1–118.

TALENT, J. A. (1965a). The stratigraphic and diastrophic evolution of central and eastern Victoria in Middle Palaeozoic times. *Proc. R. Soc. Vict.* **79**, 179–95.

TALENT, J. A. (1965b). The Silurian and Early Devonian faunas of the Heathcote district, Victoria. *Mem. Geol. Surv. Vict.* **26**.

TALENT, J. A., and SPENCER-JONES, D. (1963). The Devono-Carboniferous fauna of the Silverband formation, Victoria. *Proc. R. Soc. Vict.* **76**, 1–11.

TAYLOR, D. J. (1964). Foraminifera and the stratigraphy of the western Victorian Cretaceous sediments. *Proc. R. Soc. Vict.* **77**, 535–603.

TEICHERT, C. (1943). The Devonian of Western Australia; a preliminary review, Part I and Part II. *Am. J. Sci.* **241**, 69–94, 167–84.

TEICHERT, C., and GLENISTER, B. F. (1953). Ordovician and Silurian cephalopods from Tasmania, Australia. *Bull. Am. Paleont.* **34** (144), 187–249.

TEICHERT, C., and TALENT, J. A. (1958). Geology of the Buchan area, east Gippsland. *Mem. geol. Surv. Vict.* **21**.

THOM, B. G. (1965). Late Quaternary coastal morphology of the Port Stephens–Myall Lakes area, N.S.W. *J. Proc. R. Soc. N.S.W.* **98**, 23–36.

THOMAS, D. E. (1939). The geological structure of Victoria with respect to the Lower Palaeozoic rocks. *Min. geol. J.* **1** (4), 59–64.

THOMAS, D. E. (1947). The geology of the Eildon Dam project. *Mem. geol. Surv. Vict.* **16**.

THOMAS, D. E. (1953). Tanjilian fossils. *Min. geol. J.* **5** (2), 27.

THOMAS, D. E. (1958). The geological structure of Victoria. *J. Proc. R. Soc. N.S.W.* **92**, 182–90.

THOMAS, D. E. (1960). The zonal distribution of Australian graptolites. *J. Proc. R. Soc. N.S.W.* **94**, 1–58.

THOMAS, D. E., and SINGLETON, O. P. (1956). The Cambrian stratigraphy of Victoria. *Int. geol. Congr. 20* 2 (2), 149–63.

THOMAS, G. A. (1957). Oldhaminid brachiopods in the Permian of northern Australia. *J. palaeont. Soc. India* **2**, 174–82.

THOMAS, G. A. (1958). The Permian Orthotetacea of Western Australia. *Bull. B.M.R.* **39**.

THOMAS, G. A. (1962a). The Carboniferous stratigraphy of Western Australia. *C. r. Congr. Int. Strat. Géol. Carb.* (1958) **3**, 733–40.

THOMAS, G. A. (1962b). The Carboniferous stratigraphy of the Bonaparte Gulf Basin. *C. r. Congr. Int. Strat. Géol. Carb.* (1958) **3**, 727–32.

THOMPSON, B. N. (1960). Barrier 1:250,000 geol. Map Ser. Sheet 2B, geol. Surv. N.Z.

THOMPSON, B. N. (1961). Whangarei 1:250,000 geol. Map Ser. Sheet 2A, geol. Surv. N.Z.

THOMPSON, B. N. (1964). Quaternary volcanism of the central volcanic region. *N.Z. J. Geol. Geophys.* **7**, 45–66.

THOMSON, A. A., and EVISON, F. F. (1962). Thickness of the earth's crust in New Zealand. *N.Z. J. Geol. Geophys.* **5**, 29–45.

THOMSON, B. P. (1953). Geology and Ore Occurrence in the Cobar District. *5th Emp. Min. & Metall. Congr.*, **1**, 863–96.

THOMSON, B. P. (1966). The lower boundary of the Adelaide System and older basement relationships in South Australia. *J. geol. Soc. Aust.* **13**, 203–28.

THOMSON, B. P., COATS, R. P., MIRAMS, R. C., FORBES, B. G., DALGARNO, C. R., and JOHN-SON, J. E. (1964). Precambrian rock groups in the Adelaide geosyncline: a new subdivision. *Q. Notes geol. Surv. S. Aust.* **9**, 1–19.

THOMSON, B. P., and HORWITZ, R. C. (1961). Cambrian–Pre-cambrian unconformity in Sellick Hill–Normanville area of South Australia. *Aust. J. Sci.* **24**, 40.

TINDALE, N. B. (1933). Geological notes on the Cockatoo Creek and Mount Liebig country, Central Australia. *Trans. R. Soc. S. Aust.* **57**, 206–17.

TINDALE, N. B. (1959). Ecology of primitive aboriginal man in Australia, in *Biogeography and Ecology in Australia.* Junk, The Hague, pp. 36–51.

TOMLINSON, J. G. (1961). Ordovician fossils from Thangoo No. 1 and Thangoo No. 1A Western Australia. *Publs. Petrol. Search Subsidy Acts Aust.* **14**, 24–27.

TOMLINSON, J. G. (1967). Devonian fish and a plant from the Amadeus Basin, Northern Territory. *Bull. B.M.R.* **80.**

TRAVES, D. M. (1955). The geology of the Ord–Victoria region, Northern Australia. *Bull. B.M.R.* **27.**

TRAVES, D. M. (1956). Upper Proterozoic and Cambrian geology in northwestern Australia. *Int. geol. Congr. 20* **2** (2), 75–90.

TURNER, F. J. (1938). Progressive regional metamorphism in southern New Zealand. *Geol. Mag.* **75**, 160–74.

TWIDALE, C. R. (1956). Chronology of denudation in northwest Queensland. *Bull. geol. Soc. Am.* **67**, 867–82.

VALENTIN, H. (1961). The central west coast of Cape York Peninsula. *Aust. Geogr.* **8**, 65–72.

VALENTINE, J. W. (1965). Quaternary Mollusca from Port Fairy, Victoria, Australia, and their palaeoecologic implications. *Proc. R. Soc. Vict.* **78**, 15–73.

VALLANCE, T. G. (1953). Studies in the metamorphic and plutonic geology of the Wantabad-gery–Adelong–Tumbarumba district, N.S.W. Part 1. Introduction and metamorphism of the sedimentary rocks. *Proc. Linn. Soc. N.S.W.* **78**, 90–121.

VAN ANDEL, TJ. H., CURRAY, J. R., and VEEVERS, J. J. (1961). Recent carbonate sediments of the Sahul Shelf—northwestern Australia. *Coastal and Shallow Water Res. Conf.*, Nat. Sci. Fdn. and Off. nav. Res., pp. 564–7.

VAN DIJK, D. C. (1959). Soil features in relation to erosional history in the vicinity of Canberra. *Soil Publ. C.S.I.R.O. Aust.* **13**, 1–41.

VEEVERS, J. J. (1959). Devonian brachiopods from the Fitzroy Basin, Western Australia. *Bull. B.M.R.* **45**, 1–220.

VEEVERS, J. J., MOLLAN, R. G., OLGERS, F., and KIRKEGAARD, A. G. (1964a). The geology of the Emerald 1:250,000 sheet area, Queensland. *Rep. B.M.R.* **68.**

VEEVERS, J. J., RANDAL, M. A., MOLLAN, R. G., and PATEN, R. J. (1964b). The geology of the Clermont 1:250,000 sheet area Queensland. *Rep. B.M.R.* **66.**

VEEVERS, J. J., ROBERTS, J., KAULBACK, J. A., and JONES, P. J. (1964c). New observations on the Palaeozoic geology of the Ord River area, Western Australia and Northern Territory. *Aust. J. Sci.* **26**, 352–4.

VEEVERS, J. J., and WELLS, A. T. (1961). The geology of the Canning Basin, Western Australia. *Bull. B.M.R.* **60.**

VINE, R. R. (1964). New Tertiary stratigraphic units—western Queensland. *Qd. Govt. Min. J.* **65**, 470–4.

VINE, R. R., and DAY, R. W. (1965). Nomenclature of the Rolling Downs Group, northern Eromanga Basin, Queensland. *Qd. Govt. Min. J.* **66**, 417–21.

VOISEY, A. H. (1957). Erosion surfaces around Armidale, N.S.W. *J. Proc. R. Soc. N.S.W.* **90**, 128–33.

VOISEY, A. H. (1958*a*). Further remarks on the sedimentary formations of New South Wales. *J. Proc. R. Soc. N.S.W.* **91**, 165–89.

VOISEY, A. H. (1958*b*). The Manilla syncline and associated faults. *J. Proc. R. Soc. N.S.W.* **91**, 209–14.

VOISEY, A. H. (1959*a*). Australian geosynclines. *Aust. J. Sci.* **22**, 188–98.

VOISEY, A. H. (1959*b*). Tectonic evolution of north-eastern New South Wales, Australia. *J. Proc. R. Soc. N.S.W.* **92**, 191–203.

VOISEY, A. H., and WILLIAMS, K. L. (1964). The geology of the Carroll–Keepit–Rangari area of New South Wales. *J. Proc. R. Soc. N.S.W.* **97**, 65–72.

VON DER BORCH, C. (1965*a*). The distribution and preliminary geochemistry of modern carbonate sediments of the Coorong area, South Australia. *Geochim. cosmochim. Acta* **29**, 781–99.

VON DER BORCH, C. (1965*b*). Distribution of detrital minerals in recent carbonate sediments from the Sahul Shelf, northern Australia. *J. geol. Soc. Aust.* **12**, 333–9.

WADE, MARY (1964). Application of the lineage concept to biostratigraphic zoning based on planktonic foraminifera. *Micropaleontology* **10**, 273–90.

WADE, R. T. (1935). *The Triassic fishes of Brookvale, New South Wales.* British Museum (Natural History), London.

WALKER, D. B. (1959). Palaeozoic stratigraphy of the area to the west of Borenore, N.S.W. *J. Proc. R. Soc. N.S.W.* **93**, 39–46.

WALKER, P. H. (1962). Terrace chronology and soil formation on the south coast of New South Wales. *J. Soil Sci.*, **13**, 178–86.

WALPOLE, B. P. (Ed.) (1962*a*). Geological notes in explanation of the tectonic map of Australia. *B.M.R.*

WALPOLE, B. P. (1962*b*). Mount Evelyn, N.T. 1:250,000 Geological Series Sheet D53/5. *Explan. Notes B.M.R.*

WALPOLE, B. P., and CROHN, P. W. (1965). Katherine–Darwin metalliferous province. *8th Commonw. Min. Metall. Congr.* **1**, 168–75.

WANLESS, H. R. (1960). Evidences of multiple Late Paleozoic glaciation in Australia. *Int. geol. Congr.* **21** (12), 104–10.

WARD, W. T. (1965). Eustatic and climatic history of the Adelaide area South Australia. *J. Geol.* **73**, 592–602.

WARD, W. T., and JESSUP, R. W. (1965). Changes of sea-level in Southern Australia. *Na'ure, Lond.* **205**, 791–2.

WARNER, R. A., and HARRISON, J. (1961). Discovery of Middle Cambrian fossils in New South Wales. *Aust. J. Sci.* **23**, 268.

WASSERBURG, G. J., CRAIG, H., MENARD, H. W., ENGEL, A. E. J., and ENGEL, CELESTE (1963). Age and composition of a Bounty Islands granite and age of a Seychelles Island granite. *J. Geol.* **71**, 785–9.

WATERHOUSE, J. B. (1958*a*). The occurrence of *Atomodesma* Beyrich in New Zealand. *N.Z. J. Geol. Geophys.* **1**, 166–77.

WATERHOUSE, J. B. (1958*b*). The age of the Takitimu group of western Southland. *N.Z. J. Geol. Geophys.* **1**, 604–10.

WATERHOUSE, J. B. (1959). A new species of *Maccoyella* from Raukumara Peninsula, with a revision of *M. magnata* Marwick. *N.Z. J. Geol. Geophys.* **2**, 459–500.

WATERHOUSE, J. B. (1963*a*). Permian gastropods of New Zealand. Part 1. Bellerophontacea and Euomphalacea. *N.Z. J. Geol. Geophys.* **6**, 88–112.

WATERHOUSE, J. B. (1963*b*). Permian gastropods of New Zealand. Part 2. Pleurotomariacea (in part). *N.Z. J. Geol. Geophys.* **6**, 115–54.

WATERHOUSE, J. B. (1963*c*). Permian Gastropods of New Zealand. Part 3. Pleurotomariacea (concluded). *N.Z. J. Geol. Geophys.* **6**, 587–622.

WATERHOUSE, J. B. (1963*d*). The Permian faunal succession in New Zealand. *J. geol. Soc. Aust.* **10**, 165–76.

WATERHOUSE, J. B. (1964*a*). Permian stratigraphy and faunas of New Zealand. *Bull. geol. Surv. N.Z.* **72**.

WATERHOUSE, J. B. (1964*b*). Permian Brachiopoda of New Zealand. *Palaeont. Bull. Wellington* **35**.

WATERHOUSE, J. B., and VELLA, P. (1965). A Permian fauna from north-west Nelson, New Zealand. *Trans. R. Soc. N.Z. (Geol.)* **3** (5), 57–84.

WEBB, A. W., COOPER, J. A., and RICHARDS, J. R. (1963). K–Ar ages on some central Queensland granites. *J. geol. Soc. Aust.* **10**, 317–24.

WEBB, A. W., and McDOUGALL, I. (1964). Granites of Lower Cretaceous age near Eungella, Queensland. *J. geol. Soc. Aust.* **11**, 151–3.

WEBB, A. W., McDOUGALL, I., and COOPER, J. A. (1963). Retention of radiogenic argon in glauconites from Proterozoic sediments, Northern Territory, Australia. *Nature, Lond.* **199** (4890), 270–1.

WEBB, B. P., and HORWITZ, R. (1959). Notes on the boundaries of the Marinoan Series of the Adelaide System. *Aust. J. Sci.* **21**, 188–9.

WELLMAN, H. W. (1956). Structural outline of New Zealand. *Bull. N.Z. Dep. scient. ind Res.* **121**.

WELLMAN, H. W. (1959). Divisions of the New Zealand Cretaceous. *Trans. R. Soc. N.Z.* **87**, 99–163.

WELLMAN, H. W. (1962). New graptolite localities in New Zealand. *N.Z. J. Geol. Geophys.* **5**, 642–5.

WELLMAN, H. W., and WILSON, A. T. (1964). Notes on the geology and archaeology of the Martin's Bay district. *N.Z. J. Geol. Geophys.* **7**, 702–21.

WELLS, A. T., FORMAN, D. J., and RANFORD, L. C. (1965*a*). Geological reconnaissance of the Rawlinson–Macdonald area, Western Australia. *Rep. B.M.R.* **65**.

WELLS, A. T., FORMAN, D. J., and RANFORD, L. C. (1965*b*). Geological reconnaissance of the north-west Amadeus Basin. *Rep. B.M.R.* **85**.

WELLS, A. T., STEWART, A. J., and SKWARKO, S. K. (1965*c*). Geology of the south-eastern part of the Amadeus Basin. *Rep. B.M.R.* **88**.

WELLS, B. E. (1956). Geology of the Casterton district. *Proc. R. Soc. Vict.* **68**, 85–110.

WHITE, A. H. (1964). The stratigraphy and structure of the Upper Palaeozoic sediments of the Somerton–Attunga district, N.S.W. *Proc. Linn. Soc. N.S.W.* **89**, 203–17.

WHITE, A. H. (1965). Tarecla, N.S.W. Geological Map of New England 1:100,000 Sheet 8/300. Univ. New England, Armidale, N.S.W.

WHITE, D. A. (1954). The Geology of the Strathbogie igneous complex, Victoria. *Proc. R. Soc. Vict.* **66**, 25–52.

WHITE, D. A. (1961). Geological history of the Cairns–Townsville hinterland, North Queensland. *Rep. B.M.R.* **59**.

WHITE, D. A. (1962). Georgetown, Qd. 1:250,000 Geological Series Sheet E/54-12. *Explan. Notes B.M.R.*

WHITEHOUSE, F. W. (1936). The Cambrian faunas of north-eastern Australia. *Mem. Qd. Mus.* **11**, 59–112; (1939), **11**, 179–282.

WHITEHOUSE, F. W. (1940). Studies in the late geological history of Queensland. *Pap. Dep. Geol. Univ. Qd.* **2** (1), 1–74.

WHITEHOUSE, F. W. (1948). The geology of the Channel Country of south-western Queensland. *Tech. Bull. Dep. publ. Lds. Qd.* **1**, 10–28.

WHITEHOUSE, F. W. (1963). The sandhills of Queensland—coastal and desert. *Qd. Nat.* **17**, 1–10.

WHITING, J. W. (1954). Limestone deposits, Parish Braylesford, County Gresham. *Annu. Rep. Dep. Mines N.S.W.* (1950), **87**.

WILKINS, R. W. T. (1963). Relationships between the Mitchellian, Cheltenhamian and Kalimnan stages in the Australian Tertiary. *Proc. R. Soc. Vict.* **76**, 39–59.

WILKINSON, J. F. G. (1958). The petrology of a differentiated teschenite sill near Gunnedah, New South Wales. *Am. J. Sci.* **256**, 1–39.

WILKINSON, J. F. G. (1962). Mineralogical, geochemical, and petrogenetic aspects of an analcite–basalt from the New England district of New South Wales. *J. Petrology* **3**, 192–214.

WILLETT, R. W. (1950). The New Zealand Pleistocene snow line, climatic conditions and suggested climatic effects. *N.Z. J. Sci. Technol.* **32B**, 18–48.

WILLIAMS, G. E. (1964). The geology of the Kinglake district, central Victoria. *Proc. R. Soc. Vict.* **77**, 273–327.

WILLIS, I. (1965). Stratigraphy and structure of the Devonian strata at Baton River, New Zealand. *N.Z. J. Geol. Geophys.* **8**, 35–48.

WILSHIRE, H. G. (1959). Contact metamorphism adjacent to a teschenite intrusion. *J. geol. Soc. Aust.* **6**, 11–20.

WILSON, A. F. (1958). Advances in the knowledge of the structure and petrology of the Precambrian rocks of south-western Australia. *J. Proc. R. Soc. West. Aust.* **41**, 57–83.

WILSON, A. F., COMPSTON, W., JEFFERY, P. M., and RILEY, G. H. (1960). Radioactive ages from the Precambrian rocks in Australia. *J. geol. Soc. Aust.* **6**, 179–95.

WILSON, D. D. (1963). Geology of Waipara Subdivision. *Bull. geol. Surv. N.Z.* **64**.

WOLF, K. H. (1965). Petrogenesis and paleoenvironment of Devonian algal limestones of N.S.W. *Sedimentology* **4**, 113–78.

WOOD, B. L. (1952). Paleozoic and Mesozoic stratigraphy and structure in Southland. *Rep. 7th Sci. Congr. R. Soc. N.Z.* 106–14.

WOOD, B. L. (1960). Fiord 1:250,000 geol. Map Ser. Sheet 27, geol. Surv. N.Z.

WOOD, B. L. (1962). Wakatipu 1:250,000 geol. Map Ser. Sheet 22, geol. Surv. N.Z.

WOOD, B. L. (1963), Structure of the Otago Schists. *N.Z. J. Geol. Geophys.* **6**, 641–80.

WOODS, J. T. (1961). Mesozoic and Cainozoic sediments of the Wrotham Park area. *Qd. Govt. Min. J.* **62**, 228–32.

WOODS, J. T. (1962). Fossil marsupials and Cainozoic continental stratigraphy in Australia: a review. *Mem. Qd. Mus.* **14**, 41–49.

WOPFNER, H. (1960). On some structural development in the central part of the Great Australian Artesian Basin. *Trans. R. Soc. S. Aust.* **83**, 179–93.

WOPFNER, H. (1963). Post-Winton sediments of probable Upper Cretaceous age in the central Great Artesian Basin. *Trans. R. Soc. S. Aust.* **86**, 247–53.

WRIGHT, A. J. T. (1965). Implications of the Devonian geology of the Mudgee district. *Aust. J. Sci.* **37**, 237–8.

WRIGHT, C. W. (1963). Cretaceous ammonites from Bathurst Island, northern Australia. *Palaeontology* **6**, 597–614.

WRIGHT, R. L. (1963). Deep weathering and erosion surfaces in the Daly River Basin, Northern Territory. *J. geol. Soc. Aust.* **10**, 151–63.

YOUNG, D. G. (1964). Stratigraphy and petrography of north-east Otago loess. *N.Z. J. Geol. Geophys.* **7**, 839–63.

Unpublished References

BASTIAN, L. V. (1962). Geological completion report, bores BMR 4 and BMR 4A. Canning Basin, Western Australia. Rec. B.M.R. 1962/168.

COOK, P. J. (1963). The geology of Yuendumu Native Reserve, Northern Territory. Rec. B.M.R. 1963/37.

CROHN, P. W., and OLDERSHAW, W. (1964). The geology of the Tennant Creek one-mile sheet area. Rec. B.M.R. 1964/79.

DICKINS, J. M. (1960). Cretaceous marine macrofossils from the Great Artesian Basin in Queensland. Rec. B.M.R. 1960/69.

DICKINS, J. M. (1964). Correlation of the Permian of the Hunter Valley, New South Wales and the Bowen Basin, Queensland. Rec. B.M.R. 1964/96.

DICKINS, J. M., MALONE, E. J., and JENSEN, A. R. (1962). Subdivision and correlation of the Middle Bowen Beds. Rec. B.M.R. 1962/87.

DOW, D. B., GEMUTS, I., PLUMB, K. A., and DUNNET, D. (1964). The geology of the Ord River region, Western Australia. Rec. B.M.R. 1964/104.

EVANS, P. R. (1962a). Palynological observations of F. B. H. Flaxman's Hill No. 1 Well. Rec. B.M.R. 1962/57.

EVANS, P. R. (1962b). Microfossils associated with the "Bundamba Group" of the Surat Basin, Queensland. Rec. B.M.R. 1962/115.

EVANS, P. R., and HODGSON, E. A. (1963). A correlation of the Tertiary of A. O. G. Wentworth No. 1, Woodside Oil Balranald No. 1 and Woodside Oil Bundy No. 1 Wells, Murray Basin. Rec. B.M.R. 1963/95.

FORMAN, D. J. (1964). Preliminary tectonic maps of the Amadeus Basin 1:500,000. Rec. B.M.R. 1964/34.

GELLATLY, D. C., DERRICK, G. M., and PLUMB, K. A. (1965). The geology of the Lansdowne 1:250,000 Sheet SE 52/5 Western Australia. Rec. B.M.R. 1965/210.

HAITES, T. B. (1962). A review of Murray Basin geology for Planet Exploration Co. Pty. Ltd. (Courtesy of Planet Exploration.)

HARMS, J E. (1959). The geology of the Kimberley Division, Western Australia and of an adjacent area of the Northern Territory. M.Sc. Thesis, Univ. Adelaide.

JENSEN, A. R., GREGORY, C. M., and FORBES, V. R. (1964). The geology of the Taroom 1:250,000 sheet area and the western third of the Mundubbera 1:250,000 sheet area. Rec. B.M.R. 1964/61.

LUCAS, K. G. (1962). The geology of the Cooktown 1:250,000 sheet area, North Queensland. Rec. B.M.R. 1962/149.

LUCAS, K. G. (1964). The geology of the Cape Melville 1:250,000 sheet area, North Queensland. Rec. B.M.R. 1964/93.

MALONE, E. J., JENSEN, A. R., GREGORY, C. M., and FORBES, V. R. (1962). Progress report on the Bowen Basin regional survey, season 1961. Rec. B.M.R. 1962/72.

MILLIGAN, E. N. (1964). The regional geology of the northern half of the Alcoota 1:250,000 sheet area, N.T. Rec. B.M.R. 1964/43.

MOLLAN, R. G., EXON, N. F., and KIRKEGAARD, A. G. (1964). The geology of the Springsure 1:250,000 sheet area, Queensland. Rec. B.M.R. 1964/27.

OLGERS, F., WEBB, A. W., SMIT, J. A. J., and COXHEAD, B. A. (1964). The geology of the Baralaba 1:250,000 sheet area, Queensland. Rec. B.M.R. 1964/26.

RANDAL, M. A., and BROWN, G. A. (1962). Additional notes on the geology of the Camooweal 4-mile sheet area. Rec. B.M.R. 1962/49.

RAYNER, E. O. (1962). The mineralogy and genesis of the iron-rich copper ores of the Cobar province, N.S.W. Ph.D. Thesis, Univ. N.S.W.

REYNOLDS, M. A., (1963). The sedimentary basins of Australia and New Guinea. Rec. B.M.R. 1963/159.

REYNOLDS, M. A., and PRITCHARD, P. W. (1964). The geology of the Glenormiston 1:250,000 sheet area. Rec. B.M.R. 1964/28.

ROBERTS, H. G., HALLIGAN, R., and GEMUTS, I. (1965). Geology of the Mount Ramsay 1:250,000 sheet area, E/52-9, Western Australia. Rec. B.M.R. 1965/156.

SKWARKO, S. K. (1962). Notes on Australian Lower Cretaceous palaeogeography. Rec. B.M.R. 1962/11.

SKWARKO, S. K. (1963). Mesozoic fossils from the Gibson Desert, central Western Australia. Rec. B.M.R. 1963/2.

SMITH, J. W. (1963). Explanatory notes to accompany Gordon Downs 1:250,000 sheet SE52-10. Rec. B.M.R. 1963/120.

SMITH, K. G. (1960). Summary of the geology of the Hay River 4-mile sheet, Northern Territory. Rec. B.M.R. 1960/73.

SMITH, K. G. (1967). Geology of the Georgina Basin. *Rec. B.M.R.* 1967/61.

SMITH, K. G., and MILLIGAN, E. N. (1963). The geology of the Elkedra 1:250,000 sheet, Northern Territory. Rec. B.M.R. 1963/46.

SMITH, K. G., and VINE, R. R. (1960). Summary of the geology of the Tobermory 4-mile geological sheet. Rec. B.M.R. 1960/71.

SMITH, K. G., VINE, R. R., and MILLIGAN, E. N. (1961). Revisions to the Stratigraphy of the Hay River, Huckitta and Tobermory 4-mile Sheets, Northern Territory, Rec. B.M.R. 1961/65.

SPENCE, A. G. (1964). Tanami/the Granites airborne magnetic and radiometric survey, Northern Territory 1962. Rec. B.M.R. 1964/102.

VINE, R. R., CASEY, D. J., and JOHNSON, N. E. A. (1964). Progress report 1963 on the geology of part of the north eastern Eromanga Basin, Queensland. Rec. B.M.R. 1964/39.

WELLS, A. T. (1963). Reconnaissance geology by helicopter in the Gibson Desert, Western Australia. Rec. B.M.R. 1963/59.

WELLS, A. T., RANFORD, L. C., and COOK, P. J. (1963). The Geology of the Lake Amadeus 1:250,000 sheet area: Palaeontological Appendix by Joyce G. Tomlinson. Rec. B.M.R. 1963/51.

WELLS, A. T., RANFORD, L. C., COOK, P. J., STEWART, A. J., and SHAW, R. D. (1965d). The geology of the north-eastern part of Amadeus Basin. Rec. B.M.R. 1965/108.

WHITE, A. J. R. (1956). Ph.D. Thesis, Univ. London.

Map References

Note:—4244/14619 = Lat. 42° 44′ S, Long. 146° 19′ E.

AUSTRALIA

Adamsfield	4244/14619	Cargo	3325/14849
Adelaide	3456/13836	Cessnock	3250/15121
Albany	3502/11753	Clermont	2249/14738
Alice Springs	2342/13353	Cloncurry	2042/14030
Andersons Creek	4112/14649	Cobar	3130/14549
Arcadia	2519/14850	Condobolin	3305/14709
Armidale	3031/15139	Constance Headland	2356/12317
Arnhem Land	1310/13430	Cooleman Caves	3527/14843
Avon River	3803/14716	Cooma	3614/14908
Bacchus Marsh	3741/14427	Coorong, The	3600/13930
Barkly Tableland	1900/13800	Cootamundra	3439/14802
Barrington	2300/15128	Copley	3032/13826
Barrow Creek	2133/13353	Cowra	3350/14841
Baryulgil	2913/15236	Dampier Peninsula	1730/12255
Bass Strait	3920/14530	Dandenong Ranges	3750/14521
Batemans Bay	3543/15011	Dawson Valley	2400/14950
Bathurst	3325/14934	Delegate	3703/14856
Beaconsfield	4112/14649	Derby	1718/12338
Bindi	3707/14750	Dirk Hartogs Island	2550/11305
Blinman	3106/13840	Douglas Creek	2250/14740
Blue Mountains	9990/15015	Drake	2856/15224
Bombala	3654/14914	Eildon	2314/14225
Borenore	3315/14858	Esk	2714/15225
Boulia	2254/13954	Eungella	2111/14824
Bourke	3006/14556	Everard Range	2705/13228
Bowral	3428/15025	Eyre Peninsula	3400/13545
Brisbane	2730/15301	Fitzroy	1811/12535
Broken Hill	3157/14126	Fleurieu Peninsula	3530/13830
Broome	1758/12214	Flinders Island	1411/14415
Buchan	3730/14811	Flinders Ranges	3125/13845
Bungunnia	3353/13945	Forbes	3323/14801
Burdekin River	1939/14730	Furneaux Islands	4010/14805
Burra	3340/13856	Geraldton	2846/11436
Burt Range	2602/12729	Gidgealpa	2756/14003
Cabawin	2720/15015	Gilberton	1917/14340
Camden	3403/15042	Giles Range	2200/13225
Camooweal	1955/13807	Giralia	2241/11421
Canberra	3520/14910	Glasshouse Mountains	2654/15255
Cania	2438/15058	Glenelg	3735/14140
Canoblas	3318/14904	Gogano	2340/15002
Canowindra	3334/14840	Goodradigbee	3508/14841
Cape Otway	3851/14331	Goulburn	3445/14943
Cape Range	2210/11400	Groote Eylandt	1400/13640
Cape York Peninsula	1200/14230	Gundagai	3504/14806

Harts Range	2310/13450	Mount Dromedary	3612/15002
Hawker	3153/13825	Mount Fitton	2958/13932
Heathcote	3655/14443	Mount Gambier	3750/14046
Heron Island	2327/15155	Mount Garnet	1741/14507
Hill End	3302/14925	Mount Howie	2623/14054
Hillgrove	3034/15154	Mount Isa	2044/13930
Hopkins River	3824/14231	Mount Kosciusko	3627/14816
Huckitta	2238/13530	Mount Lofty Ranges	3500/13850
Hunter River	3250/15142	Mount Morgan	2339/15023
Iragana Hills	2435/12615	Mount Mulligan	1651/14452
Ivanhoe No. 1 Well	3254/14418	Mount Painter	3013/13921
Jenolan	3349/15002	Mount Wellington	3735/14649
Kalgoorlie	3045/12128	Mudgee	3236/14935
Kangaroo Hills	1857/14541	Mulgildie	2458/15107
Kangaroo Island	3550/13706	Mundubbera	2536/15118
Katherine	1428/13216	Murray River Mouth	3526/13910
Kempsey	3105/15250	Murrurundi	3146/15050
Kiewa Valley	3616/14701	Nandewar Mountains	3030/15100
King Island	3950/14400	Nebine–Eulo Ridge	2700/14730
Kinglake	3731/14521	Newcastle	3255/15145
King Leopold Range	1730/12545	North West Cape	2145/11410
Lake Eyre	2840/13710	Nowra	3453/15036
Lake Frome	3048/13948	Nymagee	3204/14620
Lake Torrens	3137/13802	Nyngan	3134/14711
Lapstone Monocline	3300/15050	Olary	3217/14019
Leigh Creek	3032/13826	Orange	3317/14906
Lilydale	3745/14521	Pandieburra No. 1 Well	2645/13925
Lithgow	3329/15009	Parkes	3308/14811
Liverpool Range	3145/15045	Peake and Denison Ranges	2830/13600
Lochinvar	3242/15127	Petermann Ranges	2500/12946
Lord Howe Island	3133/15905	Pilbara	2115/11818
Loxton Bore	2300/14527	Pincombe Range	1533/12855
Macdonnell Ranges	2345/13320	Pine Mountain	2737/15246
Mackay	2109/14912	Point Cygnet	4314/14704
Macleay River	3050/15300	Police Creek	1648/12626
Macpherson Ranges	2820/15300	Port Augusta	3230/13746
Maitland	3244/15133	Port Keats	1405/12935
Mallee	3500/14200	Port Phillip	3807/14448
Mandurama	3339/14905	Portland	3820/14136
Manning River	3150/15240	Queanbeyan	3521/14914
Mansfield	3703/14605	Renmark North	3408/14043
Maralinga	2945/13135	Riverine Plain	3500/14500
Maryborough	2532/15242	Riverton	3410/13845
Mary Kathleen	2044/14000	Rockhampton	2323/15030
Mary River	2600/15230	Roma	2635/14847
Melbourne	3750/14500	Roopena	3257/13723
Minnie Range	2005/12643	Rough Range	2226/11404
Mitta Mitta River	3612/14711	Rough Range No. 1 Well	2222/11405
Molong	3306/14852	Rum Jungle	1301/13100
Moonie	2744/15015	Rylstone	3248/14958
Mootwingee	3117/14218	Seaham	3240/15144
Mornington Island	1630/13930	Snowy Plains	3716/14645
Morwell	3814/14624	Snowy River	3700/14900
Mount Barney	2816/15242	Sofala	3305/14942
Mount Bonner	1207/13633	Spero Bay	4238/14519

Springleigh	2434/14444	Waratah Bay	3851/14604
Stanwell	2329/15019	Warnbro Sound	3220/11543
Stradbroke Island	2735/15328	Warrumbungle Range	3127/14910
Strathbogie Range	3654/14545	Warwick	2814/15201
Swan Hill	3521/14334	Wee Jasper	3509/14842
Sydney	3353/15112	Weipa	1240/14155
Tabberabbera	3735/14723	Wellington	3233/14857
Taemas	3500/14845	Wentworth No. 1 Bore	3348/14158
Tamworth	3106/15056	Werrie Basin	3120/15040
Tanami	1959/12943	West Coast Range	4200/14530
Taree	3154/15228	Whyalla	3302/13735
Tarlton	2247/13648	Wilkinson Range	2759/12447
Tennant Creek	1939/13412	Williamsbury	2354/11456
Texas	2851/15110	Wilpena	3107/13948
The Granites	2035/13021	Woolmulla No. 1 Well	3001/11511
Toko Range	2305/13820	Wooltana	3025/13925
Tolarno	3247/14223	Wreck Island	2320/15158
Tower Hill	3820/14215	Yallourn	3811/14620
Townsville	1915/14648	Yarrangobilly	3539/14829
Trundle	3255/14743	Yarrol	2457/15121
Tyers	3809/14628	Yass	3450/14855
Urandangi	2136/13818	Yorke Peninsula	3500/13730
Wagga	3507/14722	Yuendumu	2216/13149
Walhalla	3757/14627	Zeehan	4153/14520

NEW ZEALAND

Alfred River	4221/17214	Curio Bay	4638/16910
Amuri Bluff	4233/17332	Dun Mountain	4120/17317
Aorangi	3754/17808	D'Urville Island	4050/17350
Awakino	3839/17438	Eglinton Valley	4500/16757
Awatere Valley	4200/17330	Fairlie	4406/17050
Banks Peninsula	4345/17250	Flora Track	4110/17242
Batley	3612/17420	Gebbies Pass	4341/17238
Baton River	4117/17240	Golden Bay	4040/17250
Baton Valley	4120/17243	Gore	4607/16858
Bay of Islands	3510/17410	Great Barrier	3610/17525
Benmore Dam	4435/17012	Grey–Inangahua Depression	4210/17145
Blenheim	4132/17358	Haast Pass	4405/16922
Bobs Cove	4505/16830	Harper Pass	4243/17152
Bounty Islands	4743/17905	Hikurangi	3756/17804
Bruce Bay	4335/16935	Hokianga Harbour	3530/17325
Buller Gorge	4150/17135	Hokonui Hills	4600/16835
Campbell Island	5233/16908	Hollyford Valley	4440/16807
Cape Kidnappers	3929/17717	Huntly	3735/17510
Cape Providence	4601/16628	Kahurangi Point	4047/17211
Chatham Islands	4400/17630	Kaikoura Range	4200/17340
Clarence Valley	4209/17335	Kaitangata	4615/16950
Clent Hills	4335/17125	Kapuni	3930/17407
Clinton	4615/16925	Karioi	3752/17448
Cobb Valley	4108/17238	Kawhia Harbour	3805/17447
Collingwood	4041/17241	Koranga	3830/17725
Coopers Beach	3459/17334	Kowhitirangi Hill	4253/17100
Coromandel	3630/17530	Lake Cobb	4103/17231
Coverham	4149/17403	Lake Waikaremoana	3845/17705

Lake Wakatipu	4505/16830	Red Hills	4420/16818
Leslie River	4114/17233	Reefton	4707/17152
Little Barrier Island	3611/17505	Ross	4254/17048
Livingstone Range	4505/16802	Rotorua	3810/17615
Lodestone Peak	4110/17244	Ruahine Range	4000/17605
Malvern Hills	4325/17140	Seymour River	4215/17325
Manawatu Gorge	4019/17548	Shag Point	4528/17048
Mangaotane Valley	3807/17745	Shag Valley	4525/17040
Marakopa River	3817/17445	Slaty Creek	4042/17226
Mataura Island	4627/16848	Solander Islands	4637/16653
Mataura River	4610/16853	South Kaipara	3630/17418
Mayor Island	3715/17615	Stewart Island	4700/16800
Milford Sound	4435/16750	Taitai	3753/17810
Moeraki Peninsula	4523/17052	Takaka	4052/17249
Mokau River	3842/17437	Takitimu Mountains	4540/16750
Motu	3815/17733	Tapuwaeroa Valley	3752/17813
Mount Arthur	4113/17242	Tararua Range	4055/17520
Mount Cook	4335/17007	Taringatura Hills	4555/16810
Mount Egmont	3918/17404	Three Kings Islands	3410/17210
Mount Ngauruhoe	3910/17540	Timaru	4423/17114
Mount Owen	4133/17233	Tinui	4053/17605
Mount Peel	4107/17235	Tongariro National Park	3908/17538
Mount Potts	4330/17055	Tophouse	4146/17254
Mount St. Mary	4443/17021	Trelissick	4315/17150
Mount Somers	4343/17124	Upper Buller Valley	4205/17250
Mount Tongariro	3908/17542	Waihi Beach	3725/17555
Murchison	4150/17220	Waimakariri Valley	4325/17205
Naseby	4502/17010	Waipahi	4608/16916
Ngahape	4107/17555	Waipara	4303/17247
North Range	4545/16815	Waipawa	3956/17636
Nugget Point	4627/16950	Waipiata	4512/17010
Oamaru	4506/17057	Waipoua	3520/17330
Ohai	4555/16758	Wairakei	3925/17605
Onekaka	4047/17244	Wairaki	4550/16750
Otaio Gorge	4430/17100	Wairarapa	4100/17600
Otapiri Valley	4558/16825	Wairoa Gorge	4125/17306
Paturau River	4041/17229	Waiuta	4217/17149
Pepin Island	4109/17326	Wakamarama Range	4115/17230
Pikikiruna Range	4051/17252	Wangaloa	4615/17000
Pirongia	3800/17506	Wanganui	3956/17500
Port Waikato	3723/17445	Wangapeka	4126/17232
Preservation Inlet	4610/16635	Whangarei	3543/17420
Raukokere	3739/17753	Whangaroa Bay	3503/17348
Raukumara Range	3800/17800		

Index

Note. The suffix "f" indicates a figure or table facing the appropriate page

393